STATE TAXATION OF ELECTRIC, NATURAL GAS, AND OTHER PUBLIC UTILITIES

COORDINATING AUTHORS: **William F. Kimble**, Partner
KPMG, Houston

Glenn D. Todd, Senior Manager
KPMG, Pittsburgh

TECHNICAL REVIEW AUTHOR: **David M. Vistica**, Partner
KPMG, Northern Virginia

CONTRIBUTING AUTHORS: **Wesley Bond**
KPMG, Atlanta

Leah A. Durner
KPMG, Washington National Tax Practice, Washington, D.C.

Justin J. Hyland
KPMG, Houston

Philip M. Seabrease
KPMG, San Francisco

CCH INCORPORATED
Chicago

ISBN: 0-8080-0679-7

4025 W. Peterson Ave.
Chicago, IL 60646-6085
1 800 248 3248
http://tax.cchgroup.com

Printed in the United States of America

Preface

State Taxation of Electric, Natural Gas, and Other Public Utilities explores how regulation and deregulation have affected the state tax policies impacting the utility industry. Specifically, it explores the impact deregulation has had on the overall and regional imposition of the following state and local taxes: gross receipts taxes, sales and use taxes, income taxes, franchise taxes, and property taxes. Further, it presents an in-depth discussion of the state taxation of emerging industries, particularly trading and marketing companies, energy services companies, and independent power projects. Also highlighted are industry-specific technical issues including nexus, business and non-business income, allocation and apportionment of income, and discriminatory taxes.

More than half of all states have enacted legislation or are studying the restructuring of their state's utility industries. As deregulation continues to change the utility industry and its existing suppliers, federal, state, and local taxing authorities will be forced to restructure their taxing policies. As taxing strategies evolve on all levels, the utility industry will have to respond with countermeasures and effective planning.

The information in this book is general in nature and based on authorities that are subject to change. While we have worked hard to present the latest information in this book, each tax practitioner should always research the current status of issues in his or her jurisdiction, or consult with a tax advisor on the applicability of any information provided herein to a specific situation. That said, we hope that *State Taxation of Electric, Natural Gas, and Other Public Utilities* provides tax practitioners with a comprehensive understanding of the utility industry so that they can be responsive to their clients' changing needs.

William F. Kimble
Glenn D. Todd
David M. Vistica

February 2002

About the Authors

William F. Kimble is the national industry director for KPMG's Energy Power and Natural Resources Practice and also serves KPMG's State and Local Tax Practice as partner-in-charge of the National Utility Practice. He is also a member of KPMG's board of advisors to the utility industry. He is a Certified Public Accountant and a graduate of Southern Methodist University. Mr. Kimble has testified before the National Association of Regulatory Utility Commissioners on state and local tax issues in the deregulation of the electric industry. He has also spoken on behalf of the American Gas Association on state and local tax issues in the deregulation of the gas utility industry. Mr. Kimble is a frequent contributor of articles to *Electric Light & Power, Utility Spotlight, Electric Perspectives, Public Utilities Fortnightly, Gas Daily,* and *World Energy*. He is based in KPMG's Houston office.

Glenn D. Todd is a senior manager with KPMG's State and Local Tax Practice and serves as KPMG's Mid-Atlantic State and Local Tax Utility Practice leader. He is also a member of KPMG's board of advisors to the utility industry. Prior to joining the Utility Practice, he served in KPMG's Washington National Tax Practice, providing technical support and product development for KPMG's State and Local Tax Practice. Mr. Todd has authored or coauthored articles on various state and local tax topics for publications such as *Tax Analysts BNA Portfolio Series, The State and Local Tax Lawyer, State and Local Tax Insights, The NYU State and Local Tax Symposium, Electric Light & Power,* and *The Income Tax Alert*. He has an LL.M. (with distinction) from Georgetown University Law Center, a J.D. (magna cum laude) from Capital University Law School, and a B.S. in Accounting from Duquesne University. Mr. Todd is based in KPMG's Pittsburgh office.

David M. Vistica is a partner with KPMG's State and Local Tax Practice and serves as KPMG's tax industry leader for the Northeast and Mid-Atlantic utility practice. He is also a member of KPMG's board of advisors to the utility industry. He is a Certified Public

Accountant, a member of the American Institute of Certified Public Accountants, and a member of the Virginia Society of CPAs. He has served as the state liaison between the State Tax Committee of the Virginia Society of CPAs and the Virginia Department of Taxation. Prior to joining KPMG, he served for four years in the Virginia Department of Taxation's Office of Tax Policy. There he drafted legislation, regulations, rulings, and protests for corporate and individual income taxes and sales taxes, and assisted in economic development efforts for the state of Virginia. Mr. Vistica is a frequent speaker on state and local tax topics and has been an adjunct professor of accounting. He has a Master of Science in Taxation from Bentley College and a B.S. from Husson College. Mr. Vistica is based in KPMG's Tyson's Corner office in northern Virginia.

Acknowledgments

Many thanks to the contributing authors whose depth of knowledge and experience was integral to this book's accuracy and completion.

Wesley Bond is a senior manager and a member of KPMG's State and Local Tax Practice with an emphasis in the utility and independent power generation industries. He is also a member of KPMG's board of advisors to the utility industry. Mr. Bond is responsible for the marketing and delivery of state tax solutions and for servicing clients in a wide range of professional services. He has written several articles on tax planning and incentive opportunities for utilities and independent power generators. He is also familiar with all areas of state and local taxation, including income and franchise taxes, sales and use taxes, property taxes, and utility taxes. Mr. Bond is a Certified Public Accountant and a member of the American Institute of Certified Public Accountants. He is a graduate of Georgia Southern University and the University of Georgia. Mr. Bond is based in KPMG's Atlanta office.

Leah A. Durner is a senior manager with KPMG's Washington National Tax Practice in Washington, D.C. She serves as a national technical resource for KPMG's State and Local Tax Practice by advising on the multistate aspects of corporate income and franchise taxes, sales and transactions taxes, employment taxes, property taxes, and unclaimed property. Ms. Durner has also worked in the Atlanta and Raleigh offices of KPMG, consulting with clients on tax planning and tax controversy resolution. Prior to joining KPMG, Ms. Durner worked in the financial accounting and reporting department of a major electric utility as well as a public accounting firm. She is a graduate of Wake Forest University School of Law and holds a B.S. in Accounting from the University of North Carolina at Charlotte.

Justin J. Hyland is a manager with KPMG's State and Local Tax Practice with an emphasis in the utility and independent power producer sectors. He is also a member of KPMG's board of advisors to the utility industry. Mr. Hyland has been involved in the design and implementation of strategic tax structures for multiple new merchant power plants throughout the United States. He has also helped restructure project entities and transactions to produce savings in property taxes, sales taxes, and income and franchise taxes. In addition, Mr. Hyland represents clients in the utility, energy, manufacturing, and airline industries in property tax appeals on valuation issues. He has also conducted valuations of companies' intangible assets for income and property tax purposes. Mr. Hyland is a graduate of Rice University and is based in KPMG's Houston office.

Philip M. Seabrease is the Western area leader for KPMG's State and Local Tax Utility Practice. He is also a member of KPMG's board of advisors to the utility industry. Mr. Seabrease is responsible for the marketing and delivery of state tax solutions specific to utilities and independent power producers and for servicing clients in a wide range of professional services. He has worked in all areas of state and local taxation, including income and franchise taxes, sales and use taxes, property taxes, and utility taxes. He is a Certified Public Accountant and a graduate of the University of Baltimore. Mr. Seabrease is based in KPMG's San Francisco office.

We also gratefully acknowledge the assistance of **Philip R. Pulliam** and **Jill A. Waugh** in the preparation of this publication. Mr. Pulliam is a supervising senior tax specialist in KPMG's Northern Virginia State and Local Tax Practice, and Ms. Waugh is a senior administrative assistant in KPMG's Pittsburgh State and Local Tax Practice.

TABLE OF CONTENTS

DETAILED TABLE OF CONTENTS

Paragraph

PART 1 DEREGULATION AND REGULATION

CHAPTER 1 DEREGULATION OF PUBLIC UTILITIES

CHAPTER 2 REGULATION OF THE UTILITY INDUSTRY

Paragraph

PART 3 INDUSTRY-SPECIFIC TECHNICAL ISSUES

CHAPTER 7 NEXUS

CHAPTER 8 BUSINESS AND NONBUSINESS INCOME

Paragraph

CHAPTER 9 ALLOCATION AND APPORTIONMENT OF INCOME

Paragraph

CHAPTER 10 DISCRIMINATORY TAXES

Page

APPENDICES — RELEVANT SOURCE DOCUMENTS

APPENDIX A

APPENDIX B

APPENDIX C

APPENDIX D

INDEX

Part 1

DEREGULATION AND REGULATION

Chapter 1

DEREGULATION OF PUBLIC UTILITIES

¶ 101 Overview

For decades, public utilities have been a consistent source of revenues for state and local jurisdictions nationwide. In 1997, prior to deregulation, just the investor-owned electric utilities paid over $13.9 billion in state and local taxes.[1] Many state and local jurisdictions impose a number of taxes exclusively on utilities, causing utility companies to collect those taxes from their customers. Examples of taxes collected by utility companies include gross receipts taxes, power generation taxes, transmission/pole taxes, and utility user taxes.

Most current state and local tax statutes were enacted under the presumption that public utilities would always be regulated entities able to pass taxes on to their customers through their recoverable cost of service. This has and will continue to present numerous problems as states deregulate, both in the loss of tax revenues and in the ability of public utility companies to compete.

Loss of tax revenues. Deregulation may produce significant shortfalls in the state and local tax revenues collected by jurisdictions (see ¶ 305). These revenue shortfalls could result from any of the following:

- Lower electric and natural gas prices
- Declining property values
- Cross-border sales taxed at lower rates (or not taxed at all)
- Less heavily taxed utility service providers displacing the regulated utilities

[1] Edison Electric Institute, *Statistical Yearbook of the Electric Utility Industry* (Washington, D.C.: Edison Electric Institute, 1997). See also the bar graph at ¶ 320.03.

Some states have recognized some or all of these issues and attempted to address them in their deregulation bills. For example, the New Jersey Board of Public Utilities has stated that

> [its] proposed reforms are intended . . . to prevent the tax revenue erosion which would result under the current tax laws when electric competition is implemented.[2]

Ability to compete. Deregulation may also put utility companies at a competitive disadvantage if states do not address their current tax statutes. Prior to deregulation, many regulated utilities were taxed under different methodologies and rates than their competitors, and, as a result, many utilities argue that they pay higher taxes. In addition, several studies have concluded that cross-border sales are taxed at lower rates, if taxed at all.[3]

Deregulation of the electric industry has reached almost every state (see ¶ 105). In addition, most states have either enacted legislation deregulating the natural gas industry or have such legislation pending (see ¶ 110).

¶ 105 Deregulation of the Electric Industry

In the electric industry, 24 states have enacted electric utility restructuring legislation or regulatory reforms so that retail access is or will soon be available to all or some of their customers. However, seven of those states have recently passed legislation to delay the implementation of retail access, and California has ordered the suspension of direct retail access. For a map showing each state's restructuring activity, see below.

[2] New Jersey Board of Public Utilities, *Proposed Findings and Recommendations* (January 1997).

[3] Pennsylvania Public Utility Commission, *Report and Recommendations to the Governor and General Assembly on Electric Competition* (July 1996).

Status of State Electric Industry Restructuring Activity [4]

[1]These States have either enacted enabling legislation or issued a regulatory order to implement retail access. Retail access is either currently available to all or some customers or will soon be available. Some States are currently running pilot programs, and they will begin to implement retail access in the near future: Arizona, Connecticut, Delaware, District of Columbia, Illinois, Maine, Maryland, Massachusetts, Michigan, New Hampshire, New Jersey, New York, Ohio, Pennsylvania, Rhode Island, Texas, and Virginia.

[2]These States have either passed legislation or issued regulatory orders to delay implementing retail access: Arkansas, Montana, Nevada, New Mexico, Oklahoma, and Oregon. Although West Virginia passed legislation that approved the PSC's plan to restructure and implement retail access, the process is delayed until a bill for tax reform is enacted.

[3]The CPUC ordered suspension of direct retail access.

[4]These States have not enacted enabling legislation to restructure the electric power industry or implement retail access: Alabama, Alaska, Colorado, Florida, Georgia, Hawaii, Idaho, Indiana, Iowa, Kansas, Kentucky, Louisiana, Minnesota, Mississippi, Missouri, Nebraska, North Carolina, North Dakota, South Carolina, South Dakota, Tennessee, Utah, Vermont, Washington, Wisconsin, and Wyoming.

¶ 110 Deregulation of the Natural Gas Industry

Deregulation of the natural gas industry took place in two distinct transformations. First, the Natural Gas Policy Act of 1978 (NGPA) dealt with changing the form and scope of wellhead price regulation. The NGPA's intention was that market forces would determine the supply, demand, and price of natural gas sold by producers. The NGPA

[4] Energy Information Administration of the U.S. Department of Energy, *Status of State Electric Industry Restructuring Activity as of February 2002,* http://www.eia.doe.gov/cneaf/electricity/chg_str/regmap.html.

was followed by the Federal Energy Regulatory Commission (FERC) Order 436 on October 9, 1985. FERC Order 436 transformed interstate pipelines from nondiscriminatory transport into open-access transport. It marked the beginning of the end for pipelines as monopolistic sellers of gas and transportation. Capacity on pipelines was to be allocated on a "first-come first-served" basis. Pipelines were transformed from regulated monopoly sellers of gas to regulated transporters of gas. In addition, producers and local distribution companies (LDCs) took ownership of the aggregating and packaging of gas supplies for LDCs and large retail customers.

The second distinct transformation of the natural gas industry occurred in the early 1990s beginning with FERC Order 636. FERC Order 636 completed the transformation of interstate pipelines from resellers of gas to open-access transporters of gas. For a map showing the status of each state's natural gas deregulation, see below.

Status of Natural Gas Residential Choice Programs by State [5]

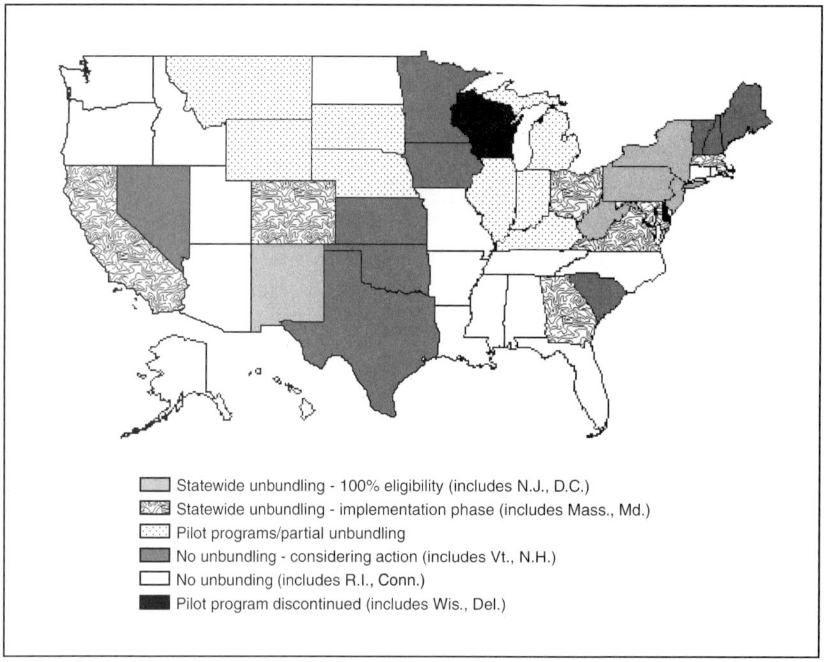

[5] Energy Information Administration of the U.S. Department of Energy, *Status of Natural Gas Residential Choice Program by State as of December 2001,* http://www.eia.doe.gov/oil_gas/natural_gas/restructure/restructure.html.

Chapter 2

REGULATION OF THE UTILITY INDUSTRY

¶ 201 Overview

Historically, the chief difference between a public utility and other commercial and industrial enterprises has been the public utility's ability to operate as a monopoly within its service area. The privilege to be the sole provider of a particular service within certain geographic bounds has historically been granted to utilities because of the huge capital investment required for providing the service and the need to construct facilities on public rights-of-way for delivering the service to customers. The theory has been that user charges and congestion on the rights-of-way will be minimized, even in the absence of competition among several providers, by appropriately regulating the authorized sole provider.

This chapter provides an overview of utility regulation and the role regulation has played in the development of the utility industry. The regulation of various utilities is handled by several federal and state regulatory bodies (see ¶ 205), and regulation has generally meant that utilities are required to seek permission or give notice to regulators before engaging in certain transactions. In addition, utilities need to follow the requirements for regulatory reporting (see ¶ 210), regulatory accounting (see ¶ 215), and, of course, rate making, which has traditionally been a central part of the regulation of utilities (see ¶ 220). The chapter further explains the segments of the natural gas industry (see ¶ 225) and the electric industry (see ¶ 230). The final section of this chapter provides an overview of the major federal legislative and regulatory reforms that have helped shape the electric industry's power marketing segment (see ¶ 235).

¶ 205 Federal and State Regulators

Federal regulatory agencies have generally governed the *interstate* operations of electric and natural gas public utilities, while state regulatory agencies have governed the *intrastate* operations.

Federal regulatory agencies. A few well-known federal regulatory agencies and their Web addresses are listed below.

- The Federal Energy Regulatory Commission (FERC) (formally the Federal Power Commission (FPC)) regulates interstate electric and gas pipeline utilities: http://www.ferc.fed.us.
- The Nuclear Regulatory Commission (NRC) (formerly the Atomic Energy Commission (AEC)) regulates the construction and operations of nuclear generating facilities: http://www.nrc.gov.
- The Securities and Exchange Commission (SEC) regulates interstate utility companies that are registered under the Public Utility Holding Company Act of 1935 (PUHCA): http://www.sec.gov.

State regulatory agencies. Each individual state has a regulatory agency (or body) that controls its intrastate operations of public utilities. The name of each state's regulatory agency varies from state to state, but the most commonly used names are "Public Utilities Commission" and "Public Service Commission." In general, the state regulatory bodies and the FERC have the authority to designate areas of operations, fix rates to be charged for services rendered, prescribe accounting policies through the medium of uniform charts of accounts (systems of accounts), issue special rulings regarding accounting policy in specific instances, process complaints by customers in an attempt to reach equitable conclusions in disputes between customers and the utility, and prescribe methods of operations, if necessary.

It is common to find electric public utility companies subject to regulation by both state and federal regulatory authorities; the state commission having jurisdiction over *intrastate* operations and retail rates, and the FERC having jurisdiction over *interstate* operations and wholesale rates. It is typical, in such companies, that the main portion of operations is intrastate and that the state has primary jurisdictional authority.

A listing of each state's regulatory agency and Web address is shown below.

State Regulatory Agencies and Their Web Addresses

State	*Acronym of Regulatory Agency*	*Web Address of Regulatory Agency (http://)*
Alabama	PSC	www.psc.state.al.us/
Alaska	RCA	www.state.ak.us/rca/
Arizona	ACC	www.cc.state.az.us/
Arkansas	PSC	www.state.ar.us/psc/
California	PUC	www.cpuc.ca.gov/
Colorado	PUC	www.dora.state.co.us/puc/
Connecticut	PUC	www.state.ct.us/dpuc/
Delaware	PSC	www.state.de.us/delpsc/
District of Columbia	PSC	www.dcpsc.org/
Florida	PSC	www.scri.net/psc/pas_toc.html
Georgia	PSC	www.psc.state.ga.us/
Idaho	PUC	www.puc.state.id.us/
Illinois	ICC	www.icc.state.il.us/
Indiana	URC	www.ai.org/iurc/index.html
Iowa	IUB	www.state.ia.us/government/com/util/util.htm
Kansas	KCC	www.kcc.state.ks.us/
Kentucky	PSC	www.psc.state.ky.us/
Louisiana	PSC	www.lpsc.org/
Maine	PUC	www.state.me.us/mpuc/
Maryland	PSC	www.psc.state.md.us/psc/
Massachusetts	DTE	www.magnet.state.ma.us/dte/
Michigan	PSC	www.cis.state.mi.us/mpsc/
Minnesota	PUC	www.state.mn.us/ebranch/puc/
Mississippi	PSC	www.psc.state.ms.us/
Missouri	PSC	www.psc.state.mo.us/
Montana	PSC	www.psc.state.mt.us/
Nebraska	PSC	www.nol.org/home/NPSC/
Nevada	PUC	www.state.nv.us/puc/
New Hampshire	PUC	www.puc.state.nh.us/
New Jersey	BPU	www.bpu.state.nj.us/
New Mexico	PRC	www.nmprc.state.nm.us/

State	*Acronym of Regulatory Agency*	*Web Address of Regulatory Agency (http://)*
New York	DPS	www.dps.state.ny.us/
North Carolina	UC	www.ncuc.commerce.state.nc.us/
North Dakota	PSC	www.psc.state.nd.us/
Ohio	PUC	www.state.oh.us/puc/
Oklahoma	OCC	www.occ.state.ok.us/
Oregon	PUC	www.puc.state.or.us/
Pennsylvania	PUC	www.puc.paonline.com/
Rhode Island	PUC	www.ripuc.org/
South Carolina	PSC	www.psc.state.sc.us/
South Dakota	PUC	www.state.sd.us/puc/
Tennessee	TRA	www.state.tn.us/tra/
Texas	PUC	www.puc.state.tx.us/
Utah	PSC	wwww.psc.state.ut.us/
Vermont	PSD	www.state.vt.us/psd/
Virginia	SCC	www.state.va.us/scc/
Washington	UTC	www.wutc.wa.gov/
West Virginia	PSC	www.psc.state.wv.us/
Wisconsin	PSC	www.psc.state.wi.us/
Wyoming	PSC	www.psc.state.wy.us/

National association of regulatory agencies. Also influential in the regulation of public utilities and in establishing uniform charts of accounts, although not a regulatory body, is the National Association of Regulatory Utility Commissioners (NARUC), whose mission is to improve the quality and effectiveness of public regulation.

¶ 210 Regulatory Reporting

One of the ways that utility regulators fulfill their oversight functions is through monitoring the compliance of the regulated utilities through regulatory reporting. The requirements for such reporting vary considerably from one commission to another. Beyond basic financial information, regulatory reporting often includes operational and statistical information. Such information is usually broken down by type of regulated utility operation (electric vs. gas) and often by function (generation, transmission, and distribution).

The Federal Energy Regulatory Commission (FERC) requires all utilities subject to the 1935 Federal Power Act (16 U.S.C.) and the 1938 Natural Gas Act (15 U.S.C.) to submit annual reports: "Form 1" for major electric utilities and "Form 2" for major natural gas companies. State regulatory commissions generally require annual reports from electric and gas utilities subject to their regulatory jurisdiction. Some may permit the filing of FERC forms while others have their own reporting formats. In addition, regulatory bodies may require that certain information be reported more frequently (quarterly or even monthly).

¶ 215 Regulatory Accounting

Along with regulatory reporting comes regulatory accounting. Utilities operate under a chart of accounts mandated by regulatory commissions. The chart of accounts dictates how financial transactions are recorded. The system of accounts prescribed by a regulatory commission with primary rate jurisdiction commonly includes all the accounts used by the company. Utilities are permitted to maintain records in any manner they wish as long as such records can be summarized into the accounts prescribed by the respective regulatory commission for required periodic reports. Utility plant accounts are numerous and contain considerable detail regarding the costs to be capitalized during construction. The extent of the detail indicates the importance of any construction work in progress and of the utility plant to the regulatory body.

From the standpoint of a regulatory commission, the accounting prescribed for a public utility is regarded as a tool of regulation. The regulatory commission, in carrying out its responsibility, requires substantial uniformity of accounting by all of the utilities under its jurisdiction. Transactions must be accounted for in conformity with the rate-making philosophy of the regulatory commission so that the data submitted to the commission is in usable and consistent form for monitoring the operations of the utility. Various uniform systems of accounts have been developed for use by the different types of utilities. The uniform systems of accounts of the Federal Energy Regulatory Commission (FERC) and the National Association of Regulatory Utility Commissioners (NARUC) are very similar. The various state commissions have basically adopted either the FERC system or the NARUC system of accounts.

The FERC uniform system of accounts provides basic account descriptions and accounting definitions that are useful in understanding the information that must be reported on Forms 1 and 2. The

FERC's accounting regulations for jurisdictional electric companies and natural gas companies are found at Title 18, Parts 101, 102, and 352 of the Code of Federal Regulations. A sample of the FERC uniform system of accounts for electric plants is shown below.

FERC Uniform System of Accounts for Electric Plants

Type of Electric Plant	*FERC Uniform Account Number and Description*	
1. INTANGIBLE PLANT	301	Organization
	302	Franchises and consents
	303	Miscellaneous intangible plant
2. PRODUCTION PLANT		
A. STEAM PRODUCTION	310	Land and land rights
	311	Structures and improvements
	312	Boiler plant equipment
	313	Engines and engine driven generators
	314	Turbogenerator units
	315	Accessory electric equipment
	316	Miscellaneous power plant equipment
B. NUCLEAR PRODUCTION	320	Land and land rights (Major only)
	321	Structures and improvements (Major only)
	322	Reactor plant equipment (Major only)
	323	Turbogenerator units (Major only)
	324	Accessory electric equipment (Major only)
	325	Miscellaneous power plant equipment (Major only)
C. HYDRAULIC PRODUCTION	330	Land and land rights
	331	Structures and improvements
	332	Reservoirs, dams, and waterways
	333	Water wheels, turbines and generators
	334	Accessory electric equipment
	335	Miscellaneous power plant equipment
	336	Roads, railroads, and bridges

Type of Electric Plant	*FERC Uniform Account Number and Description*	
D. Other Production	340	Land and land rights
	341	Structures and improvements
	342	Fuel holders, producers, and accessories
	343	Prime movers
	344	Generators
	345	Accessory electric equipment
	346	Miscellaneous power plant equipment
3. Transmission Plant	350	Land and land rights
	351	[Reserved]
	352	Structures and improvements
	353	Station equipment
	354	Towers and fixtures
	355	Poles and fixtures
	356	Overhead conductors and devices
	357	Underground conduit
	358	Underground conductors and devices
	359	Roads and trails
4. Distribution Plant	360	Land and land rights
	361	Structures and improvements
	362	Station equipment
	363	Storage battery equipment
	364	Poles, towers and fixtures
	365	Overhead conductors and devices
	366	Underground conduit
	367	Underground conductors and devices
	368	Line transformers
	369	Services
	370	Meters
	371	Installations on customers' premises
	372	Leased property on customers' premises
	373	Street lighting and signal systems
5. General Plant	389	Land and land rights
	390	Structures and improvements
	391	Office furniture and equipment
	392	Transportation equipment
	393	Stores equipment

Type of Electric Plant	*FERC Uniform Account Number and Description*
	394 Tools, shop and garage equipment
	395 Laboratory equipment
	396 Power operated equipment
	397 Communication equipment
	398 Miscellaneous equipment
	399 Other tangible property

¶ 220 Rates

A public utility generally operates under a monopoly franchise issued by the government (either state or federal, depending on the jurisdiction). In the absence of competition, the consumers' interests are protected by having a regulatory commission participate in the process of establishing the prices that a utility is permitted to charge for the services it provides. In the event either the utility or consumers feel that the commission has not acted fairly, recourse is available through the state and federal court systems.

The rate-making process is usually initiated by a utility company preparing and filing a "rate case" with an applicable commission. The rate case is designed to show the "revenue requirements" that are necessary to permit the utility to recover its reasonable expenses of operation plus earn a fair return on net assets devoted to providing its utility service. The rate adjustment required is measured by the difference between the utility's revenue requirements and the annualized revenue that would be produced by the utility's current rate schedule. The commission will usually suspend the utility's requested increase to conduct an investigation of the data supporting the utility's request. The investigation is usually conducted in a public hearing format where all qualified persons (i.e., company representatives, the staff of the commission, and recognized intervenors) have an opportunity to present evidence and/or cross-examine company witnesses about details of the company report.

.01 Recovery of Reasonable Costs of Operation

Revenues must be set in a way that permits a utility to recover its reasonable costs of operation including a "return" to cover interest expense, preferred stock dividends, and earnings on common stock. The return is often expressed as a percentage (rate of return) applied to the rate base. This system of setting revenues is called "cost-of-service rate making."

To determine a utility's reasonable costs of operation, a commission usually requires the utility to present details of its actual experience during a recent 12-month "test period." Although revenues and expenses for the test period will initially be "per books," the utility (and later the commission) will propose certain pro forma adjustments to "normalize" conditions in the test period and to provide for certain "known and measurable changes" that have occurred and need to be reflected in rates of future periods. Examples of pro forma adjustments to normalize test-period conditions include adjustments to revenues or expenses for abnormal weather, unusual maintenance expenses, or unusual operating experiences. An example of a pro forma adjustment for a known change that occurred subsequent to the test period, or that must occur by contractual terms at about the time the new rates are to go in effect, is a required pay increase for union employees.

Some commissions have permitted the use of partial or fully forecasted test years. The use of forecasted or future test years allows the utility to set rates prospectively based on projections of future operating results.

The rate-making process results in a series of approved rate schedules at which the utility will sell its services to its various classes of customers—industrial, commercial, and residential—and to various categories within each class. The art of apportioning revenues to be collected from each class of customers and determining the form of rate to be used is called "rate design." Rate design involves considerations such as the cost of service for each class, historical rates, revenue stability, and conservation.

> ***CAUTION:*** It should be noted that the rate-making process does not guarantee results. The utility is merely afforded the opportunity to earn a fair return based on conditions during the particular test period. Conditions may change quickly (e.g., higher fuel costs, heavy maintenance, growth, rising labor costs) and the anticipated return to the utility may not be realized. The remedy is another rate case. The situation, therefore, is dynamic and, especially in periods of inflation, the utility may have to file new rate cases frequently. Once a rate term, or condition of service, has been approved by a regulatory body, the length of time it will remain in effect could vary from only a relatively short time to many years.

.02 Revenue Requirements

The rates of a public utility are fundamentally the prices charged for the utility's product or services. These prices, together with the rules and regulations governing the rendering of service, are almost universally subject to regulation by state and federal commissions and, in some cases, municipalities. A sample of calculations used in determining utility revenue requirements is shown below.

Simplified Calculations Used to Determine
Utility Revenue Requirements

Revenue Requirements = Cost of Service
+ Return on Rate Base

Cost of Service = Cost of Operations
+ Maintenance Expenses
+ Administrative and General Expenses
+ Depreciation
+ Property and Other Non-Income Taxes
+ Income Taxes

Return on Rate Base = Allowed Rate of Return
× Rate Base

Allowed Rate of Return = Weighted Cost of Capital

Capital = Long-Term Debt
+ Preferred Stock
+ Common Equity

Rate Base = Plant in Service
+ Working Capital
+ Regulatory and Certain Other Assets
− Accumulated Depreciation
− Accumulated Deferred Income Taxes
− Certain Liabilities

The essential difference between utility pricing and the pricing of other commodities rests upon the differences between the markets. In the traditional utility market, competition by suppliers of the same service is limited, but the market is not free from competition per se. For example, gas utilities face competition from regulated electric utilities as well as unregulated coal, oil, and liquefied petroleum gas dealers.

¶ 225 Natural Gas Industry Segments

The natural gas industry consists of three segments: production, transmission, and distribution. These three segments have existed since the natural gas industry began to emerge in the early 1900s. The production segment consists of the exploration, production, gathering, and processing of natural gas for its sale to consumers. The transmission segment includes the transportation of gas to distribution centers through large diameter pipelines. The distribution segment consists of the delivery of gas to local consumers through small diameter gas mains.

This paragraph (¶ 225) will focus primarily on the transmission and distribution segments because they are the last segments in the industry to deregulate. Transmission and distribution of natural gas is the business of interstate pipelines and local distribution companies (LDCs).

Interstate transmission pipelines. The interstate pipelines that connect the production of gas to the ultimate consumers functioned as merchants or resellers of gas until the 1980s. At that time, the interstate pipelines purchased gas from producers and sold gas to distribution companies or to other pipelines that would resell to distributors.

Local distribution companies. The retail portion of the industry, however, has traditionally been the function of local gas utilities (local distribution companies, or LDCs). Until recently, all LDCs were resellers of gas. Since the 1980s, LDCs have also begun to act as carriers of gas purchased by or for industrial customers as well as large commercial customers.

See ¶ 110 for deregulation of the natural gas industry and ¶ 205 for regulators of the natural gas industry.

.01 Restructuring the Distribution Segment

The downstream portion of the natural gas industry is currently going through the same types of changes and decisions that pipelines faced years earlier. LDCs have gained access to commodity markets and unbundled transmission and storage. LDCs must choose whether to delegate these services or coordinate these functions themselves. As history has shown, producers and marketers now want direct access to the LDCs' captive customer base by using the LDCs' lines. The gas distribution segment is currently confronting the issues of a more open, market-driven industry. State regulatory agencies are confronted with the issue of opening the gas industry within the city gate.

¶ 230 Electric Industry Segments

Historically, the operations of the electric utility industry fall into three main segments: generation, transmission, and distribution.

.01 Generation

One of the unique characteristics of the electric generation industry is that it must supply an energy "load" to its customers that varies from year to year, from month to month, from day to day, and from hour to hour. The overall system load requirements must be met, even though peakloads vary significantly. To meet the load in the most economical manner, baseload requirements are met by operating large generators that produce the least expensive power. As the load increases, the next least expensive generators are placed into service in succession. This is referred to as "economic dispatch."

To some extent, the nature of the load will govern the type of generating units that will be placed in service. Steam, water, diesel engines, or gas turbine engines may power the generators. Steam plants may burn fossil fuel (coal, gas, or oil) or nuclear fuel to produce steam. The type of fuel used in a steam generator is a matter of economics. Coal is relatively inexpensive on a cost-per-mmBTU (million British thermal unit) basis but is expensive to haul long distances. Steam generators in the Northeast and Northwest are more often gas- or oil-fired or fueled by nuclear energy because there is no significant coal supply in close proximity and the extra transportation costs make it an uneconomical source of fuel. Nuclear fuel is one of the least expensive types of fuel. However, the cost of constructing a nuclear generating facility can outweigh the benefit of the low fuel cost.

Hydroelectric generation. A water-powered generating plant is referred to as a "hydro" plant. Hydro generation is typically the least expensive fuel source, but unless there are assured, adequate supplies of water, it cannot be relied on as a primary power source for a baseload on a year-round basis. In the absence of adequate water supplies, the newest, largest, and most efficient steam generators usually supply the baseload. Older, less efficient steam generators usually supply the intermediary load and are available for providing the baseload in an emergency or when the normal baseload generators are being repaired.

It takes several hours to build up steam to full pressure, and the steam plants are not always suitable for meeting peak demand that will last for only an hour or two. To meet peak demand, the industry relies on diesels and gas turbines, which can be turned on and off quickly, and pumped storage hydro-generators. Diesel and gas turbines usually require less capital to build but have a relatively high fuel cost while in operation. Recent technological advancements in generation technology have resulted in the development of advanced gas-fired turbine generators that are cleaner and more efficient than older models. The new generators can be built and placed into operation quickly, providing an alternative to adding more expensive baseload capacity at central station plants.

Pumped storage hydro projects have the effect of "storing" low-cost baseload energy for use during peak periods. During the night, when the load on the entire system is low, water is pumped into a high reservoir. Energy for pumping is obtained from the system's most efficient (baseload) generators. The water is released to flow downhill through hydroelectric turbines that generate electricity during the day when demand for electricity is high.

Cogeneration facilities. Cogeneration facilities simultaneously produce two forms of useful energy, such as electric power and steam, using the same fuel source. Cogeneration facilities use significantly less fuel to produce electricity and steam (or other forms of energy) than would be needed to produce the two separately. Thus, by using fuels more efficiently, cogeneration facilities can make a significant contribution to the nation's effort to conserve its energy resources. Small power production facilities use biomass, waste, or renewable resources, such as wind, solar energy, and water, to produce electric power. Reliance on these sources of energy can reduce the need to consume traditional fossil fuels to produce electric power.

Power pools. Another factor relating to the type, size, and siting of generators has been the growth of power pools. Power pools are comprised of electric utility companies that combine their resources to ensure reliable and economic flow of electricity for all of the customers served within their combined service territories. The participating utilities in a pool agree to regional generation planning for the entire service area covered by the pool. This permits each company to share the benefits of large baseload generators, the size and efficiency of which may not be economically feasible for any one company alone.

Lengthy agreements and operating procedures govern the rights and obligations of participants in a power pool. Generally, such agreements provide for the operation of all generating facilities within a region on a one-system basis. This is accomplished through central dispatching of the most economical generating equipment in the combined system. The process of economic dispatching on a combined-system basis results in certain member companies producing energy in excess of their own load requirements (sellers) while other member companies produce less energy than their own load requirements (buyers). This production differential is termed "interchange" or "purchased power" and is billed monthly by selling companies to the buying companies through established wholesale power markets.

.02 Transmission

As the generators have become larger, the geographic area each generating plant serves has increased and the power is carried over greater distances. Energy is the product of voltage and current, as indicated in the equation below:

$$\textbf{Energy} = \textbf{Voltage} \times \textbf{Current}$$

A given amount of energy can be the product of high voltage and low current, or low voltage and high current. Economically, it is cheaper to carry energy long distances at high voltage with a lower current because the transmission lines lose less energy and require less copper content in the wires. These savings more than offset the cost of the strong, high pylons needed to carry the high voltage wires.

Interconnections. In order to ensure continuity of service to all of its customers, a utility "interconnects" its own transmission system so that generating units can serve the entire area. Utilities within a regional area may also be interconnected to provide for interchange of power during peak periods or in time of emergency for any one utility in the region. Similarly, there are regional interconnections affording, when necessary, the transmission of energy produced in one section of the nation to another section having generation problems. All interconnections are metered for measuring the flow of energy.

Wheeling and displacement. "Wheeling" is the transmission of power and/or energy by a utility for the benefit of other utility systems. Wheeling might be done as a matter of course in a power pool. In other interconnected utilities, wheeling might be done by specific negotiation between three or more utilities. For example, Utility A is interconnected with Utility B, but not C. Utility C, however, is connected to B and happens to have the energy available that A wishes to purchase. With no special wheeling contract in existence, A might arrange for the purchase from B of the amount it needs, and B would in turn purchase it from C. This requires only a sequence of two-party arrangements and is referred to as "displacement."

.03 Distribution

When energy is delivered to households or factories, it is necessary to do so at usable voltage levels. The typical household receives its electricity at about 110V (volts) for ordinary lighting and 220V for heavier appliances. At these low voltages, it is permissible to string wires on the usual wooden poles, or to place the wires underground.

The sequence, then, is:

Generation → Transmission → Distribution
(High Voltage) (Low Voltage)

The electric component that raises and lowers the alternating voltage is the transformer, which operates on the principle of magnetic induction, has no moving parts, and is highly efficient. The size of the transformer depends on the power it must handle. Transmission transformers vary in size depending on the stage of step up or step down that is required. Distribution transformers, often seen on top of residential poles, are relatively small.

The use of energy is metered to measure the flow, providing the basis for billing. Electric energy is measured in kilowatts, one kilowatt being equivalent to 1.341 horsepower. A kilowatt-hour (kWh) is equal to the use of one kilowatt for one hour and is the unit of energy measurement for electric service delivered to customers.

¶ 235 Electric Power Marketing

Deregulation of the electric power industry (see ¶ 105) has led to the creation of a new segment within the industry: power marketers. Recent federal and state legislative and regulatory reforms have introduced competition to the power generation segment and the electric power markets. As the states move through the deregulation process, states are requiring that electric utilities separate their power generation operations from their regulated transmission and distribution operations. This has created both an opportunity and a need for the newly deregulated power producers or their nonregulated marketing affiliates to participate in competitive power marketing activities to maintain market share. This paragraph (¶ 235) provides an overview of the major federal legislative and regulatory reforms that have helped shape the electric industry's power marketing segment and concludes (¶ 235.03) with a discussion of some of the market characteristics that continue to drive its dynamic growth.

.01 Background

Prior to deregulation, regulated electric utilities did not engage in traditional marketing activities. Historically operated as natural monopolies, these entities have been regulated at both the federal and state level to control entry, prices, and profits. Utilities operated under exclusive franchise rights granted by state regulatory authorities that obligated them to provide "bundled" utility services to customers within their designated service area but precluded them from providing similar services outside of their geographical service area. Expenditures for on-system generation capital improvements have historically been subject to regulatory review and approval while retail and wholesale electric rates have been set by state regulatory authorities at levels that allowed the utilities to recover their cost of service plus a reasonable rate of return on their invested capital. When initially developed, the regulatory scheme was put into place to alleviate public concerns that large, unregulated utilities could use market power to artificially raise prices. With both commodity price and capital commitments subject to the command and control of state regulators, competition did not influence either the supply or demand for utility services.

> ***COMMENT:*** A general consensus has been reached among industry regulators, economists, and federal and state legislators that the power generation segment of the electric power industry will operate more efficiently in a competitive environment. Most industry observers agree that recent advancements in power generating technology will be brought to market more efficiently in a market-based competitive environment. It is also believed that regional electricity price variations can only be reduced through opening the wholesale and retail power markets to competition.

See Part 2 (Chapters 4, 5, and 6) for a detailed discussion of the emerging industries resulting from deregulation: trading and marketing companies, energy services companies, and independent power projects.

.02 Major Federal Legislative and Regulatory Reforms

Over the last 20 years there have been several major federal legislative and regulatory reforms enacted that were designed to open both the wholesale and retail power markets to competition.

Public Utility Regulatory Policies Act of 1978 (PURPA). PURPA (P.L. 95-617) authorized a certain class of nonutility independent power producers—qualified facilities (QFs)—to sell power to regulated utilities at prices mandated by state regulators. The prices were typically set at the utilities' "avoided cost," or the cost that the utility would have otherwise incurred to produce a similar amount of power. Incumbent utilities were required to purchase power produced by the QFs; this provided the utilities with a reliable source of power without incurring additional capital expenditures. In most cases, the QFs entered into long-term power purchase agreements with the incumbent utilities at 1980 price levels.

The QF program was largely responsible for the recent technological advancements in the power generation segment. The program resulted in the development of advanced power generation facilities that were cleaner and used less fuel than the power plants being used by the incumbent utilities at the time. Most industry observers credit the QF program with introducing competition to the power generation segment since this was the first time independent power producers were able to retain profits derived from efficiency gains without having to pass them through to customers. PURPA was somewhat limited in scope and did not provide these benefits to the larger independent power producers. Nonetheless, PURPA has had a significant impact on the growth of nonutility power generation capacity and has resulted in significant technology advances within the industry. It is estimated that approximately half of the electric power generation capacity added in the United States during the 1990s was attributable to independent power producers operating QF facilities.

Although the QFs were selling power in the wholesale markets to the incumbent regulated utilities, they were not actively engaged in competitive power marketing. Their prices were fixed by regulatory mandate (based on the incumbent utility's "avoided" costs) and, in most cases, they were selling 100 percent of their output to a single purchaser. They did not assume any of the market risk now being assumed by the new nonregulated power marketers.

National Energy Policy Act of 1992 (NEPACT). NEPACT (P.L. 102-486) authorized the Federal Energy Regulatory Commission (FERC) to require electric utilities to provide wholesale transmission service (wholesale wheeling) at cost from any requesting electric-generating entity, or facility, to another utility for the purpose of making wholesale power sales. This opened the interstate transmission networks to the independent power generators and the regulated utilities, and gave them access to the national wholesale power markets for the first time. NEPACT allowed QFs to apply for and receive wholesale wheeling orders from FERC. NEPACT also created an additional class of independent power producers—exempt wholesale generators (EWGs)—who are exempt from regulation under the PUHCA provisions. Unlike the QFs authorized under PURPA, NEPACT allowed investor-owned utilities to own majority interests in EWG facilities without violating the federal PUHCA restrictions.

> ***PLANNING NOTE:*** If a qualifying exempt wholesale generator (EWG) provides power to a regulated affiliate, those power sales will continue to be subject to regulatory review by state public service commissions, but sales made in the competitive wholesale power market to unrelated third parties can be made at market-based prices.

NEPACT specifically places retail wheeling (the practice of selling transmission services to another for the purpose of selling electricity to the ultimate consumer) under the jurisdiction of the individual states. Thus, state public service commissions across the country are now in the process of addressing this issue. At the time of this writing, 24 states have adopted legislation or regulatory reforms designed to open their retail power markets to competition. However, seven of those states have recently passed legislation to delay the implementation of retail access, and California has ordered the suspension of direct retail access. See the map showing each state's restructuring activity at ¶ 105.

Prior to NEPACT, most wholesale power sales were transacted between utilities who shared physical interconnects on the transmission system. Each utility was responsible for maintaining the appropriate voltages at the shared interconnects to allow the power to flow uninterrupted across the transmission grid. This contributed to the overall reliability of the transmission and distribution system. Wholesale power that was delivered across multiple transmission systems was generally purchased and resold at each system interconnect in route. However, this resulted in a somewhat closed system since uncooperative transmission owners and operators could use their market position to discriminate against competitors and other independent power producers.

FERC Orders 888 and 889. On April 24, 1996, the Federal Energy Regulatory Commission (FERC) issued two final orders that further encourage wholesale power competition. Orders 888 and 889 require public utilities that own, control, or operate transmission lines in interstate commerce to:

1. provide both network and point-to-point service under open-access tariffs for wholesale transactions on an open, nondiscriminatory basis;
2. file for open transmission-tariffs and take transmission service (including ancillary services such as scheduling, dispatching, and other related services) for their own wholesale electricity sales and purchases under the new tariffs;
3. develop and maintain same-time information systems that will give existing and potential users the same access to transmission information that the public utility enjoys; and
4. unbundle transmission and distribution services from generating and power marketing functions and communications.

With Order 888, FERC specifically offered its support for the concepts related to the formation of Independent System Operators (ISOs), although it does not require transmission companies to either form or join existing ISOs. The rules for ISOs may be determined by the public service commission for each state. Once an ISO is formed, it will become responsible for ensuring nondiscriminatory, open-access transmission and the planning and security of the utilities' combined bulk transmission systems.

.03 Market Characteristics of Electric Power Marketing

With the issuance of Federal Energy Regulatory Commission (FERC) Orders 888 and 889 in 1996, all major federal regulatory reforms were in place to allow open market characteristics to develop in the industry's power marketing segment. With market access to industrial, commercial, and residential customers on a national basis, the number of registered power marketing companies began to grow rapidly. As of December 1, 2001, there were 506 independent power marketers registered with FERC (up from 157 registered marketers at the end of 1995). These new power marketing entities are being formed largely by unregulated affiliates of the regulated public utilities, by independent power producers, and by unregulated subsidiaries of natural gas marketing companies. The explosive growth in this sector has been accompanied by intense competition. Of those 506 marketers listed with FERC, the status of 14 was listed as pending, and the status of 70 was listed as terminated, succession, cancellation, withdrawal, or merger (see http://www.ferc.fed.us/electric/pwrmkt/). In the end, there are expected to be only 10 to 15 large trading and marketing operations in the United States.

> ***CAUTION:*** The shakeout has already begun due to the volatility in the markets. Several marketers with significant losses have already exited the business. The volatility will continue, largely due to the nature of the commodity—it cannot be stored. Only the marketers that can efficiently link power generation with integrated energy service offerings will survive.

Most large power marketers now offer a full complement of energy services to their customers in addition to simply providing wholesale electric power. Service offerings may include risk management, energy project financing, energy audits, facilities management, and self-generation project planning. Many companies now look to act as single-source energy providers under which the power marketer proposes to reduce the customer's total energy costs in return for a percentage of the savings realized. This type of service is expected to spread quickly throughout the industry in the next several years as energy users and suppliers develop new and innovative products to reduce energy costs in a highly competitive market.

Chapter 3

DEREGULATION OF THE ELECTRIC INDUSTRY AND ITS EFFECTS ON TAX POLICY

¶ 301 Overview

State and local jurisdictions are concerned about the potential tax revenue loss likely to accompany deregulation of the electric industry (see ¶ 305). In each region of the country, states are at various stages of deregulation (see ¶ 315). Depending on the stage of deregulation, a state's ability to collect revenue by imposing traditional taxes on electric utilities, such as gross receipts and property taxes (as well as other state taxes, such as sales and use taxes, franchise taxes, and income taxes), will have been affected (see ¶ 320). Moreover, state tax legislation to account for deregulation has been lacking (see ¶ 325).

¶ 305 Potential Revenue Loss

State and local jurisdictions are concerned about the potential tax revenue loss likely to accompany deregulation of the electric industry. For decades, in-state utilities paying utility-only taxes have been a consistent source of revenues for states and localities nationwide. Therefore, very little reason has existed to change tax legislation that in some cases is seriously antiquated. As a result, members of the established utility industry have alerted states to the potential for an unlevel state-tax playing field when the electric industry is deregulated and have advocated for state tax reform so that their utilities can meet competitive pricing. As a result, most states have recognized a need to reexamine utility tax laws along with deregulation.

States who have chosen to tackle deregulation legislation have done so with two primary goals: (1) accommodating in-state traditional utilities and (2) achieving tax revenue neutrality. Accommodation of in-state utilities is generally being achieved by creating some form of short-term transactional charge on consumers to help utilities recover "stranded costs" (see ¶ 310), plus legislating the same taxation on utilities and energy markets alike. Achieving tax revenue neutrality during deregulation will likely involve more dramatic changes.

¶ 310 Stranded Costs

Prior to deregulation, utilities made significant investments to upgrade and expand electric generation assets on the assumption that they would be guaranteed a rate of return on those investments. However, as a result of deregulation, there is no guarantee that these "stranded costs" will ever be recovered. Therefore, most deregulation legislation includes a recovery mechanism for stranded costs. This mechanism generally consists of a transition charge, which allows the utility to collect the stranded cost from ratepayers (i.e., customers) for a certain period of time.

For a discussion of other fees and charges that are passed through to consumers, see ¶ 320.

¶ 315 State Analysis of Deregulation by Region

There has been a surge of activity in legislatures and public utility commissions in most states to examine retail competition. In the absence of national legislation, states have set their own pace in restructuring and deregulating the electric industry.[1]

Within the deregulation arena, most states fall into one of four categories (see map at ¶ 105). The most rapidly deregulating states, where restructuring legislation has already been enacted, include Pennsylvania, Illinois, and most of the New England states. In those states, high electricity costs (above the national average) have helped lead to the dismantling of many utility regulations and the welcoming of competition. Not far behind is New York, where comprehensive regulatory orders have been issued. Twenty-six states, the largest in number if not in population or electricity usage, are taking a slower approach to utility restructuring. They claim that the economic and social costs of restructuring have not been fully examined and that full competition will benefit a select few at the expense of the average consumer. Included in these states are Alabama, Colorado, Florida, and Utah. Finally, California, due to recent events, has suspended deregulation.

.01 Midatlantic

Pennsylvania. Pennsylvania was one of the first states to offer its residents the right to choose electric generation suppliers. In 1996, the

[1] James R. Dukart, "States Race to Compete," *Utility Business*, March 1999, Vol. 2, Iss. 3, p. 30.

state Legislature passed, and Gov. Ridge signed, the Electricity Generation Customer Choice and Competition Act. The law gave consumers the right to choose electric generation suppliers beginning with one-third of consumers by January 1999, two-thirds by January 2000, and all consumers by January 2001. However, subsequent legislation, House Bill 2286, was introduced in March 1998 to accelerate retail choice for all consumers by two years, to January 1999.

In addition, the law required electric companies to design pilot programs. In September 1997, the program offered 230,000 customers the ability to choose their electric generation supplier. Approximately 1 million customers applied, and 230,000 were selected based on a lottery.

Enacted in December 1996, House Bill 1509 allowed the recovery of "stranded costs."[2] In order to recover stranded costs, the Public Utilities Commission (PUC) must approve the amount requested by each utility generator. The PUC has allowed utilities to use reasonable mitigation measures or securitization. To date, a majority of the amounts requested for stranded costs have been approved. Transition charges paid by utility customers will be used to recover stranded costs and will appear on customer bills.

As of September 1999, 450,000 Pennsylvania customers (approximately 9 percent of eligible customers) had switched to a different supplier. (This was three times the number of California customers who switched suppliers.) The number of customers participating in electricity open markets increased to 787,846 as of April 2001. However, just three months later, as of July 1, 2001, only 591,596 customers were participating. About half of these customers are former PECO Energy customers who are buying power at below-market cost. The ability to buy electricity at below-market cost is due to Pennsylvania's discount power program, which was designed to encourage customers to switch to alternative generation suppliers. Rising wholesale prices have caused many commercial and industrial customers to return to their traditional electric utility supplier.

.02 Midwest

Illinois. During the early part of 1996, Central Illinois Light Company (CILCO) and Illinois Power conducted retail wheeling test programs.[3] The Illinois Power pilot included only large customers. The CILCO pilot included all classes of customers. By November 1998, CILCO requested the termination of its pilot program for retail choice,

---

[2] Penn. House Bill 1509, Act 139 (December 1996). See ¶ 310 for a discussion of stranded costs.

[3] "Wheeling" is discussed at ¶ 230.02.

"Power Quest." CILCO stated that the program had served the purpose of showing that retail choice works in Illinois.

In December 1997, the Electric Service Customer Choice and Rate Relief Act was enacted. The law provided for rate cuts for ComEd and Illinois Power, effective August 1998. The law required that certain commercial and industrial markets be opened to competition by October 1999, and all customers, including residential, have a choice of electric generation suppliers by May 2002. Customers who choose an alternative supplier must pay transition charges until 2006. In addition, the law allows for the recovery of stranded costs based on a formula for lost revenue.

Enabled by the Restructuring Law enacted in December 1997,[4] ComEd sought Illinois Commerce Commission (ICC) approval of a bond issue in April 1998. By law, the proceeds from bonds were to be used to refinance debt and equity in preparation for competition. The following month, the ICC approved ComEd's plan to offer nonresidential customers hourly rates under its "Hourly Energy Pricing" program. Under the program, hourly energy prices (1) would be priced on a dollar-per-kilowatt-hour basis, (2) would vary hour by hour, and (3) would be market based, reflecting the marginal (or incremental) cost of purchasing nonfirm energy on a daily basis on the open market.

In August 1998, the phase-in of rate cuts took effect. The state's largest utilities, Illinova and ComEd, cut rates by 15 percent; another 5 percent reduction is due by May 2002. Smaller utilities will phase-in 5 percent reductions by May 2002. To date, Illinois Power customers have saved about $12.5 million.

In March 1999, enrollment of *nonresidential* consumers for choice of their electric generation supplier began in the CILCO service territory. Up to one-third of all Illinois nonresidential consumers were eligible to choose alternative suppliers by October 1, 1999, and as of December 2000, all nonresidential consumers were able to choose their supplier. By May 2002, all Illinois *residential* consumers will also be able to choose their supplier.

Subsequent legislation was enacted in July 1999 to amend the restructuring law. Senate Bill 24 (SB 24) sped up the transition to retail choice by requiring the first third of commercial and industrial customers to have retail choice by October 1, 1999, the second third by June 1, 2000, and the final third by October 1, 2000. Under SB 24, residential customers were to receive a 5 percent rate reduction by October 1, 2001, which was seven months earlier than under the original restructuring law. This new legislation also increased the rate cap for utilities

[4] 35 ILCS 620/1a *et seq.*

by 2 percent, promoted cogeneration, and required ComEd to allocate $250 million to a special fund to be used for environmental and energy efficiency initiatives.

Michigan. In June 1997, the Public Service Commission (PSC) set forth an order laying out the framework for electric industry restructuring. By January 1998, the PSC completed rehearing orders introducing competition in the state's electric utility market. The phase-in schedule allowed 2.5 percent of Consumer's Energy and Detroit Edison customers retail access as early as March 1998, adding another 2.5 percent in June 1998, January 1999, January 2000, and January 2001, with all consumers to have retail access by 2002.

The PSC proposed in January 1998 a plan allowing for the full recovery of stranded costs using exit fees through 2007. By November 1998, the Michigan Senate Technology and Energy Committee passed a bill to implement retail competition beginning with 7.5 percent of consumers and extending to all consumers by January 2002. The bill allowed collection of transition fees and recovery of stranded costs through 2007.

Retail competition, however, was stalled when the Michigan Legislature adjourned in December from its 1998 session without passing a restructuring bill. Meanwhile, the PSC began to move forward with its plan to open the retail electric market by 2002. On June 29, 1999, the Michigan Supreme Court ruled that the PSC lacked statutory authority to move forward with its plan to open the retail market.

Restructuring legislation was introduced on January 25, 2000, and Public Act 141 of 2000 and companion Public Act 142 were signed into law on June 3, 2000. The comprehensive restructuring legislation required that all consumers have retail choice by January 2002. Residential customers of Detroit Edison and Consumers Energy were to receive an immediate 5 percent rate reduction. The reduced rates were frozen until at least December 31, 2003. Rates for large commercial and industrial consumers were also capped through 2003, and rates for small business consumers were capped at their current levels through 2004. The law also authorized stranded cost recovery and securitization (refinancing of debt) and gave the PSC authority to implement restructuring and retail competition.

The PSC issued a series of orders to implement the restructuring legislation. Among the orders was a directive to Detroit Edison and Consumers Energy to file revised tariffs to implement retail access programs and an order to all other investor-owned utilities to file restructuring plans to implement retail access. The PSC also issued an order establishing the framework for alternative electric suppliers to participate in retail electric markets under the restructuring law. In January 2001, the PSC issued a final order authorizing Detroit Edison to securitize $1.77 billion in costs by issuing bonds, which allowed the electric supplier to implement a 5 percent rate reduction.

Ohio. During 1996, the Public Utilities Commission (PUC) adopted guidelines for "interruptible buy-through contracts," allowing power purchases from alternative suppliers in order to avoid interruptions. In December 1996, the PUC adopted guidelines for Conjunctive Electric Services. The two-year test program allowed customers to band together for collective billing under rates designed for the group. (This pilot was an experiment in innovative pricing and did not allow retail wheeling.)

The PUC approved the first tariff allowing consumers to aggregate and negotiate the price for electricity in June 1998. By July 1998, the PUC approved consumer protection standards. The improved standards addressed new service installation, meter testing, disconnects, complaint resolution, outage reporting, and utility reporting requirements.

In February 1998, the Legislative Joint Committee on Electric Deregulation's plan was adopted. Retail access was set to begin by January 2000 and included a five-year transition period. Utilities were allowed to receive "transmission revenues" in the form of nonbypassable wire charges to partially recover stranded costs after relinquishing control of transmission to an Independent System Operator.

The following month, identical bills to deregulate the electric power industry were introduced in the Ohio House and Senate. The co-chairs, Rep. Mead and Sen. Johnson, of the legislative Joint Committee on Electric Deregulation sponsored the bills. The proposed legislation would have allowed retail competition beginning in January 2000 and would have set a five-year transition period to full competition by December 2004.

In August 1998, representatives of the major investor-owned utilities, in response to requests from the General Assembly, began developing a consensus framework for a restructuring proposal. Their proposal recommended that all consumers have a choice of suppliers by January 1, 2001.

The 1998 legislative session closed without action on restructuring bills. The Senate president pushed for addressing deregulation early in 1999, and the PUC chairman also urged the state to make deregulation a top priority. In February 1999, House Bill 5 and Senate Bill 3 were introduced to restructure the electric power industry. A pressing issue concerned a tax policy to ensure that schools and local governments would not be harmed by deregulation through the erosion of their tax base.

In March 1999, Rep. Mead and Sen. Johnson introduced restructuring legislation that would phase-in competition over five years beginning in 2001 and allow stranded cost recovery between $5 billion and $11 billion. Clearing the way for the PUC to move ahead with plans for a conjunctive billing service, a lawsuit aimed at blocking conjunctive service regulations was thrown out of court in August 1998. On July 6, 1999, the governor signed Senate Bill 3, allowing for retail competition to begin in January 2001 and be completed by December 2005.

Between July and October 2000, the PUC approved the restructuring plans of five utilities in the state, including requests for the recovery of transition and stranded costs, which ranged from $13 million (Monongahela Power) to $7 billion (First Energy).

.03 Northeast

New Jersey. The Board of Public Utilities (BPU) issued an order releasing its Energy Master Plan for public comment in January 1997. The proposal called for a phase-in of retail choice giving all New Jersey residents and businesses the ability to select their electric supplier by April 2001. After reviewing comments and proposals, the BPU issued an order adopting and releasing its final report for the Energy Master Plan in April 1997. The revised plan accelerated the time line for retail competition. It was planned that competition would be phased-in beginning with 10 percent by October 1998, 35 percent by April 1999, 50 percent by October 1999, 75 percent by April 2000, and all consumers by July 2000.

In July 1997, the four investor-owned electric utilities in the state submitted three filings each to the BPU: (1) a rate unbundling filing, (2) a stranded cost filing, and (3) a restructuring filing. In September 1997, an initial decision on the four investor-owned utilities' restructuring filings was set for May 1998.

A pilot program started by Jersey Central Power & Light in September 1997 for customers in the Monroe township was extended through December 31, 1998, and an allowance was made for an extension until competition was begun.

In a ruling on Public Service Electric & Gas's (PSE&G) restructuring plan, an Administrative Law Judge (ALJ) opined that PSE&G should recover from customers most of its stranded costs and it would have to cut rates by 10 percent to 12 percent. Another ALJ issued an initial decision on Atlantic City Electric Co.'s stranded costs and unbundling filings, agreeing that stranded cost estimates were acceptable and should be recovered. Legislative and BPU approval would be needed to implement utility restructuring plans.

Both the New Jersey Assembly and the Senate scheduled a vote on restructuring legislation for January 12, 1999. Assembly Bill 10 allowed for retail competition by August 1999, a 10 percent rate reduction, and stranded cost recovery through securitization. The bill did not require divestiture of electric generation assets, but various utilities announced the sale of generation assets in the state.

In January 1999, the issue of municipal aggregation delayed the bill until at least January 25. Finally, in February 1999, legislation was enacted in New Jersey to restructure the electric power industry. The law allowed for all consumers to have retail choice by August 1999. The law called for current rates to be immediately reduced by 5 percent, and then reduced by another 10 percent over three years. The law also allowed for utility generators to recover stranded costs through a wire charge paid by consumers.

In December 2000, the New Jersey Supreme Court upheld the BPU's orders for PSE&G's restructuring and securitization. This decision allowed PSE&G to proceed with its implementation of the restructuring plan pursuant to the BPU's orders. Under the BPU's orders, PSE&G customers received an additional 2 percent rate reduction and PSE&G was allowed to sell securitization bonds totaling $2.5 billion, the proceeds of which were to retire outstanding debt or equity.

New York. In May 1996, the Public Service Commission (PSC) issued a decision to restructure New York's electric industry. The Competitive Opportunities Case adopted the goal of having a competitive wholesale market by 1997 and a competitive retail market by early 1998. Electric utilities were notified that they were required to submit restructuring plans by October 1996. The decision also stated that utilities should have a reasonable opportunity to recover stranded costs consistent with the goals of restructuring. In 1998, in order to recover stranded costs, various sales of hydro plants, power plants, and fossil-fuel-fired generation plants took place among several companies, subject to approval by state and federal regulatory authorities.

In addition, the Public Utilities Commission (PUC) stated in an order that it would determine each utility's allowable recovery of stranded costs. Utilities were instructed to use creative means to reduce the amount of stranded costs prior to consideration and to include stranded cost recovery plans in their restructuring filings.

In July 1996, the PUC approved one company's pilot program, "Power Pick," allowing industrial consumers retail access to competitive generation suppliers. The program began in May 1998. In June 1997, the PUC approved a pilot program for more than 17,600 qualified farmers and food processors, beginning in November 1997.

In November 1998, the PSC ordered utilities to inform customers of the sources of their electricity and their amount of environmentally "clean" power beginning April 2000. Then in February 1999, the PSC ordered utilities to submit monthly reports in 1999, and quarterly reports thereafter, in order to allow the PSC to monitor competition.

While the transition to complete retail competition began at different times and progressed at different rates in the service territories of the different utilities, as of July 2001, all customers of the state's major regulated electric utilities had the right to choose their suppliers.

.04 Southeast

Florida. In October 1997, the Florida Legislature formed a special subcommittee to track restructuring developments in other states. At the same time, the House Committee on Utilities and Communication sponsored informal hearings on electricity restructuring issues.

House Bill 1888 (HB 1888) was introduced and referred to committee in March 1998. The bill would deregulate the electric power industry and allow retail access by 2001. However, HB 1888 faced strong opposition and died in committee without a hearing, reflecting both the strong opposition from utilities and lack of consumer interest.

In response to competitive pressures that could lower electric bills for large consumers, the Public Service Commission (PSC) approved discount rates (up to 20 percent) for new and expanding businesses in August 1998. The Florida Alliance for Lower Electric Rates Today opposed the discounts, instead proposing statewide competition for all consumers.

In April 1999, the PSC approved a merchant plant to be built in New Smyrna by Duke Energy. The combined cycle gas plant will have a photovoltaic unit to offer a "green" pricing option as part of the plant's marketing. The utilities in the state opposed the plant, but the PSC stated that the plant, and other merchant plants proposed to be built, could help solve the state's reserve margin problem, lack of photovoltaics, and market share concerns. However, in April 2000, the Florida Supreme Court reversed the PSC's order approving the Duke merchant plant proposal. The Court held that the PSC did not have the authority to approve the merchant plant under the Florida Electric Power Plant Siting Act of 1973.

As of January 2000, neither the legislature nor the PUC was actively pursuing restructuring for retail access in Florida. In response to the legislature's failure to address the restructuring of Florida's electric power industry, Gov. Bush signed an executive order appointing a 17-member Energy 2020 Study Commission. The Commission was charged with studying retail competition and future energy demand in Florida. In February 2001, the Commission released an interim report that included recommendations for the development of a competitive wholesale electricity market in Florida. The Commission submitted its final report to Gov. Bush on December 1, 2001. The Commission's final report adopted five goals and developed specific objectives, strategies, and tasks to achieve these goals: (1) promoting energy efficiency and public benefits, (2) assuring an adequate and reliable supply of energy, (3) improving energy infrastructure, (4) preserving the environment, and (5) preparing Florida for new technologies and renewable resources.

.05 Southwest

Texas. In January 1997, the Public Utilities Commission (PUC) issued three reports as directed by the Texas Legislature. Volume 1 discussed the scope of competition in the electric industry in Texas; Volume 2 included an investigation into retail competition; and Volume 3 focused on recovery of stranded costs and competition.

West Texas Utilities began a pilot program in October 1997, allowing approximately 1,000 customers in San Angelo to support the development of renewable energy resources by adding certain amounts to monthly bills and receiving increments of power from renewable energy sources.

In April 1998, the PUC notified utilities about its recommendations for deregulation. In July 1998, the PUC approved Texas-New Mexico's (T-NM's) five-year transition plan providing residential customers an immediate 3 percent rate reduction and another 3 percent in January 2000 and January 2001, totaling 9 percent over three years. Also, the plan provided for full recovery of stranded costs through a Competitive Transition Charge. In addition, the plan included a pilot program to allow all retail consumers a choice of electric generation providers by 2003.

As part of T-NM's transition to competition, the PUC approved a price reduction for their customers that was retroactive to January 1998. This resulted in a credit on the bills of customers. The price reduction was part of T-NM's plan to reduce residential rates by 9 percent and commercial rates by 3 percent over a five-year transition period.

The PUC also proposed a means by which utilities could recover stranded costs. In May 1998, the PUC's revisions to their plan for deregulation would allow securitization of stranded assets, estimated to be $4.5 billion if retail competition occurred in 2001. By deferring full competition one more year, stranded costs would decrease to $3.3 billion. Delaying competition until 2003 would decrease stranded costs to $2.3 billion.

In June 1998, the Texas Legislature was expected to consider four bills to open electricity to competition when it convened in January 1999. A hearing was held with the Texas Industrial Electric Consumers that claimed residential customers would also benefit from deregulation.

Restructuring legislation bills were filed in both the House (House Bill 349) and Senate (Senate Bill 7) in February 1999. The bills would open the Texas retail electricity market to competition by January 1, 2002. To limit market power, the bills limited ownership of generating capacity to 20 percent of the state's total capacity. In addition, the bills froze rates and required companies to split their generation, transmission, and distribution assets. In March, the Senate approved Senate Bill 7 (SB 7) and in June, the Texas Legislature adopted it.[5] SB 7 made the PUC responsible for stranded cost recovery (estimated between $4 billion and $9 billion) and reduced rates by 6 percent from 2002 until 2005 (or until utilities lose 40 percent of their consumers to competition).

In April 2000, the utilities filed restructuring plans with the PUC. The plans addressed the mandated rate reduction of 6 percent after January 1, 2002, how the utilities would implement retail choice by 2002, and how they would separate their businesses into divisions for generation, retail provider, and delivery.

The PUC adopted rules for the "providers of last resort" (POLRs) in October 2000 to ensure continuity of service once retail competition begins in 2002. Under the PUC rules, electric service providers who are chosen to be POLRs (through a competitive bidding process) will provide service to customers in areas of open competition whose current service providers went out of business or dropped the consumer. The rules also provide that the POLRs must offer a fixed, nondiscountable, seasonally differentiated rate to three classes (residential, small non-residential, and large nonresidential). The POLR service is not intended to be competitive, innovative, or anything other than basic service.

The next step for Texas was to institute a pilot program. Initially the program was to begin on June 1, 2001, with enrollment starting in February 2001. The program was open to customers in the investor-

[5] Texas Senate Bill 7, Ch. 405 (1999 Texas Laws).

owned utility (IOU) service territories, and if more than 5 percent chose to enroll, a lottery would be held to choose participants. A high level of interest necessitated a lottery to choose participants. Beginning in June, 5 percent of each customer class in each of the IOUs would be allowed to choose their electric supplier. The official opening of the pilot program was delayed twice, from the original date of June 1, to July 6, to July 31. However, the schedule for full retail access was still set to begin in January 2002.

In August 2001, the PUC considered delaying the implementation of retail competition beyond January 2002 in some areas of East Texas. No companies had offered service in these areas during the pilot program, thus no customers had requested service by an alternate provider.

Under SB 7, ownership of generating capacity was limited to 20 percent of Texas' total capacity. This provision was designed to increase the pool of available power for new retail suppliers entering the market and to promote competition in the electric market. In September 2001, each generation company affiliated with a former monopoly utility company started selling entitlements to at least 15 percent of its installed generation capacity as required by SB 7.

In October 2001 and again in November, the PUC delayed retail choice in areas of Texas, citing reasons such as lack of an RTO (Regional Transmission Organization) in the region, no retail electric suppliers, absence of marketing by retail providers, and wholesale electricity markets were as yet competitive. These delays affected customers in Southeast Texas and those Texas customers covered by the Southwest Power Pool.

.06 West

California. California has been at the forefront of utility deregulation. In December 1995, the California Public Utilities Commission (PUC) issued a final order to deregulate the electric power industry and phase-in retail competition in conjunction with Assembly Bill 1890,[6] which formally restructured the electric utility industry and opened electric generation to competition. The plan was then amended to allow retail competition for all consumers simultaneously, beginning in January 1998 and extending through March 1998.

In August 1997, Senate Bill 477 [7] was passed allowing utilities to issue bonds (securitize) to recover their stranded investments. These

[6] Calif. Assembly Bill 1890, Ch. 854 (1996 Calif. Laws).

[7] Calif. Senate Bill 477, Ch. 275 (1997 Calif. Statutes).

bonds would then be paid for by a transition charge passed through to all utility customers.

On March 31, 1998, the PUC issued a final order officially opening the electric industry market to competition effective for all consumers in investor-owned utility (IOU) service territories. Jurisdiction of transmission lines was transferred from state to federal authority with 70 percent of the transmission grid under control of the Independent System Operator (ISO). This made California the first state to introduce a statewide competitive electric industry.

In 1998, other states that were considering restructuring legislation were closely tracking California's progress to gauge its success. California's deregulation did create the desired result: lower electricity prices. In 1996, California customers paid an average of 9.5 cents per kilowatt-hour for electricity, which was well above the national average of 6.9 cents. The prices after deregulation did drop significantly and were expected to continue to drop over the next few years. Along with lowering prices, opening competition brought about choice to the consumer and innovation on the part of the supplier.

As of April 1999, after one year of deregulation, about 30 percent of industrial consumers and 1 percent of residential consumers had switched from the incumbent utility to an alternative supplier. As of January 15, 2000, almost one-third of large industrial customers had switched suppliers, whereas only about 2 percent of residential customers had opted for retail choice.

As deregulation expanded, California considered establishing a new energy "superagency" to plan and site new electric and gas transmission. The California Energy Reliability Agency would replace the California Energy Commission and the Electricity Oversight Board as well as certain functions of the California PUC and the California ISO. Since utilities and competitive generators sit on the Cal-ISO, elected officials were concerned the ISO board's objectives would be at odds with public interest. If the ISO board allowed congestion and restricted supply, prices would be driven up in conjunction with utility and generator interests. The agency would determine the locale of transmission lines and gas pipelines, develop future transmission, certify new generators, exercise eminent domain, and administer energy-efficiency programs.[8] To date, the California Energy Reliability Agency has not been established.

California's success with deregulation, however, was short lived. Not all electric customers were experiencing the price drops expected to

[8] U.S. Department of Energy, *Electric Utility Restructuring Weekly Update* (April 2, 1999). http://www.eren.doe.gov/electricity–restructuring/weekly.html.

continue under deregulation. In the summer of 2000, San Diego Gas & Electric (SDG&E) customers, who were paying market rates for electricity, saw their electric bills nearly triple compared to the prices they paid the summer before. In August 2000, the Senate passed emergency legislation to roll back and freeze rates for all SDG&E customers, and the bill was signed into law (with some revisions) in September.

The experience of SDG&E's customers was only the beginning of the problem for California. During January 2001, the ISO issued a Stage Three Electrical Emergency almost daily. Stage Three means that electric reserves fell below 1.5 percent and that rolling blackouts may be necessary to maintain the system's integrity. Three bills, Assembly Bill 5, Assembly Bill 6, and Senate Bill 7, were passed into law that same month to address the state's energy crisis.

Assembly Bill 5 (AB 5) required the ISO to replace its interested board members (utilities and competitive generators sat on the board) with disinterested members appointed by the governor. AB 5 also required the ISO to list daily the plants that were not operational on its Internet site. Assembly Bill 6 (AB 6) required generating plants owned by California utilities prior to June 1997 remain under the PUC's jurisdiction. AB 6 also forbade those plants from being sold prior to January 2006. Senate Bill 7 (SB 7) addressed the utilities' growing inability to purchase electricity to meet their consumers' demands due to financial problems. Southern California Edison (SCE) and Pacific Gas & Electric both had their credit ratings downgraded to "junk bond" status, and thus were unable to obtain financing to purchase electricity. SB 7 authorized the Department of Water Resources to spend $400 million to purchase electricity and sell it to consumers through utilities.

Gov. Davis released his plan to rescue California's nearly bankrupt utilities in March 2001. The plan called for the purchase of the utilities' transmission systems, expected parent companies to contribute significant amounts to the utilities for debt payment, and prohibited the sale of generating facilities currently owned by the utilities. To pay creditors, utilities would be allowed to sell secured revenue bonds. Senate Bill 33 authorized the governor to initiate a plan to purchase the utilities' transmission facilities. Gov. Davis reached an agreement with SCE to purchase its transmission system for an estimated $2.67 billion.

In June 2001, Gov. Davis signed a bill into law creating the California Consumer Power and Conservation Financing Authority. This new agency is to ensure that California has an adequate supply of power at reasonable prices. The agency has the authority to construct new power plants, issue up to $5 million in bonds, require efficiency and environmental improvements to existing power plants, and direct new energy efficiency and renewable energy programs.

In October 2001, the PUC suspended retail choice in California.

Arizona. In April 1996, the Arizona Legislature began exploring deregulation with House Bill 2504 (HB 2504). HB 2504 established a Joint Committee to study electric industry restructuring. Two years later in May 1998, HB 2663[9] was enacted and gave the Arizona Corporate Commission (ACC) authority to open territories to retail competition. The ACC planned to open 20 percent of the market to competition by December 31, 1998, and 100 percent of the market by December 31, 2000. The law also extended deregulation to municipals and other publicly owned utilities, such as the Salt River Project.

Tucson Electric Company (TEC) was one of the first utilities to file a divestiture plan with the ACC. The ACC order on stranded costs provided utilities either of the following two options:

1. *Divestiture of assets.* The amount of recoverable stranded costs would be the difference between the value of electric generation assets under traditional regulation and their market value after an auction process.
2. *Transition revenues methodology.* The ACC "would provide sufficient revenues necessary to maintain financial integrity for a period of 10 years," allocating stranded costs among consumers and shareholders as deemed "to be in the public interest."

The ACC approved TEC's divestiture plan and recovery of 100 percent of stranded costs in November 1998. The agreement supported the creation of a transmission company owned by TEC and TEC's acquisition of Arizona Public Power's transmissions assets. The agreement called for open retail access in TEC's market by January 1, 1999, beginning with 20 percent of the load.

In January 1999, the ACC's decision[10] against a restructuring plan between the ACC, Arizona Public Service Company (APS), and Tucson Electric Power (TEP) delayed deregulation over the settlement for stranded costs.

At the same time, the Salt River Project (SRP) opened approximately 20 percent of their market to retail competition. However, only one alternative supplier (PG&E) was licensed to sell to commercial and

[9] Ariz. House Bill 2663, 2nd Ariz. Legis., Sess. 43 (May 1998).

[10] Decision on Electric Deregulation, January 11, 1999, Decision No. 61311, Docket No. RE-00000C-94-0165.

industrial consumers. SRP's restructuring plan included a 5.4 percent rate reduction for consumers remaining with SRP.

> ***COMMENT:*** The SRP is not under jurisdiction of the ACC and thus has not been affected by the court ruling that delayed competition in the investor-owned utilities' territories.

By April 1999, the Public Service Commission (PSC) approved a new plan that allowed retail competition to begin later that year. In the new plan, utilities were given four options to recover stranded costs: (1) calculating lost net revenue due to restructuring, (2) selling assets, (3) determining revenue to financial ratios, or (4) a combination of the three.

In September 1999, the ACC approved APS's restructuring settlement agreement. Under the agreement, APS was to open 20 percent of the load in its territory to competition on October 1, 1999, and residential rates were to be reduced by 7.5 percent over a four-year period. Additionally, large consumers' rates were to be reduced by 5 percent over a three-year period. The ACC also approved of APS collecting $350 million in stranded costs over five years.

One month later, in October 1999, the ACC issued a recommendation to approve TEP's restructuring settlement. The settlement provided for TEP to open 20 percent of the load in its territory to competition by January 2000, and 100 percent by January 2001. Rates were to be reduced by 1 percent and frozen through 2008. The settlement also allowed TEP to recover $450 million in stranded costs by collecting a Competition Transition Charge (CTC) and an additional $638 million in stranded costs through a "floating" CTC.

There has been much opposition to the opening of Arizona's electric market. The Arizona Consumers Council and the Arizona Center for Law in the Public Interest have filed numerous lawsuits, with varying results, challenging such things as the ACC's Electric Competition Rules and the ACC's approval of APS's restructuring settlement.

¶ 320 Traditional Taxation of Utilities

For decades, state and local taxes paid by in-state utilities have been a reliable source of revenues for states and localities. Public utilities represent a huge source of revenue to state and local governments both as taxpayers and tax collectors. In 1997, investor-owned electric utilities paid in excess of $13.9 billion in state and local taxes.[11]

[11] Edison Electric Institute, *Statistical Yearbook of the Electric Utility Industry* (Washington, D.C.: Edison Electric Institute, 1997). See also the bar graph at ¶ 320.03.

Public utilities are subject to general taxes and special taxes at the state and local level. General taxes are imposed on most corporations doing business within the taxing jurisdiction. Examples of general taxes include state income taxes, franchise taxes, sales and use taxes, and property taxes. In addition, public utilities are subject to special taxes unique to the electric utility industry. These special taxes may be imposed in addition to (or in lieu of) general taxes or other taxes. Some of the most common types of special taxes include gross receipts taxes, administrative fees for funding state regulatory commissions, kilowatt-hour taxes, and public utility license taxes.

Generally, gross receipts taxes and property taxes have comprised the major portion of state and local taxes paid by utilities each year. For example, in 1994, investor-owned electric utilities paid a collective $5.4 billion in property and ad valorem taxes, $4 billion in gross receipts taxes, $1.5 billion in miscellaneous taxes, $2 billion in state income and franchise taxes, and $0.6 billion in regulatory fees and other local utility charges.[12] These figures are shown as percentages in the pie chart below.

Traditional State and Local Taxes Paid by Investor-Owned Electric Utilities Prior to Deregulation

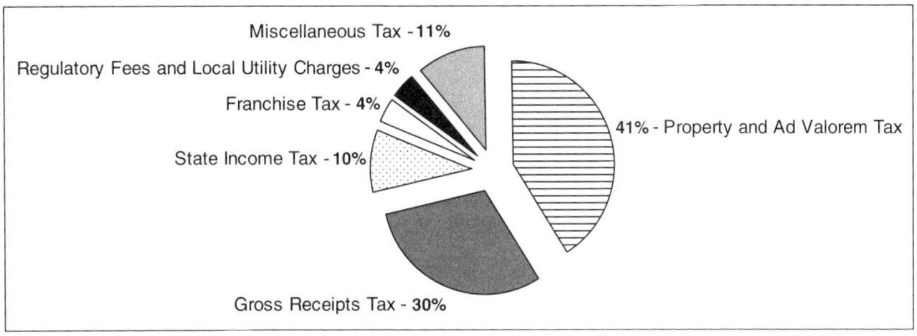

.01 Gross Receipts Tax

The gross receipts tax, or gross earnings tax, is the most common form of special tax imposed on utilities. A gross receipts tax is applied to a utility's gross revenues without deduction for most expenditures or operating costs. Gross receipts taxes may be imposed at a single rate or at graduated rates. Usually, gross receipts taxes are imposed only on sales to customers within the taxing state. Since the tax is imposed on

[12] National Council on Competition and the Electric Industry, *Federal, State and Local Tax Implications of Electric Utility Industry Restructuring* (October 1996). See ¶ 325 for a detailed discussion of the changes to tax methodologies brought about by deregulation.

gross receipts, a utility will still be liable for the tax even if the utility operated in a net operating loss position.

.02 Property Tax

Property taxes have generally been local governments' primary source of tax revenue. Property taxes are a relatively stable source of revenue and are relatively easy to administer. Because property taxes are a principal source of revenue for local governments, wide discretion is given to the property tax boards in the assessment process. One such latitude is that property tax rates can be adjusted annually to compensate for fluctuations in the tax base. Property taxes are often used by local governments to fund schools, roads, and other local services.

Property taxes are imposed on the owners of property located in a taxing jurisdiction. Property taxes are generally characterized as "ad valorem" because they are assessed on the value of property on a prescribed assessment date each year (frequently January 1). Real property is subject to tax in virtually every jurisdiction imposing a property tax. Personal property used in a trade or business is also subject to property taxation in most states. The rate of tax is usually applied to the assessed value of the property. In states that do not impose a tax on personal property (or the rate is lower for personal property), statutes have been enacted to classify some types of personal property of utilities as real property.

The utility industry is highly capital intensive. Utility generation, transmission, and distribution assets create a significant tax base for property taxes. The valuation of utility property is administered in a variety of ways. In a majority of states, real and personal property of regulated utilities is centrally assessed by the state assessor. The state assessor then apportions the tax base among local taxing jurisdictions. Other states assess utility property at the local level.

There are various methods of valuation used in the assessment process of utilities. Under the "unit method" of valuation, the assessor estimates the "unit value" of the entire utility. The "unit value" can be based on (1) the cost of the utility's taxable assets, (2) the income earned by the utility, or (3) the value placed by the financial markets upon the utility's debt and equity securities, or (4) some combination of the three. Another method assesses utility property based on the value of each specific item of property.

> ***CAUTION:*** Difficulty often arises in assessing utility property. The assessed value may be based either on original cost or fair market value of the property. However, utility assets historically are not readily marketable, and, therefore, fair market valuation is at best judgmental. Valuation based on a financial market ap-

proach or an income approach is often difficult, if not impossible, to ascertain for specific properties. Consequently, on many occasions, assessed value of utility property may be based on a form of depreciated cost rather than fair market value. Regardless of the valuation method used, valuation of utility property remains a subjective process.

Property located in multiple jurisdictions. Often, in addition to the variety of valuation methodologies used, utility property is located within the jurisdictions of multiple taxing authorities. The lack of uniformity may create disparity in allocating value among jurisdictions, resulting in a heavier burden of taxation compared to other property. In addition, a utility's service market is usually restricted by regulatory mandate, thus prohibiting the utility from shifting its property assets to jurisdictions with lower property tax rates. As a result, in numerous states, utilities pay disproportionately higher property taxes.

Ohio property taxes on utilities. Regulated utilities in Ohio were traditionally taxed at a higher rate than nonregulated entities through disparate property tax assessments. Prior to the 1999 deregulation legislation, all utility property in Ohio was assessed at 88 percent of its value, while the property value of nonregulated entities was assessed at 25 percent of its value.

Beginning with the 2001 tax year, the taxable personal property of a rural electric company in Ohio is assessed at 50 percent of the true value of the taxable transmission and distribution property and 25 percent of the true value of all other taxable property. The taxable transmission and distribution property of an electric company is still assessed at 88 percent of its true value, but all other taxable property is assessed at 25 percent of its true value. However, some personal property leased to an electric or rural electric company and used directly in the rendition of a public utility service (as well as boilers, machinery, equipment, and personal property used to generate or distribute electricity when some of the electricity is not distributed to others) continues to be assessed at 100 percent for production equipment and 88 percent for all other taxable property until January 1, 2002.[13]

.03 "Invisible" Source of State and Local Tax Revenues

Generally, special taxes such as gross receipts taxes and state regulatory commission administrative fees are imposed exclusively on electric utilities. Under the traditional cost-of-service approach to rate making, these taxes have been embedded in the utility rates and passed

---

[13] Ohio Rev. Code § 5727.111.

on to the customers in a transparent fashion. In addition, states impose various taxes on the utility customers, such as sales and use taxes or utility user taxes, which require the utilities to act as tax collectors for taxes imposed on their customers. Thus, before deregulation, most utilities had been acting as quasi-tax collectors for the state and local governments, collecting the general and special taxes imposed on the utilities as well as the various taxes imposed on their customers. Under the traditional system, state and local governments benefit from receiving substantial and reliable revenue streams that the utilities helped in collecting and administering. The utilities were not adversely affected due to recovery of the taxes through rates. However, often utility customers have been unaware that a significant amount of their utility bill was comprised of taxes. Shown below is a bar graph illustrating the billions of dollars of taxes paid by the electric utilities in years prior to deregulation.

Dollar Amount of State and Local Taxes Paid by Investor-Owned Electric Utilities Prior to Deregulation [14]

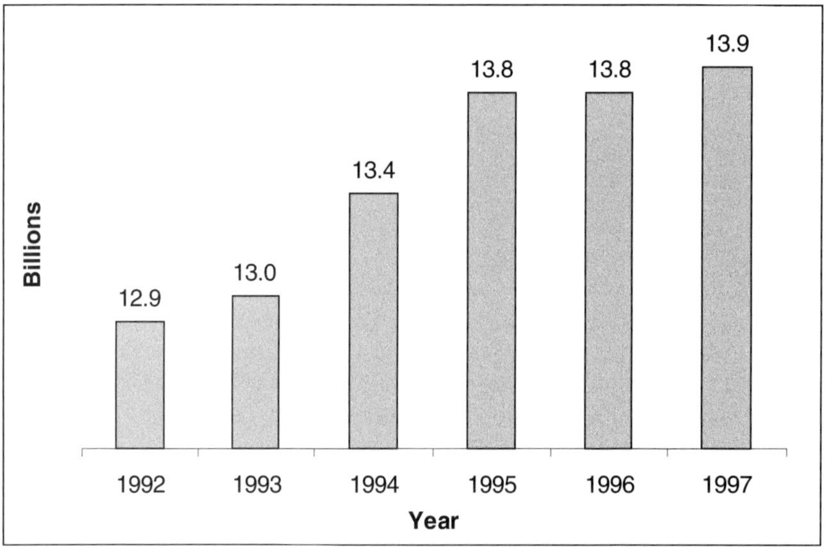

[14] Edison Electric Institute, *Statistical Yearbook of the Electric Utility Industry* (Washington, D.C.: Edison Electric Institute, 1997).

¶ 325 Effect of Deregulation on Specific State and Local Taxes

With the issuance of Federal Energy Regulatory Commission (FERC) Orders 888 and 889 in 1996, all major federal regulatory reforms were in place to allow open market characteristics to develop in the electric industry's *wholesale* power markets.[15] Whether *retail* markets would be open to competition has largely been left to the individual states. Although several federal bills have been introduced that were designed to open the retail markets to competition, most of the deregulation activity has taken place at the state level.

The initial deregulation efforts originated in states with relatively high electricity rates. State regulators in these states believed that open competition in the retail markets would lead to lower electricity rates, more product choices, better customer service, and perhaps less need for federal and state regulation. In states where electricity rates are below the national average, the deregulation process has not moved as quickly.

In the electric industry, according to the Energy Information Administration of the U.S. Department of Energy, as of February 2002, 24 states have enacted electric utility restructuring legislation or regulatory reforms. However, seven of those states have recently passed legislation to delay the implementation of retail access, and California has ordered the suspension of direct retail access.[16]

For decades, taxes paid by utilities have been a consistent source of revenues for state and local tax jurisdictions nationwide. In 1997, investor-owned electric utilities paid in excess of $13.9 billion in state and local taxes.[17] State and local jurisdictions are therefore justifiably concerned by the potential loss of tax revenues that may accompany deregulation.

Illinois restructuring legislation. In its electric utility restructuring legislation, the Illinois General Assembly specifically acknowledged the need to reform the state's utility tax regime:

> The General Assembly finds that the deregulation and restructuring of the electric utility industry in this State mandated and implemented by this amendatory Act of 1997, including the unbundling of services and the authorization of competition in the provision of those services such that consumers may in the future transact with multiple providers to obtain the services that were formerly provided by a

[15] See ¶ 235.02 for a summary of the major federal legislative and regulatory reforms that have been enacted to date.

[16] See the map showing each state's restructuring activity at ¶ 105.

[17] See the bar graph detailing taxes paid by electric utilities at ¶ 320.03.

> single franchised monopoly supplier of electricity, renders the system of taxation embodied in the Public Utilities Revenue Act impracticable and infeasible. The General Assembly further finds that the deregulation and restructuring of the electric utility industry necessitate changes to the existing system of taxation in order to preserve revenue neutrality in tax collections for the State . . . to avoid placing any supplier engaged in the business of distributing, supplying, furnishing, selling, transmitting or delivering electricity at a competitive disadvantage, to minimize additional administrative costs and burdens of collection, and to avoid the imposition of increased tax burdens on individual consumers of electricity, particularly residential electric users.

Most states' tax systems. A majority of the states have tax regimes that do not appropriately deal with the changes brought about by deregulation. In most states' existing utility tax systems, electric rates are based on the regulated model where in-state utilities provide "bundled" utility services to all customers residing in their designated service areas. In a deregulated environment, state regulators lose control over electric rates, thus introducing uncertainty in the corresponding state tax revenues.

> ***PLANNING NOTE:*** Even though competition will increase the number of energy providers in a particular market and, it is hoped, reduce prices, regulated utilities are expected to lose customers to out-of-state suppliers who may not be subject to the state's utility tax regime.

Some of the more significant issues confronting state regulators and tax administrators as they attempt to modify existing tax systems to fit within a deregulated environment are discussed by specific tax below (¶ 325.01–¶ 325.05).

.01 Gross Receipts Tax

Prior to deregulation, most states subjected electric utilities to a different tax regime than other businesses. Many states impose gross receipts taxes on regulated electric utilities, often in lieu of corporate income taxes or property taxes. In a 1996 study conducted by The National Council on Competition and the Electric Industry, it was found that approximately 30 percent of state and local taxes paid by investor-owned electric utilities were comprised of gross receipts taxes.[18]

States that rely heavily on utility gross receipts taxes are expected to experience declines in state tax revenues after deregulation due to

[18] National Council on Competition and the Electric Industry, *Federal, State and Local Tax Implications of Electric Utility Industry Restructuring* (October 1996).

several factors. Most restructuring calls for electric rate reductions, which correspondingly lead to reductions in gross receipts taxes from in-state sales of electricity. In addition, out-of-state energy providers may not be subject to the state's gross receipts taxes. Still more state and local tax revenue may be lost as a result of noncompliance.

Replacing with corporate income tax or consumption tax. To address the potential revenue shortfall based on gross receipts, state tax administrators have considered various tax alternatives. As a result, many deregulated states have eliminated their gross receipts tax, replacing it with either a corporate income tax or a consumption tax.

Pennsylvania. Pennsylvania took a unique route in addressing its gross receipts tax issue. On December 3, 1996, Pennsylvania Gov. Tom Ridge signed into law the Electricity Generation Customer Choice and Competition Act. The legislation contains various tax provisions designed to prevent any major tax revenue losses caused by the sweeping deregulation legislation. Prior to deregulation, Pennsylvania subjected electric companies to five separate state-level taxes including the utility gross receipts tax, the corporate net income tax, the capital stock/franchise tax, the sales and use tax, and the utility realty tax. In fiscal year 1996, these five taxes raised for the state more than $1 billion from the electric utilities, with gross receipts taxes accounting for nearly half of the total.[19]

When enacting deregulation legislation, the Pennsylvania Legislature added safeguards to the legislation to ensure that the source and level of tax revenues were maintained. The revenue-neutral reconciliation (RNR) formula is designed to prevent losses to the general funds of Pennsylvania during the transition period to a competitive electricity market. The RNR formula adjusts the utility gross receipts tax rate up or down depending on whether the total receipts would otherwise vary from the preexisting levels of tax.

The RNR takes fiscal 1995–1996 as the base year and adjusts the gross receipts tax rate upward during years that total receipts fall below the base level. The tax rate is adjusted downward during years that total gross receipts rise. The base year receipts total (1995–1996) is multiplied by a fraction, the numerator being the total kilowatt-hours consumed in the year at issue, and the denominator being total kilowatt-hours consumed in 1995. The total cash payments from all utility taxes for the year at issue are then subtracted from the product. The result is then divided by the previous year's gross receipts for all utilities. The end result is the replacement utility gross receipts tax

[19] Federation of Tax Administrators, *Switching on Competition: The Tax Implication of Consumer Choice in Pennsylvania* (1996).

rate. If the end result is negative, it becomes the rate that determines the taxpayers' credit.

The RNR provisions ensured the maintenance of the gross receipts tax base by redefining the legal incidence of the gross receipts tax to include any sale of electricity occurring in the state. The restructuring legislation defines retail sales of generation as those deemed to occur at the meter of the retail consumer. In addition, "doing business in this commonwealth" and "engaged in electric light and power business . . . in this commonwealth" includes obtaining a license or certification from the Commission to supply electric energy. Thus, virtually every supplier who sells electricity to a consumer in Pennsylvania is subject to the gross receipts taxes. If the supplier fails to impose the gross receipts tax, the legislation provides for a compensating "use" tax to be collected at the point of first sale to an in-state company. The legislation also allows a distributor to seek indemnification from a supplier if the distributor becomes liable for the tax because of the supplier's failure to remit the tax. These provisions help ensure that Pennsylvania will collect tax on electricity generated by out-of-state generators, power brokers, and aggregators that is sold to in-state purchasers.

> ***PLANNING NOTE:*** Pennsylvania deregulation legislation seeks to modify the gross receipts tax regime rather than to eliminate it, clearly preferring to maintain the status quo. However, the steps taken to strengthen viability of the gross receipts tax may be suspect. Forcing a nexus upon out-of-state power providers will probably be challenged in the courts on constitutional grounds. Although the revenue-neutral reconciliation formula is designed to provide a reliable source of revenue for the state, its complexity may limit its effectiveness. By maintaining a relatively high tax burden, the Pennsylvania tax regime may create a disincentive for new electricity providers to enter the market, which clearly runs counter to the stated goals of deregulation. Most other states have opted for less complicated alternatives than the restructuring enacted in Pennsylvania.

Connecticut. Connecticut limited the scope of its gross receipts tax in light of the unbundling of the electric utility industry. Effective January 1, 2000, Connecticut eliminated the gross receipts tax on electric *generation.* However, a new replacement gross receipts tax was imposed (8.5 percent of gross receipts for nonresidential and 6.8 percent of gross receipts for residential) on electric *distribution* companies and municipal electric companies for electric *transmission* services.[20]

---

[20] CGS § 12-264, § 12-265.

Maryland. Maryland adopted similar changes in its franchise tax structure. Beginning January 1, 2000, utilities will continue to pay a franchise tax on *transmission* and *distribution* of electricity at a rate of 2 percent of gross receipts derived from business in Maryland. However, the utility franchise tax will not apply to *generation* activity and will be replaced with a consumption tax at 0.062 cents for each kilowatt-hour of electricity delivered by a public service company for final consumption in the state.[21]

Illinois. In Illinois, the deregulation legislation converted the state's gross receipts tax to an excise tax imposed on the customers for the privilege of consuming electricity. Illinois adopted a 10-tier sliding scale of rates for its electricity excise tax ranging from 0.33 cents per kilowatt-hour for the first 2,000 kilowatt-hours consumed in a month, to 0.202 cents per kilowatt-hour for electricity consumed in excess of 20 million kilowatt-hours.[22]

Virginia. The Virginia deregulation legislation eliminated the state gross receipts tax, the local gross receipts tax, and the State Corporation Commission special assessment tax on electric suppliers. Instead, beginning January 1, 2001, consumers of electricity were subject to a declining block consumption tax. This declining block consumption tax is levied at rates of [23]

1. $0.00155 for the first 2,500 kilowatt-hours consumed,
2. $0.00099 for between 2,500 and 50,000 kilowatt-hours, and
3. $0.00075 for power consumed in excess of 50,000 kilowatt-hours.

Consumption taxes in other states. Most states are choosing to replace existing gross receipts taxes with consumption taxes. There are two methods that can be used to measure consumption taxes, either as a percentage of the selling price of the electricity or as a fixed amount per kilowatt-hour delivered or consumed. States opting for or contemplating consumption tax based on kilowatt-hour include Arizona, Arkansas, Illinois, Maryland, New Hampshire, New Jersey, Ohio, Oklahoma, and Oregon.

> ***PLANNING NOTE:*** The two methods of measuring consumption taxes can produce significantly different effective electricity tax rates between and among the different classes of electricity consumers. A tax based on kilowatt-hours consumed will be price sensitive to the extent that higher prices can cause electricity consumption to decline, but the same tax will also cause revenues to be unresponsive to inflationary increases in electricity prices in

[21] Md. Code Ann. § 8-403(b).

[22] 35 ILCS 640/2-4.

[23] Va. Code § 58.1-2900(A)(1)–(3).

future years. A kilowatt-hour-based tax may have a potentially negative impact on industrial and commercial consumers of electricity. Because industrial and commercial consumers purchase larger quantities of electricity, they may currently pay less per kilowatt-hour than residential users due to price discounts they receive for quantity. Switching to a kilowatt-hour-based system may cause industrial and commercial consumers to pay a greater portion of the tax than they had under a gross-receipts-based system. States can overcome this possibility of a shifting tax burden by adopting a sliding scale of rates for its consumption tax.

.02 Sales and Use Tax

Deregulation has resulted in significant changes to traditional transaction taxes, including sales taxes, use taxes, and consumption taxes. A sales tax can be broadly defined as a tax imposed on the retail sale price of tangible personal property purchased for use or consumption in a taxing state. Its counterpart, the use tax, is designed to tax transactions not otherwise subject to the state sales tax. A consumption tax is levied on the consumption of a product or service by an end-user.

Prior to deregulation, some states imposed a sales tax on electricity while other states offered specific sales and use tax exemptions for electricity sales. Under deregulation, new challenges to the sales tax structure are presented when the sale of electricity becomes unbundled (i.e., the various components of electricity production, transmission, distribution, and service become separated and priced individually). In those states that already subject the sale of electricity to a state sales tax, deregulation could erode the sales tax base if the sales tax statutes are not updated to capture the corresponding transportation charges. In such states, sales and use taxes will typically apply to the "retail sale of electricity," which often is not clearly defined. Sales tax statutes will therefore need to be revised to include all phases of the electricity sale from generation to the ultimate distribution.

Some states that have previously exempted the sale of electricity from a sales tax have now enacted legislation to impose a sales tax on the transmission and distribution of electricity. For example, New Jersey imposed a 6 percent sales tax on the sale of electricity effective January 1, 1998. Even when a state's sales tax base is clearly defined, its sales tax revenues may possibly erode from any price reductions in the sale of electricity brought on by mandatory rate reductions or as a result of open competition.

Imposing a consumption tax on distribution companies is appealing because it may alleviate the "nexus" issues associated with tax collection responsibilities (see Chapter 7 for a discussion of nexus).

Proposals include changing the sales tax collection point from the utility to the consumer, with the collection taking place through the meter owner. As discussed at ¶ 325.01, many states are replacing or augmenting their gross receipts tax structures with a consumption tax based on kilowatt-hours imposed at graduated rates.

While some states have enacted legislation aimed at bolstering sales taxes on electricity, other states such as New York have looked to reduce or eliminate state sales taxes related to electricity to provide a more competitive energy environment within the state. Beginning September 1, 2000, New York state and local sales and use tax rates imposed on receipts from the sale of natural gas service or electric service (including the transportation, transmission, or distribution of natural gas or electricity, but not including the sales of natural gas or electricity) were reduced by 25 percent, with subsequent reductions annually until the tax on such services is eliminated as of September 1, 2003.[24]

.03 Income Tax

Most states impose a corporate income tax on corporations doing business in their states. Prior to deregulation, states varied on whether they imposed a corporate income tax on regulated electric utilities in the following ways. Some states subjected their regulated electric utilities to their corporate income tax just like any other business. Another group of states exempted utilities from corporate income tax if they were subject to the state gross receipts tax. Still another group of states excluded from the calculation of corporate income tax any receipts from providing electricity, so in effect, only nonutility receipts were subjected to the corporate income tax. Also, a few states imposed the corporate net income tax as well as the gross receipts tax on their regulated electric utilities.

Effect of deregulation. For those states that already impose a corporate income tax on electric utilities, their corporate tax revenue may decline in a deregulated environment. Industry profits formerly protected by regulated monopoly status may decline due to open competition, lowering prices, stranded costs, and restructuring costs. Many states that have previously exempted electric utilities from the corporate income tax have enacted legislation imposing the general corporate income tax on electric utilities. For example, New Jersey now subjects utilities to its 9 percent corporate income tax. In Virginia, most electric suppliers, except for electric cooperatives became subject to Virginia's 6 percent corporate income tax beginning January 1,

[24] N.Y. Tax Law § 1105-C.

2001.[25] Prior to that date, the utilities were instead subject to a gross receipts tax.

The tax revenues generated from a corporate income tax, however, will not normally compare to those generated from a state-level gross receipts tax. The corporate income tax may also present more uncertainty for a state's tax revenue base.

Although a corporate income tax may appear to be a viable alternative to some of the other taxes imposed on electric utilities, many of the same issues brought about by electric utility deregulation hinder the administration of the corporate income tax. For example, in a regulated environment, a vertically integrated public utility was not normally presented with nexus issues since it frequently owned and operated generation, transmission, and distribution assets within its designated service area. With the advent of competition and the interstate sale of electricity involving multiple parties including sellers, buyers, brokers, and third-party owners of transmission and distribution systems, traditional rules for nexus (see Chapter 7) and apportionment (see Chapter 9) may be impractical.

Taxing the ultimate customer. Based on a state's treatment of the sale of electricity, either as a sale of an intangible service or as a sale of a tangible product, alternative tax apportionment methodologies may apply. Sales of intangibles or services are generally sourced to the state where the income-producing activity occurred. Sales of tangible personal property are generally sourced to the destination of the customer. Under the Uniform Division of Income for Tax Purposes Act (UDITPA) (see ¶ 805), receipts from the sale of electricity are generally sourced to the location of the ultimate user of electricity. Due to the unique nature of the electric industry, it may be difficult to determine the ultimate customer. In a regulated environment, it is less difficult to identify the customer since the regulated electric utility often owns the generation, distribution, and transmission assets serving a specific region. However, in a deregulated environment, with the increase of players in the marketplace, such as independent power producers, power marketers, and the sale of electricity on an open transmission grid, the ultimate consumer may not be easily identified.

Apportionment formulas. Issues also arise in the apportionment formulas (see Chapter 9) used to apportion taxable income for electricity providers in a deregulated environment. Examples are found in the following two states.

North Carolina. In North Carolina, public utilities are required to use a single-factor apportionment method based on sales when calculat-

[25] Va. Code § 58.1-400.2.

ing their North Carolina taxable income.[26] Under North Carolina tax law, a public utility is defined

> as any corporation that is subject to control by one or more of the following entities: the North Carolina Utilities Commission, the Federal Communications Commission, the Interstate Commerce Commission, the Federal Power Commission, or the Federal Aviation Agency; and that owns or operates for public use any plant, equipment, property, franchise, or license for the transmission of communications, the transportation of goods or persons, or the production, storage, transmission, sale, delivery, or furnishing of electricity, water, steam, oil, oil products, or gas.

In North Carolina's deregulated environment, electric generation companies may no longer qualify as public utilities as defined above. Most nonregulated businesses are required to use a three-factor apportionment formula for determining their North Carolina taxable income. For taxpayers with operations and assets in multiple states, changing from the single-factor apportionment method to the three-factor apportionment method can have a dramatic effect on the taxpayer's North Carolina income tax liability. Although North Carolina has moved relatively slowly on deregulation compared to other states, it will need to address the issue of income tax apportionment in order to achieve a revenue-neutral result under deregulation.

Ohio. Ohio's deregulation legislation specifically addressed apportionment and allocation issues and provided a new sales factor apportionment formula for the sales of electric transmission and distribution services.[27] Under the new legislation, applicable beginning with the 2002 tax year, sales of transmission or distribution of electricity are to be apportioned to Ohio based on the ratio of the wire mileage of the taxpayer's transmission or distribution lines located in Ohio divided by the wire mileage of the taxpayer's transmission or distribution lines located everywhere.[28] Until other states issue specific guidance on apportionment and allocation issues, electric utilities will continue to have difficulty forecasting their state income tax liabilities.

.04 Franchise Tax

A franchise tax is an excise tax imposed for the privilege of doing business, owning property, or engaging in other activities within a state. In most states, a franchise tax is typically imposed on the level of capital employed in the taxing state, although some states impose it on net income. Still other states compute the franchise tax based on gross receipts. Franchise taxes levied based upon gross receipts or net income

---

[26] N.C. Gen. Stat. § 105-130.4.

[27] Ohio Rev. Code § 5733.059.

[28] See ¶ 315.02 for new Ohio tax legislation regarding electric utility deregulation.

are discussed at ¶ 325.01. For the purposes of this discussion, franchise taxes are those taxes measured by the level of capital employed in a taxing state.

Prior to deregulation, most states exempted regulated utilities from such taxes, instead subjecting them to the gross receipts tax. Some states, such as North Carolina and Pennsylvania, imposed a franchise tax on their electric utilities in addition to other taxes. As states move through the deregulation process, it is more likely that electric utilities, just as any other business, will be subject to a corporate franchise tax based on the level of capital employed.

.05 Property Tax

Deregulation of the electric industry (as well as natural gas and other public utilities) has brought about numerous changes to the property tax methodologies in a number of states. The following five states, California, Massachusetts, Montana, Ohio, and Pennsylvania, illustrate a number of such changes in the property tax assessment rules.

California.

Property subject to tax. All real and tangible personal property in the state is subject to tax unless specifically exempt. There is no tax on intangible property.

A public utility is defined in the California Constitution as

> a line, plant, or system for the transportation of people or property, for the transmission of telephone or telegraph messages, for the production, generation, transmission, or distribution of electricity, water, heat, and light, or for the provision of wharfages directly or indirectly to common carriers.[29]

Assessment procedure. The passage of California Assembly Bill 1890 (AB 1890) provided for the restructuring of the electric industry by opening generation facilities to competition. AB 1890 required certain investor-owned utilities to sell their California generation assets. This raises the issue as to who has the authority to assess power generation plants following AB 1890.[30]

The California State Board of Equalization (SBE) proposed Property Tax Rule 905 to clearly delineate which facilities should continue to be assessed by the SBE and which facilities should be assessed by local county assessors. Those facilities that were assessed by the SBE would continue to be assessed by the SBE. In addition, all new electric

[29] Calif. Constitution, Article XII, Sec. 3.

[30] Calif. Assembly Bill 1890 (Ch. 854 Laws 1996) is codified as Calif. Civil Code § 955.1.

generation facilities constructed pursuant to a certificate by the California Public Utilities Commission would also be assessed by the SBE. Any new power generating facility commissioned in the future and not part of a regulated "public utility" would be subject to local jurisdiction.

The California State Board of Equalization (SBE) annually values and assesses all of the taxable public utility property in the state.[31] Under the state constitution, the SBE must assess pipelines, flumes, canals, ditches, and aqueducts located within two or more counties. The SBE must also assess property owned or used by any regulated railway, telegraph, telephone, and car company operating on in-state railways, and companies transmitting or selling natural gas or electricity.

Public utility property is assessed by the SBE as unitary property, nonunitary property, or operating nonunitary property. Properties that are operated as a unit in a primary function of the assessee are assessed as unitary property. Nonunitary properties are properties that are not valued by the use of the principle of unit valuation. Operating nonunitary properties are properties that the assessee and its regulatory agency consider to be operating as a unit, but the SBE considers not part of a unit in the primary function of the assessee.[32]

Master Settlement Agreement. Since 1991 California has assessed utility property in accordance with the provisions of the Master Settlement Agreement (MSA). Under this agreement, value is determined by a basic formula of historical costs less depreciation, less 25 percent of the assessee's deferred tax reserve.

> ***CAUTION:*** With the expiration of the MSA on January 1, 1999, it remains unclear how the SBE will continue to determine fair market value. There is a growing consensus that with the availability of a large number of recent sales, the state may use the sales or market approach for valuing generation property. For state assessed property, there are no statutory provisions limiting annual increases in taxable value.

Most local assessors when determining fair market value rely on historical costs less depreciation. However, each assessor may use any of the three traditional approaches to value: cost, income, or sales. Under county assessment, the valuation provisions of Article XIII A (Proposition 13) protect the taxpayer by establishing a base year value and placing a 2 percent limit on annual assessment increases.

Basis and rate of tax. Public utility property is subject to tax to the same extent and in the same manner as other property.[33]

---

[31] Calif. Rev. & Tax. Code § 721.

[32] Calif. Rev. & Tax. Code § 723 and § 723.1.

[33] Calif. Constitution, Article XIII, Sec. 19.

The assessed value of unitary and operating nonunitary property is allocated among the counties where parts of the unitary and operating nonunitary property are situated, and the tax rate for the particular taxing jurisdiction is applied.[34] A single countywide tax rate area is required in each county for the assignment of the assessed value of unitary and operating nonunitary property of state assessees other than railroads.[35]

Massachusetts.

Property subject to tax. Property tax is imposed on all property in Massachusetts unless it is specifically exempt.[36] Real property may be classified in no more than four classes, according to its use. The rate of tax on property may differ by class, but it must be proportionate by property within the same class.[37]

In November 1997, the Massachusetts Legislature enacted Section 38H to Chapter 59 of the Massachusetts General Laws to restructure the electric industry and provide customers with rate cuts and retail choice. As part of the deregulation act, the legislation provided that utilities must make transition payments to municipalities for property devaluation that causes lost property tax revenue as a byproduct of deregulation. Through 2000, utilities were paying the entire difference between the property taxes actually collected on the facilities and the property taxes collected in 1997, the tax year prior to deregulation. From 2001 through 2009, the transition payments on the difference decrease by 10 percent each year. The only exception from the transition payments clause is for facilities that are currently under payment in lieu of tax (PILOT) agreements with municipalities.

Pipelines that are used to transmit natural gas or petroleum, including products or byproducts, for a distance of at least 25 miles are taxed as personal property and are assessed to the owner by the assessors of each city and town where the pipeline is located. However, this treatment does not apply if the owner is a gas or electric company.[38] A pipeline must be assessed by the local board at the valuation that is certified by the Commissioner, unless the taxpayer successfully challenges the Commissioner's valuation.[39]

Telecommunications equipment, such as underground wires, conduits, and appurtenant equipment installed pursuant to local ordinances,[40] are exempt up to 75 percent of their value.[41] The valuation of

[34] Calif. Rev. & Tax. Code § 745.

[35] Calif. Rev. & Tax. Code § 100.

[36] Mass. Constitution, Article IV, Sec. 36; Mass. Gen. L., Chapter 59, § 2A.

[37] Mass. Constitution, Article IV, Sec. 36.

[38] Mass. Gen. L., Chapter 59, § 3C and § 38A.

[39] Mass. Gen. L., Chapter 59, § 38A.

[40] Ordinances adopted under the provisions of Mass. Gen. L., Chapter 166 § 22C and § 22D (Telephone and Telegraphic Companies).

[41] Mass. Gen. L., Chapter 59, § 5 (Sixteenth 1A).

machinery, poles, wires, and underground conduits, wires, and pipes of all telephone and telegraph companies is annually determined by the Commissioner of Revenue.

Assessment procedure. Cities and towns must determine the fair cash valuation of real property for the purpose of taxation on January 1 of each year.[42] The fair cash value determined is the assessed valuation of the property.[43]

In certified cities or towns, the assessed valuation of real property subject to taxation is then classified into one of four classifications. The resulting amount is the taxable valuation of each class of property. The amount of tax due and payable is determined by applying the local tax rate to the assessed valuation of the property.[44]

Montana.

Property subject to tax.

Almost all property whether real, tangible, or intangible is subject to taxation.[45] Exemptions from taxation are limited and specific in scope. "Property" includes all matters and things, real, personal, and mixed, which are capable of private ownership.[46]

Utilities are assessed for property owned directly as well as for the value of property owned by a government agency but used by the utility.[47] The personal property and franchises of gas and water companies are listed and assessed in the county, town, or district where the principal works are located. Gas and water mains and pipes laid in roads, streets, or alleys are personal property.[48]

A utility must file an annual statement with the Department of Revenue. The statement must be signed and sworn to by the appropriate officer, or in the case of an association, one of the persons forming the association, and contain: [49]

1. the total number of miles of utility property in the state on the immediately preceding December 31 (for a multistate utility, the statement must list total miles within the state and total miles outside the state);
2. the total value of all property and plant, and the total value of the portion of the property and plant located within the state;
3. a complete description of the property located inside the state, including points of entrance and exit from the state, and points of entrance and exit within each county in the state, plus the

[42] Mass. Gen. L., Chapter 59, § 2A(a).
[43] Mass. Gen. L., Chapter 59, § 38.
[44] Mass. Gen. L., Chapter 59, § 38.
[45] Mont. Code Ann. § 15-1-101 and § 15-6-101.
[46] Mont. Code Ann. § 15-1-101(p).
[47] Mont. Code Ann. § 15-8-201 and § 15-24-1203(1).
[48] Mont. Code Ann. § 15-8-404(3).
[49] Mont. Code Ann. § 15-23-301.

total number of miles in each county in the state on the immediately preceding December 31; and

4. any other information required by the Department.

Utility property for purposes of the owner's statement includes telephone, telegraph, microwave, electric power, or transmission lines; natural gas pipeline; oil pipeline; canal; ditches; flumes; or other property other than real estate not included in a right-of-way, and that constitutes a single and continuous property throughout more than one county or state.[50]

Assessment procedure. There are no specific provisions for valuation of public utility property. Property is assessed for valuation purposes at 100 percent of market value except as otherwise provided.[51] "Market value" is the value at which property would change hands between a willing buyer and a willing seller, neither being under any compulsion to buy or sell and both having reasonable knowledge of the relevant facts relating to the property.[52] If construction cost is used as one approximation of market value, the Department must consider depreciation.[53]

Effective October 1, 1999, and applicable after 1999, to tax years beginning after 1999, if the Department uses the capitalization of net income method as one approximation of market value and sufficient, relevant information on comparable sales and construction cost exists, the Department must rely on two methods that provide a similar market value as the better indicators of market value.[54]

Basis and tax rate. The ad valorem tax on real and personal property is the main source of revenue for local governments in Montana. An assessment of all kinds of property within the state, except property specifically exempted from taxation by statute, is made annually between January 1 and the second Monday in July by the Department of Revenue.[55]

Property is initially assessed at full market value, but then is taxed based on the percentage of value applicable to the classification into which the property falls.[56]

Class 7 property includes property used and owned by persons, corporations, or other organizations that are engaged in the business of furnishing telephone communication services exclusively to rural areas and cities or towns of 800 persons or less. Class 7 property also includes property owned by telephone and electric cooperatives serving less than

[50] Mont. Code Ann. § 15-23-301.
[51] Mont. Code Ann. § 15-8-111(1).
[52] Mont. Code Ann. § 15-8-111(2)(a).
[53] Mont. Code Ann. § 15-8-111(2)(b).
[54] Mont. Code Ann. § 15-8-111(2)(c).
[55] Mont. Code Ann. § 15-8-201.
[56] Mont. Code Ann. § 15-6-101 and § 15-8-111.

95 percent of the electricity consumers or telephone users within the incorporated limits of a city or town (except rural elective cooperative properties),[57] electric transformers and meters, light and power substation machinery, natural gas measuring and regulation station equipment owned by noncentrally assessed public utilities.

To qualify for Class 7 property, the circuit miles for each station on a telephone system must be more than one mile. Class 7 property is taxed at 8 percent of market value. Effective January 1, 2000, unless other contingent events occur, Class 7 property will not include property used and owned by persons, corporations, or other organizations that are engaged in the business of furnishing telephone communication services exclusively to rural areas and cities or towns of 800 persons or less, or cooperative rural telephone associations serving less than 95 percent of electricity consumers. In addition, the provision that the circuit miles for each station must be more than a mile is deleted.[58]

Class 8 property includes all oil and gas production machinery, fixtures, and equipment, including pumping units, oil field storage tanks, water storage tanks, water disposal injection pumps, gas compressor and dehydrator units, communication towers, gas metering shacks, treaters, gas separators, water flood units, gas boosters, and similar equipment that is skidable, portable, or movable, tools that are not exempt under Mont. Code Ann. § 15-6-201(1)(r), and supplies, except those included in Class 5.[59]

Class 9 property includes centrally assessed allocations of an electric power company, or centrally assessed allocations of an electric power company that owns or operates transmission or distribution facilities, or both, including if Congress passes legislation that allows the state to tax property owned by an agency created by Congress to transmit or distribute electrical energy, allocations of properties constructed, owned, or operated by a public agency created by Congress to transmit or distribute electric energy produced at privately owned generating facilities, not including rural electric cooperatives. However, rural electric cooperatives' property used for the sole purpose of serving customers representing less than 95 percent of the electric consumers located within the incorporated limits of a city or town of more than 3,500 persons where a centrally assessed electric power company also owns property is included. Class 9 property is taxed at 12 percent of market value.[60]

---

[57] See description of rural electric cooperative properties in Mont. Code Ann. § 15-6-141(1)(a).

[58] Mont. Code Ann. § 15-6-137.

[59] Mont. Code Ann. § 15-6-138.

[60] Mont. Code Ann. § 15-6-141.

Ohio.

Property subject to tax. Ohio is in the midst of a legislative process to deregulate the electric industry. One of the major issues being addressed in pending deregulation legislation is what is the appropriate tax policy and structure to promote competition in the electric industry while maintaining an adequate level of school funding.

A "public utility" is defined to include: [61]

1. an electric company, including a rural electric company, when engaged in the business of generating, transmitting, or distributing electricity within Ohio for use by others;
2. a natural gas company, when engaged in the business of supplying natural gas for lighting, power, or heating purposes to consumers within Ohio;
3. a pipeline company, when engaged in the business of transporting natural gas, oil, or coal or its derivatives through pipes or tubing, either wholly or partially within Ohio;
4. a waterworks company, when engaged in the business of supplying water through pipes or tubing, or in a similar manner, to consumers within Ohio;
5. a water transportation company, when engaged in the transportation of passengers or property, by boat or other watercraft, over any waterway, whether natural or artificial, from one point within Ohio to another point within the state, or between points within the state and points without the state; or
6. a heating company, when engaged in the business of supplying water, steam, or air through pipes or tubing to consumers within Ohio for heating purposes—referred to as an electric company, a natural gas company, a pipeline company, a waterworks company, a water transportation company, a heating company, or a rural electric company—meaning any nonprofit corporation, organization, association, or cooperative engaged in the business of supplying electricity to its members or persons owning an interest therein in an area the major portion of which is rural.

The terms "public utility," "electric company," "natural gas company," "pipeline company," "waterworks company," "water transportation company" and "heating company" do not include: [62]

---

[61] Ohio Rev. Code Ann. § 5727.04, § 5727.01(A), § 5727.01(C), and § 5727.01(D).

[62] Ohio Rev. Code Ann. § 5727.02.

- any person who is engaged in some other primary business to which the supplying of electricity, heat, natural gas, water, water transportation, steam, or air to others is incidental;
- any person who supplies electricity, natural gas, water, water transportation, steam, or air to its tenants, whether for a separate charge or otherwise; or
- any person whose primary business in Ohio consists of producing, refining, or marketing petroleum or its products.

Public utilities are not exempted from the assessment and taxation of their property. The property tax base of all public utilities, except railroads, consists of real and tangible personal property owned and located in Ohio on December 31 of the preceding year. The taxable property that must be assessed by the Tax Commissioner is: [63]

- for a railroad company, all real and tangible personal property owned or operated by it in Ohio on December 31 of the preceding year;
- for a water transportation company, tangible personal property owned or operated in Ohio on December 31 of the preceding year and all watercraft owned or operated in Ohio during the preceding calendar year;
- for all other public utilities and interexchange telecommunications companies, all tangible personal property that on December 31 of the preceding year was both located in Ohio and owned or leased (under a sale/leaseback transaction) by the company.

PLANNING NOTE: In *Duquesne Light Co. v. Tracy,*[64] the Ohio Board of Tax Appeals (BTA) reversed in part the Tax Commissioner's decision concerning property tax exemptions and nontaxable costs for a public utility's pollution control facility. Ohio's property tax statutes require a utility's taxable property to be valued at its capitalized book cost. The court in this instance, however, found that this did not imply that utility property was automatically subject to Ohio public utility property tax. It found the statute provided a method for valuing property if it was taxable, without specifying which property was taxable. As a result, items such as air pollution control equipment, obsolete machinery, and certain intangible items (i.e., engineering drawings) were to be excluded from the utility's tangible personal property tax base.

[63] Ohio Rev. Code Ann. § 5727.01(E) and § 5727.06(A).

[64] *Duquesne Light Co. v. Tracy,* Ohio Board of Tax Appeals, Case Nos. 95-K-40, (November 6, 1998).

The Supreme Court of Ohio has vacated the BTA decision and order granting exemptions for air pollution control facilities and engineering drawings from Ohio public utilities property tax. The cause was remanded to the BTA for further proceedings.[65] Pending the final outcome of this case, the Ohio BTA has issued a "joint motion to stay hearing date" in a number of other pending cases.

Assessment procedure. The Tax Commissioner assesses the real estate of railroads and the tangible personal property of all public utilities; county auditors assess all other public utility real estate.[66] Annually, the Tax Commissioner, guided by the public utility's report and other evidences, must determine the true value and the taxable value based on the percentages of true value at which the property is required to be assessed. On or before the 1st Monday in October, the Tax Commissioner must assess the taxable property of each public utility, and notify the public utility of the proposed total taxable value of its taxable property, including any proposed penalty.[67]

For most public utility personal property, true value is the capitalized cost less the composite annual allowances that vary according to the actual age and expected life of the property. The true value of electric company production equipment and all taxable property of a rural electric company is 50 percent of capitalized cost; current gas stored underground is valued at the cost of the gas; noncurrent gas stored underground is valued at 35 percent of cost. For railroad real and personal property, the unitary method is used to value the railroad's entire railroad system.[68]

Basis and rate of tax. Real property is assessed at 35 percent of true value. Personal property is assessed at 88 percent of true value, except for the following: personal property of railroads and water transportation companies is assessed at 25 percent; rural electric companies are assessed at 50 percent; production equipment of electric companies is assessed at 100 percent; interexchange telephone companies and local exchange telephone company (added to the tax rolls beginning in tax year 1995) are assessed at 25 percent.[69]

Most other taxpayers are assessed at 25 percent of their property's true value. Accordingly, the effective tax rate on electric production equipment is significantly higher than the tax rate for other taxpayers both within Ohio and neighboring states. Legislation enacted in Ohio in 1999 lowers the assessment ratio on *generation* property to 25 percent but maintains the 88 percent ratio on *transmission* and *distribution* property for tax year 2001 and thereafter.[70]

---

[65] Ohio Supreme Court, 88 Ohio St. 3d 1459, 726 N.E. 2d 502 (April 3, 2000).

[66] Ohio Rev. Code Ann. § 5713.01 and § 5727.06(A).

[67] Ohio Rev. Code Ann. § 5727.10 and § 5727.23.

[68] Ohio Rev. Code Ann. § 5727.11 and § 5727.12.

[69] Ohio Rev. Code Ann. § 5715.01, § 5727.111, § 5727.12.

[70] Ohio Rev. Code Ann. § 5727.111(E)(2).

Pennsylvania.

Property subject to tax. All real property in Pennsylvania is subject to property tax unless specifically exempted. Real property is ordinarily assessed against the record owner. Separate rules exist for public utility real property.

There is no property tax assessed on tangible personal property in Pennsylvania, although certain types of tangible personal property are treated and taxed as if they were real property. Local governments may also impose a special intangibles tax on intangible personal property.

The public utilities real property tax (PURTA) is imposed on public utilities. Effective retroactively to January 1, 1998, a "public utility" is defined as

> any person, partnership, association, corporation or other entity furnishing public utility service under the jurisdiction of the Pennsylvania Public Utility Commission or other corresponding regulatory agency of any other state or of the U.S. on December 31 of the tax year, and any electric cooperative corporation, municipality or municipality authority furnishing public utility service.

It does not include any public utility furnishing public utility sewage services, or municipality or municipality authority furnishing public utility services on December 31 of the tax year.[71]

Effective retroactively to January 1, 1998, "utility realty" is defined by Pennsylvania statutes as

> all lands, buildings, towers, smokestacks, dams, dikes, canals, cooling towers, storage tanks, reactor structures, pump houses, supporting foundations, enclosing structures, supporting structures, containment structures, reactor containment outer shells, reactor containment vessels, turbine buildings, recovery tanks, solid waste area enclosures, primary auxiliary buildings, containment auxiliary safeguard structures, fuel buildings, decontamination buildings, and all other structures and enclosures that are physically affixed to the land, regardless of how these structures and enclosures are designated and without regard to the structures' classification for purposes of local real estate tax.[72]

"Utility realty" does not include machinery and equipment, or, after December 31, 1999, land and improvements that are indispensable to the generation of electricity, that are owned directly or indirectly by the public utility or its affiliate at the end of the tax year. The property must be located in Pennsylvania, used to furnish, produce,

[71] Pa. Stat. Ann., Title 72, § 8101-A(2).

[72] Pa. Stat. Ann., Title 72, § 8101-A(3).

distribute, or transport public utility service and must be subject to local real estate tax in effect on April 23, 1968.[73]

Assessment procedure. As part of Pennsylvania's 1996 Electric Choice Act, the generation component of the electric utility business was deregulated. Generation facilities now fall outside the scope of PURTA and will be taxed in the same manner as all other property.

Effective retroactively to January 1, 1998, elected and appointed assessors must assess, value, and enroll utility realty in the same manner as provided for assessment, valuation, and enrollment of other real property. However, after December 31, 1998, assessors must *enroll* utility realty separately from other real property owned by a utility or a utility's affiliate or associate.[74]

> ***PLANNING NOTE:*** Certain valuation issues will come to the forefront as local assessors begin the process of appraising and taxing generation plants for the first time. Significant debate exists within the utility industry as to the determination of what is real or personal property for certain components of integrated generation facilities.

Whereas the majority of previously regulated facilities have been appraised on an historical cost less depreciation method, the deregulated market will demand alternative valuation methods be used to value generation facilities.

The general statutory rule is that all property must be assessed for all county and municipal purposes according to the actual value thereof, and at such rates and prices for which it would separately sell in good faith. In arriving at actual value, the price at which property may actually have been sold either in the base year or the current taxable year may be considered but is not controlling. Instead, the actual or estimated selling price may be increased or decreased to accomplish equalization with other similar property in the taxing district. In arriving at an actual value, the actual cost, comparable sales, and income approaches must be considered in conjunction with one another.[75]

"Market value" means the price that a purchaser, who is willing but not obligated to buy, would pay an owner, who is willing but not obligated to sell, taking into consideration all uses to which the property is adapted and might in reason be applied.[76]

Basis and rate of tax. Effective retroactively for tax year 1998, the Department of Revenue became responsible for calculating the millage

[73] Pa. Stat. Ann., Title 72, § 8101-A(3).

[74] Pa. Stat. Ann., § 8105-A(a).

[75] Pa. Stat. Ann., Title 72, § 5020-402.

[76] See *In re Lehigh & Wilkes-Barre Coal Co.'s Assessment,* 298 Pa 294, 148 A. 301 (1929); appeal after remand, 300 Pa. 564, 151 A. 359 (1930).

rate to apply to utility realty on or before November 1, 1999. The Department then notified the utility of the rate and the taxable value of its utility realty. For tax year 1999, the Department was responsible for calculating the millage rate on or before August 1, 2000. Before 1998, the tax was imposed at the rate of 30 mills upon each dollar of the state taxable value of the public utility realty at the end of the preceding calendar year.[77]

.06 Lack of Change to Tax Law

States not planning to deregulate in the next few years have not made changes to tax laws to account for electricity deregulation. While high-cost electricity states aggressively deregulate, and states like Ohio and New Jersey follow close behind, nearly half of the states may be labeled reluctant, if not actually opposed, to rapid utility deregulation. Twenty-three states have formed the "Low-Cost Electricity States Initiative" and sent a letter to Congress opposing national deregulation. Low-cost states want to be given a greater voice in discussions about electric utility reform.[78]

Other states moving toward deregulation of utilities are satisfied with current tax laws and have no plans to make changes. The remaining states on the road to deregulation recognize the need to change current tax laws, but have failed to initiate changes.

Some states proposing legislation to open retail electricity markets to competition in the next four years have not included specific tax law changes. They would rather open the markets first and deal with any inconsistent tax treatment of out-of-state providers and in-state utilities second. Most legislation includes some means for in-state utilities to recover stranded costs through a competition transition charge. Other states have no proposals pending.

The need for utility taxation is not obvious or necessary in states where deregulation is not guaranteed. In 1996 and 1997, utility deregulation bills failed in 19 states. However, in a number of those states, revised electric industry restructuring legislation was included in later legislative sessions. Whether deregulation's momentum becomes stalled based on recent events in California remains uncertain. Ultimately, if competitive markets result in significant savings for consumers, the pressure on the legislatures of slower states to speed along deregulation will build.

---

[77] Pa. Stat. Ann., Title 72, § 8102-A (b).

[78] James R. Dukart, "States Race to Compete," *Utility Business*, March 1999, Vol. 2, Iss. 3, p. 30.

Part 2

STATE TAXATION OF EMERGING INDUSTRIES

Chapter 4

TRADING AND MARKETING COMPANIES

¶ 401 Overview

The recent convergence of the increasingly competitive electric and natural gas industries has enabled the largest trading and marketing companies to now dominate the top ten market positions in both electricity and natural gas. The convergence of the two industries is being driven by the large utility companies' desires to increase their nontraditional customer base and to provide "one-stop" *energy* shopping for their customers. Their asset portfolios may include natural gas production, storage, transportation, and distribution assets, as well as nonregulated electric generation assets located throughout the country. These megamarketers now trade huge blocks of electricity and natural gas, including both physical and financial products, from sophisticated trading floors that in some cases operate 24 hours a day.

Sales are routinely made with physical deliveries occurring in states where the marketers conduct no other business activities and may not otherwise be subject to state regulation. As the states continue to enact legislation in response to deregulation, industry-specific "nexus" and apportionment issues will need to be resolved (see ¶ 410 and ¶ 415). In addition, some of the emerging industry-specific state and local tax issues now confronting trading and marketing companies will need to be addressed, such as choice of business entity (¶ 405), interstate commerce exemptions (¶ 420), and issues related to commodity exchanges (¶ 425) and financial derivatives and risk trading (¶ 430).

¶ 405 Choice of Business Entity

Convergence of the electric and natural gas industries has led to the creation of several new trading and marketing companies. As the consolidation trend continues in these industries, many more marketing ventures will likely be formed over the next five years. In most cases, the choice of business entity (or choice of classification in the case of limited liability companies) will determine how these entities and their owners will be taxed by the states in which they operate.

Regular corporations and partnerships. Entities that elect to operate as regular corporations will be taxed directly in most states and will be subject to state income, franchise, and gross receipts taxes. Most states do not impose income taxes directly on partnerships, but instead tax each corporate partner on his or her share of income from the venture. However, states vary widely in how general partners and limited partners are taxed and in how partnership income is apportioned among and between the states.

Limited liability companies (LLCs). LLCs with more than two members may elect for federal tax purposes to be classified as either an association (which is taxed as a regular corporation under federal rules) or as a partnership. Single-member LLCs may elect to be classified as either a "disregarded entity" (which is taxed as a division of its parent) or as a regular corporation. Most states follow the federal law classifications of LLCs for state income tax purposes. However, a notable exception is Texas—it imposes its income/franchise tax directly on LLCs regardless of their federal income classification, yet it does not impose its income/franchise tax on partnerships.[1]

Competitive pressures. Many states impose gross receipts taxes on trading and marketing companies; however, since the taxes are not consistently applied to all legal entities, a trading and marketing company's choice of a business entity can be critical. In some circumstances, competition has cut trading and marketing profit margins so deeply that the imposition of even a modest gross receipts tax will often negate the entire profit earned on any particular sale. Note how the choice of entity could affect a company in the following two states.

New York. New York previously imposed a "utility" franchise tax (in lieu of the normal corporate income or franchise tax) on every corporation, joint-stock company, or association formed for, or principally engaged in, supplying water, steam, or gas (when delivered through mains or pipes), or electricity.[2] The 0.75 percent franchise tax applied to all sales (both wholesale and end-user) without reduction or credit for the related costs of goods sold. However, New York does not apply the tax to partnerships, and does not allow the tax to be indirectly passed through to *corporate limited partners* that are not otherwise engaged in the day-to-day business operations of the partnership.[3]

---

[1] Texas Code Ann. § 171.001(b)(3)(A).

[2] N.Y. Tax Law § 186.

[3] *GTE Spacenet Corp., etc. v. New York State Department of Taxation and Finance, et al,* 223 A.D.2d 468, 637 N.Y.S.2d 362 (1996).

CAUTION: The New York Section 186 tax was repealed and the Section 186-a tax (a related tax) was phased out by legislation signed on May 15, 2000.[4]

Indiana. Another state where choice of business entity can be critical for trading and marketing companies is Indiana.

Corporations doing business in Indiana must pay the higher of [5]

1. the Indiana gross income tax based upon its Indiana gross receipts at a rate of 1.2 percent, or
2. the Indiana adjusted gross income tax at a rate of 3.4 percent.

The Indiana gross income tax is imposed on a corporation's total gross receipts from Indiana sources. Two rates of tax are provided under the gross income tax system. The rate that applies depends on the nature of transactions that generates the gross receipts. Generally, the lower rate of 0.3 percent is applied to receipts generated from wholesaling, retailing, and other specifically designated business activities. The higher rate of 1.2 percent is applied to receipts derived from services, investments, utility operations, and certain other activities. Specifically, the receipt of gross income from "producing, transmitting, furnishing, wholesaling, or retailing electrical energy" is subject to the higher 1.2 percent rate.[6]

The Indiana adjusted gross income tax is similar to a traditional income tax since it is based on federal taxable income before subtracting any net operating loss and special deductions. Indiana also has a corporate supplemental net income tax (based on the apportioned net income minus the greater of the gross income tax liability or the adjusted gross income tax liability) at a rate of 4.5 percent.

LLCs and limited liability partnerships (LLPs) are generally not subject to Indiana income tax. However, the individual and corporate partners and/or members must pay Indiana state and local income tax on their Indiana source income. LLCs are classified as corporations or partnerships for Indiana income tax purposes in the same manner that they are classified for federal tax purposes.

Partnerships doing business in Indiana compute the gross income tax by including net partnership income (or loss) in the calculation of gross income rather than the gross revenues earned by the partnership.[7] Therefore, a significant amount of the Indiana gross receipts tax may be reduced or eliminated by entities conducting business as a partnership (rather than a corporation) in Indiana.

---

[4] N.Y. A.B. 1106 (May 15, 2000).

[5] Ind. Code § 6-2.1-2-3 and Ind. Code § 6-3-2-1.

[6] Ind. Code § 6-2.1-2-5.

[7] Ind. Regulation, Rule 45 IAC 1.1-2-13.

¶ 410 Nexus-Creating Trading and Marketing Activities

Trading and marketing companies routinely conducting business in interstate commerce may look to Public Law 86-272 (P.L. 86-272) (see ¶ 705.01) to protect them from state income taxes in destination states when their only business activities in the destination state consist of soliciting orders for the purchase and sale of electric power, natural gas, and similar commodities.

However, P.L. 86-272 (Sec. 101) only affords protection when a company's income is derived from interstate commerce and when the company's only business activities performed in the destination state during a tax year are limited to either, or both, of the following:

> (1) the solicitation of orders by such person, or his representative, in such State for sales of tangible personal property, which orders are sent outside the State for approval or rejection, and, if approved, are filled by shipment or delivery from a point outside the State; and
>
> (2) the solicitation of orders by such person, or his representative, in such State in the name of or for the benefit of a prospective customer of such person, if orders by such customer to such person to enable such customer to fill orders resulting from such solicitation are orders described in paragraph (1).

Natural gas is generally treated as tangible personal property in most states, and although electricity is not commonly regarded as tangible personal property, it is considered as such for some state tax purposes. In states that classify natural gas and/or electricity as tangible personal property, a state's argument that an out-of-state marketer selling into the state has substantial nexus may be strengthened, allowing such states to impose other types of taxes on the marketer (i.e., taxes other than income taxes).[8]

> ***PLANNING NOTE:*** When analyzing whether P.L. 86-272 will protect a marketer from paying state income taxes, review the details from the following three issues: (1) the nature of the marketer's solicitation activities to be performed in the state during the tax year in question, (2) whether such activities will be conducted by employees or independent contractors, and (3) whether delivery will be made by "common carrier."

While all regulated interstate natural gas pipelines are designated as common carriers, that designation is not as clear when it comes to assets used for electric transmission and distribution activities. As a result of open-access legislation, electric transmission systems will oper-

[8] For a discussion of general nexus issues, see ¶ 705.

ate in practice much like common carriers. However, many of the early transmission agreements entered into between the electric utilities and power marketers provided specifically that a utility's transmission services were not considered as part of its capacity as a common carrier, but instead represented the utility's capacity-leasing transactions.

CAUTION: If a transaction is properly cast as a leasing transaction, a state may strongly argue that a power marketer's activities have exceeded the threshold of activity protected by P.L. 86-272 (i.e., the marketer entered into an equipment-leasing transaction with a utility in a destination state rather than utilizing a common carrier).

.01 Back-to-Back Sales

Another issue that frequently arises in connection with nexus determinations (and therefore tax determinations) for wholesale marketers is "back-to-back" sales. Marketers often simultaneously purchase and sell identical blocks of electric power or natural gas either to alleviate inadvertent oversupply positions or to take advantage of favorable strike prices between the purchase and sell transactions. These types of transactions were at issue in a recent Montana State Tax Appeal Board case that found that a Montana pipeline company's recurring, simultaneous back-to-back sales established sufficient nexus for Montana's Corporation License Tax purposes. By successfully asserting nexus, the state was able to significantly increase the company's Montana Corporation License Tax liability by being able to include the gross revenues from the back-to-back sales at issue in the company's Montana sales factor.[9]

¶ 415 Allocation and Apportionment of Gross Receipts in Book-Out Transactions

While Chapter 9 gives a general discussion of allocation and apportionment, this section specifically relates to those involving electricity book-out transactions. Electricity marketers engage in various types of transactions, including physical deliveries and book-outs. A "physical delivery" involves the actual physical flow of electricity from a generator to a purchaser and will generally be apportioned to where the purchaser is located.[10] A "book-out transaction" is one in which

[9] *The Williams Companies, Inc. and Subsidiaries v. The Department of Revenue of the State of Montana*, MT STAB, No. CT-1996-1, Montana State Tax Appeal Board (December 31, 1998). For a more detailed discussion of this case, see ¶ 715.03; also, see Appendix E, p. 335, for a reproduction of this case. For a discussion of the sales factor, see ¶ 940.

[10] Assuming electricity is considered tangible personal property, receipts from the sales of electricity would be sourced to its destination under the laws of a majority of states; see the discussion of the Uniform Division of Income for Tax Purposes Act (UDITPA) and Multistate Tax Commisson (MTC) regulations at ¶ 925.

electricity is bought and sold by marketers in an effort to satisfy unplanned increases in the demand for energy. In a book-out, a marketer is both the seller and ultimate purchaser of a quantity of electricity (e.g., marketer A sells to marketer B, who sells to marketer C, who sells back to marketer A).

Accordingly, a marketer ends up owing a certain quantity of electricity to one party but being owed a like quantity from another party. Rather than actually completing a long series of physical sales and deliveries, the amounts are offset against one another, with the parties recognizing the related financial gain or loss. Thus, in a book-out transaction there is no actual physical delivery of power.

Book-out transactions are entered into by companies largely because of fluctuations in the value of the commodity of energy. As demand increases, generators of electricity (either affiliated with the marketer or not) often need to buy excess capacity because they cannot increase their production enough to satisfy demand. As electricity marketers seek to have the rights to electricity on hand to satisfy this demand, they often buy and sell to one another, resulting in book-outs. Because the profit margins on these sales are extremely low, issues such as apportionment and jurisdiction to impose state and local taxes become very important.

The complexities surrounding book-out transactions become especially evident in the context of apportionment. Because there is no physical flow of power, there is an issue as to whether a book-out transaction is a sale of tangible personal property or a sale of intangible property. The general rule for income tax purposes is that receipts from the sale of tangible personal property are sourced according to destination. Conversely, under the general rule applicable to receipts from sources other than tangible personal property, income is sourced on the basis of where the activities that gave rise to the income were performed, based on cost of performance (typically the commercial domicile or headquarters of the income recipient).[11]

If a book-out transaction is more properly characterized as the assignment of rights to a particular block of electricity, then it should be considered the sale of an intangible. In that case, the income would likely be allocated to the location where the traders are located, based on cost of performance. Alternatively, if the transactions are more properly characterized as sales of electricity, which would most likely be considered tangible personal property, then the income would generally be apportioned or otherwise attributed to the destination state.

[11] UDITPA Sec. 16; MTC Reg. IV.16.

CAUTION: Determining where a particular block of electricity is "destined" can be difficult. Thus, until guidance is forthcoming from the states, the sourcing of these transactions will likely remain uncertain.

Ohio's allocation and apportionment formula. Ohio's recently enacted electric deregulation law included a unique industry-specific allocation and apportionment formula that applies to sales of electric transmission and distribution services beginning with the 2002 tax year.[12] The law provides a new sales factor for use in determining when net income arising from sales of these services will be apportioned to Ohio under the state's franchise tax. This was a particularly important component of the deregulation legislation, because before enactment of the law, electric utilities were not subject to the regular corporate franchise tax in Ohio because they were subject to the former utility gross receipts tax.[13] Under the deregulation law, electric transmission and distribution services will be apportioned to Ohio as follows:

- Sales of the *transmission* of electricity are in Ohio in proportion to the ratio of the wire mileage of the utility company's transmission lines located in Ohio, divided by the wire mileage of the utility company's transmission lines located everywhere. Transmission wire mileage must be weighted for the voltage capacity of each line.
- Sales of the *distribution* of electricity are in Ohio in proportion to the ratio of the wire mileage of the utility company's distribution lines located in Ohio, divided by the wire mileage of the utility company's distribution lines located everywhere. Distribution wire mileage is prohibited from being weighted for the voltage capacity of each line.

For a utility company that has transmission or distribution lines in Ohio, the price charged for the transmission and distribution of electricity must be apportioned to Ohio as stated above if (1) the contract for the sale of electricity includes the seller's or the seller's related-member's obligation to transmit or distribute the electricity and if (2) the sales contract separately identifies the price charged for the transmission or distribution of electricity. Any remaining portion of the sales price of the electricity must be apportioned in accordance with the rule for determining the situs of electricity sales. Under the deregulation law, any entity that makes a sale of electricity must apportion the sale to Ohio in the following instances:

---

[12] Ohio Rev. Code § 5733.05.

[13] Ohio Rev. Code § 5733.09. For a discussion of the sales factor, see ¶ 940.

- Electricity sales that are made directly or indirectly to a customer to the extent the customer consumes the electricity in Ohio. (The law defines a "customer" as a person who purchases electricity for consumption either by that person or by the person's related member, and the electricity is not for resale directly or indirectly to any person other than a related member.)
- Electricity sales that are made directly or indirectly to a related member where the related member directly or indirectly sells electricity to a customer to the extent the customer consumes the electricity in Ohio.
- Electricity sales if the seller or the seller's related member directly or indirectly delivers the electricity to a location in Ohio or directly or indirectly delivers the electricity exactly to the border of Ohio and another state.
- Electricity sales if the seller or the seller's related member directly or indirectly directs the delivery of the electricity to a location in Ohio or directly or indirectly directs the delivery of the electricity exactly to the border of Ohio and another state.

If the situsing provisions prescribed above do not fairly represent the extent of the business's (i.e., utility company's) or the business's related member's activity in Ohio, the business may request, or the Tax Commissioner may require, in respect to all or part of a business's or related member's sales, if reasonable:

- separate accounting,
- the exclusion of one or more additional situsing factors that will fairly represent the business's and the related member's sales in Ohio, or
- the inclusion of one or more additional situsing factors that will fairly represent the business's and the related member's sales in Ohio.

¶ 420 Interstate Commerce Exemptions

In addition to the nexus provisions discussed at ¶ 410, many state gross receipts tax statutes provide for a specific exemption for transactions in interstate commerce. When interstate commerce exemptions are specifically provided, a state's ability to assess a tax on trading and marketing companies will generally be limited to transactions that both originate and terminate in the taxing state (i.e., intrastate sales).

.01 Illinois Interstate Commerce Laws

Illinois imposes a utility gas revenue tax on all companies engaged in the business of distributing, supplying, furnishing, or selling natural gas to persons (other than municipal corporations operating local transportation systems) for use or consumption and not for resale. However, Illinois law specifically provides that such taxes are not to be imposed on any business engaging in interstate commerce (or on any business protected from such taxation by the Constitution and statutes of the United States).[14] The following general principles apply in determining whether any particular transaction is considered interstate commerce, and therefore not subject to the utility gas revenue tax: [15]

1. When a utility company delivers gas through continuous mains, lines, and pipes from a point in Illinois to a point outside of Illinois, the transaction is considered interstate commerce, and the company is not liable for tax on any gross receipts it received from such a delivery.
2. When a utility company not engaged in business in Illinois delivers gas through continuous mains, lines, or pipes from a point outside of Illinois to a point within Illinois, the transaction is considered interstate commerce, and the company is not liable for tax on such receipts. However, if a utility company is engaged in Illinois in the business of distributing, supplying, furnishing, or selling natural gas brought within Illinois for use or consumption and not for resale, such transactions do not constitute interstate commerce, and the tax will apply.
3. When a utility company delivers natural gas through continuous mains, lines, or pipes from one point in Illinois to a second point in Illinois, the transaction is not considered interstate commerce, and the company will be liable for the tax on those receipts. This rule applies irrespective of whether a portion of the continuous mains, lines, or pipes through which the gas passes are situated outside of Illinois.
4. When a utility company distributes, supplies, furnishes, or sells gas to a single customer under a contract calling for the delivery of gas partly outside of Illinois, the company is liable for the tax on that portion of gross receipts from the contract accruing from service furnished within Illinois.

Currently, Illinois does not impose a gas use tax for natural gas used or consumed within the state, so the gas revenue tax provides the only mechanism for collecting tax revenues at the state level related to the consumption of natural gas in Illinois. Municipalities are also authorized to impose local taxes on companies engaged in the business of distributing, supplying, furnishing, or selling gas for use or consumption within the corporate limits of the municipality; the local taxes are

---

[14] Ill. Rev. Stat. ch. 35, para. 615/2.

[15] Ill. Admin. Code tit. 86, § 470.155.

subject to the same prohibitions against any taxing of transactions that are considered interstate commerce. Presently, the only municipality that imposes a local tax is Chicago.[16]

The Supreme Court of Illinois construed the meaning of the interstate commerce exemption in *Mississippi River Fuel Corp. v. Hoffman.*[17] In *Mississippi River Fuel,* the Court held that an interstate pipeline company that sold and delivered natural gas to Illinois customers, and which transported gas through pipelines from points outside of Illinois, was engaged in interstate commerce and, therefore, was not liable for the gas revenue tax.

The facts of *Mississippi River Fuel* indicated that the company's gas-distributor-owned pipelines extended from Louisiana north into Illinois. The pipelines were used to transport gas to Illinois customers for their own use or for the purpose of resale. All gas sold was subject to written contracts between the parties providing the delivery terms and conditions. The gas was delivered in the same form in which it was transported and may have been temporarily stored in Illinois prior to delivery. No mention was made as to where title to the gas passed to Illinois customers or where the contracts between the parties were entered into or executed. The court found that such activity is "very clearly sales in interstate commerce" and, therefore, not subject to the gas revenue tax.

¶ 425 Commodity Exchanges

Trading and marketing companies frequently exchange their physical commodities (i.e., their products) with each other to help control transportation costs and to aggregate a large volume of commodities at established trading hubs or storage terminals.

> **Example:** Agar Inc., an integrated oil and gas producer, owns and operates oil and gas properties in the Gulf of Mexico and also owns an oil storage terminal in Tulsa, Oklahoma, a large trading hub. Benz Inc., also an oil and gas producer, owns and operates oil and gas properties throughout Oklahoma, and an oil refinery in Houston, Texas. In order to minimize the transportation costs associated with transporting their oil production to their respective storage and refining locations, Agar Inc. and Benz Inc. enter into an exchange agreement. Under the exchange agreement, Agar Inc. agrees to deliver a specified amount and grade of its Gulf of

[16] Chicago Department of Revenue, *Informational Bulletin,* Vol. 3, No. 3 (August 1998).

[17] 35 ILCS 615/2 in *Mississippi River Fuel Corp. v. Hoffman,* 4 Ill. 2d 468, 123 N.E. 2d 503 (1954). See Appendix E, p. 295, for a reproduction of this case.

Mexico crude oil to Benz Inc.'s oil refinery in Houston. Benz Inc. agrees to deliver a like volume and grade of its Oklahoma crude oil to Agar Inc.'s oil storage terminal in Tulsa.

.01 Methods of Accounting

There are two methods of accounting that the industry generally uses for commodity exchanges. Each method of accounting can lead to significantly different allocation and apportionment results.

Cash sale method. Using the "cash sale" method, Agar Inc., in the example above, would record its delivery of crude oil to Benz Inc. in Houston as a sale, and record the corresponding Houston sales proceeds. The crude oil Agar Inc. receives from Benz Inc. in Tulsa would be recorded as an inventory purchase. Assuming Agar Inc. resells the crude "purchased" from Benz Inc. to a third-party purchaser in Tulsa, those transactions would be recorded as sales. Under this cash sale method of accounting, Agar Inc. will recognize a similar amount of sales in both states.

Inventory method. The second method of accounting used for product exchanges is generally referred to as the "inventory" method. Under the inventory method, Agar Inc., in the example above, would treat its physical delivery of crude oil to Benz Inc. in Houston as an inventory adjustment rather than a sale. The only sales proceeds Agar Inc. would recognize would be from a third-party purchaser in Tulsa; no sales proceeds would be allocated to Houston.

Some states specifically exclude gross revenues related to exchanges from the determination of the sales factor.[18] Physical commodity exchanges are very common in the crude oil markets and may be a model for alternatives in the wholesale electricity markets as more nonregulated independent power producers enter the market.

¶ 430 Financial Derivatives and Risk Trading

By their nature, trading and marketing transactions typically produce very small profit margins, forcing marketers to buy and sell huge blocks of power and natural gas to earn a reasonable economic return. This tends to expose marketers to more commodity price risk than virtually any other industry. To manage the inherent commodity price risk, trading and marketing companies enter into hedging transactions using established exchange-traded futures contracts, new exchange-based electricity derivatives, private forward contracts and swaps, and traditional insurance. These types of transactions often

[18] La. Rev. Stat. Ann. § 47:287.95(I). See ¶ 940 for a discussion of the sales factor.

create unique apportionment and allocation issues for state tax purposes. There appears little doubt that the gains or losses realized from trading in these types of instruments produce business income; however, there is still some uncertainty as to how the income derived from this activity should be apportioned among and between the states.

States that have adopted the Uniform Division of Income for Tax Purposes Act (UDITPA), but not the Multistate Tax Commission (MTC) regulations, require income from sales (other than sales of "tangible personal property") to be apportioned to the state where the "income-producing activity" occurs.[19] The determination of where the "income-producing activity" occurs for intangible property is based on where the greatest proportion of the cost of performance is incurred. Therefore, under a UDITPA "cost-of-performance" analysis, gains and losses derived from financial hedging transactions should, therefore, be apportioned to the state where the hedging activities are performed.

The state that gets apportioned a trading and marketing company's income activity will normally be where the company's trading floor is located. Under UDITPA's general apportionment rules, the gross income from intangible property sales should be used in calculating a company's sales apportionment factor. However, UDITPA contains a deviation rule that allows states to require companies to use net income rather than gross income in the determination of the sales apportionment factor if use of the gross income results in an apportionment ratio that does not fairly reflect income.[20] Although there are no safe harbors provided in the regulation on what constitutes a "distortion," California courts have held that a 36 percent difference in the factor would not constitute a distortion whereas a 250 percent difference in the factor would be distortive.[21]

A different interpretation applies in states that have adopted the Multistate Tax Commission (MTC) regulations. In August 1997, the MTC amended and updated Regulation IV.18.(c), which addressed special rules for the sales factor.[22] The amendment provided that when apportioning business income derived from the disposition of intangibles, the *net* gain (but not less than zero) rather than the *gross proceeds* from the sale should be included in the determination of the sales apportionment factor. The regulation specifically addressed the treatment of investment securities, trading account assets, federal funds, securities purchased and sold under agreements to resell or repurchase, options, futures contracts, forward contracts, notional prin-

[19] UDITPA Sec. 16; MTC Reg. IV.16. See ¶ 920 for a complete discussion of UDITPA and the MTC.

[20] UDITPA Sec. 18.

[21] *In the Matter of the Appeal of Merrill, Lynch, Pierce, Fenner & Smith, Inc.*, California State Board of Equalization, No. 89-SBE-017 (1989).

[22] For a discussion of MTC Reg. IV.18, see ¶ 940.02. Also see Appendix B, p. 159, for a reproduction of the MTC Regs.

cipal contracts such as swaps, equities, and foreign currency transactions.

According to the MTC, the amendment did not represent a substantive change but rather clarified the original intent of MTC Regulation IV.18(c). The amendment was prompted by state tax cases where companies included the gross receipts from the short-term investment and reinvestment of principal in the sales factor and, consequently, had a distortive apportionment result. Although the final regulation provides for net gains to be included in the determination of the sales factor, the company retains the right to include gross receipts provided it is not distortive to the apportionment formula.

.01 *Sherwin-Williams* Cases: Indiana and Tennessee

Sherwin-Williams has twice been challenged in its attempt to include principal realized from the sale of investments in the denominator of its sales factor. Both the Indiana Tax Court and the Court of Appeals of Tennessee concluded that the Sherwin-Williams' calculation did not fairly represent Sherwin-Williams' income in either state. In each case, each court focused on the statutory meaning of "gross receipts" to determine whether the denominator of the sales factor could be increased to include the claimed capital amount.

The Indiana Tax Court was the first to reject Sherwin-Williams' apportionment, holding that "gross receipts" for the purpose of the sales factor does not include the return of working capital realized from investment securities. The court noted the great potential for abuse because Sherwin-Williams could use the same principal many times while reinvesting in short-term securities, rolling over the principal of the previously sold investment.[23]

The Court of Appeals of Tennessee agreed, explicitly citing the Indiana decision, but it did not base its holding on the state's definition of "gross receipts." Instead, the court applied Tennessee's alternative apportionment provision, § 67-4-812(a), to circumvent the otherwise applicable plain meaning rule which gave the court discretion to apportion income in a manner more accurately representing the company's business in the state.[24]

.02 Texas

Texas (a non-UDITPA state) has provided specific guidance on how income derived from certain financial transactions (swaps and exchange-traded futures) should be apportioned for Texas franchise tax purposes. Under the Texas apportionment rules, a company may only

---

[23] *The Sherwin-Williams Company v. Indiana Department of State Revenue*, 673 N.E.2d 849 (1996).

[24] *The Sherwin-Williams Company v. Ruth E. Johnson*, 989 S.W.2d 710 (1998), rev. denied.

net the payments it receives against the payments it makes if the payments are derived from the sale of capital assets or investments.[25] Because swap transactions were found not to meet either of these definitions, swap payments received by the company were required to be included in the company's gross receipts without being offset by swap payments made by the company.[26]

In an earlier letter ruling, exchange-traded futures contracts were found to meet the definition of "capital asset" in Franchise Tax Rule 3.557(b)(1) or the definition of "investment" in Franchise Tax Rule 3.557(b)(6). Pursuant to Tax Rule 3.557(e)(3), the net gains and losses from the sales of these types of contracts must therefore be added together to determine the total receipts from such transactions. Unless the specific buyer of an exchange-traded futures contract can be identified by the buyer (which is highly unlikely), the net gain from exchange-traded futures contracts are allowed to be apportioned at 6.5 percent to Texas pursuant to Rule 3.557(e)(35).[27]

[25] See Franchise Tax Rules 3.549(e)(3) and 3.557(e)(3).

[26] Texas Comptroller of Public Accounts Letter Ruling 9606T1415G12 (June 18, 1996).

[27] Texas Comptroller of Public Accounts Letter Ruling 9508L1389E03 (August 17, 1995).

Chapter 5

ENERGY SERVICES COMPANIES

¶ 501 Overview

The utility industry is in a state of transition. As deregulation unfolds, companies are finding it advantageous to pursue new and innovative approaches to the energy marketplace. Besides power trading and marketing (see Chapter 4), innovative companies are providing energy services ranging from energy portfolio management to electric generation facility design. These energy services are emerging as the utility industry's new direction in a competitive marketplace.

Deregulation has also facilitated a new generation of energy consulting services. Most major utilities now offer marketing services, whereby the company serves as the sole marketing partner for wholesale power traders and producers. In addition, services on the operational side have increased, with many large utilities now assisting clients in maximizing the efficiency with which they purchase, manage, and use multiple fuel sources. Other utilities are offering their vast experience in plant construction and innovation to help energy producers maximize their generation capacity.

Accompanying deregulation comes fundamental state income and franchise tax issues (see ¶ 505), sales and use (transaction) tax issues (see ¶ 510), and property tax issues (see ¶ 515), some apparent, some not as apparent, that will challenge many of these energy services companies. Since state tax systems were designed to deal with traditional vertically integrated utility companies, energy services companies will operate within an unsettled state tax environment for years to come.

¶ 505 Income and Franchise Tax Issues

Energy services companies will likely encounter diverse state revenue policies for income and franchise taxes. The key issues in these policies include unitary groups, nexus, gross receipts tax repeal, and apportionment formulas.

.01 Unitary Groups

Unitary states, in their search for ways to enhance revenue from utility companies, may attempt to pull energy services companies into the same unitary groups as the regulated entities with which they are affiliated. Classifying a company in a unitary group involves a subjective facts and circumstances approach. If a state considers a corporation's business activity that occurs outside of the state so interrelated and interdependent with the corporation's business activity within the state, then the company has an integrated interstate business, and the state is justified in pulling the income generated outside of the state into the state's apportionment calculation. However, classification of any energy services company as a member of a unitary group may arguably be economically inaccurate and subject to attack by the company, depending on which of the four traditionally followed unitary tests the state uses in seeking to tax the energy services company.[1] While the traditional vertically integrated utility companies are heavily regulated with a controlled rate base and captive consumer base, energy services companies are typically unregulated, leaving their growth to be determined by a totally different set of market-based forces, and they may have a corporate mission quite different from that of their regulated affiliates.

.02 Nexus

A second issue that may be encountered in state policies is whether the presence of electricity or natural gas creates nexus within a state for income tax purposes. (See ¶ 701 and ¶ 705 for a discussion of nexus.) When energy is delivered within the traditional vertically integrated structure of a utility company, the nexus issue would likely not arise because such an in-state entity would be providing electrical service to a captive customer base. However, with components of the electric industry being unbundled, the following fundamental question could arise, especially in the context of energy services companies that do not own the transmission or distribution infrastructure: Is the provision of electric power the sale of a service or the sale of tangible personal property?

In one sense it may be difficult to argue that a power trader in a remote state selling power to a purchaser in another state is providing that purchaser a service, as was the case in the traditional regulated market. However, if electricity can be defined as tangible personal property, it may be difficult for a state to assert nexus under the

---

[1] *Butler Brothers v. McColgan*, 315 US 501 (US SCt 1942) (three unities test); *Edison California Shores v. McColgan*, 183 P2d 16 (Cal. 1947) (contribution and dependency test); *Mobil Oil Corp. v. Commissioner*, 445 US 425 (1980) (Mobil Oil test); Multistate Tax Commission Regulations (MTC Reg.) IV.1.(b) (unitary business test).

Commerce Clause. A state would have to argue with the Supreme Court's substantial physical presence rationale in *Quill Corp. v. North Dakota* [2] as well as the limitations placed on such sales by Public Law 86-272 (see ¶ 705.01), a law that states previously did not encounter within the state monopoly environment. Nevertheless, some states are taking aggressive approaches to assert jurisdiction over out-of- state providers.

Pennsylvania. Pennsylvania has dealt with nexus issues surrounding its gross receipts tax by expanding the boundaries of its "doing business" concept to include any direct and indirect activities in the state that establish or maintain a market for the sale of electricity, including obtaining a license from the state's Public Utility Commission.[3] Pennsylvania has taken the process one step further in attempting to bypass the issues of jurisdiction by requiring all out-of-state and in-state providers of electricity to obtain a license from the Public Utility Commission.[4] The licensing process includes a certification by the company that they will be "subject to all taxes imposed by the state." [5] However, the constitutionality of these provisions may be suspect if a taxpayer has little or no physical presence within the taxing state. (See ¶ 705).

New York. Some states have taken aggressive approaches to pull out-of-state energy marketers within their taxing jurisdiction. New York has taken the position that the state's utility taxes apply to out-of-state natural gas marketers whose sales are to points of delivery within the state.[6]

> ***CAUTION:*** The New York Section 186 tax was repealed and the Section 186-a tax (a related tax) was phased out by legislation signed on May 15, 2000.[7]

New York has also taken the position that both the state's utility franchise tax and gross receipts tax apply to the delivery of electricity, whenever the point of sale is in New York. Such a delivery and sale is sufficient to indicate that an out-of-state corporation is doing business in the state, regardless of whether an out-of-state marketer has the traditional indicia of physical presence in New York, such as offices or employees in the state.[8]

---

[2] *Quill Corp. v. North Dakota,* 504 US 298, 112 SCt 1904 (1992).

[3] 66 Pa. Cons. Stat. Ann. § 2810(j).

[4] Pennsylvania Electric Generation Customer Choice and Competition Act, Act 138 of 1996, P.L. 802.

[5] 66 Pa. Cons. Stat. § 2809(c)(1)(iv).

[6] N.Y. Tax Law § 186, § 186-a.

[7] N.Y. A.B. 1106 (May 15, 2000).

[8] *New York Advisory Opinion,* TSB-A-91(11)C (1991). (This Advisory Opinion is discussed in detail at ¶ 715.01.)

.03 Gross Receipts Tax Repeal

A third way states have shifted their taxation of utilities is by repealing their special utility gross receipts taxes, while also choosing to pull such taxpayers within the reach of their traditional income tax.

Pennsylvania. Pennsylvania recently enacted House Bill 1331, providing for the repeal of the state's gross receipts tax on natural gas, effective January 1, 2000.[9]

Ohio. In Ohio, a law was recently passed that, among other provisions, removes the requirement that electric companies and rural electric companies pay the public utility excise tax on gross receipts.[10] Instead, these entities will be subject to the state's corporation franchise tax beginning in 2002.

New Jersey. Effective January 1, 1998, New Jersey also repealed its gross receipts tax on utilities, thereby subjecting utilities to the New Jersey corporate income tax.[11]

> ***PLANNING NOTE:*** As more states attempt to subject out-of-state energy providers to their corporate income and franchise taxes, the aforementioned issues of unitary groups, nexus, and gross receipts tax repeal will become a top priority for utility tax planners.

.04 Apportionment Formulas

As states attempt to impose corporate income taxes on electricity and natural gas providers, the energy services companies will encounter challenging issues regarding the differing apportionment approaches that various states apply. Many states apply a special apportionment formula to all entities that are defined under their state laws as regulated utilities and/or pipeline/transportation companies. Such formulas are often based on an alternative measure for the sales factor, such as cubic foot miles for natural gas pipeline entities.[12]

> ***PLANNING NOTE:*** Several issues may arise dealing with apportionment. First, will states choose to classify an energy services company (whether engaged in consulting or trading and marketing activities) as a public utility for the purpose of their income/franchise tax? If so, will the state continue to apply an alternative apportionment formula to the subject company—a formula that is not well-suited to energy services companies? This uncertainty could lead to an increased level of petitions to state departments of

---

[9] "Pennsylvania Lawmakers OK Repeal of Gross Receipts Tax on Natural Gas," *State Tax Notes Today,* 1999 STT 118-18 (June 18, 1999).

[10] Ohio R.C. § 5727.30.

[11] N.J. A.B. 2825, Ch. 162 (July 14, 1997).

[12] See S.C. Code Ann. Sec. 12-6-2310(40; Fla. Stat. § 220.151(2); Fla. Admin. Code Ann. Rule 12C-1.0151(2).

Revenue to request the use of alternative apportionment formulas. Ultimately this pressure could force state governments to tackle the difficult issues of apportionment, especially of interstate electricity trading in which the physical nature of electricity transmission (i.e., the inability to store electricity and the commingling nature of electricity on a common transmission grid) challenges conventional methodologies.

¶ 510 Sales and Use (Transaction) Tax Issues

One of the largest emerging players in the interstate utility industry are power marketers, entities that sell unbundled electricity or natural gas to a retail customer by using third-party transmission/distribution facilities or transportation pipelines. As the flow of electricity among networks of aggregators and other traders becomes more complex, many states may find that their transaction taxes (such as gross receipts or sales taxes), designed to tax wholly intrastate transactions, are difficult to apply to these transactions. Determining whether such sales of electricity are of an interstate or intrastate nature will be critical in applying such taxes to the deregulated utility marketplace.[13]

Determining where title to electricity is passed or transferred will also be of central importance. While many power trading contracts provide for both a path of transmission and a point of legal title transfer, it remains to be seen whether states will respect the terms of such contracts, or instead try to pull such sales into their state transaction tax base by asserting title to the electricity transferred within their borders. One case decided by the Indiana Tax Court did respect the delivery terms provided in a contract for the sale of power, holding that a sale of electricity by an Indiana generator occurred out of state.[14]

> ***CAUTION:*** The above Indiana Tax Court case concerned the state's *gross income tax;* whether such respect would be afforded to the contractual terms of a *sales and use tax* or *gross receipts tax* remains to be seen.

As more and more states begin to deal with a decreasing property tax base and, consequently, lower tax revenues, state courts may find it less feasible from a policy standpoint to allow the contract of sale to guide their determinations on this issue. Already, some states have not proven to be as accommodating. For example, Pennsylvania law now

[13] Marc. M. Lewis, "Electric Utility Deregulation: A Shock to State and Local Taxation," *Journal of Multistate Taxation,* March/April 1998, Vol. 8.

[14] *Indiana-Kentucky Electric Corp. v. Indiana Dept. of State Revenue,* 598 N.E.2d 647 (Ind. Tax Ct., 1992).

provides that the retail sale of electricity is deemed to occur at the meter of the retail customer for purposes of a gross receipts tax.[15]

However, whether an energy services company is even subject to a state's transaction tax could be a complex determination. Unlike traditional vertically integrated suppliers of electricity or natural gas, power traders and marketers will often sell natural gas or electricity while maintaining minimal (if any) physical presence in the purchaser's state. The U.S. Supreme Court's decision in *Quill Corp. v. North Dakota* established a substantial physical presence standard for determining when nexus exists with a state in the context of sales and use taxes.[16] (See ¶ 705 for a detailed discussion of nexus issues.) With the emergence of power marketers and traders bringing unbundled offerings to the forefront, the question may arise whether a seller of gas or electricity will have nexus with a state merely by selling to a purchaser in that state without having a physical presence, such as infrastructure or employees. Many such entities will have used third-party marketing agents or a transmission, distribution, and transportation infrastructure to transport electricity or natural gas.

.01 Missouri's *Consolidated Fuel Corp.*

The nexus issue was addressed by the Missouri Administrative Hearing Commission in *Consolidated Fuel Corp. v. Director of Revenue.*[17] The Commission held that Consolidated Fuel Corp. (CFC), a wholesale supplier of natural gas to Missouri natural gas customers, had nexus with the state and thus upheld an assessment for the sales and use tax. CFC had no physical presence in the state and used contracts with pipeline operators to transport and meter all gas that was sold to Missouri customers.

The Commission held that nexus was created by CFC's solicitation of sales in the state through an in-state agent, as well as its servicing of clients, stating that "a seller who systematically solicits sales in a state through independent contractor agents has sufficient nexus with that state to support the use tax collection duty." (See ¶ 715.04 for a detailed discussion of this case.) However, this fact pattern may have left the Commission an easy route of resolution because CFC was using an agent to create an in-state presence. The outcome could be much more uncertain in a case that involves a wholesale trader who, although purposely directing its economic activities toward a state, maintains no physical presence whatsoever with the state, through agent or otherwise.

---

[15] 66 Pa. Cons. Stat. Ann. § 2810(j).

[16] *Quill Corp. v. North Dakota,* 504 US 298; 112 SCt 1904 (1992).

[17] *Consolidated Fuel Corp. v. Director of Revenue,* Missouri Administrative Hearing Commission, No. 92-000230RV (April 29, 1993). See Appendix E, p. 253, for a reproduction of this case.

Example: A power trader in State A sells large amounts of capacity to a purchaser in State B. If those sales are made on power trading markets in other states, arguably the power trader, which may be supplying enormous amounts of power to the purchaser, may not have nexus with State B where the purchaser is located.

PLANNING NOTE: Utilities may also encounter more aggressive modern approaches to sales and use tax nexus, akin to the emergence of "economic nexus" with income taxation, whereby a state claims that a gas or electric trader is purposefully directing activities at the state while in turn receiving the benefits from the state in the form of a state regulated and protected transmission grid and/or distribution system. Alternatively, states may pursue more consumer-oriented taxation whereby use taxes become more prevalent, avoiding nexus issues altogether.

The *Consolidated Fuel* decision also raises another important issue concerning various costs that will be subject to sales and use taxation. As sales of unbundled electricity and natural gas continue to increase, with separate charges for distribution, metering, and actual power sold, the question arises as to what portion of the sale price will be subject to a state's sales and use tax regimes. In some states, a sales and use tax may not apply to charges for transmission, delivery, or metering.[18]

In *Consolidated Fuel,* the Commission disputed CFC's contention that transportation charges should not be included in the use tax base because they are fees for services that are not part of the sale. The Commission interpreted the Missouri sales and use statute, which states that the "sales price is the consideration including charges for services . . . paid or given or contracted to be paid or given, by the purchaser . . . including any services that are a part of the sale," as including charges for transportation. The Commission also stressed the ability of the actual end-user customers to choose an alternative delivery method, concluding that the end-users' lack of choice in delivery method dictated that such costs should be included in the tax base.

Other states, such as New Jersey, in the spirit of this decision, have changed their sales and use tax systems to "provide that receipts from charges for the transportation of energy are not exempt from the tax." [19] The state of New York altered its sales and use tax regime to

[18] Marc. M. Lewis, "Electric Utility Deregulation: A Shock to State and Local Taxation," *Journal of Multistate Taxation,* March/April 1998, Vol. 8. (citing Minn. Stat. § 297A.01, subd. 8, providing that "sales price" does not include charges for transportation occurring after a sale is completed); Me. Admin. Rel., Instructional Bulletin No. 39(5)(a)(I) (providing that delivery charges are not taxable even if not separately stated on the customer's invoice as long as separate statement is available in vendor's records); Ill. Reg. § 130.415 (providing that Illinois exempts delivery charges from sales where the buyer and seller agree on transportation charges separately from the selling price).

[19] N.J. Revised Statutes § 54:32B-8.11 (1998).

provide that fees charged by utilities for getting electricity or gas to a customer are subject to state and local sales and use tax.[20] Such fundamental changes will likely become commonplace as states attempt to pull more utility companies within the reaches of their transaction taxes, particularly in response to shrinking property tax revenues.

¶ 515 Property Tax Issues

Growth in the energy services sector has led to the increased importance of intellectual property, in particular each company's "brand name." Traditionally, for property tax purposes, regulated electric and natural gas utilities have been valued based upon their income streams rather than by their traditional fair market dollar value, an approach that has guided the valuation of nonregulated entities. Essentially, the income-producing capacity of the entire utility company was determined, and this capacity was prorated to the various taxing jurisdictions where the company had real or personal property.

Going forward, the real value of energy services companies could lie in the income streams that are produced by their brand names. Whether states choose to classify such companies as utilities for property tax purposes will be a fundamental issue in the near term, particularly since energy services companies may not have significant levels of real and personal property, but instead the bulk of their value consists of intellectual property.

> ***PLANNING NOTE:*** Many utilities may begin to set up intangible holding companies under which the parent company is charged a fee for the use of the name thereby decreasing the income stream being produced by the regulated entity. The "lost income" would simply be directed to entities that may not be subject to the income-stream-based property tax valuation method.
>
> ***CAUTION:*** States faced with the prospect of a decreasing property tax base under the traditional valuation system after deregulation may attempt to alter the manner in which utility property is valued, or if the states remain under the income stream approach, they may attempt to include the income that is going out to the intangible holding companies as part of the property tax base.

Furthermore, the introduction of increased competition into the energy marketplace by state legislation may strain profit margins even further, especially in industries such as power marketing where profit

---

[20] New York TSB-M-99(1.1)S; "New York Postpones Implementation of Sales Taxation of Certain Utilities," *State Tax Notes Today*, 1999 STT 71-27 (March 31, 1999).

margins are thin to start with.[21] This could put even greater downward pressure on the property tax base of many utility companies, and present significant opportunities for these entities to pursue lower valuations and realize significant tax savings.[22]

In response to these transaction tax issues, states may choose to reform their overall approach to taxing energy companies. In 1999, the Ohio Senate passed Senate Bill 3, a sweeping deregulation bill that, in addition to providing for a competitive marketplace, included protection for local tax jurisdictions from pending revenue declines.[23] While SB 3 reduced the assessment on all tangible personal property of electric companies and rural electric companies used in generation from 88 percent to 25 percent, the bill introduced a new kilowatt-hour tax on electric distribution companies beginning in 2001. A large portion of the funds are earmarked for local school districts and other local governmental subdivisions.

¶ 520 *General Motors Corp. v. Tracy:* Is the Playing Field Level for Energy Services?

In *General Motors Corp. v. Tracy* (see ¶ 1005 for a detailed discussion of this case), the U.S. Supreme Court upheld an Ohio use tax statute that exempted natural gas purchases from state public utilities, while taxing purchases from out-of-state marketers.[24] In its reasoning, the Court defended the charge that the tax discriminated against interstate commerce, stating that the two taxpayers were "not similarly situated." The Court took special note of the fact that while out-of-state marketers served a noncaptive business consumer base, the state regulated natural gas utility served a captive residential customer base dependent upon the assurances of affordable natural gas. The Supreme Court's decision indeed asks more questions than it answers.

While deregulation has taken place in a number of states, many states still heavily regulate utilities. Perhaps the biggest question facing energy services companies (and power marketers and wholesale traders) is to what extent the Supreme Court's opinion in *General Motors* will be used by states to protect their existing state monopolies in the near term. While the two taxpayers may not have been similarly situated in the *General Motors* decision, what will happen when a

[21] "How Profitable is Power Marketing," of "Energy Insight," *PointCast Network Energy News,* June 7, 1999.

[22] See Michael Shapiro and Steven P. Schneider, "Effects of Deregulation on Property Taxes," *National Real Estate Investor,* Vol. 41, No. 6, pg. 36 (May 1999), for concise discussion of the effects of deregulation on popular valuation methodologies.

[23] See "Ohio Senate Ok's Electricity Deregulation Bill," *State Tax Notes Today,* 1999 STT 102-26 (May 26, 1999).

[24] *General Motors Corp. v. Tracy,* 519 US 278; 117 SCt 811 (1997). See Appendix E, p. 264, for a reproduction of this case.

power marketer is selling to a similar residential customer base? There is a chance that energy services companies could be facing an uneven playing field for years to come. However, the counterargument to this concern, which some observers have pointed out, is that the *General Motors* decision arguably rests on a precise set of facts and would be difficult to pigeonhole into other situations.[25] Either way, the Supreme Court's decision should be a source of uncertainty regarding protective state tax regimes.

[25] Marc. M. Lewis, "Electric Utility Deregulation: A Shock to State and Local Taxation," *Journal of Multistate Taxation,* March/April 1998, Vol. 8.

Chapter 6

INDEPENDENT POWER PROJECTS

¶ 601 Overview

The former regulated energy market allowed producers, wholesalers, and retailers of electricity to have access to a captive customer base. Changing market trends and increased competition, however, have dramatically changed the landscape of a once secure, largely government-regulated industry. The restructuring via deregulation of the electric utility industry has essentially opened the doors for a new and different breed of power producer and power service provider. Nonutility electric generation facilities, including cogeneration facilities and independent power projects, are becoming the standard for the energy industry.

For electric utility customers, deregulation is expected to bring about cheaper electricity and enhanced services, and the increasingly competitive industry is struggling to identify ways to minimize operating costs and increase the bottom line. While cheaper and more economical generation and transmission methods can only be obtained through improved technology, certain operating costs, such as the tax liability of power generation facilities, can vary significantly from one locality to another.

The risks involved in the power generation business are comparable to any other business. Currently, at least within many geographic regions, there is a demand for generation facilities. Hence, the industry is moving to fill that demand. As a result of this movement, competition is increasing among those involved, from the selection of sites and markets to securing the turbines to be used in a facility.

For generation facilities, whether regulated or nonregulated, property taxes represent a significant, recurring expense on a facility's income statement. Because of the increased competition and the number of nonregulated players entering the market, independent power project development managers within the industry are scrutinizing the property tax as a potential means of minimizing operating expenses. Because of the need and the potential to cut property tax expenses, managers will be examining the methods of assessment (see ¶ 605); methods of valuation, including the cost approach, income approach, stock and debt approach, and market approach (¶ 610); planning opportunities such as relocation or expansion incentives (¶ 615), payments or fees in lieu of taxes (¶ 620), and pollution control exemptions (¶ 625); valuating generation facilities (¶ 630); determining "fair market value" (¶ 635); taxable vs. nontaxable properties (¶ 640); and which locality has jurisdiction to assess property taxes (¶ 645).

Additionally, since property taxes are an above-the-line expense, or at least should be, they are expected to become more in line with the nonregulated entities' property tax expense as deregulation takes place. Historically, the property taxes paid on the property of public utilities, including power generation facilities, have exceeded the taxes paid by nonregulated entities. This disparity is due largely to the regulation of the industry and the utilities' ability to pay the tax and flow the expense through to the customers. In some jurisdictions, the property tax revenue attributable to utilities makes up over 90 percent of the jurisdiction's total revenue base. In attaining this level of disparity, jurisdictions often apply clearly biased statutes and methodologies targeting utilities. For instance, in the state of Ohio, property taxes have historically been assessed at 88 percent of fair market value for utilities, while nonutilities are assessed at 25 percent of fair market value.

> ***PLANNING NOTE:*** In Ohio, beginning with the 2001 tax year, the taxable transmission and distribution property of an electric company will still be assessed at 88 percent of true value, but all other taxable property (i.e., generation property) will be assessed at 25 percent of true value.[1]

For additional discussions of property taxes, see also ¶ 320.02 and ¶ 325.05.

¶ 605 Methods of Assessment

The basis for any property tax assessment begins with a determination of the value of the property in question, in this case, an independent power project. This determination of value is typically performed by either the local municipality (typically the city or county) or the state. If the value is determined at the local level, the property (or properties) within a particular county, city, or other municipality is valued by that particular jurisdiction. For state assessed properties, the state determines the value of the property, although the property tax revenue is often used to fund local programs. In the past, regulated entities, including electric utilities, have gener-

[1] Ohio Rev. Code § 5727.111.

ally been centrally assessed by states rather than locally assessed by the locality where the property is located.

¶ 610 Valuation

In most jurisdictions, the basis for property tax assessments of electric generation facilities will involve the use of one or more of the four following approaches.

.01 Cost Approach

Under the cost approach to valuation, the value of property is measured by the cost required to produce an exact replica (reproduction cost) or a functional equivalent (replacement cost). The cost approach is based on the "principle of substitution" that provides that an informed buyer would not pay any more for a particular asset than the cost of acquiring or constructing an asset having the same utility.

The next step in the cost approach to valuation is to reduce the reproduction or replacement cost by the facility's accumulated depreciation. Depreciation should account for all elements of aging, including physical deterioration, and functional and economic obsolescence.

The cost approach is typically computed by taking the original cost of an asset and deducting an estimated depreciation amount, which is taken from a standard depreciation table. This method of valuation is rarely accurate because of the cost indexes and the unreliability of the standard depreciation tables that are used.

.02 Income Approach

The income approach to valuation measures the capitalization of the future income stream attributable to a specific property. The capitalization rate is composed of the rate of return required by debt holders and equity holders and is weighted by the relative proportions of the debt and equity within a company's structure.

Given the weaknesses of the cost approach to valuation, the income approach provides a more accurate estimate of the property in question.

> ***CAUTION:*** A major weakness of the income approach, however, is the inability to separate the income and relative capitalized value among taxable and nontaxable assets, including intangible items such as goodwill and wholesaling marketing contracts in place.

.03 Stock and Debt Approach

The stock and debt approach to valuation relies on the basic accounting principle that the value of the property is equivalent to the value of the debt plus equity, or stock, of the entity in question. This method presents many issues in its application, however, especially in the attribution of the corporation's stock and debt to the property being valued. It is rarely used on its own to value generation facilities.

.04 Market Approach

The market approach to valuation simply involves using recent sales of similar properties to ascertain the value of the property in question. For electric generation facilities, however, this method is of little use since sales of similar properties simply do not occur on a regular basis. Additionally, the listed purchase price of a generation facility oftentimes includes an amount paid for nontaxable assets, including power purchase agreements, fuel contracts, and an "entry fee" into a newly deregulated market.

¶ 615 Relocation or Expansion Incentives

Since new generation facilities do not require a significant number of employee operators, states and local jurisdictions hesitate to provide the facilities with relocation or expansion incentives. And while a new generation facility does not create hundreds of new jobs, it also does not burden the local infrastructure with the need for new schools, roads, etc. In many jurisdictions, a generation facility would, however, provide a significant increase to the local property tax base, and jurisdictions are often willing to provide significant incentives, such as training, financing, and site selection services in order to attract such a facility.

> ***PLANNING NOTE:*** Electric companies and independent power project development managers should recognize that location incentives provided by any jurisdiction are negotiable and should be pursued.

¶ 620 Payments or Fees in Lieu of Taxes (PILOT or FILOT)

To secure a fixed, guaranteed revenue stream, many jurisdictions are willing to negotiate a payment or fee in lieu of taxes (PILOT or FILOT) arrangement with generation facilities. A PILOT or FILOT arrangement provides a fixed revenue stream for the jurisdiction, even when the project is not successful, while providing a fixed, and oftentimes lesser, expense for the project manager. The profitability of such a project can be more accurately forecasted over the project's life.

The notion of generating-facility owners negotiating PILOT agreements has become increasingly popular with the advent of broad deregulation in the electric utility sector. With traditional utility facilities being sold at a brisk pace and independent power projects springing up throughout the country, local taxing jurisdictions are being faced with issues not previously contemplated, such as tax windfalls and losses. To secure a fixed, guaranteed revenue stream, many jurisdictions are willing to negotiate a PILOT agreement with generation facilities. Utilities and independent power producers are also willing to enter into PILOT agreements if the terms can provide them with a reasonable expense that minimizes their future risk of increased property taxes while not adversely affecting projected financial performance.

¶ 625 Pollution Control Exemptions

In most states, a property that helps mitigate or eliminate air, noise, or water pollution may be exempted from property tax, sales tax, and/or the property factor of the state's income tax apportionment formula. To obtain such exemptions, an application must usually be made to the state's environmental authorities. A certification from the environmental authorities that the property helps eliminate or mitigate pollution is then required to be submitted to the appropriate taxing authorities to secure the exemptions.

¶ 630 Valuating Electric Generation Facilities

Assessors in most states are required to assess electric generation facilities at 100 percent of each facility's fair market value. Historically, assessors have used net book value or rate base value as a primary appraisal indicator for valuating these facilities since market transactions were rare when utilities were regulated.

Because of the significant changes in the electric utility industry, the methods historically used by assessors to valuate generation facilities may be outdated. On one hand, the income-producing capabilities of many plants will no longer be constrained by regulators, causing an increase in the market value of those facilities. On the other hand, increased competition in the marketplace will reduce the value of other facilities. Additionally, because of the increase in sales and transfers of generation facilities, the market approach to valuation (see ¶ 610.04) might quickly become a primary indicator of their fair market value.

The answer to the question, What is fair market value?, will differ by jurisdiction for similar assets. The significant task in each assessment is insuring the valuation is agreeable to both parties.

> ***PLANNING NOTE:*** Outside appraisers, experienced in the electric utility industry, can often provide assistance to independent power projects by preparing a separate, independent appraisal to be used in negotiations with the local tax assessor.

¶ 640 Taxable vs. Nontaxable

Each jurisdiction taxes electric power generation facilities differently for property tax purposes. Certain states will consider an entire generation facility as taxable real property, while others will tax the land and buildings as real property and the machinery and equipment as personal property. Most jurisdictions do not purport to tax intangible assets; however, the determination of the existence and value of the intangible, nontaxable assets remains an issue in property taxation. In determining the economics of a power generation facility, a basic understanding of what is taxable versus what is nontaxable is critical to the independent power project development manager.

Many states do not tax the tangible personal property of utilities. Working through the maze of state statutes is a science unto itself and often requires the assistance of experienced local professionals. For example, in the state of Pennsylvania, a public utility's "utility realty" is considered taxable. Utility realty is defined in the state's statutes as

> All lands, together with all buildings, towers, smokestacks, dams, dikes, canals, cooling towers, storage tanks, reactor structures, pump houses, supporting foundations, enclosing structures, supporting structures, containment structures, reactor containment outer shells, reactor containment vessels, turbine buildings, recovery tanks, solid waste area enclosures, primary auxiliary buildings, containment auxiliary safeguard structures, fuel buildings, decontamination buildings, and, all other structures and enclosures whatsoever which are physically affixed to the land, no matter how such structures and enclosures are designated and without regard to the classification thereof for local real estate taxation purposes, but not including machinery and equipment, whether or not housed within such building, structure or enclosure, or after December 31, 1999, land and improvements to land that are indispensable to the generation of electricity, located within this Commonwealth that at the end of the taxable year are owned by a public utility or its affiliate either directly or by or through a subsidiary and are used or in the course of development or construction for use, in whole or in part, in the furnishing, including producing, storing, distributing or transporting,

of public utility service and which are not subject to local real estate taxation under any law in effect on April 23, 1968.[2]

Of course, and as always, there are specific exemptions from the above definition that often further complicate the issue, making clarity of taxation even further remote.

¶ 645 Jurisdiction to Assess Property Taxes

The annual property taxes on an electric power generation facility are determined by which state division has the authority to assess property taxes. The issue is not only whether the property will be centrally assessed by the state or locally assessed by the locality/ county, but whether a regulated public utility will be subjected to differing property tax assessment procedures and valuation methods than a nonregulated entity. In Pennsylvania, for example, a public utility is assessed by the Pennsylvania Department of Revenue under the Public Utility Realty Tax Act of 1971 (PURTA). A question exists, however, whether a nonregulated generation facility qualifies as a public utility for purposes of PURTA.

PLANNING NOTE: Minimizing the annual property tax expense for an electric power generation facility is a task worth undertaking. This task must always be completed to determine the overall economics of an independent power project. A proactive, timely approach to the recurring property tax expenditure can result in significant savings over the life of a project.

---

[2] Pa. Stat. Ann., Title 72, § 8101-A(3).

Part 3

INDUSTRY-SPECIFIC TECHNICAL ISSUES

Chapter 7

NEXUS

¶ 701 Overview

In a regulated environment, customers must purchase electricity from the local utility at "bundled" rates that cover the utility's related generation, transmission, and distribution costs. Because the local utility typically owns and operates in-state power generation, transmission, and/or distribution assets, the utility is clearly subject to state and local taxation. As such, public utilities have historically been a reliable source of tax revenues, including the gross receipts tax, franchise tax, sales and use tax, and property tax.

With the advent of deregulation, customers can purchase power from the local utility, from the local utility's marketing affiliate, or other in-state power producers or marketers. Or customers can purchase power directly from out-of-state suppliers. If an in-state supplier is selected, there will be little or no effect on tax collections since the supplier will typically be subject to the full complement of state and local taxes. However, when an out-of-state power supplier is selected, traditional gross receipts or sales and use taxes may either not apply or would not be collected since the out-of-state supplier may not be subject to either tax in the delivery state. Faced with the potential loss of a significant amount of state and local tax revenue, state tax administrators have had to reexamine their utility tax regimes and identify replacement sources of revenue. In addition, most states have become very aggressive in asserting their rights to tax the out-of-state power suppliers.

A 1998 tax policy review for the electric and natural gas utility industries in Washington, D.C., concluded that:

> If the gross receipts tax is left unchanged, and deregulation continues, unregulated energy firms may enter the market and gain a cost advantage (perhaps 11.1%) over the regulated industries by not having to pay the gross receipts tax. Such firms are likely to have no legal nexus in the District, so the city may not be able to tax their receipts. The prospective competitive advantage from unequal taxation of these unregulated firms would, in all likelihood, lead to a flow of energy sales to the lower cost firms outside the District, leading to

> a decline in tax receipts from D.C.-based firms as well as a decline in the business of these firms. Accordingly, the employment base of the utilities in the District will decline, weakening its economic development impact.[1]

The report to the D.C. Tax Revision Committee contemplated a change in the gross receipts tax to extend it to out-of-state sellers, stating "the nexus issue is non-trivial, court challenges from non-D.C.-based energy firms are inevitable, and such litigation may prove successful." Similar changes in other states have not been challenged in the courts to date; however, such challenges are inevitable.

Although many states have recognized the need to modify their tax systems to reflect the dramatic changes in the industry, devising a system of taxation that entirely avoids nexus concerns is difficult. Under general constitutional law, for a state to tax an out-of-state entity, the entity must have sufficient nexus, or contacts, with the state.[2] Often, however, the only contacts out-of-state electricity marketers have with a state is that they sell electricity to customers located in the state.

Despite the risk of constitutional challenge, states have continued to legislate changes to their tax regimes to prevent or replace potential revenue losses caused by deregulation. New taxes have been imposed on the consumers of energy, rather than energy sellers. Also, states have asserted that aggressive nexus positions applied to traditional taxes already in place (see ¶ 705, ¶ 710, and ¶ 715). In addition, licensing or in-state office requirements (see ¶ 720 and ¶ 725) have been imposed that seek to force out-of-state power marketers to subject themselves to the jurisdiction of the state. These attempts often run the risk of violating constitutional nexus requirements, especially as states attempt to assert jurisdiction over out-of-state power marketers.

¶ 705 General Nexus Principles

Even if aggressive nexus positions and licensing requirements are supported by a particular state's "doing business" statute, they still may not be consistent with the jurisdictional requirements imposed by the U.S. Constitution and federal law. Under general nexus principles, states can only tax out-of-state corporations when there is a sufficient connection, or nexus, between the business being conducted by the corporation and the taxing state, as required by the Commerce and Due Process Clauses of the Constitution.

---

[1] Rodney D. Green, "A Report to the Washington, D.C., Tax Revision Commission," *Tax Policy Review for the Electric and Natural Gas Utility Industries in Washington, D.C.* (January 1998).

[2] See *Complete Auto Transit v. Brady,* 430 US 274, 97 SCt 1076 (1977 US SCt), discussed fully at ¶ 705.

The main limitation on a state's ability to tax out-of-state corporations is the Commerce Clause, which gives the U.S. Congress the authority to regulate commerce among the states. Even in the absence of congressional action, states are still prohibited from interfering with interstate commerce. The U.S. Supreme Court has held that a tax on interstate commerce will not satisfy the Commerce Clause unless the activity taxed has a substantial nexus with the state.[3] Under *Complete Auto Transit,* a tax will not withstand Commerce Clause scrutiny unless the tax

1. is applied to an activity that has a substantial nexus with the taxing state;
2. is fairly apportioned;
3. does not discriminate against interstate commerce; and
4. is fairly related to the services provided by the state.

The U.S. Supreme Court has interpreted substantial nexus to mean that a corporation must be physically present in a state before that state can impose a tax on it.[4] Furthermore, the *Quill* case provides that the degree of presence necessary to establish substantial nexus must exceed a slightest presence, such that the presence of a *de minimis* amount of property in the state will not be sufficient.

> ***CAUTION:*** It is important to recognize, however, that *Quill* dealt specifically with the imposition of sales and use taxes. Thus, the physical presence, bright-line test set forth by the Supreme Court in *Quill* and *National Bellas Hess* has been regarded by some to only apply to sales and use taxes.[5]

Several states have taken the position that a physical presence is not necessary to establish substantial nexus for taxes other than the sales and use tax.[6] However, a recent Tennessee court of appeals decision held that a financial institution with no physical presence in the state did not have substantial nexus for an excise tax despite the existence of a Tennessee statute basing nexus on economic (not physical) presence.[7]

---

[3] *Complete Auto Transit, Inc. v. Brady,* 430 US 274, 97 SCt 1076 (1977 US SCt).

[4] *Quill Corporation v. North Dakota,* 504 US 298, 112 SCt 1904 (1992 US SCt). See Appendix E, p. 305, for a reproduction of this case.

[5] See Multistate Tax Commission, *National Nexus Program Bulletin 95-1* (December 20, 1995) which states: "There is a question of whether the substantial nexus standard for imposition of use tax collection as preserved in *Quill* or a lower nexus standard applies to income taxes, franchise taxes based upon income, and other comparable taxes."

[6] See *Geoffrey, Inc. v. South Carolina Tax Comm'n,* 437 SE2d 13 (S.C. 1993), *cert. denied,* 114 SCt 550 (1993) (corporation that licensed intangible assets in South Carolina established substantial nexus for South Carolina income tax purposes). See also, e.g., Ind. Code § 6-5.5-3-1; Mass. Gen. Laws ch. 63, § 1; Tenn. Code Ann. § 67-4-806 (statutes providing that financial institutions will be considered to have nexus in the state on the basis of economic presence factors, such as the number of customers located in the state).

[7] *J.C. Penney Nat'l Bank v. Johnson,* 19 SW3d 831 (Tenn. Court of Appeals 1999); Tenn. Code Ann. § 67-4-806 (statute providing that financial institutions will be considered to have nexus in the state on the basis of economic presence factors, such as the number of customers located in the state).

.01 Public Law 86-272

Federal law prohibits the imposition of an income tax on certain out-of-state sellers even though they may have sufficient contacts with a taxing state to establish nexus under the Due Process and Commerce Clauses of the U.S. Constitution. Under Public Law 86-272 (P.L. 86-272),[8] a state may not impose a corporate net income tax on an out-of-state seller whose only activity within the state during the year is the solicitation of orders for sales of tangible personal property within the state, provided that orders are approved and the property is delivered from outside the state.

Although electricity is not normally considered to be tangible personal property, it is considered such in some states. In states where electricity is classified as tangible personal property, a state's ability to tax out-of-state power marketers making in-state sales may be strengthened. For example, for Pennsylvania sales and use tax purposes, "tangible personal property" includes, among other things, natural, manufactured, and bottled gas, steam, and electricity when these things are not purchased directly by the user solely for his own residential use.[9] Presumably, electricity sold by out-of-state marketers to commercial users should qualify as tangible personal property for Pennsylvania sales and use tax purposes, raising the issue of whether P.L. 86-272 would apply to such a transaction. However, to qualify for P.L. 86-272 protection, all aspects of the statute must be satisfied. Thus, in analyzing whether P.L. 86-272 would apply, it is necessary to examine other issues, including but not limited to (1) the nature of the electricity marketer's in-state solicitation activities, (2) whether such activities are conducted by employees or independent contractors, and (3) whether delivery is made by "common carrier." Although P.L. 86-272 applies only to net income taxes (not the gross receipts taxes typically levied on utilities), many states have or are considering changing their laws to impose the general corporate income tax on electric utilities. (See ¶ 325 and ¶ 505.)

¶ 710 Applying General Nexus Principles to the Utility Industry

The imposition of a tax on out-of-state energy providers, in general, that have no physical presence in the taxing state may not be consistent with the Constitution's general nexus principles as applied by the Supreme Court. But under *Koch Fuels v. Clark* [10] (see ¶ 715.02), an out-

---

[8] Public Law 86-272 (1959), 15 U.S.C. § 381. See Appendix C, p. 241, for a reproduction of P.L. 86-272.

[9] 61 Pa. Code § 31.1(3)(ii).

[10] *Koch Fuels, Inc. v. Clark*, 676 A2d 330 (R.I. 1996), *cert. denied*, 519 US 930 (1996). See Appendix E, p. 287, for a reproduction of this case.

of-state fuel marketer that used a common carrier to deliver fuel to Rhode Island customers established substantial nexus in the state because title to the fuel did not pass until it reached the purchaser's flange inside the state, and the seller maintained possession of and control over the fuel until the delivery point. While *Koch Fuels* deals with fuel rather than electricity or natural gas, states may assert similar nexus arguments in the electric and natural gas industries.

Constitutional issues are heightened within the electric industry where, due to differences in the mode of transportation and delivery, it is more difficult to prove that an out-of-state seller has established a physical presence in the state. This is why electricity contracts often specify that title to the electricity passes at an "interconnect" or "grid," or other "pooling" point which may be located outside the purchaser's state. An "interconnect" is defined as a point where the transmission lines from two or more utilities connect while a "grid" is an interconnection of transmission lines where the flow of electricity (from multiple utilities) is controlled. In all cases, title may actually pass at a point outside the purchaser's state, thus reducing the likelihood that an out-of-state seller will have the substantial nexus necessary to be subjected to a tax.

¶ 715 Nexus Developments in the Utility Industry

In the 1990s, significant nexus developments occurred in New York, Rhode Island, Montana, and Missouri. The four cases are described below (¶ 715.01–¶ 715.04).

.01 *New York Advisory Opinion,* TSB-A-91(11)C

New York has taken the position that its utility taxes apply to out-of-state natural gas marketers whose sales are to points of delivery within the state.[11] The conclusion in this *Advisory Opinion* is based on the fact that title to the natural gas did not pass to the purchaser until it reached a delivery point inside the state of New York. Because the out-of-state marketer held title to the natural gas in the state until delivery to the New York customer, it was concluded that substantial nexus was established and that New York could constitutionally impose a tax on the out-of-state marketer.

> ***CAUTION:*** Note that *New York Advisory Opinion,* TSB-A-91(11)C (1991), which applies specifically to natural gas utilities, predates electric deregulation. Nevertheless, it is believed that

[11] New York Advisory Opinion, TSB-A-91(11)C (1991).

New York would take the position that the *Advisory Opinion* applies, by analogy, to the electric industry.

New York imposes two separate taxes on utilities: (1) a franchise tax on the "gross earnings" of companies that both furnish utility services and are regulated by the state Department of Public Service and (2) a gross receipts tax on the "gross operating income" of businesses engaged in the delivery of electricity.[12] Based on TSB-A-91(11)C, when an out-of-state corporation's point of sale is in New York, the New York Department of Taxation and Finance may take the position that the sales activity is sufficient to indicate that the out-of-state corporation is doing business in the state.[13] Thus, regardless of whether an out-of-state marketer has the traditional indicia of physical presence in New York, such as offices or employees in the state, New York may seek to assert its taxing jurisdiction on sales made into the state.

CAUTION: The New York § 186 tax was repealed and the Section 186-a tax (a related tax) was phased out by legislation signed on May 15, 2000.[14]

.02 Rhode Island's *Koch Fuels, Inc. v. Clark*

The Rhode Island Supreme Court held that Koch Fuels [15] had met the physical presence requirements of the Commerce Clause by selling fuel oil to customers in Rhode Island, thus subjecting Koch Fuels to Rhode Island's gross receipts tax. Koch Fuels is a Delaware company engaged in the sale and distribution of fuel oil. Among its customers was New England Power, based in Rhode Island, to which it shipped oil originating in Texas, Pennsylvania, or Massachusetts by common carriers. Upon receiving a deficiency notice for Rhode Island's gross receipts tax, Koch Fuels paid the assessment under protest and filed a complaint claiming that the state's imposition of the tax was in violation of both the Equal Protection and Commerce Clauses of the U.S. Constitution.

In addressing the nexus issue, the state supreme court rejected Koch Fuels' contentions that it did not maintain the requisite physical presence for a gross receipts tax under the Commerce Clause. The court reasoned that by maintaining title, possession, and risk of loss over the fuel oil until it reached the flange in Rhode Island, Koch Fuels had established the necessary physical presence with the state. In particular, the court noted that while not owning the common carrier

> Koch's fuel represented the entire and exclusive cargo of the vessel . . . [and] [o]n the basis of Koch's complete control over the oil shipments, the exclusive nature of the common carrier's contract, *the*

---

[12] N.Y. Tax Law § 186 and § 186-a.

[13] *New York Advisory Opinion,* TSB-A-91(11)C (1991).

[14] N.Y. A.B. 1106 (May 15, 2000).

[15] *Koch Fuels v. Clark,* 676 A2d 330 (R.I. 1996), *cert. denied,* 519 US 930 (1996). See Appendix E, p. 287, for a reproduction of this case.

unique nature of the cargo, and the fact that the sales were consummated upon delivery in Rhode Island . . . Koch's activities created in practical effect a physical presence within [the] state.

Although the fuel oil shipments were made by common carrier, the court also noted that Koch Fuels caused the oil to be imported into Rhode Island through its negotiations, and it held title, risk of loss, and possession of the oil up until the moment of delivery inside the state. In addition, the court found that the payment of the gross receipts tax was reasonable related to the services that the state provided to Koch Fuels. The provision by Rhode Island of shipping facilities and the maintenance of emergency equipment in case of an environmental disaster were found to be sufficiently related to the tax imposed by the state.

PLANNING NOTE: Rhode Island paid particular heed to the terms of the sales contracts, including the provisions that provided for title, possession, and control of the fuel oil to be retained by Koch Fuels, the seller, until it arrived in the state. Had Koch Fuels surrendered title to the fuel oil at the time it was loaded on the ship or if it had commingled its fuel with that of another supplier on the ship (as would naturally happen in the delivery of electricity or natural gas), it is questionable whether the state would have found Koch Fuels to have the requisite physical presence in Rhode Island. Additionally, a majority of the court's physical presence reasoning, while applicable to fuel oil, would be difficult to apply to a transfer of electricity or natural gas by third-party transmission or pipeline facilities.

CAUTION: The *Koch Fuels* decision may have questionable application to the sale of electricity or natural gas. First, as mentioned above, transmission of both electricity and natural gas requires instant commingling in a common transportation system. Second, complete control cannot be maintained by a seller of electricity or natural gas (one of the factors that the *Koch* court relied on was that the fuel oil ship could be called back, an impossible feat once electricity or natural gas is released to a transmission facility or pipeline), nor can electricity or natural gas ever be an exclusive unit of cargo transported by a third-party facility.

.03 *Williams Companies, Inc. v. Montana*

In *Williams Companies, Inc. v. Montana,* the Montana State Tax Appeal Board (STAB) held that Northwest Alaskan Pipeline Company (NWA) had taxable nexus with the state of Montana because of its role in importing Canadian natural gas into the United States and, therefore, subjecting itself to the state's corporation license tax.[16] NWA, a subsidiary of Williams Companies, Inc., entered into agreements to purchase Canadian natural gas at the international border, import the gas into the United States, and resell it to several U.S. purchasers. The board rendered its decision notwithstanding the fact that NWA did not have employees and did not own any gas pipelines, compressor stations, or other pipeline parts within the state. However, NWA held a permit from the Federal Energy Regulatory Commission (FERC) that authorized it to import and resell natural gas.

What is noteworthy about the board's decision is that the presence of federal regulatory oversight guided the board's determination that the physical transfer of natural gas had taken place in Montana, and not at the international border as claimed by the NWA. NWA argued that it did not have nexus with the state of Montana, claiming instead that its purchase and subsequent transfer of natural gas took place simultaneously at the international border before entering the United States. NWA asserted that the purchase and transfer occurred in a "nanosecond," in the "dead zone" or boundary between the United States and Canada.

The board highlighted the fact that NWA was importing gas under authority granted by FERC, and asserted further that had the sales not taken place within the United States, this organization would not and could not assert jurisdiction over the transactions. Specifically, the board stated that

> NWA is the first owner of the natural gas subject to FERC regulation and, as such, the transactions are recognized as occurring in FERC jurisdiction within the U.S. . . . Because of geography it follows then that, if the transactions occur within the U.S., they are occurring in Montana.

On this same note, the Montana Department of Revenue had pointed to several FERC filings by NWA indicating that delivery of the gas actually took place in Idaho and Montana, and not at the international border as NWA had claimed.

It is noteworthy that the board reached this decision despite the evidence offered by NWA that it neither transported the gas to the border nor into the United States, but rather, merely effectuated title transfer. NWA claimed and offered testimony that it acquired title to the gas at the international border and then immediately transferred title to a series of purchasers in the United States. The board acknowl-

[16] *Williams Companies, Inc. v. Montana,* MT STAB, No. CT-1996-1 (December 31, 1998). See Appendix E, p. 335, for a reproduction of this case.

edged that NWA was not a shipper and that the purchasers of the gas arranged for and paid for the pipeline transportation of the purchased gas. Nevertheless, the board was more compelled by the presence of regulatory oversight when determining where transfer of the natural gas took place.

.04 *Consolidated Fuel Corp. v. Director of Revenue of Missouri*

In *Consolidated Fuel Corp. v. Director of Revenue of Missouri,* the Missouri Administrative Hearing Commission upheld an assessment of use tax on Consolidated Fuel Corp. (CFC).[17] In so doing, the commission concluded that CFC had created nexus with the state by systematically soliciting sales of natural gas to Missouri customers through an independent agent, even though CFC lacked any other physical presence in the state.

The facts indicate that CFC had no facility, employees, real property, or personal property in Missouri. Instead, CFC contracted with pipeline operators to transport and meter its gas. These contracts were written to give CFC title to the gas at all times until it passed from CFC to its customers upon delivery.

CFC's independent agent in Missouri, Comet Industries, would solicit Missouri gas consumers on the company's behalf, mostly by telephone using prepared lists of potential consumers. On occasion, its employees did make visits to customers. The agent was not authorized to enter into contracts. In addition, the agent serviced the Missouri accounts by maintaining monthly contact with each customer and troubleshooting problems.

In summarizing their reason for upholding the use tax, the Administrative Hearing Commission stated:

> Where the tax liability concerned is the use tax collection duty, that is, the vendor's use tax, a special "bright line" rule replaces the first prong of the *Complete Auto Transit* test: a state may not impose the use tax collection duty upon an out-of-state seller whose only contact with the forum state is by common carrier or the United States Mail.[18]

However, CFC's contacts with Missouri were more than common carrier or U.S. mail. CFC systematically solicited sales in Missouri through its agent, Comet, and, therefore, CFC had sufficient nexus with the

---

[17] *Consolidated Fuel Corp. v. Director of Revenue,* Missouri Administrative Hearing Commission, No. 92-000230RV (April 29, 1993). See Appendix E, p. 253, for a reproduction of this case.

[18] *Consolidated Fuel Corp.* (see n. 17) citing *Quill Corp. v. North Dakota,* 504 US 298, 112 SCt 1904, 1914-16 (1992); *National Bellas Hess, Inc. v. Department of Revenue of Illinois,* 386 US 753 (1967 US SCt).

state to support the use tax collection duty.[19] Thus, Missouri had sufficient nexus with CFC to impose the use tax collection duty on it.[20]

¶ 720 Licensing Requirements

Some states, anticipating nexus issues, have sought to avoid the issue of obtaining jurisdiction over out-of-state electricity and natural gas marketers by requiring out-of-state marketers to register with the state and consent to its taxes before being permitted to sell in the state.

Pennsylvania (electricity). In November 1996, Pennsylvania enacted legislation phasing in direct retail access to all customers over a three-year period beginning in 1998.[21] Pennsylvania's statute includes a requirement that out-of-state and in-state providers obtain a license from the Pennsylvania Utility Commission before selling electricity in the state.

As part of the licensing process, all providers must certify that they will be "subject to all taxes imposed" by the state.[22] Additionally, power providers who were not filing returns before, but wish to obtain licensing to continue marketing in the state, will be subject to the capital stock/franchise tax at the rate of 12.75 mills per dollar value of capital stock apportionable to Pennsylvania as well as the public utility realty tax (PURTA) at the rate of 42 mills per dollar of taxable value of any utility realty they purchase in Pennsylvania.[23] Even the gross receipts tax statute was written to include out-of-state sellers by defining that all sales of electricity and related services, including generation from out-of-state sources, are sales of electric energy by an "electric light company." [24]

The provision further provides that sales of electricity are within Pennsylvania if the meter of the customer is within Pennsylvania. In cases where out-of-state suppliers do not remit the gross receipts tax, Pennsylvania law provides for a compensating use tax to be collected on the first sale to an in-state company.[25] Another provision goes so far as to state that the electric distribution company's tariff shall provide that if the distributor becomes liable for the use tax, the supplier will indemnify the distributor, a type of contractual method of charging the tax back to the supplier.[26]

---

[19] *Tyler Pipe Industries, Inc. v. Washington State Dept. of Revenue*, 483 US 232 (1987); *Scripto, Inc. v. Carson*, 362 US 207, 80 SCt 619 (1960).

[20] *Consolidated Fuel Corp. v. Director of Revenue*, Missouri Administrative Hearing Commission, No. 92-000230RV (April 29, 1993).

[21] Pennsylvania Electric Generation Customer Choice and Competition Act, Act 138 of 1996 (P.L. 802).

[22] 66 Pa. C.S. § 2809(c)(1)(iv).

[23] 72 Pa. P.S. § 7601; P.S.C.A. § 1102-A(a).

[24] 66 Pa. C.S. § 2810(I)–§ 2810(L).

[25] 66 Pa. C.S. § 2806(G)(3)(III) and § 2809(C)(2).

[26] 66 Pa. C.S. § 2810(M).

Connecticut (natural gas). Similar provisions have been enacted by states that have deregulated the natural gas industry. In Connecticut, a 5 percent gross earnings tax is imposed on companies whose principal business is "manufacturing, selling, or distribution" of natural gas.[27] If a business that is not a municipal gas utility, gas company, or gas pipeline sells natural gas to an end-user in Connecticut, it must register with the Department of Public Utility Control and become subject to the tax.[28] Thus, out-of-state natural gas marketers must register with the state and pay the tax.

Consent to state taxation. Under such licensing requirements, all out-of-state marketers must consent to state taxation in order for them to be licensed to sell in the state, potentially side-stepping the issue of whether constitutional nexus exists to support the imposition of tax. The question remains, however, whether these licensing requirements are imposed on out-of-state sellers in violation of the Commerce Clause nexus requirements. In addition, to the extent that the activities of out-of-state electricity marketers fall within the protection of P.L. 86-272 (see ¶ 705.01), consent requirements that subject out-of-state marketers to a net-income-based tax may be inconsistent with the statute. But see, *Heublein, Inc. v. South Carolina Tax Comm'n,*[29] in which P.L. 86-272 protection was not available to a liquor dealer whose activities exceeded the scope of P.L. 86-272, even though it only engaged in the unprotected activities to comply with South Carolina's alcoholic beverage regulations.

> ***CAUTION:*** State regulatory schemes that serve a legitimate local purpose are valid even if they cause an entity to lose its P.L. 86-272 protection, and the state may subject such entities to a net income tax. Nevertheless, it is not clear that the state consent requirements imposed on utilities serve an independent, local purpose other than taxation. Further, it should be noted that most licensing requirements do not require entities to engage in activities that would exceed the protection of P.L. 86-272, but rather, simply require them to consent to taxation.

¶ 725 In-State Office Requirements

Other states, rather than require that out-of-state companies register to collect tax, have employed more subtle means of avoiding the nexus issues. New Jersey, for example, as part of its deregulation legislation, requires out-of-state suppliers of energy to have an in-state

[27] Conn. Gen. Stat. § 16-27.

[28] Conn. Act 95-114 § 1.

[29] *Heublein, Inc. v. South Carolina Tax Comm'n,* 409 US 275 (1972).

office.[30] As part of deregulation, the New Jersey Legislature found that to maintain continued safety, reliability, and consumer protection, and to ensure accessibility to electricity and natural gas suppliers, certain regulatory authority, including the authority to require electricity and natural gas suppliers to maintain an office within the state, was necessary. The legislation goes on to require that electric power and natural gas suppliers maintain an office in New Jersey for accepting service of process, maintaining the records required by the New Jersey Board of Public Utilities, and ensuring accessibility to the board, consumers, and electric public utilities.

PLANNING NOTE: This in-state office requirement will likely make any nexus challenges moot because otherwise out-of-state energy suppliers will have a physical presence in New Jersey that is generally considered sufficient to meet the constitutional nexus standards (see ¶ 705).

[30] Electric Discount and Energy Competition Act, N.J. Statute § 48:3-49 (2000).

Chapter 8

BUSINESS AND NONBUSINESS INCOME

¶ 801 Overview

Attributing income from a company doing business in multiple states is done by classifying all income as either business income or nonbusiness income. Business income is apportioned to each of the states in which the company is doing business whereas nonbusiness income is generally allocated to a specific state. Many states with a corporate income tax have adopted the Uniform Division of Income for Tax Purposes Act (UDITPA) that instructs how to ascribe the income of companies that are subject to tax in multiple states (see ¶ 805). Not all states follow the UDITPA method of apportionment; among the non-UDITPA states, some specifically allocate only certain types of income while others allocate all types of income (see ¶ 810). In addition, many states follow the Multistate Tax Commission (MTC) regulations, which offer guidelines for specific types of income (see ¶ 815).

¶ 805 Uniform Division of Income for Tax Purposes Act (UDITPA)

The Uniform Division of Income for Tax Purposes Act (UDITPA) (which is fully reproduced with comments in Appendix A, p. 151) states that "business income" means:

> income arising from transactions and activity in the regular course of the taxpayer's trade or business and includes income from tangible or intangible property if the acquisition, management, and disposition of the property constitute integral parts of the taxpayer's regular trade or business operations.[1]

"Nonbusiness income" has simply been defined as all income other than business income.[2]

PLANNING NOTE: Deregulation provides utilities the opportunity to review their tax positions on gains or losses generated by

[1] UDITPA Sec. 1(a).

[2] UDITPA Sec. 1(e).

disposing of portions of their existing businesses. Prudent tax planning may convert business income otherwise subject to apportionment into allocable nonbusiness income. Depending on where the allocable nonbusiness income is sourced, a favorable result can occur.

Most states interpret UDITPA as incorporating two alternative tests for determining whether income is business income. The tests are referred to as the "transactional test" and the "functional test." In the majority of states, if either test is satisfied, the income will be classified as business income.

.01 Transactional Test

The first clause in the UDITPA definition is the focus of the transactional test. Income will be considered business income if it arises from "transactions and activities in the regular course of the taxpayer's trade or business." In applying this test, the focus is on the type of transaction giving rise to the income and how the transaction relates to the taxpayer's regular trade or business.

The frequency and regularity of sales transactions are important factors in determining whether the proceeds of a sale constitute business income under the transactional test. In *Western Natural Gas Co.,*[3] the Kansas Supreme Court held that the sale by a company of all its assets in complete liquidation was not a transaction in the regular course of the taxpayer's business. Therefore, the gain did not constitute business income subject to apportionment.

.02 Functional Test

Under the functional test, income is considered apportionable business income if the acquisition, management, and disposition of the asset that generates the income constitutes an integral part of the taxpayer's regular trade or business operations. The functional test focuses on the relationship of the asset giving rise to the taxable income, and the business itself.

An Illinois court of appeal held that either the transactional test or the functional test could be applied to classify gains as business income. In *Kroger,*[4] the taxpayer underwent a corporate restructuring in which it disposed of various tangible and intangible assets, including leasehold interests in real property. According to the court, the

> second definition refers to the conditions of ownership of property by the taxpayer; it is not limited to a taxpayer's trade or business, such

[3] *Western Natural Gas Co. v. McDonald,* 202 Kan. 98, 446 P2d 781 (1968).

[4] *Kroger Co. v. Department of Revenue,* 284 Ill. App. 3d 473, 673 NE2d 710 (1996).

as Kroger's retail business, but includes operations of the taxpayer's business, such as the sale of leasehold interests.

Some states, such as Tennessee, have statutorily reversed judicial opinions when the courts have interpreted UDITPA to imply only the application of the transactional test.[5] Under the statutory rule, Tennessee employs both the transactional and functional tests as alternatives for determining whether income is business income.

The regulations interpreting UDITPA by the Multistate Tax Commission (MTC) (see ¶ 815) construe UDITPA to establish a presumption in favor of apportionment. The regulations state that "the income of the taxpayer is business income unless clearly classifiable as nonbusiness income." [6] Therefore, states in which the MTC regulations have been adopted and states that adopt the functional test as an alternative test (through judicial opinion or statute), are likely to classify income obtained from a transaction as business income subject to apportionment, even when the income would otherwise be allocable as nonbusiness income.

.03 Allocation of Nonbusiness Income

Under UDITPA, the following items of nonbusiness income are allocated based either on the situs of the property or the commercial domicile of the company:

- Rents and royalties from real property are allocated to the state in which the property is located.[7]
- Rents and royalties from tangible personal property are allocated to the state in which the property is located, or the state of commercial domicile if the taxpayer is not organized under the laws or taxable in the other state.[8]
- Gains and losses from real property are allocated to the state in which the property is located.[9]
- Gains and losses from tangible personal property are allocated to the state of situs of the property at the time of sale, or to the state of commercial domicile if the taxpayer is not taxable in the state of sale.[10]
- Gains and losses from intangible property are allocated to the taxpayer's state of commercial domicile.[11]
- Interest and dividends are allocated to the taxpayer's state of commercial domicile.[12]

[5] Tenn. Code § 67-4-804.
[6] MTC Reg. IV.1.(a).
[7] UDITPA Sec. 5.
[8] UDITPA Sec. 5.
[9] UDITPA Sec. 6.
[10] UDITPA Sec. 6.
[11] UDITPA Sec. 6.
[12] UDITPA Sec. 7.

- Patent and copyright royalties are allocated to the state in which utilized, such as in manufacturing or printing, but if the taxpayer is not taxable in that state, the royalties are allocable to the taxpayer's state of commercial domicile.[13]

¶ 810 Non-UDITPA States

Not all states follow the Uniform Division of Income for Tax Purposes Act (UDITPA) practice of apportioning business income and allocating nonbusiness income. Some states specifically allocate certain types of income and others apportion all types of income. A few states distinguish between apportionable and allocable income using criteria other than the business/nonbusiness standard. For instance, a state may allocate all items of a certain type of income. South Carolina, for example, allocates income based on whether it is derived from interest, dividends, or gains from the sale of real property.[14] Similarly, Louisiana allocates income from rents, royalties, construction services, interest, dividends, and gains or losses.[15]

The states that apportion all types of income, known as full-apportionment states, frequently legislate a presumption that income received by a taxpayer is related to its business and, hence, is to be included in the apportionable tax base.

The U.S. Supreme Court, in a series of decisions, concluded that only income from the taxpayer's unitary business is considered apportionable income. Income that is unrelated to the taxpayer's unitary business is nonbusiness income subject to allocation.[16] The Court held that New Jersey could not tax the gain Allied-Signal derived from the sale of a minority stock interest in ASARCO because ASARCO was not part of Allied-Signal's unitary business conducted in New Jersey. Furthermore, the ASARCO stock served as an investment function, not as an operational function. The Court therefore rejected New Jersey's full apportionment method of taxation. Refusing to abandon the unitary business principle for distinguishing between apportionable business income and allocable nonbusiness income, the Court easily concluded that ASARCO was not engaged in a unitary business with Allied-Signal in New Jersey. However, the Court held that a unitary business determination is not the exclusive means of meeting the constitutional requirements for apportioning income.

The Court introduced a new functional test for classifying income: the operational test versus the investment test. Under this test, a

---

[13] UDITPA Sec. 8.

[14] S.C. Code § 12-7-1120.

[15] La. Rev. Stat. § 47:287.92.

[16] *Allied-Signal, Inc. v. Director, Division of Taxation,* 504 US 768, 112 SCt 2251 (1992).

transaction or activity may create business income if it serves an operational function, rather than an investment function. For example, the Court pointed out that interest earned by a corporation on short-term bank deposits used as working capital may be apportionable even though the bank and corporation are not engaged in a unitary business. Likewise, income received from the stock of a company held by a corporation to ensure a steady supply of raw materials for the corporation's production process would presumably constitute apportionable income even if the supplier was not a part of the taxpayer's unitary business.

The Court rejected a "business purpose" test, stating that the mere fact that an intangible asset was acquired pursuant to a long-term corporate strategy of acquisitions and dispositions does not convert an otherwise passive investment into an operational function.

Following *Allied-Signal,* it would appear that full apportionment might be unconstitutional, at least in application to certain companies. Therefore, some full-apportionment states, such as Massachusetts and Virginia, have reacted to *Allied-Signal* by issuing administrative releases to reflect the Court's decision excluding some income that would otherwise be included in the apportionable income base.

The effect of *Allied-Signal* is less dramatic in states that have traditionally recognized a business/nonbusiness income distinction. Although *Allied-Signal* does not adopt the UDITPA functional and transactional tests (see ¶ 805), it appears in many instances that the result under the UDITPA tests, particularly the functional test, and the result under *Allied-Signal* would be the same.[17]

¶ 815 Multistate Tax Commission Regulations

The Multistate Tax Commission (MTC) regulations interpret the Uniform Division of Income for Tax Purposes Act (UDITPA) provisions. To the extent that a particular state adopts them, in whole or in part, the MTC regulations set forth standards for determining whether certain types of income constitute business or nonbusiness income; business income being apportioned to the states in which the taxpayer is doing business, and nonbusiness income being allocated to one state, usually the state of commercial domicile. (See Appendix B, p. 159, for a reproduction of the MTC regulations.)

For allocating income, commercial domicile is defined under UDITPA as the "principal place from which the trade or business of

[17] See *Matter of the Appeal of American Biltrite Inc.,* California State Board of Equalization, No. 92-SBE-026 (Nov. 19, 1992), and *Ross-Araco Corp. v. Commonwealth of Pennsylvania,* 544 Pa. 74; 674 A.2d 691 (Pa. SCt 1996).

the taxpayer is directed or managed." [18] The criteria typically used to determine the commercial domicile of a company include the site of the board of directors' meetings, location of stockholder meetings, location and residence of the officers, and location of corporate records and bank accounts, etc.

.01 Rents from Tangible Personal Property

Rents received from property "used" in or "incidental [to]" a company's trade or business are business income. An example of business income includes rents received in a rental car business at an airport. However, rents received by a grocery store operator from lease of a building purchased with surplus funds as an investment would be considered nonbusiness income.[19]

.02 Gains and Losses from Sales of Property

Gains and losses from dispositions of real or personal property are business income if the property was used in the company's trade or business. However, if the property was used for the production of nonbusiness income or otherwise was excluded from the property factor as a nonbusiness asset before its sale or other disposition, the gain or loss will constitute nonbusiness income. An example of business income includes the gain (or loss) from the sale of a manufacturing plant by a manufacturer. However, the gain (or loss) from the sale by a grocery store operator of an office building previously used as corporate headquarters, but vacated and rented to an unrelated investment company for the past five years, is nonbusiness income.[20]

.03 Interest

Interest is business income if the intangible generating the interest is used or arose from the trade or business or when the purpose of acquiring and holding the intangible is related to or incidental to such trade or business operations. An example of business income includes interest income from installment sale receivables and temporary investments of working capital. However, interest income from long-term investments unrelated to a company's regular trade or business (e.g., funds derived from sale of a subsidiary that is invested pending a decision by management as to application and use) is nonbusiness income.[21]

.04 Dividends

Dividends are business income if the stock arose out of or was acquired in the regular course of the company's trade or business

[18] UDITPA Sec. 1(b).
[19] MTC Reg. IV.1.(c)(1).
[20] MTC Reg. IV.1.(c)(2).
[21] MTC Reg. IV.1.(c)(3).

operations or when the purpose of acquiring and holding the stock is related to or incidental to the company's trade or business. An example of business income includes dividends received on stock from a minority investment in a supplier. However, dividends received by a manufacturer on stock held for investment and that are unrelated to its manufacturing business constitute nonbusiness income.[22]

.05 Patent and Copyright Royalties

Patent and copyright royalties are business income if the patent or copyright arose out of, or was created in, the regular course of the company's trade or business operations or when the purpose for acquiring and holding the patent or copyright is related to or incidental to such trade or business operations. An example of business income includes royalties received by a company engaged in the music publishing business from music copyrights acquired upon the acquisition of a smaller music publishing company. In contrast, royalties received by this same company on the patent of a type of phonograph needle acquired upon the acquisition of another company are nonbusiness income (the company does not manufacture or sell phonographs or phonographic equipment).[23]

---

[22] MTC Reg. IV.1.(c)(4).

[23] MTC Reg. IV.2.(b)(2).

Chapter 9

ALLOCATION AND APPORTIONMENT OF INCOME

¶ 901 Overview

A multistate corporation [1] is often required to pay income taxes to more than one state, assuming the corporation has taxable nexus in more than one state (see Chapter 7 for a discussion of nexus). However, the multistate corporation has the right to divide its income tax base among the states where it has taxable nexus so that each state only taxes a reasonably determined portion of the corporation's income. Under the Due Process and Commerce Clauses of the U.S. Constitution, states are required to provide a fair apportionment or division of a multistate taxpayer's income tax base. A state is constitutionally prohibited from taxing income that is not connected with business conducted in the state.

Unlike the federal methodology, states generally do not use a system of corporate income tax credits to prevent multiple taxation. Instead, the states attempt to divide the tax base among the states where the corporation does business so that each state taxes only a fair proportion of the corporation's income.

Commercial domicile. Although states are constitutionally required to divide the income tax base of a multistate taxpayer, the "home" state generally imposes certain conditions that must be satisfied before a domiciliary corporation can divide its income. Generally, the corporation must be engaged in some activity outside the state. Most home states, as a condition precedent to the division of income, require a domiciliary corporation to be "engaged in business," "doing business," "carrying on business," or, most frequently, to be "taxable" in at least one other state.

A corporation's "home" state is generally its state of commercial domicile. This may or may not be the corporation's state of incorporation. For example, California defines commercial domicile as "the

[1] The term "corporation" is used throughout this chapter because LLCs, partnerships, and certain other business entities are often not subject to state income taxes.

principal place from which the trade or business of the taxpayer is directed or managed."[2] Essentially, a corporation's state of commercial domicile is determined by the place where realistic control of its functions is located.

Taxability by a state other than commercial domicile. Most states limit division of income to corporations that have income from business activity "which is taxable both within and without this state."[3] Such a taxpayer is deemed to be taxable in another state if[4]

- in that state the corporation is subject to a net income tax, a franchise tax measured by net income, a franchise tax for the privilege of doing business, or a corporate stock tax; or
- that state has jurisdiction to subject the taxpayer to a net income tax regardless of whether or not, in fact, the other state imposes such a tax.

Methods of apportionment. There are three basic methods of dividing the income tax base of a multistate corporation among the states where it is taxable. These methods are separate accounting (¶ 905), specific allocation (¶ 910), and formulary apportionment (¶ 915). Many states use formulary apportionment as prescribed by the Uniform Division of Income for Tax Purposes Act (UDITPA) and/or by the Multistate Tax Commission (MTC) regulations (¶ 920 and ¶ 925). Generally, formulary apportionment is comprised of three components: the property factor (¶ 930), the payroll factor (¶ 935), and the sales factor (¶ 940).

The UDITPA method of apportionment is not followed by all states; some states use other apportionment formulas (¶ 945). Also, because the standard formula is not suitable for all businesses, both UDITPA and MTC regulations provide for alternative methods of apportionment. Additionally, many states provide alternative formulas for specialized industries (¶ 950).

¶ 905 Separate Accounting

Under the separate accounting method, the activities of a corporation within a state are considered separate and distinct from those outside of the state. The corporation attempts to assign each item of revenue and expense to the state where it is generated.

.01 Weaknesses of Separate Accounting

Separate accounting has three major weaknesses:

[2] Cal. Rev. & Tax Code § 25120(b).

[3] UDITPA Sec. 2.

[4] UDITPA Sec. 3.

1. It can be quite costly and time consuming since separate books must be maintained for each operation and for each state where business is conducted.
2. The determination of reasonable profit and transfer prices is a matter of judgment, particularly where no comparable prices are available. As a result, a distortion of income often occurs.
3. The separate accounting method ignores the realities of the business world. A business does not operate in a vacuum. The operations of the business in one state usually contribute to the operations of the business in another state. It is most often impractical and impossible to separately determine the profits of one component of an integrated business operation.

.02 When to Use Separate Accounting

As a result of the above weaknesses, separate accounting in the state tax area is generally used in limited instances. Usually, separate accounting is used in the following industries, which by their nature lend themselves to this approach: mining, banking, oil and gas, construction, and hotels.

CAUTION: Most states do not allow the use of separate accounting for general manufacturing or merchandising corporations unless it can be proved that the preferred method (i.e., formulary apportionment, discussed at ¶ 915) drastically distorts the income otherwise attributed to the state.

¶ 910 Specific Allocation

Specific allocation is similar to separate geographical accounting, but it is applied only to certain classes of income. Under specific allocation, these classes of income are traced to their source or other connection with a state and attributed solely to that state. For example, rents from real property might be allocated to the state where the real property is located.

.01 Weaknesses of Specific Allocation

The major weakness of the specific allocation method is that more than one state may have claim to the specified element of income. For example, if a corporation manufactured goods in one state, warehoused them in a second, maintained a sales office in a third, and sold the goods to a customer in a fourth, each state would have some claim to receive the income from the sale of these goods. To avoid taxing the corporation on greater than 100 percent of its income, some sort of arbitrary rule would have to be adopted uniformly by all states to determine the specific attribution of income, by type, to each state. Such a rule could unduly benefit one state to the detriment of the others.

.02 When to Use Specific Allocation

Specific allocation is generally used only for allocating the income from certain types of transactions. Income that is typically subject to specific allocation rules includes: rents from real and tangible property, royalties from patents and copyrights, dividend income, and interest income. Generally, the income is sourced to the state where the property is located or to the corporation's commercial domicile.

> ***CAUTION:*** In most states, allocation is further limited to only those items listed above and is applied only if the income is not connected with the corporation's regular trade or business, i.e., if they constitute nonbusiness income.

¶ 915 Formulary Apportionment

Under formulary apportionment, there is no attempt to trace items of income to the state where the income was generated. Formulary apportionment divides a multistate corporation's tax base among the states where it does business by applying a fraction representing the ratio of in-state factors to total factors. The factors generally include some combination of receipts, payroll, and/or property.

Formulary apportionment merely approximates the amount of income of a business that should be attributed to a particular state. Apportionment is the method most relied on by the states to divide the income of a corporation. Because it is difficult to determine the amount of income that is generated by a multistate corporation's operations in any one state, the use of a statutory formula can provide a rough approximation of the corporation's income reasonably attributable to its operations in the state.

The formula most frequently used is the so-called "Massachusetts formula," or standard apportionment formula, which consists of three evenly weighted factors: property, payroll, and sales. A corporation first ascertains the income that is to be apportioned and then multiplies that amount by the arithmetical average of three ratios:

1. In-state property to total property
2. In-state payroll to total payroll
3. In-state sales to total sales

Many states have modified the standard formula by giving additional weight to the sales factor in the calculation and/or eliminating one or more of the factors.

A corporation's taxable income times the above apportionment factor represents the apportioned tax base.

¶ 920 UDITPA and the Multistate Tax Commission

UDITPA. The Uniform Division of Income for Tax Purposes Act (UDITPA) is a model act drafted in 1957 by the National Conference of Commissioners on Uniform State Tax Laws in response to a widely recognized need for a uniform method of dividing income for tax purposes among the states. The primary purpose for the creation of UDITPA was twofold:

1. To promote uniformity in the allocation practices among the states that impose tax on or measured by the net income of a corporation.
2. To relieve the pressure for congressional legislation in the field.

UDITPA is directed principally at the division of income of manufacturing and merchandising businesses, but its major provisions are applied by many states to all industries. (A full reproduction of UDITPA with comments is shown in Appendix A, p. 151.)

Multistate Tax Commission. Citing a need for uniformity, two organizations, the National Association of Attorneys General and the National Legislative Council, formulated the Multistate Tax Compact in 1966. The Multistate Tax Compact created the Multistate Tax Commission (MTC), established a joint audit program for multistate taxpayers, and adopted UDITPA as an optional method of apportionment for member states.

Twenty-one states are members of the Multistate Tax Compact. These states, some with modifications, have enacted UDITPA into law. In addition, 16 states are associate members of the commission. Current membership (shown below) is composed primarily of western states.

States That Have Enacted UDITPA

Alabama	Idaho	New Mexico
Alaska	Kansas	North Dakota
Arkansas	Maine	Oregon
California	Michigan	South Dakota
Colorado	Minnesota	Texas
District of Columbia	Missouri	Utah
Hawaii	Montana	Washington

Currently headquartered in Washington, D.C., the Multistate Tax Commission is comprised of one member from each state that is a party to the Compact. Its purpose is to increase uniformity in state and local tax laws. In addition to proposing uniform regulations interpreting UDITPA, the commission administers the joint audit program authorized by the Compact.

¶ 925 Formulary Apportionment Under UDITPA and MTC Regulations

The Uniform Division of Income for Tax Purposes Act (UDITPA) and the Multistate Tax Commission (MTC) regulations are significant because they demonstrate an earnest attempt by the states at self-regulation. Although not all states have adopted UDITPA or the MTC regulations, the regulations establish a nonbinding conceptual framework for dividing the income of a multistate business. Any proposed regulations are merely advisory and not binding on any state unless specifically adopted by the state.

Under UDITPA and the MTC regulations, business income is subject to formulary apportionment, while nonbusiness income is subject to specific allocation. Business income is apportioned by the standard apportionment formula that equally weights three factors. This formula compares the ratio of in-state to overall property (¶ 930), payroll (¶ 935), and sales (¶ 940).

The apportionment formula yields a percentage that determines the portion of a corporation's business income included in a particular state's taxable income. The larger the numerators of the apportionment factors for a given state, the more income that will be apportioned to that state.

UDITPA and the MTC regulations set forth rules for determining the apportionment factors. The rules for each factor establish what items are included in the factors, the timing of entry and removal from the factors, the evaluation of items included in the factors, and how items are assigned to a particular state and included in that state's apportionment factor numerator. While most states follow the general approach set forth by UDITPA and the MTC regulations, there are numerous exceptions and differences between states and between UDITPA and the MTC as they relate to public utilities. (See Appendix A, p. 151, for a reproduction of UDITPA with comments; Appendix B, p. 159, for MTC Regulations.)

.01 Public Utilities Under UDITPA

Expressly excluded from UDITPA's coverage are three kinds of taxpayers: [5]

[5] UDITPA Sec. 2.

1. Individuals, to the extent their income is derived from personal services
2. Financial organizations
3. Public utilities

UDITPA defines "public utility" as

> any business entity which owns or operates for public use any plant, equipment, property, franchise, or license for the transmission of communications, transportation of goods or persons, or the production, storage, transmission, sale, delivery, or furnishing of electricity, water, steam, oil, oil products, or gas.[6]

.02 Public Utilities Under the Multistate Tax Compact

In contrast to the definition provided in UDITPA, "public utility" is defined in the Multistate Tax Compact as [7]

> any business entity
>
> (1) which owns or operates any plant, equipment, property, franchise, or license for the transmission of communications, transportation of goods or persons, except by pipe line, or the production, transmission, sale, delivery, or furnishing of electricity, water or steam; and
>
> (2) whose rates of charges for goods or services have been established or approved by a Federal, State or local government or governmental agency.

Differences in the definitions are discussed below at ¶ 925.03.

.03 How Differences Between UDITPA and the Multistate Tax Compact Affect Public Utilities

The differences between UDITPA and the Multistate Tax Compact may be significant for public utilities depending on whether a state has adopted either for its method of apportioning income. While UDITPA defines a public utility as businesses operated for "public use," the Compact narrows its definition to businesses whose rates or charges are established by a governmental agency. Pipelines are not included in the Compact's definition of public utility, but they are included by UDITPA. Unlike the Compact, UDITPA includes "storage" as an activity and "oil, oil products, or gas" as products that could cause a business to be considered a public utility. The Compact further deviates from UDITPA by allowing a business that derives a greater percentage of its income from non-public utility activities to elect to allocate and apportion its entire income under the general Compact guidelines.[8]

---

[6] UDITPA Sec. 1(f).

[7] Multistate Tax Compact Article IV.1.(f).

[8] Multistate Tax Compact Article IV.2.

PLANNING NOTE: Public utilities may find some elective flexibility in determining where income is taxed if a state has adopted UDITPA or the Multistate Tax Compact for its allocation and apportionment basis.

¶ 930 Property Factor

Under UDITPA and the MTC regulations, the property factor consists of a corporation's real and tangible personal property owned or rented and used during the tax period in the regular course of the corporation's trade or business.[9] Intangible property is not included in the property factor. Only property used to produce business income, not property that produces nonbusiness income, is included in the property factor.

Property enters the property factor when the property is used or is capable of being used in the corporation's trade or business. For example, idle plant facilities are included, but plant construction-in-progress is not included until available for use.[10] Property is removed from the property factor only when

> its permanent withdrawal is established by an identifiable event such as its conversion to the production of nonbusiness income, its sale, or the lapse of an extended period of time (normally, five years) during which the property is held for sale.[11]

Valuation of property. Owned property is valued at the average original cost, which is generally the basis of the property for federal income tax purposes at the time of acquisition, adjusted for additions, improvements, and partial dispositions. Fair market value is not used, nor is accumulated depreciation taken into account.[12]

Generally, the average value of property owned by a corporation is determined by averaging the values at the beginning and ending of the tax period. Averaging by monthly values may be allowed or required by the tax administrator if substantial fluctuations in the values of property exist or if property is acquired after the beginning of the tax period or disposed of before the end of the tax period.[13]

Rented property is valued at eight times the net annual rental rate, which includes amounts paid in lieu of rents, such as real estate taxes, interest, insurance, or repairs, or any other items that are required to be paid by the terms of the lease, not including amounts paid as service charges, such as utilities, janitor services, etc. Under the

---

[9] UDITPA Sec. 10; MTC Reg. IV.10.(a).

[10] MTC Reg. IV.10.(b).

[11] MTC Reg. IV.10.(b).

[12] MTC Reg. IV.11.(a).

[13] MTC Reg. IV.12.

MTC regulations, rents are reduced by subrentals received unless the subrents constitute business income.[14]

¶ 935 Payroll Factor

Under UDITPA and the MTC regulations, the payroll factor consists of amounts paid by the corporation in the regular course of its trade or business for compensation during the tax period. Compensation consists of taxable wages, salaries, commissions, and any other form of remuneration paid to employees for personal services. Amounts paid to independent contractors are not included. An officer of a corporation is considered an employee.[15]

The employer determines wages for the payroll factor based on its overall method of accounting (i.e., cash or accrual). If payroll is capitalized in the cost basis of a self-constructed asset, the payroll is nevertheless included in the payroll factor.[16] Payroll connected with the production of nonbusiness income is excluded from both the numerator and the denominator of the payroll factor.[17] For example, if an employee's only duty is the management of a corporation's investment portfolio that is not part of the corporation's regular trade or business, the salary paid to this employee is excluded from the payroll factor.

Compensation paid in the state. The numerator of the payroll factor is the total compensation paid by the corporation in the state during the tax period.[18] Under the MTC regulations, compensation is paid in the state and included in the state's payroll numerator if the employee's service is performed entirely within the state. If the employee's service is performed both within and without the state, the compensation is deemed to be paid in the state by applying the following hierarchy: [19]

1. If the service performed without the state is incidental to the employee's service within the state.
2. If the employee's base of operation is in the same state or if there is no base of operation in any state in which some part of the service is performed and the service is directed or controlled from within the state.
3. If the base of operations or the place from which the service is directed or controlled is not in any state in which some part of the service is performed and the employee's residence is in the state.

---

[14] MTC Reg. IV.11.(b).
[15] UDITPA Sec. 13; MTC Reg. IV.13.(a).
[16] MTC Reg. IV.13.(a)(2).
[17] MTC Reg. IV.13.(a)(2).
[18] MTC Reg. IV.13.(c).
[19] MTC Reg. IV.14.

This hierarchy generally follows the rules employed to source wages for state unemployment tax purposes.

These rules effectively attribute the employee's entire compensation to a single state, even though services may be performed in more than one state, unless the employee's base of operations actually moves from one state to another during the year.

> ***PLANNING NOTE:*** If payroll is properly assigned to a state where a corporation does not have nexus because its activities are limited to solicitation under Public Law 86-272 (see ¶ 705), the payroll is not thrown back to the commercial domicile state.

¶ 940 Sales Factor

Under UDITPA and the MTC regulations, all gross receipts from transactions and activities in the regular course of a corporation's trade or business are included in the sales factor.

.01 Receipts Included in the Sales Factor

The sales factor includes gross sales (less return and allowances), all interest income, service charges, carrying charges, time-price differential charges incidental to such sales, and federal and state excise taxes. The sales factor is not limited to only receipts from sales of inventory, but also includes other income such as fees and commissions received from the performance of services, rents, and lease payments received from renting real or tangible property, proceeds from the disposition of other tangible or intangible assets, and royalties and other payments received from the sale, assignment, or licensing of intangible personal property such as patents and copyrights.[20]

.02 Receipts Excluded from the Sales Factor

Certain types of gross receipts are excluded from the sales factor. Gross receipts constituting nonbusiness income are not included in the sales factor. Accordingly, gross receipts from the disposition of property are included if the gain or loss on disposition constitutes business income. The MTC regulations provide, however, that:

> Where substantial amounts of gross receipts arise from an incidental or occasional sale of a fixed asset used in the regular course of the taxpayer's trade or business, those gross receipts shall be excluded from the sales factor.[21]

---

[20] UDITPA Sec. 15; MTC Reg. IV.15.

[21] MTC Reg. IV.18.(c)(1).

The regulations further provide that:

> Insubstantial amounts of gross receipts arising from incidental or occasional transactions or activities may be excluded from the sales factor unless their exclusion would materially affect the amount of income apportioned to this state.[22]

Gross income from intangible assets is included in the sales factor only if the income-producing activity can be readily identified and localized for inclusion in the numerator of a particular state.[23]

.03 Destination State Rule

Generally, sales of tangible property are included in the numerator of the state of destination. The destination state is the state to which property is delivered or shipped.[24] Property is deemed to be delivered or shipped to a purchaser within the state if the recipient is located in the state, even if the property is ordered from outside the state.[25] Moreover, property is deemed to have been delivered or shipped to a purchaser within the state if the shipment terminates in the state, even though the purchaser subsequently transfers the property to another state.[26]

.04 Throwback Rule

Although the destination rule usually applies to the sale of tangible personal property, under UDITPA and the MTC regulations, certain sales are subject to "throwback" to prevent certain receipts from escaping inclusion in any state's sales factor numerator. Sales to a destination state where the seller is not taxable (e.g., because its activities do not exceed solicitation under Public Law 86-272), are "thrown back" to the numerator of the state from which the goods were shipped.[27]

.05 Income from Other Than Sales of Tangible Personal Property

Adaptation of the sales factor for income derived from sources other than the sale of tangible personal property may be difficult. Receipts from businesses other than manufacturing and merchandising, such as service industries, the rental of tangible property, or lending or licensing of intangible property are included in the sales numerator of the state that bears the greatest portion of the income-producing activity, measured by costs of performance. Costs of performance means direct costs consistent with generally accepted accounting principles.[28]

---

[22] MTC Reg. IV.18.(c)(2).
[23] MTC Reg. IV.18.(c)(3).
[24] MTC Reg. IV.16.(a)(2).
[25] MTC Reg. IV.16.(a)(2).
[26] MTC Reg. IV.16.(a)(3).
[27] MTC Reg. IV.16.(a)(1).
[28] MTC Reg. IV.17.

.06 Rental, Lease, or Licensing of Property and Personal Services

The MTC regulations provide special rules for the attribution of income from certain transactions. Transactions involving the rental, lease, or license of tangible personal property are attributable to a state based on the number of days the property was used in a state, compared to its total use everywhere. Gross receipts from the performance of personal services are attributable to a state to the extent such services are performed in the state. When personal services are performed in several states, each state's activities constitute a separate income-producing activity with receipts allocated between states based on the actual time of performance.[29]

¶ 945 Other Apportionment Formulas

The standard, equally weighted, three-factor UDITPA apportionment formula is not used by all states. The most common modification to the formula is to double weight the sales factor, according it twice the weight of each of the other two factors, property and payroll. This method is attractive to states because it favors domestic corporations that typically have more payroll and property in the state, and it more heavily taxes out-of-state corporations that make sales into the state.

A number of states use a formula with less than three factors, such as two-factor and single-factor formulas. For example, Iowa and Missouri permit the use of a single-factor sales formula. Colorado will allow the elective use of a two-factor formula based on property and sales.

¶ 950 Specialized Industry Formulas

The standard three-factor formula is designed for manufacturing and merchandising corporations. It is well suited for these corporations because the factors of sales, property, and payroll are related to how they do business and are appropriate estimates of the corporations' presence in a state.

The standard formula is not, however, well suited for all businesses, particularly those specialized industries where the property, payroll, and sales factors do not fairly represent where the income is generated. To allow for a more proper allocation and apportionment of income, both UDITPA and MTC have provisions for alternative methodologies.

---

[29] MTC Reg. IV.17.(4)(B)(c).

UDITPA Sec. 18 provides the following (MTC provisions provide the same):

> If the allocation and apportionment provisions of this Act do not fairly represent the extent of the taxpayer's business activity in this state, the taxpayer may petition for or the [tax administrator] may require, in respect to all or any part of the taxpayer's business activity, if reasonable:
>
> (a) separate accounting;
>
> (b) the exclusion of any one or more of the factors;
>
> (c) the inclusion of one or more additional factors which will fairly represent the taxpayer's business activity in this state; or
>
> (d) the employment of any other method to effectuate an equitable allocation and apportionment of the taxpayer's income.

Although some states use the standard formula for a variety of specialized businesses, a number of states have devised special apportionment methods that are better suited for dividing the income of such corporations among the states.

Pipelines. Many states now provide specialized apportionment formulas for transportation corporations, including pipelines. Trucking corporations apportion income in most states based on miles-per-state or ton-miles-per-state.

The MTC has not issued any regulations covering the special treatment of oil and gas pipelines since such pipelines are not designated as a special industry for which the general apportionment rules are not appropriate. Pipelines were excluded from coverage by UDITPA as a public utility. However, the MTC specifically excluded pipelines from the definition of a "public utility."

Similar to other transportation corporations, pipelines will generally apportion income by applying revenue or mileage factors determined by barrel or cubic foot miles. The methodologies employed, however, are not consistent from state to state. For example, Pennsylvania determines a ratio of a corporation's total revenue miles in the state to total revenue miles everywhere. In contrast, Massachusetts requires a pipeline to use the standard three-factor formula, while Mississippi uses a formula of property, payroll, and traffic miles.

The following states provide special industry apportionment factor rules for pipelines: Alaska, Arkansas, California, Florida, Illinois, Iowa, Kentucky, Michigan, Mississippi, Oklahoma, Pennsylvania, South Carolina, Tennessee, and Wisconsin.

Chapter 10

DISCRIMINATORY TAXES

¶ 1001 Overview

State tax regimes that can be shown to discriminate against a given company may be challenged on one of two constitutional grounds. The company may challenge a tax by asserting that it discriminates against interstate commerce in violation of the Commerce Clause of the U.S. Constitution (see ¶ 1010), or that it violates the Equal Protection Clause of either the U.S. Constitution or the applicable state constitution (see ¶ 1020). In either case, for a constitutional challenge to be successful, it must be shown that similarly situated companies are treated differently under the state's tax regime.

Historically, utilities have done business in either a single state or a small number of contiguous states. In the regulated environment, interstate commerce challenges seldom arose because utilities normally had a physical presence in each state where they operated. As the electric utility industry moves through deregulation, utilities are beginning to engage in nontraditional lines of businesses in states where they have not previously operated. In many cases, the only contact a utility will have with a state outside its service territory will be related to either gas or electricity sales made by the utility's nonregulated marketing affiliate. As a result, many out-of-state utilities are being subjected to a myriad of new state taxes. As the states seek to tax the activities of the new out-of-state power marketers (see Chapter 4), their tax regimes may violate the Commerce Clause of the U.S. Constitution by taxing out-of-state entities more heavily than in-state taxpayers.

Additionally, as the states alter their tax regimes to react to deregulation, situations may occur where a given tax violates the federal or state Equal Protection Clause (or other state uniformity provisions) by treating similarly situated taxpayers differently. The Equal Protection Clause of the U.S. Constitution has traditionally provided little protection to taxpayers because states are only required to show there is a "rationale basis" for the disparate treatment. Because regulated utilities operate much differently than nonregulated businesses, utilities have traditionally been subject to state taxes that are significantly different from the taxes that apply to nonregulated businesses. As deregulation unfolds, however, state tax regimes are often modified such that similarly situated utilities are taxed differently, or nonregulated utility affiliates are taxed differently than their nonregulated competitors. In the nonregulated environment, these modified tax systems may not survive even the modest Equal Protection Clause scrutiny.

¶ 1005 *General Motors Corp. v. Tracy*

The seminal case dealing with challenges to the constitutionality of a state tax in the gas utility industry is *General Motors Corp. v. Tracy.*[1] In *General Motors,* the U.S. Supreme Court upheld Ohio's differential treatment of public utilities and nonregulated natural gas marketers in the face of Equal Protection and dormant Commerce Clause challenges filed by in-state purchasers of out-of-state natural gas.[2] Under Ohio law, sales of natural gas by "natural gas companies," as defined by Ohio statute, are exempt from the state's sales and use tax, while sales made by taxpayers other than "natural gas companies" are subject to the tax. It is clear that in-state local distribution companies (LDCs) fit within the statutory definition of "natural gas companies." However, the Supreme Court of Ohio has determined that other sellers, such as out-of-state producers and natural gas marketers, do not.[3] Consequently, sales of natural gas made by Ohio LDCs are exempt from the state's sales and use tax, while sales made by independent producers and marketers continue to be subject to the tax.

General Motors, which purchased natural gas from an out-of-state natural gas marketer and remitted use tax, challenged the validity of the LDC's sales tax exemption on grounds that it "patently discriminated" against out-of-state marketers in violation of the dormant Commerce Clause and the Equal Protection Clause of the U.S. Constitution. The U.S. Supreme Court has repeatedly interpreted the dormant Commerce Clause as prohibiting state taxation . . . that discriminates against or unduly burdens interstate commerce and thereby "impedes free private trade in the national marketplace." [4] Nevertheless, the Court rejected General Motors' Commerce Clause argument, instead reasoning that state regulation had effectively distinguished regulated sellers from independent marketers to the point

[1] *General Motors Corp. v. Tracy,* 519 US 278, 117 SCt 811 (1997). See Appendix E, p. 264, for a reproduction of this case.

[2] Ibid.

[3] *Chrysler Corp. v. Tracy,* 652 NE2d 185 (1995).

[4] *Quill Corp. v. North Dakota,* 504 US 298, 112 SCt 1904 (1992); *Reeves, Inc. v. Stake,* 447 US 429 (1980).

that the enterprises should not be considered "similarly situated" for the facial discrimination claim.[5]

.01 U.S. Supreme Court's "Similarly Situated" Analysis

In holding that Ohio's sales and use tax exemption did not violate the Commerce Clause, the U.S. Supreme Court determined that LDCs and out-of-state marketers are not "similarly situated" taxpayers under the U.S. Commerce Clause. The Court's emphasis on this aspect of the analysis is noteworthy. First, the added weight the Court gives to the "similarly situated" analysis stands in sharp contrast with the Court's *Fulton* decision in 1996.[6] In *Fulton,* the Court held that "[s]tate laws discriminating against interstate commerce on their face are 'virtually per se invalid.' " However, in rendering its decision in *General Motors,* the Court first chose to determine whether the taxpayers in question were "similarly situated" before resolving the claim that the tax was "patently discriminatory."

Furthermore, in its analysis, the Court discounted the importance of competition between the LDCs and natural gas marketers in the deregulated marketplace when comparing the two taxpayers. The Court readily concluded that the LDCs and the out-of-state nonregulated sellers were not "similarly situated" taxpayers in a captive (i.e., regulated) natural gas market because the nonregulated marketers could not make sales directly to end-users. Consequently, it shifted its focus to the role of both parties in the noncaptive natural gas marketplace, questioning whether it was significant enough to overcome the weight of its determination regarding the regulated marketplace.

In sum, the LDC's bundled product reflects the demand of a market neither susceptible to competition by the interstate sellers nor likely to be served except by the regulated natural monopolies that have historically supplied its needs. Thus, the question raised by this case is whether the opportunities for competition between marketers and LDCs in the noncaptive market requires treating marketers and utilities as like entities for dormant Commerce Clause purposes. Although there is no *a priori* answer, a number of reasons support a decision to give the greater weight to the captive market and the local utilities' singular role in serving it and, hence, to treat marketers and LDCs as dissimilar.[7]

As noted, the Court cited three reasons for discounting the role of the noncaptive market in determining whether the taxpayers were similarly situated. First, the Court made it very clear that it was weary

---

[5] *General Motors Corp. v. Tracy,* 519 US 278, 117 SCt 811 (1997).

[6] *Fulton v. Faulkner,* 516 US 325 (1996).

[7] *General Motors Corp. v. Tracy,* 519 US 278, 117 SCt 811 (1997).

of inhibiting the ability of the states to ensure delivery of reliable natural gas service to the customers comprising the bundled captive market. For this reason, the Court was willing to make an exception to the hard and fast rule in *Fulton* to protect an industry that had been developed and shielded from potentially hazardous market forces by state regulation. Second, the Court claimed a distinct inability, both from a knowledge as well as resource standpoint, to "predict the effects of judicial intervention invalidating the Ohio tax scheme on the utilities' capacity to serve [the] captive market." Finally, the Court noted its inclination to defer to the Congress to take legislative action that would "strike the balance between the needs of the competitive and captive markets."

There are some important observations to be made about the Court's decision to discount the role of the LDC in the noncaptive market. The Court, by expressing its reservation to make a decision inhibiting the delivery of service to the bundled market, merely followed what it perceived to be a long legacy of protection, both legislative and judicial, that had allowed states to regulate and, hence, insure the delivery of natural gas to the captive market. Along these lines, the Court took special note of Section 1(b) of the Natural Gas Act of 1938, which was later interpreted by the U.S. Supreme Court in 1947 as exempting state regulation of retail sales of natural gas from the dormant Commerce Clause.[8] The Court also made further note of the extent to which Congress had acquiesced with this decision for more than 50 years:

> Indeed half a century ago we concluded that the [Natural Gas Association] NGA altogether exempts state regulation of retail sales of natural gas from the strictures of the dormant commerce clause . . . and to this day, notwithstanding the national regulatory revolution, Congress has done nothing to limit its unbroken recognition of the state regulatory authority that has created and preserved the local monopolies. The clear implication is that Congress finds the benefits of the bundled product for captive local buyers well within the realm of what the States may reasonably promote and preserve.

PLANNING NOTE: The foundation for the U.S. Supreme Court's opinion may be well entrenched for the near term. Beyond the Commerce Clause framework within which the Court rendered its decision, the reasoning here contains frequent federalist overtones, appearing to carefully define the limited role the Court should play in the deregulation landscape compared with the role of Congress and the states.

---

[8] *Panhandle Eastern Pipe Line Co. v. Public Serv. Comm'n of Ind.*, 332 US 507 (1947).

Perhaps more significant than the actual legal conclusions necessary for the Court to reach its decision is the Court's clear unwillingness to render a holding with sweeping consequences that could affect the manner in which deregulation unfolds, ever cognizant of the drastic economic effects it could lay on the doorstep of the captive marketplace. In this regard, the Court writes:

> Here we have to assume that any decision to treat the LDCs as similar to the interstate marketers would change the LDC's overall position in the non-captive market in which (we are assuming) they compete, at least at the margins, by affecting the overall size of the LDC's customer base. As we recognized in *Panhandle,* a change in the customer base could affect the LDC's ability to continue to serve the captive market where there is no such competition.

This sentiment is further highlighted by the Court's claim that they possess neither the resources nor the knowledge to make the type of economic predictions necessary to render a decision that could likely have effects on the ability of the states to ensure delivery of gas to the captive marketplace. Perhaps more than anything, the Court's pattern of reasoning indicates an unwillingness to hold such a tax unconstitutional under the Commerce Clause until real developments in the captive marketplace render some political security for a potentially sweeping decision.

.02 Continuing Validity of the Court's "Similarly Situated" Analysis

The underlying premise of the Court's reasoning, i.e., that the *"captive market is not in fact susceptible to competition,"* may or may not hold up during the deregulation process. In essence, the inquiry going forward becomes the following: at what point does a regulated entity serve the noncaptive market enough, such that its role in that market cannot be ignored in future "similarly situated" analyses? If out-of-state providers and marketers begin supplying residential natural gas, and only distribution service is provided by LDCs, one of the most compelling justifications for the Court's decision will come into question. Furthermore, if a state chooses to equalize the playing field from a tax standpoint for utilities and nonutilities and achieves success in implementing retail choice in either the residential natural gas or electricity markets, the justification for the Court's decision appears to be inapplicable.

In essence, the Court's decision focused on the sheer difference in the product being offered by the two entities at issue: the bundled product vs. the unbundled product. As these entities become more and more "similarly situated" as deregulation unfolds, the extra gateway to unconstitutionality, i.e., the "similarly situated" threshold, will become increasingly problematic.

> ***CAUTION:*** Regardless of changes in the marketplace that may occur in the years to come, the *General Motors* decision appears to add another hurdle that nonregulated marketers will need to overcome to overturn a tax that facially discriminates in favor of regulated gas or electric companies.

¶ 1010 Commerce Clause Challenges

Despite the *General Motors* decision (see ¶ 1005), other taxpayers have been successful in challenging similar taxes in similar industries. The Supreme Court of New York (New York's appellate court) ruled in *Tug Buster* that a petroleum tax imposed on out-of-state purchases violated the Commerce Clause.[9]

The petroleum tax in question was imposed on sellers that imported, or caused to be imported, petroleum into New York for consumption. In this case, Tug Buster Bouchard Corp., which operated a barge and towing service in New York, acted as the importer. Although domestic sellers of petroleum were subject to a similar tax, the court nevertheless held that the application of the petroleum tax to purchases from out-of-state sellers discriminated against interstate commerce because the tax liabilities of in- and out-of-state taxpayers could not always be presumed equal.

¶ 1015 Potential Commerce Clause Challenges

Many states have tax statutes similar in operation to the taxes questioned in *General Motors* (see ¶ 1005) and invalidated in *Tug Buster* (see ¶ 1010). New York, for example, despite the *Tug Buster* decision, continues to impose a gas import tax (the Section 189 tax) on importers of natural gas. Although the tax is meant to "complement" the Section 186 and Section 186-a taxes imposed on in-state sellers, a recent New York Court of Appeals decision has held that the gas import tax is unconstitutional under the Commerce Clause and cannot withstand scrutiny under a compensatory tax analysis.[10] The court held that the gas import tax violated the fair apportionment provision of the Commerce Clause because the tax was not internally consistent. In other words, if a neighboring jurisdiction imposed the same tax, multiple taxation would result. The state argued that the tax should be

---

[9] *Tug Buster Bouchard Corp. v. N.Y. Dept. of Taxation and Finance,* 217 AD2d 192 (N.Y. SCt 1996); affirmed 675 NE2d 1223 (N.Y. Ct App 1996).

[10] *Tennessee Gas Pipeline Co. v. Urbach,* 750 N.E.2d 52 (N.Y. Ct. App. May 1, 2001). See Appendix E, p. 327, for a reproduction of this case.

upheld do to a saving clause incorporated in the statute that provided that to the extent the tax was held unconstitutional, a credit mechanism could be employed by the court to remedy any unconstitutional imposition of tax. The court held that because the credit mechanism would have to be judicially imposed, it did not save the tax from being facially unconstitutional.

CAUTION: The New York Section 186 tax was repealed and the Section 186-a and 189 taxes were phased out by legislation signed on May 15, 2000.[11] The repeal of the 186 tax was retroactive to January 1, 2000.[12] The legislation provides for the phase-out of the 186-a tax over a five-year period, with the tax rate applicable to the gross receipts of a utility being reduced as follows: [13]

- 2.0% beginning January 1, 2001
- 1.9% beginning January 1, 2002
- 0.85% beginning January 1, 2003
- 0.4% beginning January 1, 2004
- 0% beginning January 1, 2005

The Section 189 tax is being phased out over a five-year period as well, with the following rates applicable to tax years after December 31, 2000: [14]

- 2.0% beginning January 1, 2001
- 1.9% beginning January 1, 2002
- 0.85% beginning January 1, 2003
- 0.4% beginning January 1, 2004
- 0% beginning January 1, 2005

As out-of-state and in-state sellers of natural gas and electricity begin competing in deregulated environments, taxpayers will have to continually reevaluate the application of these types of taxes.

¶ 1020 Equal Protection Clause Challenges

Although the Equal Protection Clause has traditionally offered far less protection to taxpayers than the Commerce Clause, several recent decisions have invalidated or brought into question taxing methodologies under the Equal Protection Clause or State Uniformity Clauses. For example, in *Basin Electric Power Cooperative, Inc. v. Dept. of Revenue,*[15] the Wyoming Supreme Court held that the Wyoming De-

[11] N.Y. A.B. 1106 (May 15, 2000).

[12] 2000 N.Y. Laws 11006 (Ch. 63, § § 20, 44).

[13] N.Y. Tax Law § 186a(2).

[14] Ibid.

[15] *Basin Electric Power Cooperative, Inc. v. Dept. of Revenue,* 970 P2d 841 (1998).

partment of Revenue's special valuation methodology for Basin Electric and other rural electric cooperatives was unconstitutional and invalid.

Before the Department changed its methodology, Basin Electric's property was valued in a fashion similar to investor-owned utilities. In 1994, however, the Wyoming State Board of Equalization issued an investigative report finding that the valuation of Basin Electric's property was in error and ordered the Department of Revenue to change its valuation method for rural electric cooperatives. This change resulted in an increase in the valuation of Basin Electric's system from $1.22 billion to $2.08 billion. Basin Electric challenged the valuation, arguing that it was disproportionate to the valuation of other Wyoming electric utilities and, therefore, violated the uniformity provision of the Wyoming constitution. The Wyoming Supreme Court agreed, finding that the Board's investigative report required the Department of Revenue to treat nonprofit utilities differently from investor-owned utilities, resulting in a *de facto* classification. The Court concluded that there was no rational basis for this classification.

Similarly, MCI Telecommunications Corp. successfully argued that Ohio violated the state and federal Equal Protection Clauses by classifying MCI as a public utility and subjecting it to a 100 percent assessment on its tangible personal property.[16] Ohio did not subject all long-distance providers to classification as a public utility. The Ohio court held that different entities classified and regulated in the same way by the Ohio Public Utility Commission should also be treated in the same way for tax purposes.

¶ 1025 Potential Equal Protection Clause Challenges

As deregulation continues to unfold, various court decisions will continue to have an impact on taxation.

In 1999, Ohio enacted electric utility deregulation legislation that, among other things, made significant changes in the utility property tax regime (see ¶ 325). Electric companies pay property tax on all tangible personal property in Ohio, other than certain property that is part of a pollution control facility. The assessed value is equal to the property's "true value"—as determined by statute—*times* the applicable assessment ratio. Under prior law, the "true value" of an electric company's property other than production equipment was determined by a method of valuation using cost as capitalized on the company's books and records, *less* composite annual allowances prescribed by the

[16] *MCI Telecommunications Corp. v. Limbach*, 625 NE2d 597 (1993).

Tax Commissioner. The "true value" of an electric company's production equipment was based on the property's cost as capitalized on the company's books and records *less* 50 percent of that cost as an allowance for depreciation and obsolescence. Electric company production equipment was assessed at 100 percent of its "true value," while all other property (including the utility's transmission and distribution assets) was assessed at 88 percent of its "true value."

The new law revises the manner in which "true value" is determined for production equipment that is placed into service after the law's effective date. Under the law, production equipment "true value" will be determined based on cost as capitalized on the company's books and records, *less* composite annual allowances prescribed by the Tax Commissioner. In addition, for tax year 2001 and thereafter, the assessment rate for taxable transmission and distribution property of an electric company remains at 88 percent of "true value," but all other property will be assessed at 25 percent of "true value." [17]

Because this law is related solely to the electric industry, the tax changes applicable to the electric industry were not made applicable to the natural gas industry. Thus, gas utilities will continue to be assessed based on 88 percent of the "true value" of their property, while electric utilities will be assessed based on 25 percent of the "true value" of their property, at least of non-transmission and distribution (T & D) property.

> ***PLANNING NOTE:*** The methodology for determining true value may raise challenges (as discussed above) because taxpayers operating in similar industries (electric and natural gas) will be taxed in a facially disparate fashion. Although the transmission and distribution (T & D) property of electric and natural gas utilities will continue to be taxed in a similar fashion, electric utilities may potentially gain an advantage by having the assessment on their production property reduced.

Although Equal Protection Clause challenges on similar grounds have traditionally yielded little success for taxpayers because of the great latitude granted the states in taxing different "classes" of taxpayers, the issue of the disparate property tax assessment in Ohio has already drawn attention. For example, Columbia Gas currently has an appeal before the Ohio Supreme Court that alleges that the old property tax assessment violates its constitutional rights to equal protection.[18] Columbia argues that it should be assessed based on 25 percent of true value like any other business in the state. The potential refund

---

[17] Ohio Rev. Code Ann. § 5727.111(E)(2).

[18] *Columbia Gas Company's Case Before Ohio Supreme Court Could Have Far-Reaching Effects*, 1999 STN 183-28 (September 22, 1999).

for tax years 1993 to 1998 is estimated to be approximately $180 million. The change in assessment for certain classes of electric utility property may only heighten the scrutiny the Ohio property tax scheme faces.

Appendices

RELEVANT SOURCE DOCUMENTS

Appendix A

Uniform Division of Income for Tax Purposes Act (UDITPA)

UDITPA was developed in 1957 by a multistate uniform law organization, the National Conference of Commissioners on Uniform State Laws. Under a broad framework, the Act sets uniform standards for the taxation of multistate businesses.

UDITPA is discussed at ¶ 805, ¶ 920, and ¶ 925.

SECTION 1. As used in this Act, unless the context otherwise requires:

(a) "Business income" means income arising from transactions and activity in the regular course of the taxpayer's trade or business and includes income from tangible and intangible property if the acquisition, management, and disposition of the property constitute integral parts of the taxpayer's regular trade or business operations.

COMMENT

This definition refers to "the" taxpayer's trade or business as if he had one business. It is not intended by this language to require a taxpayer having several "businesses" to use the same allocation and apportionment methods for the businesses. The language permits separate treatment of different businesses of a single taxpayer. Section 18 clearly permits separate treatment.

Income from the disposition of property used in a trade or business of the taxpayer is includible within the meaning of business income.

(b) "Commercial domicile" means the principal place from which the trade or business of the taxpayer is directed or managed.

COMMENT

The phrase "directed or managed" is not intended to permit both the state where the board of directors meets and the state where the company is managed to claim the commercial domicile. The phrase "directed or managed" is intended as two words serving the same end; not as two separate concepts.

(c) "Compensation" means wages, salaries, commissions and any other form of remuneration paid to employees for personal services.

COMMENT

This definition is derived from the Model Unemployment Compensation Act which has been adopted in all states.

Compensation paid to "employees" becomes important in the payroll fraction in section 13. If a corporation is employed to provide personal services, section 18 may be used to include compensation paid to corporations in the fraction if exclusion of compensation paid to corporate agents fails to reflect adequately the business activity in this state.

(d) "Financial organization" means any bank, trust company, savings bank, [industrial bank, land bank, safe deposit company], private banker, savings and loan association, credit union, [cooperative bank], investment company, or any type of insurance company.

COMMENT

This definition and the definition of "public utility" in subsection (f) is necessary because section 2 excludes from allocation and apportionment under this Act, income from these two types of business activity. The exclusion is proposed because some states have separate legislation for apportionment and allocation of income of such taxpayers. If not, and the state proposes to change subsection (2) so as to apply the Act to such taxpayers, this would not necessarily detract from the uniformity objective of this Act.

(e) "Non-business income" means all income other than business income.

(f) "Public utility" means [any business entity which owns or operates for public use any plant, equipment, property, franchise, or license for the transmission of communications, transportation of goods or persons, or the production, storage, transmission, sale, delivery, or furnishing of electricity, water, steam, oil, oil products or gas.]

COMMENT

It is expected that "public utility" will be defined to include all taxpayers subject to the control of the state's regulatory bodies on the theory that separate legislation will provide for the apportionment and allocation of the income of such taxpayers.

See Comment to the definition of "financial organization" for purpose of this definition. "Oil, oil products or gas" is not intended to be so restrictive as to treat differently a public utility, if any, which transmits or produces "gas products." The essential point of the definition is the requirement that the business excluded by this definition and subsection 2 be a "public utility." Private transmission lines and private production or storage companies are thus not excluded.

(g) "Sales" means all gross receipts of the taxpayer not allocated under sections 4 through 8 of this Act.

COMMENT

This all inclusive definition of sales is intended to make apportionable all income not allocated under sections 4 through 8. As indicated in the Comment to subsection 1(a) income from sales or property used in trade or business is included in apportionable income.

(h) "State" means any state of the United States, the District of Columbia, the Commonwealth of Puerto Rico, any territory or possession of the United States, any foreign country or political subdivision thereof.

SECTION 2. Any Taxpayer having income from business activity which is taxable both within and without this state, or other than activity as a financial organization or public utility or the rendering of purely personal services by an individual, shall allocate and apportion his net income as provided in this Act.

SECTION 3. For purposes of allocation and apportionment of income under this Act, a taxpayer is taxable in another state if (1) in that state he is subject to a net income tax, a franchise tax measured by net income, a franchise tax for the privilege of doing business, or a corporate stock tax, or (2) that state has jurisdiction to subject the taxpayer to a net income tax regardless of whether, in fact, the state does or does not.

COMMENT

This section defines, for purposes of section 2, where a taxpayer is "taxable both within and without this state." To bring this Act into operation a taxpayer must have income from business activity, and he must be taxable in this state, and also in some other state.

Two tests are used by this section to determine when a taxpayer is "taxable in another state." The first test is a fairly obvious one, the taxpayer is taxable in another state if he is actually subjected to the type of taxes listed in subparagraph (1).

The second test, in subparagraph (2) uses a "notion" or "hypothetical" standard rather than an actual one. Thus, if a corporation has its commercial domicile in state X, which has only a sales tax and no tax measured by net income, but that corporation has business activity in state A, which has this apportionment Act, state A must apportion the business income as provided in this Act so that some of it is allocated to state X, even though as a result of the tax system of state X a portion of the business income escapes income taxation. This is desirable in order to treat the business of all states equally, and in order to avoid having this Act as a factor in inducing a state to have an income tax. If it does not wish to tax income, that is no reason for a state which does wish to tax income to attempt to obtain more than its share of taxable income.

It should be noted that in subsection 1(h) the word "state" is defined broadly enough to include a foreign country. This means that "taxable in another state" within section 3 may mean a foreign country. The apportioning state, however, need consider only whether the foreign country "could have" taxed the income under the constitution of the United States if it had been a state.

While subparagraph (1) lists several types of taxes which might be actually in effect in another state, the reference in subparagraph (2) only to a "net income" tax is not intended to be more restricted in the hypothetical tax than the section is with respect to an actual tax.

SECTION 4. Rents and royalties from real or tangible personal property, capital gains, interest, dividends, or patent or copyright royalties, to the extent that they constitute non-business income, shall be allocated as provided in sections 5 through 8 of this Act.

COMMENT

This section is the general section on "allocating" non-business income to a state just as section 9 is the general section on apportionment of business income. Section 2 refers to an allocation and an apportionment of "net income." In "allocating" nonbusiness income to a state, the states concerned with this allocation may desire to allocate the expenses properly attributable to nonbusiness but allocable income in the same way that income is allocated so that these expenses will not be involved in determining net income from business activity where apportionment is used. Section 18 of this Code empowers the state to make this adjustment if it wishes.

SECTION 5. (a) Net rents and royalties from real property located in this state are allocable to this state.

(b) Net rents and royalties from tangible personal property are allocable to this state:

(1) if and to the extent that the property is utilized in this state, or

(2) in their entirety if the taxpayer's commercial domicile is in this state and the taxpayer is not organized under the laws of or taxable in the state in which the property is utilized.

(c) The extent of utilization of tangible personal property in a state is determined by multiplying the rents and royalties by a fraction, the numerator of which is the number of days of physical location of the property in the state during the rental or royalty period in the taxable year and the denominator of which is the number of days of physical location of the property everywhere during all rental or royalty periods in the taxable year. If the physical location of the property during the rental or royalty period is unknown or unascertainable by the taxpayer, tangible personal property is utilized in the state in which the property was located at the time the rental or royalty payer obtained possession.

COMMENT

Rents from mobile tangible property are to be allocated in accordance with section 5(c). This subsection apportions the rents by a fraction based on the number of days in the state on the assumption that the rents are generally based on time of use. If the rent itself is calculated on the basis of some factor other than time, section 18 would permit a state to substitute a fraction based on this substitute factor. Thus, if the rent for a drilling rig is calculated on the basis of number of feet drilled, the "extent of utilization" in the state might also be determined on the basis of a fraction which uses "feet drilled" rather than days in the state.

SECTION 6. (a) Capital gains and losses from sales of real property located in this state are allocable to this state.

(b) Capital gains and losses from sales of tangible personal property are allocable to this state if

(1) the property had a situs in this state at the time of the sale, or

(2) the taxpayer's commercial domicile is in this state and the taxpayer is not taxable in the state in which the property had a situs.

(c) Capital gains and losses from sales of intangible personal property are allocable to this state if the taxpayer's commercial domicile is in this state.

SECTION 7. Interest and dividends are allocable to this state if the taxpayer's commercial domicile is in this state.

SECTION 8. (a) Patent and copyright royalties are allocable to this state:

(1) if and to the extent that the patent or copyright is utilized by the payer in this state, or

(2) if and to the extent that the patent or copyright is utilized by the payer in a state in which the taxpayer is not taxable and the taxpayer's commercial domicile is in this state.

(b) A patent is utilized in a state to the extent that it is employed in production, fabrication, manufacturing, or other processing in the state or to the extent that a patented product is produced in the state. If the basis of receipts from patent royalties does not permit allocation to states or if the accounting procedures do not reflect states of utilization, the patent is utilized in the state in which the taxpayer's commercial domicile is located.

(c) A copyright is utilized in a state to the extent that printing or other publications originates in the state. If the basis of receipts from copyright royalties does not permit allocation to states or if the accounting procedures do not reflect states of utilization, the copyright is utilized in the state in which the taxpayer's commercial domicile is located.

SECTION 9. All business income shall be apportioned to this state by multiplying the income by a fraction, the numerator of which is the property factor plus the payroll factor plus the sales factor, and the denominator of which is three.

SECTION 10. The property factor is a fraction, the numerator of which is the average value of the taxpayer's real and tangible personal property owned or rented and used in this state during the tax period and the denominator of which is the average value of all the taxpayer's real and tangible personal property owned or rented and used during the tax period.

COMMENT

The property to be included in the numerator and denominator is property producing the net income to be apportioned. If net income from property is allocated property under sections 5 through 8 such property should be excluded in constructing the fraction.

SECTION 11. Property owned by the taxpayer is valued at its original cost. Property rented by the taxpayer is valued at eight times the net annual rental rate. Net annual rental rate is the annual rental rate paid by the taxpayer less any annual rental rate received by the taxpayer from sub-rentals.

COMMENT

This section is admittedly arbitrary in using original cost rather than depreciated cost, and in valuing rented property as eight times the annual rental. This approach is justified because the act does not impose a tax, nor prescribe the depreciation allowable in computing the tax, but merely provides a basis for division of the taxable income among the several states. The use of original cost obviates any differences due to varying methods of depreciation, and has the advantage that the basic figure is readily ascertainable from the taxpayer's books. No method of valuing the property would probably be universally acceptable.

In any situation where it is impossible to ascertain original cost, section 18 may be used to determine a fair value for such property. Section 18 may also be necessary to aid in determining "net annual rental value" of tangible personal property where the actual rent is so related to services that the part attributable to the object is difficult to determine.

Section 18 may also be used to determine a reasonable rental rate for this fraction where the actual rent is zero or nominal such as may be the case where a local government in attempting to induce an industry to come to a community supplies the property at a nominal rental.

SECTION 12. The average value of property shall be determined by averaging the values at the beginning and ending of the tax period but the [tax administrator] may require the averaging of monthly values during the tax period if reasonably required to reflect properly the average value of the taxpayer's property.

SECTION 13. The payroll factor is a fraction, the numerator of which is the total amount paid in this state during the tax period by the taxpayer for compensation, and the denominator of which is the total compensation paid everywhere during the tax period.

COMMENT

Payroll attributable to management or maintenance or otherwise allocable to nonbusiness property should be excluded from the fraction.

Payroll "paid" should be determined by the normal accounting methods of the business so that if the taxpayer "accrues" such matters the payroll should be treated as "paid" for purpose of this section.

SECTION 14. Compensation is paid in this state if:

(a) the individual's service is performed entirely within the state; or

(b) the individual's service is performed both within and without the state, but the service performed without the state is incidental to the individual's service within the state; or

(c) some of the service is performed in the state and (1) the base of operations or, if there is no base of operations, the place from which the service is directed or controlled is in the state, or (2) the base of operations or the place from which the service is directed or controlled is not in any state in which some part of the service is performed, but the individual's residence is in this state.

COMMENT

This section is derived from the Model Unemployment Compensation Act. This is the same figure which will be used by taxpayers for unemployment compensation purposes.

SECTION 15. The sales factor is a fraction, the numerator of which is the total sales of the taxpayer in this state during the tax period, and the denominator of which is the total sales of the taxpayer everywhere during the tax period.

COMMENT

The sales to be included in the fraction are only the sales which produce business income. Sales which produce "capital gains" are under section 6 and are to be allocated rather than apportioned.

"Total sales" means "total net sales" after discounts and returns.

SECTION 16. Sales of tangible personal property are in this state if:

(a) the property is delivered or shipped to a purchaser, other than the United States government, within this state regardless of the f.o.b. point or other conditions of the sale; or

(b) the property is shipped from an office, store, warehouse, factory, or other place of storage in this state and (1) the purchaser is the United States government or (2) the taxpayer is not taxable in the state of the purchaser.

COMMENT

The phrase "delivered or shipped to a purchaser" in this state includes shipments, at the designation of the purchaser, to a person in this state such as designating, while a shipment is enroute, the ultimate recipient.

Sales to the United States are treated separately. It is thought that this is justified because sales to the United States are not necessarily attributable to a market existing in the state to which the goods are originally shipped. This different treatment may also be justified because, if the goods are defense or war materials, it may be impossible to determine whether the goods ever come to rest in the state due to use of coded delivery instructions.

The section does not specify how sales from a subsidiary in the state to an out-of-state parent, such as a marketing corporation who thereupon redirects the goods back into the state, should be treated. If returns are not consolidated under existing state tax law, it may be necessary to use section 18 to make a fair representation of the business income in this situation.

SECTION 17. Sales, other than sales of tangible personal property, are in this state if:

(a) the income-producing activity is performed in this state; or

(b) The income-producing activity is performed both in and outside this state and a greater proportion of the income-producing activity is performed in this state than in any other state, based on costs of performance.

SECTION 18. If the allocation and apportionment provisions of this Act do not fairly represent the extent of the taxpayer's business activity in this state, the taxpayer may petition for or the [tax administrator] may require, in respect to all or any part of the taxpayer's business activity, if reasonable:

(a) separate accounting;

(b) the exclusion of any one or more of the factors;

(c) the inclusion of one or more additional factors which will fairly represent the taxpayer's business activity in this state; or

(d) the employment of any other method to effectuate an equitable allocation and apportionment of the taxpayer's income.

COMMENT

It is anticipated that this Act will be made a part of the income tax acts of the several states. For that reason, this section does not spell out the procedure to be followed in the event of a disagreement between the taxpayer and the tax administrator. The income tax acts of each state presumably outline the procedure to be followed.

Section 18 is intended as a broad authority, within the principle of apportioning business income fairly among the states which have contact with the income, to the tax administrator to vary the apportionment formula and to vary the system of allocation where the provisions of the Act do not fairly represent the extent of the taxpayer's business activity in the state. The phrases in section 18 (d) do not foreclose the use of one method for some business activity and a different method for a different business activity. Neither does the phrase "method" limit the administrator to substituting factors in the formula. The phrase means any other method of fairly representing the extent of the taxpayer's business activity in the state.

SECTION 19. This Act shall be so construed as to effectuate its general purpose to make uniform the law of those states which enact it.

SECTION 20. This Act may be cited as the Uniform Division of Income for Tax Purposes Act.

Appendix B

Multistate Tax Commission Regulations (MTC Regs.)

The following MTC Regs. were adopted February 21, 1973; as revised through July 27, 2001. They are applicable to Article IV of the Multistate Tax Compact and to the Uniform Division of Income for Tax Purposes Act. They are subject to adoption by each member state in accordance with its own laws and procedures. The numerical references of the regulations are to Article IV of the Multistate Tax Compact and its subsections.

MTC Regs. are discussed at ¶ 815, ¶ 925, and ¶ 940.

Corporate Income Tax Allocation and Apportionment Regulations

Prologue.

These Regulations are intended to set forth rules concerning the application of the apportionment and allocation provisions of Article IV of the Multistate Tax Compact. The apportionment rules set forth in these Regulations are applicable to any taxpayer having business income, regardless of whether or not it has nonbusiness income, and the allocation rules set forth in these Regulations are applicable to any taxpayer having nonbusiness income, regardless of whether or not it has business income.

The only exceptions to these allocation and apportionment rules contained in these Regulations are those set forth in Regulation IV.18 pursuant to the authority of Article IV.18 of the Compact.

These Regulations are not intended to modify existing rules concerning jurisdictional standards.

Reg. IV.1.(a). Business and Nonbusiness Income Defined.

[*Adopted February 21, 1973.*]

Article IV.1.(a) defines "business income" as income arising from transactions and activity in the regular course of the taxpayer's trade or business and includes income from tangible and intangible property if the acquisition, management, and disposition of the property constitute integral parts of the taxpayer's regular trade or business operations. In essence, all income which arises from the conduct of trade or business operations of a taxpayer is business income. For purposes of administration of Article IV, the income of the taxpayer is business income unless clearly classifiable as nonbusiness income.

Nonbusiness income means all income other than business income.

The classification of income by the labels occasionally used, such as manufacturing income, compensation for services, sales income, interest, dividends, rents, royalties, gains, operating income, nonoperating income, etc., is of no aid in determining whether income is business or nonbusiness income. Income of any type or class and from any source is business income if it arises from transactions and activity occurring in the regular course of a trade or business. Accordingly, the critical element in determining whether income is "business income" or "nonbusiness income" is the identification of the transactions and activity which are the elements of a particular trade or business. In general all transactions and activities of the taxpayer which are dependent upon or contribute to the operations of the taxpayer's economic enterprise as a whole constitute the taxpayer's trade or business and will be transactions and activity arising in the regular course of, and will constitute integral parts of, a trade or business. (See Regulation IV.1.(c) for more specific examples of the classification of income as business or nonbusiness income; see Regulation IV.1.(b) and IV.2.(b)(2) for further explanation of what constitutes a trade or business.)

Reg. IV.1.(b). Two or More Businesses of a Single Taxpayer.

[*Adopted February 21, 1973.*]

A taxpayer may have more than one "trade or business." In such cases, it is necessary to determine the business income attributable to each separate trade or business. The income of each business is then apportioned by an apportionment formula which takes into consideration the instate and outstate factors which relate to the trade or business the income of which is being apportioned.

Example: The taxpayer is a conglomerate with three operating divisions. One division is engaged in manufacturing aerospace items for the federal government. Another division is engaged in growing tobacco products. The third division produces and distributes motion pictures for theaters and television. Each division operates independently; there is no strong central management. Each division operates in this state as well as in other states. In this case, it is fair to conclude that the taxpayer is engaged in three separate "trades or businesses." Accordingly, the amount of business income attributable to the taxpayer's trade or business activities in this state is determined by applying an appropriate apportionment formula to the business income of each business.

Single trade or business. The determination of whether the activities of the taxpayer constitute a single trade or business or more than one trade or business will turn on the facts in each case. In general, the activities of the taxpayer will be considered a single business if there is evidence to indicate that the segments under consideration are integrated with, dependent upon or contribute to each other and the operations of the taxpayer as a whole. The following factors are considered to be good indicia of a single trade or business, and the presence of any of these factors creates a strong presumption that the activities of the taxpayer constitute a single trade or business:

(1) Same type of business. A taxpayer is generally engaged in a single trade or business when all of its activities are in the same general line. For example, a taxpayer which operates a chain of retail grocery stores will almost always be engaged in a single trade or business.

(2) Steps in a vertical process. A taxpayer is almost always engaged in a single trade or business when its various divisions or segments are engaged in different steps in a large, vertically structured enterprise. For example, a taxpayer which explores for and mines copper ores; concentrates, smelts and refines the copper ores; and fabricates the refined copper into consumer products is engaged in a single trade or business, regardless of the fact that the various steps in the process are operated substantially independently of each other with only general supervision from the taxpayer's executive offices.

(3) Strong centralized management. A taxpayer which might otherwise be considered as engaged in more than one trade or business is properly considered as engaged in one trade or business when there is a strong central management, coupled with the existence of centralized departments for such functions as financing, advertising, research, or purchasing. Thus, some conglomerates may properly be considered as engaged in only one trade or business when the central executive officers are normally involved in the operations of the various divisions and there are centralized offices which perform for the divisions the normal matters which a truly independent business would perform for itself, such as accounting, personnel, insurance, legal, purchasing, advertising, or financing.

Reg. IV.1.(c). Business and Nonbusiness Income: Application of Definitions.

[*Adopted February 21, 1973.*]

The following are rules and examples for determining whether particular income is business or nonbusiness income. (The examples used throughout these regulations are illustrative only and do not purport to set forth all pertinent facts.)

(1) Rents from real and tangible personal property. Rental income from real and tangible property is business income if the property with respect to which the rental income was received is *used* in the taxpayer's trade or business or incidental thereto and therefore is includable in the property factor under Regulation IV.10.

Example (i): The taxpayer operates a multistate car rental business. The income from car rentals is business income.

Example (ii): The taxpayer is engaged in the heavy construction business in which it uses equipment such as cranes, tractors, and earth-moving vehicles. The taxpayer makes short-term leases of the equipment when particular pieces of equipment are not needed on any particular project. The rental income is business income.

Example (iii): The taxpayer operates a multistate chain of men's clothing stores. The taxpayer purchases a five-story office building for use in connection with its trade or business. It uses the street floor as one of its retail stores and the second and third floors for its general corporate headquarters. The remaining two floors are leased to others. The rental of the two floors is incidental to the operation of the taxpayer's trade or business. The rental income is business income.

Example (iv): The taxpayer operates a multistate chain of grocery stores. It purchases as an investment an office building in another state with surplus funds and leases the entire building to others. The net rental income is not business income of the grocery store trade or business. Therefore, the net rental income is nonbusiness income.

Example (v): The taxpayer operates a multistate chain of men's clothing stores. The taxpayer invests in a 20-story office building and uses the street floor as one of its retail stores and the second floor for its general corporate headquarters. The remaining 18 floors are leased to others. The rental of the eighteen floors is not incidental to but rather is separate from the operation of the taxpayer's trade or business. The net rental income is not business income of the clothing store trade or business. Therefore, the net rental income is nonbusiness income.

Example (vi): The taxpayer constructed a plant for use in its multistate manufacturing business and 20 years later the plant was closed and put up for sale. The plant was rented for a temporary period from the time it was closed by the taxpayer until it was sold 18 months later. The rental income is business income and the gain on the sale of the plant is business income.

Example (vii): The taxpayer operates a multistate chain of grocery stores. It owned an office building which it occupied as its corporate headquarters. Because of inadequate space, taxpayer acquired a new and larger building elsewhere for its corporate headquarters. The old building was rented to an investment company under a five-year lease. Upon expiration of the lease, taxpayer sold the building at a gain (or loss). The net rental income received over the lease period is nonbusiness income and the gain (or loss) on the sale of the building is nonbusiness income.

(2) Gains or losses from sales of assets. Gain or loss from the sale, exchange or other disposition of real property or of tangible or intangible personal property constitutes business income if the property while owned by the taxpayer was used in the taxpayer's trade or business. However, if the property was utilized for the production of nonbusiness income or otherwise was removed from the property factor before its sale, exchange or other disposition, the gain or loss will constitute nonbusiness income. See Regulation IV.10.

Example (i): In conducting its multistate manufacturing business, the taxpayer systematically replaces automobiles, machines, and other equipment used in the business. The gains or losses resulting from those sales constitute business income.

Example (ii): The taxpayer constructed a plant for use in its multistate manufacturing business and 20 years later sold the property at a gain while it was in operation by the taxpayer. The gain is business income.

Example (iii): Same as (ii) except that the plant was closed and put up for sale but was not in fact sold until a buyer was found 18 months later. The gain is business income.

Example (iv): Same as (ii) except that the plant was rented while being held for sale. The rental income is business income and the gain on the sale of the plant is business income.

Example (v): The taxpayer operates a multistate chain of grocery stores. It owned an office building which it occupied as its corporate headquarters. Because of inadequate space, taxpayer acquired a new and larger building elsewhere for its corporate headquarters. The old building was rented to an unrelated investment company under a five-year lease. Upon expiration of the lease, taxpayer sold the building at a gain (or loss). The gain (or loss) on the sale is nonbusiness income and the rental income received over the lease period is nonbusiness income.

(3) Interest. Interest income is business income where the intangible with respect to which the interest was received arises out of or was created in the regular course of the taxpayer's trade or business operations or where the purpose for acquiring and holding the intangible is related to or incidental to such trade or business operations.

Example (i): The taxpayer operates a multistate chain of department stores, selling for cash and on credit. Service charges, interest, or time-price differentials and the like are received with respect to installment sales and revolving charge accounts. These amounts are business income.

Example (ii): The taxpayer conducts a multistate manufacturing business. During the year the taxpayer receives a federal income tax refund and collects a judgment against a debtor of the business. Both the tax refund and the judgment bear interest. The interest income is business income.

Example (iii): The taxpayer is engaged in a multistate manufacturing and wholesaling business. In connection with that business, the taxpayer maintains special accounts to cover such items as workmen's compensation claims, rain and storm damage, machinery replacement, etc. The moneys in those accounts are invested at interest. Similarly, the taxpayer temporarily invests *funds intended* for payment of federal, state and local tax obligations. The interest income is business income.

Example (iv): The taxpayer is engaged in a multistate money order and traveler's check business. In addition to the fees received in connection with the sale of the money orders and traveler's checks, the taxpayer earns interest income by the investment of the funds pending their redemption. The interest income is business income.

Example (v): The taxpayer is engaged in a multistate manufacturing and selling business. The taxpayer usually has *working capital and extra cash* totaling $200,000 which it *regularly invests* in short-term interest bearing securities. The interest income is business income.

Example (vi): In January, the taxpayer sold all of the stock of a subsidiary for $20,000,000. The funds are placed in an interest-bearing account pending a decision by management as to how the funds are to be utilized. The interest income is nonbusiness income.

(4) Dividends. Dividends are business income where the stock with respect to which the dividends are received arises out of or was acquired in the regular course of the taxpayer's trade or business operations or where the purpose of acquiring and holding the stock is related to or incidental to such trade or business operations.

Example (i): The taxpayer operates a multistate chain of stock brokerage houses. During the year, the taxpayer receives dividends on stock that it owns. The dividends are business income.

Example (ii): The taxpayer is engaged in a multistate manufacturing and wholesaling business. In connection with that business, the taxpayer maintains special accounts to cover such items as workmen's compensation claims, etc. A portion of the moneys in those accounts is invested interest-bearing bonds. The remainder is invested in various common stocks listed on national stock exchanges. Both the interest income and any dividends are business income.

Example (iii): The taxpayer and several unrelated corporations own all of the stock of a corporation whose business operations consist solely of acquiring and processing materials for delivery to the corporate owners. The taxpayer acquired the stock in order to obtain a source of supply of materials used in its manufacturing business. The dividends are business income.

Example (iv): The taxpayer is engaged in a multistate heavy construction business. Much of its construction work is performed for agencies of the federal government and various state governments. Under state and federal laws applicable to contracts for these agencies, a contractor must have adequate bonding capacity, as measured by the ratio of its current assets (cash and marketable securities) to current liabilities. In order to maintain an adequate bonding capacity the taxpayer holds various stocks and interest-bearing securities. Both the interest income and any dividends received are business income.

Example (v): The taxpayer receives dividends from the stock of its subsidiary or affiliate which acts as the marketing agency for products manufactured by the taxpayer. The dividends are business income.

Example (vi): The taxpayer is engaged in a multistate glass manufacturing business. It also holds a portfolio of stock and interest-bearing securities, the acquisition and holding of which are unrelated to the manufacturing business. The dividends and interest income received are nonbusiness income.

(5) Patent and copyright royalties. Patent and copyright royalties are business income where the patent or copyright with respect to which the royalties were received arises out of or was created in the regular course of the taxpayer's trade or business operations or where the purpose for acquiring and holding the patent or copyright is related to or incidental to such trade or business operations.

Example (i): The taxpayer is engaged in the multistate business of manufacturing and selling industrial chemicals. In connection with that business the taxpayer obtained patents on certain of its products. The taxpayer licensed the production of the chemicals in foreign countries, in return for which the taxpayer receives royalties. The royalties received by the taxpayer are business income.

Example (ii): The taxpayer is engaged in the music publishing business and holds copyrights on numerous songs. The taxpayer acquires the assets of a smaller publishing company, including music copyrights. These acquired copyrights are thereafter used by the taxpayer in its business. Any royalties received on these copyrights are business income.

Example (iii): Same as example (ii), except that the acquired company also held the patent on a type of phonograph needle. The taxpayer does not manufacture or sell phonographs or phonograph equipment. Any royalties received on the patent would be nonbusiness income.

Reg. IV.1.(d). Proration of Deductions.

[*Adopted February 21, 1973.*]

In most cases, an allowable deduction of a taxpayer will be applicable to only the business income arising from a particular trade or business or to a particular item of nonbusiness income. In some cases, an allowable deduction may be applicable to the business incomes of more than one trade or business and/or to several items of nonbusiness income. In such cases, the deduction shall be prorated among those trades or businesses and those items of nonbusiness income in a manner which fairly distributes the deduction among the classes of income to which it is applicable.

(1) Year to year consistency. In filing returns with this state, if the taxpayer departs from or modifies the manner of prorating any such deduction used in returns for prior years, the taxpayer shall disclose in the return for the current year the nature and extent of the modification.

(2) State to state consistency. If the returns or reports filed by a taxpayer with all states to which the taxpayer reports under Article IV of this Compact or the Uniform Division of Income for Tax Purposes Act are not uniform in the application or proration of any deduction, the taxpayer shall disclose in its return to this state the nature and extent of the variance.

Reg. IV.2.(a). Definitions.

[*Adopted February 21, 1973; amended July 27, 2001.*]

(1) "Taxpayer" means [each state should insert the definition in Article II.3. or the definition in its own tax laws].

(2) "Apportionment" refers to the division of business income between states by the use of a formula containing apportionment factors.

(3) "Allocation" refers to the assignment of nonbusiness income to a particular state.

(4) "Business activity" refers to the transactions and activity occurring in the regular course of a particular trade or business of a taxpayer.

(5) "Gross receipts" are the gross amounts realized (the sum of money and the fair market value of other property or services received) on the sale or exchange of property, the performance of services, or the use of property or capital (including rents, royalties, interest and dividends) in a transaction which produces business income, in which the income or loss is recognized (or would be recognized if the transaction were in the United States) under the Internal Revenue Code. Amounts realized on the sale or exchange of property are not reduced for the cost of goods sold or the basis of property sold. Gross receipts, even if business income, do not include such items as, for example:

1) repayment, maturity, or redemption of the principal of a loan, bond, or mutual fund or certificate of deposit or similar marketable instrument;

2) the principal amount received under a repurchase agreement or other transaction properly characterized as a loan;

3) proceeds from issuance of the taxpayer's own stock or from sale of treasury stock;

4) damages and other amounts received as the result of litigation;

5) property acquired by an agent on behalf of another;

6) tax refunds and other tax benefit recoveries;

7) pension reversions;

8) contributions to capital (except for sales of securities by securities dealers);

9) income from forgiveness of indebtedness; or

10) amounts realized from exchanges of inventory that are not recognized by the Internal Revenue Code.

Exclusion of an item from the definition of "gross receipts" is not determinative of its character as business or nonbusiness income. Nothing in this definition shall be construed to modify, impair or supersede any provision of Section IV.18.

Reg. IV.2.(b)(1). Application of Article IV: Apportionment.

[*Adopted February 21, 1973.*]

If the business activity in respect to any trade or business of a taxpayer occurs both within and without this state, and if by reason of such business activity the taxpayer is taxable in another state, the portion of the net income (or net loss) arising from such trade or business which is derived from sources within this state shall be determined by apportionment in accordance with Article IV.9. to IV.17.

Reg. IV.2.(b)(2). Application of Article IV: Combined Report.

[*Adopted February 21, 1973.*]

If a particular trade or business is carried on by a taxpayer and one or more affiliated corporations, nothing in Article IV or in these regulations shall preclude the use of a "combined report" whereby the entire business income of such trade or business is apportioned in accordance with Article IV.9. to IV.17.

Reg. IV.2.(b)(3). Application of Article IV: Allocation.

[*Adopted February 21, 1973.*]

Any taxpayer subject to the taxing jurisdiction of this state shall allocate all of its nonbusiness income or loss within or without this state in accordance with Article IV.4. to IV.8.

Reg. IV.2.(c). Consistency and Uniformity in Reporting.

[*Adopted February 21, 1973.*]

(1) Year to year consistency. In filing returns with this state, if the taxpayer departs from or modifies the manner in which income has been classified as business income or nonbusiness income in returns for prior years, the taxpayer shall disclose in the return for the current year the nature and extent of the modification.

(2) State to state consistency. If the returns or reports filed by a taxpayer for all states to which the taxpayer reports under Article IV of this Compact or the Uniform Division of Income for Tax Purposes Act are not uniform in the classification of income as business or nonbusiness income, the taxpayer shall disclose in its return to this state the nature and extent of the variance.

Reg. IV.3.(a). Taxable in Another State: In General.

[*Adopted February 21, 1973.*]

Under Article IV.2. the taxpayer is subject to the allocation and apportionment provisions of Article IV if it has income from business activity that is taxable both within and without this state. A taxpayer's income from business activity is taxable without this state if the taxpayer, by reason of such business activity (i.e., the transactions and activity occurring in the regular course of a particular trade or business), is taxable in another state within the meaning of Article IV.3.

(1) Applicable tests. A taxpayer is taxable within another state if it meets either one of two tests: (1) By reason of business activity in another state, the taxpayer is subject to one of the types of taxes specified in Article IV.3.(1), namely: A net income tax, a franchise tax measured by net income, a franchise tax for the privilege of doing business, or a corporate stock tax; or (2) By reason of such business activity, another state has jurisdiction to subject the taxpayer to a net income tax, regardless of whether or not the state imposes such a tax on the taxpayer.

(2) Producing nonbusiness income. A taxpayer is not taxable in another state with respect to a particular trade or business merely because the taxpayer conducts activities in that other state pertaining to the production of nonbusiness income or business activities relating to a separate trade or business.

Reg. IV.3.(b). Taxable in Another State: When a Corporation Is "Subject to" a Tax Under Article IV.3.(1).

[*Adopted February 21, 1973.*]

(1) A taxpayer is "subject to" one of the taxes specified in Article IV.3.(1) if it carries on business activities in a state and the state imposes such a tax thereon. Any taxpayer which asserts that it is subject to one of the taxes specified in Article IV.3.(1) in another state shall furnish to the [tax administrator] of this state upon his/her request evidence to support that assertion. The [tax administrator] of this state may request that such evidence include proof that the taxpayer has filed the requisite tax return in the other state and has paid any taxes imposed under the law of the other state; the taxpayer's failure to produce such proof may be taken into account in determining whether the taxpayer in fact is subject to one of the taxes specified in Article IV.3.(1) in the other state.

Voluntary tax payment. If the taxpayer voluntarily files and pays one or more of such taxes when not required to do so by the laws of that state or pays a minimal fee for qualification, organization or for the privilege of doing business in that state, but

(A) does not actually engage in business activity in that state, or

(B) does actually engage in some business activity not sufficient for nexus and the minimum tax bears no relationship to the taxpayer's business activity within such state, the taxpayer is not "subject to" one of the taxes specified within the meaning of Article IV.3.(1).

Example: State A has a corporation franchise tax measured by net income, for the privilege of doing business in that state. Corporation X files a return and pays the $50 minimum tax, although it carries on no business activity in State A. Corporation X is not taxable in State A.

(2) The concept of taxability in another state is based upon the premise that every state in which the taxpayer is engaged in business activity may impose an income tax even though every state does not do so. In states which do not, other types of taxes may be imposed as a substitute for an income tax. Therefore, only those taxes enumerated in Article IV.3.(1) which may be considered as basically revenue raising rather than regulatory measures shall be considered in determining whether the taxpayer is "subject to" one of the taxes specified in Article IV.3.(1) in another state.

Example (i): State A requires all nonresident corporations which qualify or register in State A to pay to the Secretary of State an annual license fee or tax for the privilege of doing business in the state regardless of whether the privilege is in fact exercised. The amount paid is determined according to the total authorized capital stock of the corporation; the rates are progressively higher by bracketed amounts. The statute sets a minimum fee of $50 and a maximum fee of $500. Failure to pay the tax bars a corporation from utilizing the state courts for enforcement of its rights. State A also imposes a corporation income tax. Nonresident Corporation X is qualified in State A and pays the required fee to the Secretary of State but does not carry on any business activity in State A (although it may utilize the courts of State A). Corporation X is not "taxable" in State A.

Example (ii): Same facts as Example (i) except that Corporation X is subject to and pays the corporation income tax. Payment is prima facie evidence that Corporation X is "subject to" the net income tax of State A and is "taxable" in State A.

Example (iii): State B requires all nonresident corporations qualified or registered in State B to pay to the Secretary of State an annual permit fee or tax for doing business in the state. The base of the fee or tax is the sum of (1) outstanding capital stock, and (2) surplus and undivided profits. The fee or tax base attributable to State B is determined by a three factor apportionment formula. Nonresident Corporation X which operates a plant in State B, pays the required fee or tax to the Secretary of State. Corporation X is "taxable" in State B.

Example (iv): State A has a corporation franchise tax measured by net income for the privilege of doing business in that state. Corporation X files a return based upon its business activity in the state but the amount of computed liability is less than the minimum tax. Corporation X pays the minimum tax. Corporation X is subject to State A's corporation franchise tax.

Reg. IV.3.(c). Taxable in Another State: When a State Has Jurisdiction to Subject a Taxpayer to a Net Income Tax.

[*Adopted February 21, 1973.*]

The second test, that of Article IV.3.(2), applies if the taxpayer's business activity is sufficient to give the state jurisdiction to impose a net income tax by reason of such business activity under the Constitution and statutes of the United States. Jurisdiction to tax is not present where the state is prohibited from imposing the tax by reason of the provisions of Public Law 86-272, 15 U.S.C.A. § § 381-385. In the case of any "state" as defined in Article IV.1.(h), other than a state of the United States or political subdivision thereof, the determination of whether the "state" has jurisdiction to subject the taxpayer to a net income tax shall be made as though the jurisdictional standards applicable to a state of the United States applied in that "state." If jurisdiction is otherwise present, that "state" is not considered as being without jurisdiction by reason of the provisions of a treaty between that state and the United States.

Example: Corporation X is actively engaged in manufacturing farm equipment in State A and in foreign country B. Both State A and foreign country B impose a net income tax but foreign country B exempts corporations engaged in manufacturing farm equipment. Corporation X is subject to the jurisdiction of State A and foreign country B.

Reg. IV.9. Apportionment Formula.

[*Adopted February 21, 1973.*]

All business income of each trade or business of the taxpayer shall be apportioned to this state by use of the apportionment formula set forth in Article IV.9. The elements of the apportionment formula are the property factor (see Regulation IV.10.), the payroll factor (see Regulation IV.13.) and the sales factor (see Regulation IV.15.) of the trade or business of the taxpayer.

Reg. IV.10.(a). Property Factor: In General.

[*Adopted February 21, 1973.*]

The property factor of the apportionment formula for each trade or business of the taxpayer shall include all real and tangible personal property owned or rented by the taxpayer and used during the tax period in the regular course of the trade or business. The term "real and tangible personal property" includes land, buildings, machinery, stocks of goods, equipment, and other real and tangible personal property but does not include coin or currency. Property used in connection with the production of nonbusiness income shall be excluded from the property factor. Property used both in the regular course of the taxpayer's trade or business and in the production of nonbusiness income shall be included in the factor only to the extent that the property is used in the regular course of the taxpayer's trade or business. The method of determining that portion of the value to be included in the factor will depend upon the facts of each case. The property factor shall include the average value of property includable in the factor. See Regulation IV.12.

Reg. IV.10.(b). Property Factor: Property Used for the Production of Business Income.

[*Adopted February 21, 1973.*]

Property shall be included in the property factor if it is actually used or is available for or capable of being used during the tax period in the regular course of the trade or business of the taxpayer. Property held as reserves or standby facilities or property held as a reserve source of materials shall be included in the factor. For example, a plant temporarily idle or raw material reserves not currently being processed are includable in the factor. Property or equipment under construction during the tax period (except inventoriable goods in process) shall be excluded from the factor until such property is actually used in the regular course of the trade or business of the taxpayer. If the property is partially used in the regular course of the trade or business of the taxpayer while under construction, the value of the property to the extent used shall be included in the property factor. Property used in the regular course of the trade or business of the taxpayer shall remain in the property factor until its permanent withdrawal is established by an identifiable event such as its conversion to the production of nonbusiness income, its sale, or the lapse of an extended period of time (normally, five years) during which the property is held for sale.

Example (i): Taxpayer closed its manufacturing plant in State X and held the property for sale. The property remained vacant until its sale one year later. The value of the manufacturing plant is included in the property factor until the plant is sold.

Example (ii): Same as above except that the property was rented until the plant was sold. The plant is included in the property factor until the plant is sold.

Example (iii): Taxpayer closed its manufacturing plant and leased the building under a five-year lease. The plant is included in the property factor until the commencement of the lease.

Example (iv): The taxpayer operates a chain of retail grocery stores. Taxpayer closed Store A, which was then remodeled into three small retail stores such as a dress shop, dry cleaning, and barber shop, which were leased to unrelated parties. The property is removed from the property factor on the date on which the remodeling of Store A commenced.

Reg. IV.10.(c). Property Factor: Consistency in Reporting.

[*Adopted February 21, 1973.*]

(1) Year to year consistency. In filing returns with this state, if the taxpayer departs from or modifies the manner of valuing property or of excluding property from or including property in the property factor used in returns for prior years, the taxpayer shall disclose in the return for the current year the nature and extent of the modification.

(2) State to state consistency. If the returns or reports filed by the taxpayer with all states to which the taxpayer reports under Article IV of this Compact or the Uniform Division of Income for Tax Purposes Act are not uniform in the valuation of property and in the exclusion of property from or the inclusion of property in the property factor, the taxpayer shall disclose in its return to this state the nature and extent of the variance.

Reg. IV.10.(d). Property Factor: Numerator.

[*Adopted February 21, 1973.*]

The numerator of the property factor shall include the average value of the real and tangible personal property owned or rented by the taxpayer and used in this state during the tax period in the regular course of the trade or business of the taxpayer. Property in transit between locations of the taxpayer to which it belongs shall be considered to be at the destination for purposes of the property factor. Property in transit between a buyer and seller which is included by a taxpayer in the denominator of its property factor in accordance with its regular accounting practices shall be included in the numerator according to the state of destination. The value of mobile or movable property such as construction equipment, trucks or leased electronic equipment which are located within and without this state during the tax period shall be determined for purposes of the numerator of the factor on the basis of total time within the state during the tax period. An automobile assigned to a traveling employee shall be included in the numerator of the factor of the state to which the employee's compensation is assigned under the payroll factor or in the numerator of the state in which the automobile is licensed.

Reg. IV.11.(a). Property Factor: Valuation of Owned Property.

[*Amended July 14, 1988.*]

(1) Property owned by the taxpayer shall be valued at its original cost. As a general rule, "original cost" is deemed to be the basis of the property for federal income tax purposes (prior to any federal adjustments) at the time of acquisition by the taxpayer and adjusted by subsequent capital additions or improvements thereto and partial disposition thereof, by reason of sale, exchange, abandonment, etc. However, capitalized intangible drilling and development costs shall be included in the property factor whether or not they have been expensed for either federal or state tax purposes.

Example (i): The taxpayer acquired a factory building in this state at a cost of $500,000 and, 18 months later, expended $100,000 for major remodeling of the building. Taxpayer files its return for the current taxable year on the calendar-year basis. Depreciation deduction in the amount of $22,000 was claimed with respect to the building on the return for the current taxable year. The value of the building includable in the numerator and denominator of the property factor is $600,000; the depreciation deduction is not taken into account in determining the value of the building for purposes of the factor.

Example (ii): During the current taxable year, Corporation X merges into Corporation Y in a tax-free reorganization under the Internal Revenue Code. At the time of the merger, Corporation X owns a factory which X built five years earlier at a cost of $1,000,000. X has been depreciating the factory at the rate of two percent per year, and its basis in X's hands, at the time of the merger is $900,000. Since the property is acquired by Y in a transaction in which, under the Internal Revenue Code, its basis in Y's hands is the same as its basis in X's, Y includes the property in Y's property factor at X's original cost, without adjustment for depreciation, i.e. $1,000,000.

Example (iii): Corporation Y acquires the assets of Corporation X in a liquidation by which Y is entitled to use its stock cost as the basis of the X assets under Section 334(b)(2) of the 1954 Internal Revenue

Code (i.e. stock possessing 80 percent control is purchased and liquidated within two years). Under these circumstances, Y's cost of the assets is the purchase price of the X stock, prorated over the X assets.

If the original cost of property is unascertainable, the property is included in the factor at its fair market value as of the date of acquisition by the taxpayer.

(2) Inventory of stock of goods shall be included in the factor in accordance with the valuation method used for federal income tax purposes.

(3) Property acquired by gift or inheritance shall be included in the factor at its basis for determining depreciation for federal income tax purposes.

Reg. IV.11.(b). Property Factor: Valuation of Rented Property.

[*Adopted February 21, 1973; amended July 14, 1988.*]

(1) Multiplier and Subrentals. Property rented by the taxpayer is valued at eight times its net annual rental rate. The net annual rental rate for any item of rented property is the annual rental rate paid by the taxpayer for the property less the aggregate annual subrental rates paid by subtenants of the taxpayer. (See Regulation IV.18.(a) for special rules when the use of such net annual rental rate produces a negative or clearly inaccurate value or when property is used by the taxpayer at no charge or is rented at a nominal rental rate.)

Subrents are not deducted when they constitute business income because the property which produces the subrents is used in the regular course of a trade or business of the taxpayer when it is producing such income. Accordingly there is no reduction in its value.

Example (i): The taxpayer receives subrents from a bakery concession in a food market operated by the taxpayer. Since the subrents are business income they are not deducted from rent paid by the taxpayer for the food market.

Example (ii): The taxpayer rents a 5-story office building primarily for use in its multistate business, uses three floors for its offices and subleases two floors to various other businesses and persons such as professional people and shops. The rental of the two floors is incidental to the operation of the taxpayer's trade or business. Since the subrents are business income, they are not deducted from the rent paid by the taxpayer.

Example (iii): The taxpayer rents a 20-story office building and uses the lower two stories for its general corporation headquarters. The remaining 18 floors are subleased to others. The rental of the eighteen floors is not incidental to but rather is separate from the operation of the taxpayer's trade or business. Since the subrents are nonbusiness income they are to be deducted from the rent paid by the taxpayer.

(2) "Annual rental rate" is the amount paid as rental for property for a 12-month period (i.e., the amount of the annual rent). Where property is rented for less than a 12-month period, the rent paid for the actual period of rental shall constitute the "annual rental rate" for the tax period. However, where a taxpayer has rented property for a term of 12 or more months and the current tax period covers a period of less than 12 months (due, for example, to a reorganization or change of accounting period), the rent paid for the short tax period shall be annualized. If the rental term is for less than 12 months, the rent shall not be annualized beyond its term. Rent shall not be annualized because of the uncertain duration when the rental term is on a month-to-month basis.

Example (i): Taxpayer A, which ordinarily files its returns based on a calendar year is merged into Taxpayer B on April 30. The net rent paid under a lease with 5 years remaining is $2,500 a month. The rent for the tax period January 1 to April 30 is $10,000. After the rent is annualized the net rent is $30,000 ($2,500 × 12).

Example (ii): Same facts as in Example (i) except that the lease would have terminated on August 31. In this case, the annualized rent is $20,000 ($2,500 × 8).

(3) "Annual Rent" is the actual sum of money or other consideration payable, directly or indirectly, by the taxpayer or for its benefit for the use of the property and includes:

(A) Any amount payable for the use of real or tangible personal property, or any part thereof, whether designated as a fixed sum of money or as a percentage of sales, profits or otherwise.

Example: A taxpayer, pursuant to the terms of a lease, pays a lessor $1,000 per month as a base rental and at the end of the year pays the lessor one percent of its gross sales of $400,000. The annual rent is $16,000 ($12,000 plus one percent of $400,000 or $4,000).

(B) Any amount payable as additional rent or in lieu of rents, such as interest, taxes, insurance, repairs or any other items which are required to be paid by the terms of the lease or other arrangement, not including amounts paid as service charges, such as utilities, janitor services, etc. If a payment includes rent and other charges unsegregated, the amount of rent shall be determined by consideration of the relative values of the rent and other items.

Example (i): A taxpayer, pursuant to the terms of a lease, pays the lessor $12,000 a year rent plus taxes in the amount of $2,000 and interest on a mortgage in the amount of $1,000. The annual rent is $15,000.

Example (ii): A taxpayer stores part of its inventory in a public warehouse. The total charge for the year was $1,000 of which $700 was for the use of storage space and $300 for inventory insurance, handling and shipping charges, and C.O.D. collections. The annual rent is $700.

(4) Exclusions. "Annual rent" does not include:

(A) Incidental day-to-day expenses such as hotel or motel accommodations, daily rental of automobiles, etc.; and

(B) Royalties based on extraction of natural resources, whether represented by delivery or purchase. For this purpose, a royalty includes any consideration conveyed or credited to a holder of an interest in property which constitutes a sharing of current or future production of natural resources from such property, irrespective of the method of payment or how such consideration may be characterized, whether as a royalty, advance royalty, rental or otherwise.

(5) Leasehold improvements shall, for the purposes of the property factor, be treated as property owned by the taxpayer regardless of whether the taxpayer is entitled to remove the improvements or the improvements revert to the lessor upon expiration of the lease. Hence, the original cost of leasehold improvements shall be included in the factor.

Reg. IV.12. Property Factor: Averaging Property Values.

[*Adopted February 21, 1973.*]

As a general rule, the average value of property owned by the taxpayer shall be determined by averaging the values at the beginning and ending of the tax period. However, the [tax administrator] may require or allow averaging by monthly values if that method of averaging is required to properly reflect the average value of the taxpayer's property for the tax period.

Averaging by monthly values will generally be applied if substantial fluctuations in the values of the property exist during the tax period or if property is acquired after the beginning of the tax period or disposed of before the end of the tax period.

Example: The monthly value of the taxpayer's property was as follows:

Month	Value	Month	Value
January	$2,000	July	$15,000
February	2,000	August	17,000
March	3,000	September	23,000
April	3,500	October	25,000
May	4,500	November	13,000
June	10,000	December	2,000
	$25,000		$95,000
		Total	$120,000

The average value of the taxpayer's property includable in the property factor for the income year is determined as follows:

$$\frac{\$120{,}000}{12} = \$10{,}000$$

Averaging with respect to rented property is achieved automatically by the method of determining the net annual rental rate of such property as set forth in Reg. IV.11.(b).

Reg. IV.13.(a). Payroll Factor: In General.

[*Adopted February 21, 1973.*]

(1) The payroll factor of the apportionment formula for each trade or business of the taxpayer shall include the total amount paid by the taxpayer in the regular course of its trade or business for compensation during the tax period.

(2) The total amount "paid" to employees is determined upon the basis of the taxpayer's accounting method. If the taxpayer has adopted the accrual method of accounting, all compensation properly accrued shall be deemed to have been paid. Notwithstanding the taxpayer's method of accounting, compensation paid to employees may, at the election of the taxpayer, be included in the payroll factor by use of the cash method if the taxpayer is required to report such compensation under that method for unemployment compensation purposes.

The compensation of any employee on account of activities which are connected with the production of nonbusiness income shall be excluded from the factor.

Example (i): The taxpayer uses some of its employees in the construction of a storage building which, upon completion, is used in the regular course of the taxpayer's trade or business. The wages paid to those employees are treated as a capital expenditure by the taxpayer. The amount of those wages is included in the payroll factor.

Example (ii): The taxpayer owns various securities which it holds as an investment separate and apart from its trade or business. The management of the taxpayer's investment portfolio is the only duty of Mr. X, an employee. The salary paid to Mr. X is excluded from the payroll factor.

(3) The term "compensation" means wages, salaries, commissions and any other form of remuneration paid to employees for personal services. Payments made to an independent contractor or any other person not properly classifiable as an employee are excluded. Only amounts paid directly to employees are included in the payroll factor. Amounts considered paid directly include the value of board, rent, housing, lodging, and other benefits or services furnished to employees by the taxpayer in return for personal services provided that such amounts constitute income to the recipient under the federal Internal Revenue Code. In the case of employees not subject to the federal Internal Revenue Code, e.g., those employed in foreign countries, the determination of whether such benefits or services would constitute income to the employees shall be made as though such employees were subject to the federal Internal Revenue Code.

(4) The term "employee" means (A) any officer of a corporation, or (B) any individual who, under the usual common-law rules applicable in determining the employer-employee relationship, has the status of an employee. Generally, a person will be considered to be an employee if he is included by the taxpayer as an employee for purposes of the payroll taxes imposed by the Federal Insurance Contributions Act; except that, since certain individuals are included within the term "employees" in the Federal Insurance Contributions Act who would not be employees under the usual common-law rules, it may be established that a person who is included as an employee for purposes of the Federal Insurance Contributions Act is not an employee for purposes of this regulation.

(5) Year to year consistency. In filing returns with this state, if the taxpayer departs from or modifies the treatment of compensation paid used in returns for prior years, the taxpayer shall disclose in the return for the current year the nature and extent of the modification.

(6) State to state consistency. If the returns or reports filed by the taxpayer with all states to which the taxpayer reports under Article IV of this Compact or the Uniform Division of Income for Tax Purposes Act are not uniform in the treatment of compensation paid, the taxpayer shall disclose in its return to this state the nature and extent of the variance.

Reg. IV.13.(b). Payroll Factor: Denominator.

[*Adopted February 21, 1973.*]

The denominator of the payroll factor is the total compensation paid everywhere during the tax period. Accordingly, compensation paid to employees whose services are performed entirely in a state where the taxpayer is immune from taxation, for example, by Public Law 86-272, is included in the denominator of the payroll factor.

Example: A taxpayer has employees in its state of legal domicile (State A) and is taxable in State B. In addition the taxpayer has other employees whose services are performed entirely in State C where the taxpayer is immune from taxation under the provisions of Public Law 86-272. As to these latter employees, the compensation will be assigned to State C where their services are performed (i.e., included in the denominator—but not the numerator—of the payroll factor) even though the taxpayer is not taxable in State C.

Reg. IV.13.(c). Payroll Factor: Numerator.

[*Adopted February 21, 1973.*]

The numerator of the payroll factor is the total amount paid in this state during the tax period by the taxpayer for compensation. The tests in Article IV.14. to be applied in determining whether compensation is paid in this state are derived from the Model Unemployment Compensation Act. Accordingly, if compensation paid to employees is included in the payroll factor by use of the cash method of accounting or if the taxpayer is required to report such compensation under that method for unemployment compensation purposes, it shall be presumed that the total wages reported by the taxpayer to this state for unemployment compensation purposes constitute compensation paid in this state except for compensation excluded under Regulation IV.13.(a). to IV.14. The presumption may be overcome by satisfactory evidence that an employee's compensation is not properly reportable to this state for unemployment compensation purposes.

Reg. IV.14. Payroll Factor: Compensation Paid in This State.

[*Adopted February 21, 1973.*]

Compensation is paid in this state if any one of the following tests, applied consecutively, are met:

(1) The employee's service is performed entirely within the state.

(2) The employee's service is performed both within and without the state, but the service performed without the state is incidental to the employee's service within the state. The word "incidental" means

any service which is temporary or transitory in nature, or which is rendered in connection with an isolated transaction.

(3) If the employee's services are performed both within and without this state, the employee's compensation will be attributed to this state:

(A) if the employee's base of operations is in this state; or

(B) if there is no base of operations in any state in which some part of the service is performed, but the place from which the service is directed or controlled is in this state; or

(C) if the base of operations or the place from which the service is directed or controlled is not in any state in which some part of the service is performed but the employee's residence is in this state.

The term "place from which the service is directed or controlled" refers to the place from which the power to direct or control is exercised by the taxpayer.

The term "base of operations" is the place of more or less permanent nature from which the employee starts his work and to which he customarily returns in order to receive instructions from the taxpayer or communications from his customers or other persons or to replenish stock or other materials, repair equipment, or perform any other functions necessary to the exercise of his trade or profession at some other point or points.

Reg. IV.15.(a). Sales Factor: In General.

[*Adopted February 21, 1973.*]

(1) Article IV.1.(g) defines the term "sales" to mean all gross receipts of the taxpayer not allocated under paragraphs (5) through (8) of Article IV. Thus, for the purposes of the sales factor of the apportionment formula for each trade or business of the taxpayer, the term "sales" means all gross receipts derived by the taxpayer from transactions and activity in the regular course of the trade or business. The following are rules for determining "sales" in various situations:

(A) In the case of a taxpayer engaged in manufacturing and selling or purchasing and reselling goods or products, "sales" includes all gross receipts from the sales of such goods or products (or other property of a kind which would properly be included in the inventory of the taxpayer if on hand at the close of the tax period) held by the taxpayer primarily for sale to customers in the ordinary course of its trade or business. Gross receipts for this purpose means gross sales less returns and allowances, and includes all interest income, service charges, carrying charges, or time-price differential charges incidental to such sales. Federal and state excise taxes (including sales taxes) shall be included as part of such receipts if the taxes are passed on to the buyer or included as part of the selling price of the product.

(B) In the case of cost plus fixed fee contracts, such as the operation of a government-owned plant for a fee, "sales" includes the entire reimbursed cost plus the fee.

(C) In the case of a taxpayer engaged in providing services, such as the operation of an advertising agency or the performance of equipment service contracts or research and development contracts, "sales" includes the gross receipts from the performance of such services including fees, commissions, and similar items.

(D) In the case of a taxpayer engaged in renting real or tangible property, "sales" includes the gross receipts from the rental, lease, or licensing the use of the property.

(E) In the case of a taxpayer engaged in the sale, assignment, or licensing of intangible personal property such as patents and copyrights, "sales" includes the gross receipts therefrom.

(F) If a taxpayer derives receipts from the sale of equipment used in its business, those receipts constitute "sales." For example, a truck express company owns a fleet of trucks and sells its trucks under a regular replacement program. The gross receipts from the sales of the trucks are included in the sales factor.

(2) Exceptions. In some cases certain gross receipts should be disregarded in determining the sales factor in order that the apportionment formula will operate fairly to apportion to this state the income of the taxpayer's trade or business. See Regulation IV.18.(c).

(3) Year to year consistency. In filing returns with this state, if the taxpayer departs from or modifies the basis for excluding or including gross receipts in the sales factor used in returns for prior years, the taxpayer shall disclose in the return for the current year the nature and extent of the modification.

(4) State to state consistency. If the returns or reports filed by the taxpayer with all states to which the taxpayer reports under Article IV of this Compact or the Uniform Division of Income for Tax Purposes Act are not uniform in the inclusion or exclusion of gross receipts, the taxpayer shall disclose in its return to this state the nature and extent of the variance.

Reg. IV.15.(b). Sales Factor: Denominator.

[*Adopted February 21, 1973.*]

The denominator of the sales factor shall include the total gross receipts derived by the taxpayer from transactions and activity in the regular course of its trade or business, except receipts excluded under Regulation IV.18.(c).

Reg. IV.15.(c). Sales Factor: Numerator.

[*Adopted February 21, 1973.*]

The numerator of the sales factor shall include gross receipts attributable to this state and derived by the taxpayer from transactions and activity in the regular course of its trade or business. All interest income, service charges, carrying charges, or time-price differential charges incidental to such gross receipts shall be included regardless of (1) the place where the accounting records are maintained or (2) the location of the contract or other evidence of indebtedness.

Reg. IV.16.(a). Sales Factor: Sales of Tangible Personal Property in This State.

[*Adopted February 21, 1973.*]

(1) Gross receipts from sales of tangible personal property (except sales to the United States Government; see Regulation IV.16.(b)) are in this state:

(A) if the property is delivered or shipped to a purchaser within this state regardless of the f.o.b. point or other conditions of sale; or

(B) if the property is shipped from an office, store, warehouse, factory, or other place of storage in this state and the taxpayer is not taxable in the state of the purchaser.

(2) Property shall be deemed to be delivered or shipped to a purchaser within this state if the recipient is located in this state, even though the property is ordered from outside this state.

Example: The taxpayer, with inventory in State A, sold $100,000 of its products to a purchaser having branch stores in several states including this state. The order for the purchase was placed by the purchaser's central purchasing department located in State B. $25,000 of the purchase order was shipped directly to purchaser's branch store in this state. The branch store in this state is the "purchaser within this state" with respect to $25,000 of the taxpayer's sales.

(3) Property is delivered or shipped to a purchaser within this state if the shipment terminates in this state, even though the property is subsequently transferred by the purchaser to another state.

Example: The taxpayer makes a sale to a purchaser who maintains a central warehouse in this state at which all merchandise purchases are received. The purchaser reships the goods to its branch stores in other states for sale. All of the taxpayer's products shipped to the purchaser's warehouse in this state constitute property delivered or shipped to a purchaser within this state.

(4) The term "purchaser within this state" shall include the ultimate recipient of the property if the taxpayer in this state, at the designation of the purchaser, delivers to or has the property shipped to the ultimate recipient within this state.

Example: A taxpayer in this state sold merchandise to a purchaser in State A. Taxpayer directed the manufacturer or supplier of the merchandise in State B to ship the merchandise to the purchaser's customer in this state pursuant to purchaser's instructions. The sale by the taxpayer is "in this state."

(5) When property being shipped by a seller from the state of origin to a consignee in another state is diverted while en route to a purchaser in this state, the sales are in this state.

Example: The taxpayer, a produce grower in State A, begins shipment of perishable produce to the purchaser's place of business in State B. While en route, the produce is diverted to the purchaser's place of business in this state in which state the taxpayer is subject to tax. The sale by the taxpayer is attributed to this state.

(6) If the taxpayer is not taxable in the state of the purchaser, the sale is attributed to this state if the property is shipped from an office, store, warehouse, factory, or other place of storage in this state.

Example: The taxpayer has its head office and factory in State A. It maintains a branch office and inventory in this state. Taxpayer's only activity in State B is the solicitation of orders by a resident salesman. All orders by the State B salesman are sent to the branch office in this state for approval and are filled by shipment from the inventory in this state. Since the taxpayer is immune under Public Law 86-272 from tax in State B, all sales of merchandise to purchasers in State B are attributed to this state, the state from which the merchandise was shipped.

(7) If a taxpayer whose salesman operates from an office located in this state makes a sale to a purchaser in another state in which the taxpayer is not taxable and the property is shipped directly by a third party to the purchaser, the following rules apply:

(A) If the taxpayer is taxable in the state from which the third party ships the property, then the sale is in that state.

(B) If the taxpayer is not taxable in the state from which the property is shipped, then the sale is in this state.

Example: The taxpayer in this state sold merchandise to a purchaser in State A. Taxpayer is not taxable in State A. Upon direction of the taxpayer, the merchandise was shipped directly to the purchaser by the manufacturer in State B. If the taxpayer is taxable in State B, the sale is in State B. If the taxpayer is not taxable in State B, the sale is in this state.

Reg. IV.16.(b). Sales Factor: Sales of Tangible Personal Property to United States Government in This State.

[*Adopted February 21, 1973.*]

Gross receipts from sales of tangible personal property to the United States Government are in this state if the property is shipped from an office, store, warehouse, factory, or other place of storage in this state. For the purposes of this regulation, only sales for which the United States Government makes direct payment to the seller pursuant to the terms of a contract constitute sales to the United States Government. Thus, as a general rule, sales by a subcontractor to the prime contractor, the party to the contract with the United States Government, do not constitute sales to the United States Government.

Example (i): A taxpayer contracts with General Services Administration to deliver X number of trucks which were paid for by the United States Government. The sale is a sale to the United States Government.

Example (ii): The taxpayer, as a subcontractor to a prime contractor with the National Aeronautics and Space Administration contracts to build a component of a rocket for $1,000,000. The sale by the subcontractor to the prime contractor is not a sale to the United States Government.

Reg. IV.17. Sales Factor: Sales Other Than Sales of Tangible Personal Property in This State.

[*Adopted February 21, 1973.*]

(1) In general. Article IV.17. provides for the inclusion in the numerator of the sales factor of gross receipts from transactions other than sales of tangible personal property (including transactions with the United States Government); under this section gross receipts are attributed to this state if the income producing activity which gave rise to the receipts is performed wholly within this state. Also, gross receipts are attributed to the state if, with respect to a particular item of income, the income producing activity is performed within and without this state but the greater proportion of the income producing activity is performed in this state, based on costs of performance.

(2) Income producing activity: defined. The term "income producing activity" applies to each separate item of income and means the transactions and activity directly engaged in by the taxpayer in the regular course of its trade or business for the ultimate purpose of obtaining gains or profit. Such activity does not include transactions and activities performed on behalf of a taxpayer, such as those conducted on its behalf by an independent contractor. Accordingly, income producing activity includes but is not limited to the following:

(A) The rendering of personal services by employees or the utilization of tangible and intangible property by the taxpayer in performing a service.

(B) The sale, rental, leasing, licensing or other use of real property.

(C) The rental, leasing, licensing or other use of tangible personal property.

(D) The sale, licensing or other use of intangible personal property.

The mere holding of intangible personal property is not, of itself, an income producing activity.

(3) Costs of performance: defined. The term "cost of performance" means direct costs determined in a manner consistent with generally accepted accounting principles and in accordance with accepted conditions or practices in the trade or business of the taxpayer.

(4) Application.

(A) In general. Receipts (other than from sales of tangible personal property) in respect to a particular income producing activity are in this state if:

(a) the income producing activity is performed wholly within this state; or

(b) the income producing activity is performed both in and outside this state and a greater proportion of the income producing activity is performed in this state than in any other state, based on costs of performance.

(B) Special rules. The following are special rules for determining when receipts from the income producing activities described below are in this state:

(a) Gross receipts from the sale, lease, rental or licensing of real property are in this state if the real property is located in this state.

(b) Gross receipts from the rental, lease, or licensing of tangible personal property are in this state if the property is located in this state. The rental, lease, licensing or other use of tangible personal property in this state is a separate income producing activity from the rental, lease, licensing or other use of the same property while located in another state; consequently, if property is within and without this state during the rental, lease or licensing period, gross receipts attributable to this state shall be measured by the ratio which the time the property was physically present or was used in this state bears to the total time or use of the property everywhere during that period.

Example: Taxpayer is the owner of 10 railroad cars. During the year, the total of the days during which each railroad car was present in this state was 50 days. The receipts attributable to the use of each of the railroad cars in this state are a separate item of income and shall be determined as follows:

$$\frac{(10 \times 50) = 500}{3650} \times \text{Total Receipts} = \text{Receipts Attributable to This State}$$

(c) Gross receipts for the performance of personal services are attributable to this state to the extent that such services are performed in this state. If services relating to a single item of income are performed partly within and partly without this state, the gross receipts from the performance of such services shall be attributable to this state only if the greater proportion of the services was performed in the state, based on costs of performance. Usually, where services are performed partly within and partly without this state, the services performed in each state will constitute a separate income producing activity; in such case the gross receipts from the performance of services attributable to this state shall be measured by the ratio which the time spent in performing the services in this state bears to the total time spent in performing the services everywhere. Time spent in performing services includes the amount of time expended in the performance of a contract or other obligation which gives rise to such gross receipts. Personal service not directly connected with the performance of the contract or other obligation, as for example time expended in negotiating the contract, is excluded from the computations.

Example (i): Taxpayer, a road show, gave theatrical performances at various locations in State X and in this state during the tax period. All gross receipts from performances given in this state are attributed to this state.

Example (ii): The taxpayer, a public opinion survey corporation, conducted a poll by means of its employees in State X and in this state for the sum of \$9,000. The project required 600 man hours to obtain the basic data and prepare the survey report. Two hundred of the 600 man hours were expended in this state. The receipts attributable to this state are \$3,000.

$$\frac{200}{600} \times \$9,000 = \$3,000$$

Reg. IV.18.(a). Special Rules: In General.

[*Adopted February 21, 1973.*]

Article IV.18. provides that, if the allocation and apportionment provisions of Article IV do not fairly represent the extent of the taxpayer's business activity in this state, the taxpayer may petition for or the tax administrator may require, in respect to all or any part of the taxpayer's business activity, if reasonable:

(1) separate accounting;

(2) the exclusion of any one or more of the factors;

(3) the inclusion of one or more additional factors which will fairly represent the taxpayer's business activity in this state; or

(4) the employment of any other method to effectuate an equitable allocation and apportionment of the taxpayer's income.

Article IV.18. permits a departure from the allocation and apportionment provisions of Article IV only in limited and specific cases. Article IV.18. may be invoked only in specific cases where unusual fact situations (which ordinarily will be unique and non recurring) produce incongruous results under the apportionment and allocation provisions contained in Article IV.

In the case of certain industries such as air transportation, rail transportation, ship transportation, trucking, television, radio, motion pictures, various types of professional athletics, and so forth, the foregoing regulations in respect to the apportionment formula do not set forth appropriate procedures for determining the apportionment factors. Nothing in Article IV.18. or in this Regulation IV.18. shall preclude [the tax administrator] from establishing appropriate procedures under Article IV.10. to 17. for determining the apportionment factors for each such industry, but such procedures shall be applied uniformly.

Reg. IV.18.(b). Special Rules: Property Factor.

[*Adopted February 21, 1973.*]

The following special rules are established in respect to the property factor of the apportionment formula:

(1) If the subrents taken into account in determining the net annual rental rate under Regulation IV.11.(b) produce a negative or clearly inaccurate value for any item of property, another method

which will properly reflect the value of rented property may be required by the [tax administrator] or requested by the taxpayer.

In no case however, shall such value be less than an amount which bears the same ratio to the annual rental rate paid by the taxpayer for the property as the fair market value of that portion of the property used by the taxpayer bears to the total fair market value of the rented property.

Example: The taxpayer rents a 10-story building at an annual rental rate of $1,000,000. Taxpayer occupies two stories and sublets eight stories for $1,000,000 a year. The net annual rental rate of the taxpayer must not be less than two-tenths of the taxpayer's annual rental rate for the entire year, or $200,000.

(2) If property owned by others is used by the taxpayer at no charge or rented by the taxpayer for a nominal rate, the net annual rental rate for the property shall be determined on the basis of a reasonable market rental rate for the property.

Reg. IV.18.(c). Special Rules: Sales Factor.

[*Adopted February 21, 1973; amended August 8, 1997.*]

The following special rules are established in respect to the sales factor of the apportionment formula:

(1) Where substantial amounts of gross receipts arise from an incidental or occasional sale of a fixed asset used in the regular course of the taxpayer's trade or business, those gross receipts shall be excluded from the sales factor. For example, gross receipts from the sale of a factory or plant will be excluded.

(2) Insubstantial amounts of gross receipts arising from incidental or occasional transactions or activities may be excluded from the sales factor unless their exclusion would materially affect the amount of income apportioned to this state. For example, the taxpayer ordinarily may include in or exclude from the sales factor gross receipts from transactions such as the sale of office furniture, business automobiles, etc.

(3) Where the income producing activity in respect to business income from intangible personal property can be readily identified, the income is included in the denominator of the sales factor and, if the income producing activity occurs in this state, in the numerator of the sales factor as well. For example, usually the income producing activity can be readily identified in respect to interest income received on

deferred payments on sales of tangible property (Regulation IV.15.(a)(1)(A)) and income from the sale, licensing or other use of intangible personal property (Regulation IV.17.(2)(D)).

Where business income from intangible property cannot readily be attributed to any particular income producing activity of the taxpayer, the income cannot be assigned to the numerator of the sales factor for any state and shall be excluded from the denominator of the sales factor. For example, where business income in the form of dividends received on stock, royalties received on patents or copyrights, or interest received on bonds, debentures or government securities results from the mere holding of the intangible personal property by the taxpayer, the dividends and interest shall be excluded from the denominator of the sales factor.

(4) (A) Where gains and losses on the sale of liquid assets are not excluded from the sales factor by other provisions under Reg. IV.18.(c)., such gains or losses shall be treated as provided in this subsection. This subsection does not provide rules relating to the treatment of other receipts produced from holding or managing such assets. If a taxpayer holds liquid assets in connection with one or more treasury functions of the taxpayer, and the liquid assets produce business income when sold, exchanged or otherwise disposed, the overall net gain from those transactions for each treasury function for the tax period is included in the sales factor. For purposes of this subsection, each treasury function will be considered separately.

(B) For purposes of this subsection, a liquid asset is an asset (other than functional currency or funds held in bank accounts) held to provide a relatively immediate source of funds to satisfy the liquidity needs of the trade or business. Liquid assets include foreign currency (and trading positions therein) other than functional currency used in the regular course of the taxpayer's trade or business; marketable instruments (including stocks, bonds, debentures, options, warrants, futures contracts, etc.); and mutual funds which hold such liquid assets. An instrument is considered marketable if it is traded in an established stock or securities market and is regularly quoted by brokers or dealers in making a market. Stock in a corporation which is unitary with the taxpayer, or which has a substantial business relationship with the taxpayer is not considered marketable stock.

(C) For purposes of this subsection, a treasury function is the pooling and management of liquid assets for the purpose of satisfying the cash flow needs of the trade or business, such as providing liquidity for a taxpayer's business cycle, providing a reserve for business contingencies, business acquisitions, etc. A taxpayer principally engaged in the trade or business of purchasing and selling instruments or other items included in the definition of liquid assets set forth herein is not performing a treasury function with respect to income so produced.

(D) Overall net gain refers to the total net gain from all transactions incurred at each treasury function for the entire tax period, not the net gain from a specific transaction.

(E) Examples.

Example (i). A taxpayer manufactures various gift items. Because of seasonal variations, the taxpayer must keep liquid assets available for later inventory acquisitions. Because the manufacturer wants to obtain a return on available funds, the manufacturer acquires liquid assets, which are held and managed in State A. The net gain resulting from all gains and losses on the sale of the liquid assets for the tax year will be reflected in the denominator of the sales factor and in the numerator of State A.

Example (ii). A stockbroker acts as a dealer or trader for its own account in its ordinary course of business. Some of the instruments sold are liquid assets. This subsection does not operate to classify those sales as attributable to a treasury function.

Reg. IV.18.(d). Special Regulation: Construction Contractors.

[*Adopted July 10, 1980.*]

The following special rules are established in respect to the apportionment of income of long-term construction contractors:

(1) In General. When a taxpayer elects to use the percentage of completion method of accounting, or the completed contract method of accounting for long-term contracts (construction contracts covering a period in excess of one year from the date of execution of the contract to the date on which the contract is finally completed and accepted), and has income from sources both within and without this state from a trade or business, the amount of business income derived from such long-term contracts from sources within this state shall be determined pursuant to this regulation. In such cases, the first step is to determine which portion of the taxpayer's income constitutes "business income" and which portion constitutes "nonbusiness income" under Article IV.1 and Reg. IV.1 thereunder. Nonbusiness income is directly allocated to specific states pursuant to the provisions of Article IV.5 to .8, inclusive. Business income is apportioned among the states in which the business is conducted pursuant to the property, payroll, and sales apportionment factors set forth in this regulation. The sum of (1) the items of nonbusiness income directly allocated to this state and (2) the amount of business income attributable to this state constitutes the amount of the taxpayer's entire net income which is subject to tax by this state.

(2) Business and Nonbusiness Income. For definitions, rules and examples for determining business and nonbusiness income see Reg. IV.1.

(3) Methods of Accounting and Year of Inclusion. For general rules of accounting, definitions and methods of accounting for long-term construction contracts see (each state adopting this Regulation should insert here reference to its laws and regulations relating in general to accounting methods of reporting income from long-term contracts. This Regulation assumes that the law of the adopting states permits the taxpayer to elect either the percentage of completion or completed contracts methods. If not, the Regulation will have to be modified to conform to an adopting state's accounting method for long-term construction contracts.)

(4) Apportionment of Business Income.

(i) In General. Business income is apportioned to this state by a three-factor formula consisting of property, payroll and sales regardless of the method of accounting for long-term contracts elected by the taxpayer. The total of the property, payroll and sales percentages is divided by three to determine the apportionment percentage. The apportionment percentage is then applied to business income to determine the amount apportioned to this state.

(ii) Percentage of Completion Method. Under this method of accounting for long-term contracts, the amount to be included each year as business income from each contract is the amount by which the gross contract price which corresponds to the percentage of the entire contract which has been completed during the income years exceeds all expenditures made during the income year in connection with the contract. In so doing, account must be taken of the material and supplies on hand at the beginning and end of the income year for use in each such contract.

Example: A taxpayer using the percentage of completion method of accounting for long-term contracts entered into a long-term contract to build a structure for $9,000,000. The contract allowed three years for completion, and as of the end of the second income year the taxpayer's books of account, kept on the accrual method, disclosed the following:

	Receipts	Expenditures
End of 1st income year	$2,500,000	$2,400,000
End of 2nd income year	4,500,000	4,100,000
Totals	$7,000,000	$6,500,000

In computing the above expenditures, consideration was given to material and supplies on hand at the beginning and end of each income year. It was estimated that the contract was 30% completed at the end of the first income year and 80% completed at the end of the second income year. The amount to be included as business income for the first income year is $300,000 (30% of $9,000,000 or $2,700,000 less expenditures of $2,400,000 equals $300,000). The amount to be included as business income for the second income year is $400,000 (50% of $9,000,000 or $4,500,000 less expenditures of $4,100,000 equals $400,000).

(iii) Completed Contract Method. Under this method of accounting business income derived from long-term contracts is reported for the income year in which the contract is finally completed and accepted. Therefore, a special computation is required to compute the amount of business income attributable to this state from each completed contract (see subdivision (5) of this regulation). Thus, all receipts and expenditures applicable to such contracts whether complete or incomplete as of the end of the income year are excluded from business income derived from other sources, as for example, short-term contracts, interest, rents, royalties, etc., which is apportioned by the regular three-factor formula of property, payroll and sales.

(iv) Property Factor. In general the numerator and denominator of the property factor shall be determined as set forth in Article IV.10 to .12, inclusive, and Reg. IV.10 to .12, inclusive. However, the following special rules are also applicable:

(A) The average value of the taxpayer's cost (including materials and labor) of construction in progress, to the extent such costs exceed progress billings (accrued or received depending on whether the taxpayer is on the accrual or cash basis for keeping its accounts) shall be included in the denominator of the property factor. The value of any such construction costs attributable to construction projects in this state shall be included in the numerator of the property factor.

Example 1: Taxpayer commenced a long-term construction project in this state as of the beginning of a given year. By the end of its second year, its equity in the costs of production to be reflected in the numerator and denominator of its property factor for such year is computed as follows:

	1st Year		2nd Year	
	Beginning	Ending	Beginning	Ending
Construction Costs . . .	0	$1,000,000		
Progress billings		600,000		
Balance 12/31—(1/1)		$ 400,000	$ 400,000	

Construction Costs—Total from beginning of project	$5,000,000
Progress billings—Total from beginning of project	4,000,000
Balance 12/31	1,000,000
Balance beginning of year	400,000
Total	$1,400,000
Average (1/2)—Value used in property factor	$ 700,000

Note: It may be necessary to use monthly averages if yearly averages do not properly reflect the average value of the taxpayer's equity; see Article IV.12 and Reg. IV.12.

Example 2: Same facts as in Example 1, except that progress billings exceeded construction costs. No value for the taxpayer's equity in the construction project is shown in the property factor.

(B) Rent paid for the use of equipment directly attributable to a particular construction project is included in the property factor at eight times the net annual rental rate even though such rental expense may be capitalized into the cost of construction.

(C) The property factor is computed in the same manner for all long-term contract methods of accounting and is computed for each income year even though under the completed contract method of accounting, business income is computed separately (see paragraph (5) below).

(v) Payroll Factor. In general the numerator and denominator of the payroll factor shall be determined as set forth in Article IV.13 and .14 and Reg. IV.13 and .14. However, the following special rules are also applicable:

(A) Compensation paid employees which is attributable to a particular construction project is included in the payroll factor even though capitalized into the cost of construction.

(B) Compensation paid employees who in the aggregate perform most of their services in a state to which their employer does not report them for unemployment tax purposes, shall nevertheless be attributed to the state in which the services are performed.

Example: A taxpayer engaged in a long-term contract in state X sends several key employees to that state to supervise the project. The taxpayer, for unemployment tax purposes, reports these employees to state Y where the main office is maintained and where the employees reside. For payroll factor purposes and in accordance with Article IV.14 and Reg. IV.14 thereunder, the compensation is assigned to the numerator of state X.

(C) The payroll factor is computed in the same manner for all long-term contract methods of accounting and is computed for each income year even though, under the completed contract method of accounting, business income is computed separately (see paragraph (5) below).

(vi) Sales Factor. In general the numerator and denominator of the sales factor shall be determined as set forth in Article IV.15—.17, inclusive, and Reg. IV.15—.17, inclusive. However, the following special rules are also applicable:

(A) Gross receipts derived from the performance of a contract are attributable to this state if the construction project is located in this state. If the construction project is located partly within and partly without this state, the gross receipts attributable to this state are based upon the ratio which construction costs for the project in this state incurred during the income year bear to the total of construction costs for the entire project during the income year, or upon any other method, such as engineering cost estimates, which will provide a reasonable apportionment.

Example 1: A construction project was undertaken in this state by a calendar year taxpayer which had elected one of the long-term contract methods of accounting. The following gross receipts (progress billings) were derived from the contract during the three income years that the contract was in progress.

	1st Year	2nd Year	3rd Year
Gross Receipts	$1,000,000	$4,000,000	$3,000,000

The gross receipts to be reflected in both the numerator and denominator of the sales factor for each of the three years are the amounts shown.

Example 2: A taxpayer contracts to build a dam on a river at a point which lies half within this state and half within state X. During the taxpayer's first income year construction costs in this state were $2,000,000. Total construction costs for the project during the income year were $3,000,000. Gross receipts (progress billings) for the year were $2,400,000. Accordingly, gross receipts of $1,600,000 ($2,000,000/3,000,000 × $2,400,000) are included in the numerator of the sales factor.

(B) If the percentage of completion method is used, the sales factor includes only that portion of the gross contract price which corresponds to the percentage of the entire contract which was completed during the income year.

Example: A taxpayer which had elected the percentage of completion method of accounting entered into a long-term construction contract. At the end of its current income year (the second since starting the project) it estimated that the project was 30% completed. The bid price for the project was $9,000,000 and it had received $2,500,000 from progress billings as of the end of its current income year. The amount of gross receipts to be included in the sales factor for the current income year is $2,700,000 (30% of $9,000,000), regardless of whether the taxpayer uses the accrual method or the cash method of accounting for receipts and disbursements.

(C) If the completed contract method of accounting is used, the sales factor includes the portion of the gross receipts (progress billings) received or accrued, whichever is applicable, during the income year attributable to each contract.

Example 1: A taxpayer which had elected the completed contract method of accounting entered into a long-term construction contract. By the end of its current income year (the second since starting the project), it had billed, and had accrued on its books a total of $5,000,000 of which $2,000,000 had accrued in the first year in which the contract was undertaken and $3,000,000 had accrued in the current (second) year. The amount of gross receipts to be included in the sales factor for the current income year is $3,000,000.

Example 2: Same facts as in example 1 except the taxpayer keeps its books on the cash basis and, as of the end of its current income year, had received only $2,500,000 of the $3,000,000 billed during the current year. The amount of gross receipts to be included in the sales factor for the current income year is $2,500,000.

(D) The sales factor, except as noted above in subparagraphs (B) and (C), is computed in the same manner, regardless of which long-term method of accounting the taxpayer has elected, and is computed for each income year even though, under the completed contract method of accounting, business income is computed separately.

(vii) Apportionment Percentage. The total of the property, payroll and sales percentages is divided by three to determine the apportionment percentage. The apportionment percentage is then applied to business income to establish the amount apportioned to this state.

(5) Completed Contract Method—Special Computation. The completed contract method of accounting requires that the reporting of income (or loss) be deferred until the year in which the construction project is completed or accepted. Accordingly, a separate computation is made for each such contract completed during the income year, regardless of whether the project is located within or without this state, in order to determine the amount of income which is attributable to sources within this state. The amount of income from each contract completed during the income year apportioned to this state, plus other business income apportioned to this state by the regular three-factor formula such as interest income, rents, royalties, income from short-term contracts, etc., plus all nonbusiness income allocated to this state is the measure of tax for the income year.

The amount of income (or loss) from each contract which is derived from sources within this state using the completed contract method of accounting is computed as follows:

(i) In the income year the contract is completed, the income (or loss) therefrom is determined.

(ii) The income (or loss) determined at (i) above is apportioned to this state by the following method:

(A) A fraction is determined for each year during which the contract was in progress. The numerator is the amount of construction costs paid or accrued in each year during which the contract was in progress and the denominator is the total of all such construction costs for the project.

(B) Each percentage determined in (A) is multiplied by the apportionment formula percentage for that particular year as determined in subparagraph (4)(vii) of this regulation above.

(C) The percentages determined at (B) for each year during which the contract was in progress are totaled. The amount of total income (or loss) from the contract determined at subparagraph (5)(i) of this regulation is multiplied by the total percentage. The resulting income (or loss) is the amount of business income from such contract derived from sources within this state.

Example 1: A taxpayer using the completed contract method of accounting for long-term contracts is engaged in three long-term contracts; Contract L in this state, Contract M in state X and Contract N in state Y. In addition, it has other business income (less expenses) during the income year 1972 from interest, rents and short-term contracts amounting to $500,000, and nonbusiness income allocable to this state of $8,000. During 1972 it completed Contract M in state X at a profit of $900,000. Contracts L and N in this state and state Y, respectively, were not completed during the income year. The apportionment percentages of the taxpayer as determined in subparagraph (4)(vii) of this regulation and the percentages of contract costs as determined in subparagraph (5)(ii) above for each year during which Contract M in state X was in progress are as follows:

	1970	1971	1972
Apportionment percentage	30%	20%	40%
Percentages of construction costs of Contract M each year to total construction costs—(100%)	20%	50%	30%

The corporation's net income subject to tax in this state for 1972 is computed as follows:

Business Income	$500,000
Apportion 40% to this state	$200,000
Add: Income from Contract M *	$252,000
Total business income derived from sources within this state	452,000
Add: Nonbusiness income allocated to this state	8,000
Net income subject to tax	$460,000

* Income from Contract M apportioned to this state:

	1970	1971	1972	Total
Apportionment percentage	30%	20%	40%	
Percent of Construction Costs	20%	50%	30%	100%
Product	6%	10%	12%	28%

28% of $900,000 = $252,000

Example 2: Same facts as in Example 1 except that Contract L was started in 1972 in this state, the first year in which the taxpayer was subject to tax in this state. Contract L in this state and Contract N in state Y are incomplete in 1972.

The corporation's net income subject to tax in this state for 1972 is computed as follows:

Business income	$500,000
Apportion 40% to this state	$200,000
Add: Income from Contract M *	108,000
Total business income derived from sources within this state	$308,000
Add: Nonbusiness income allocated to this state	8,000
Net income subject to tax	$316,000

* Income from Contract M apportioned to this state:

	1970	1971	1972	Total
Apportionment percentage	0	0	40%	
Percent of Construction Costs	20%	50%	30%	100%
Product	0	0	12%	12%

12% of $900,000 = $108,000

Note: Only 12% is used to determine the income derived from sources within this state since the corporation was not subject to tax in this state prior to 1972.

Example 3: Same facts as in example 1 except that the figures relate to Contract L in this state and 1972 is the first year the corporation was taxable in another state (see Article IV.2 and .3 and Reg. IV.2(b)(1) and .3. Contracts M and N in states X and Y were started in 1972 and are incomplete.

The corporation's net income subject to tax in this state for 1972 is computed as follows:

Business income	$500,000
Apportion 40% to this state	$200,000
Add: Income from Contract L *	738,000
Total business income derived from sources within this state	$938,000
Add: Nonbusiness income allocated to this state	8,000
Net income subject to tax	$946,000

* Income from Contract L apportioned to this state:

	1970	1971	1972	Total
Apportionment percentage	100%	100%	40%	
Percentage of Construction Costs	20%	50%	30%	100%
Product	20%	50%	12%	82%

82% of $900,000 = $738,000

(6) Computation for Year of Withdrawal, Dissolution or Cessation of Business—Completed Contract Method. Use of the completed contract method of accounting for long-term contracts requires that income derived from sources within this state from incomplete contracts in progress outside this state on the date of withdrawal, dissolution or cessation of business in this state be included in the measure of tax for the taxable year during which the corporation withdraws, dissolves or ceases doing business in this state.

The amount of income (or loss) from each such contract to be apportioned to this state by the apportionment method set forth in subparagraph (5)(ii) of this regulation shall be determined as if the percentage of completion method of accounting were used for all such contracts on the date of withdrawal, dissolution or cessation of business. The amount of business income (or loss) for each such contract shall be the amount by which the gross contract price from each such contract which corresponds to the percentage of the entire contract which has been completed from the commencement thereof to the date of withdrawal, dissolution or cessation of business exceeds all expenditures made during such period in connection with each such contract. In so doing, account must be taken of the material and supplies on hand at the beginning and end of the income year for use in each such contract.

Example: A construction contractor qualified to do business in this state had elected the completed contract method of accounting for long-term contracts. It was engaged in two long-term contracts; Contract L in this state was started in 1971 and completed at a profit of $900,000 on 12/16/73. The taxpayer withdrew on 12/31/73. Contract M in state X was started in 1972 and was incomplete on 12/31/73. The apportionment percentages of the taxpayer as determined at subdivision (4) of this regulation, and percentages of construction costs as determined in subparagraph (5)(ii) of this regulation for each year during which Contract M in state X was in progress are as follows:

	1971	1972	1973	Total
Apportionment percentage	30%	20%	40%	
Percentage of Construction Costs:				
Contract L, this state	20%	50%	30%	100%
Contract M, state X	0	10%	25%	35%

The corporation had other business income (net of expenses) of $500,000 during 1972 and $300,000 during 1973. The gross contract price of Contract M (state X) was $1,000,000 and it was estimated to be 35% completed on 12/31/73. Total expenditures to date for Contract M (state X) were $300,000 for the period ended 12/31/73.

The measure of tax for the taxable year ended 12/31/73 is computed as follows:

	Taxable Year 1973	
	Income Year 1972	Income Year 1973
Business income	$500,000	$300,000
Apportionment percentage to this state	20%	40%
Amount apportioned to this state	$100,000	$120,000
Add: Income from contracts:		
L * (this state)		$252,000
M ** (state X)		$ 6,000
Total business income derived from sources within this state	$100,000	$378,000

* Income from Contract L apportioned to this state:

	1971	1972	1973	Total
Apportionment percentage	30%	20%	40%	
Percentage of construction costs	20%	50%	30%	100%
Product	6%	10%	12%	28%

28% of $900,000 = $252,000

** Income from Contract M apportioned to this state:

	1971	1972	1973	Total
Apportionment percentage	0	20%	40%	
Percentage of Construction Costs	0	10%	25%	35%
Product	0	2%	10%	12%

12% of $50,000*** = $6,000

*** Computation of apportionable income from Contract M based on percentage of completion method:

Total Contract Price	$1,000,000
Estimated to be 35% completed	$ 350,000
Less: total expenditures to date	300,000
Apportionable income	$ 50,000

Reg. IV.18.(e). Special Rules: Airlines.

[*Adopted July 14, 1983.*]

The following special rules are established in respect to airlines:

(1) In General. Where an airline has income from sources both within and without this state, the amount of business income from sources within this state shall be determined pursuant to IV. of the Multistate Tax Commission except as modified by this regulation.

(2) Apportionment of Business Income.

(i) General Definitions. The following definitions are applicable to the terms used in the apportionment factor descriptions.

A. "Value" of owned real and tangible personal property shall mean its original cost. (See Article IV.11. and Regulation IV.11(a).)

B. "Cost of aircraft by type" means the average original cost or value of aircraft by type which are ready for flight.

C. "Original cost" means the initial federal tax basis of the property plus the value of capital improvements to such property, except that, for this purpose, it shall be assumed that Safe Harbor Leases are not true leases and do not affect the original initial federal tax basis of the property. (See Regulation IV.11(a).)

D. "Average value" of property means the amount determined by averaging the values at the beginning and ending of the income year, but the (insert here the appropriate title of the administrative agency) may require the averaging of monthly values during the income year if such averaging is necessary to reflect properly the average value of the airline's property. (See Article IV.12. and Regulation IV.12.)

E. The "value" of rented real and tangible personal property means the product of eight (8) times the net annual rental rate. (See Article IV.11. and Regulation IV.11(b).)

F. "Net annual rental rate" means the annual rental rate paid by the taxpayer.

G. "Property used during the income year" includes property which is available for use in the taxpayer's trade or business during the income year.

H. "Aircraft ready for flight" means aircraft owned or acquired through rental or lease (but not interchange) which are in the possession of the taxpayer and are available for service on the taxpayer routes.

I. "Revenue service" means the use of aircraft ready for flight for the production of revenue.

J. "Transportation revenue" means revenue earned by transporting passengers, freight and mail as well as revenue earned from liquor sales, pet crate rentals, etc.

K. "Departures" means for purposes of these regulations all takeoffs, whether they be regularly scheduled or charter flights, that occur during revenue service.

(ii) Property Factor.

A. Property valuation. Owned aircraft shall be valued at its original cost and rented aircraft shall be valued at eight (8) times the net annual rental rate in accordance with Article IV.11. and Regulation IV.11. The use of the taxpayer's owned or rented aircraft in an interchange program with another air carrier will not constitute a rental of such aircraft by the airline to the other participating airline. Such aircraft shall be accounted for in the property factor of the owner. Parts and other expendables, including parts for use in contract overhaul work, will be valued at cost.

B. The denominator and numerator of the property factor. The denominator of the property factor shall be the average value of all of the taxpayer's real and tangible personal property owned or rented and used during the income year. The numerator of the property factor shall be the average value of the taxpayer's real and tangible personal property owned or rented and used in this state during the income year.

In determining the numerator of the property factor, all property except aircraft ready for flight shall be included in the numerator of the property factor in accordance with Article IV.10.-.12, inclusive. Aircraft ready for flight shall be included in the numerator of the property factor in the ratio calculated as follows:

Departures of aircraft from locations in this state weighted as to the cost and value of aircraft by type compared to total departures similarly weighted.

(iii) The Payroll Factor.

The denominator of the payroll factor is the total compensation paid everywhere by the taxpayer during the income year. (See Article IV.13.-.14) The numerator of the payroll factor is the total amount paid in this state during the income year by the taxpayer for compensation. With respect to non-flight personnel, compensation paid to such employees shall be included in the numerator as provided in Article IV.13.-.14. With respect to flight personnel (the air crew aboard an aircraft assisting in the operations of the aircraft or the welfare of passengers while in the air), compensation paid to such employees shall be included in the ratio of departures of aircraft from locations in this state, weighted as to the cost and value of aircraft by type compared to total departures similarly weighted, multiplied by the total flight personnel compensation.

(iv) Sales (Transportation Revenue) Factor.

The transportation revenue derived from transactions and activities in the regular course of the trade or business of the taxpayer and miscellaneous sales of merchandise, etc., are included in the denominator of the revenue factor. (See Article IV.1. and Regulation IV.1) Passive income items such as interest, rental income, dividends, etc., will not be included in the denominator nor will the proceeds or net gains or losses from the sale of aircraft be included. The numerator of the revenue factor is the total revenue of the taxpayer in this state during the income year. The total revenue of the taxpayer in this state during the income year is the result of the following calculation:

The ratio of departures of aircraft in this state weighted as to the cost and value of aircraft by type, as compared to total departures similarly weighted multiplied by the total transportation revenue. The product of this calculation is to be added to any non-flight revenues directly attributable to this state.

(3) Records. The taxpayer must maintain the records necessary to arrive at departures by type of aircraft as used in these regulations. Such records are to be subject to review by the respective state taxing authorities or their agents.

EXAMPLES OF THE MANNER IN WHICH THE MULTISTATE TAX COMMISSION AIRLINE REGULATION WOULD APPLY TO SPECIFIC FACT SITUATIONS

Example 1: Assume the following facts for an airline for A tax year:

1. It has ten 747s ready for flight and in revenue service at an average cost per unit of $40,000,000 for nine of the aircraft. It

rents the tenth 747 from another airline for $9,000,000 per year. At eight times rents, the latter is valued at $72,000,000 for apportionment purposes. The total 747 valuation is, therefore, $432,000,000 for property factor denominator purposes.

2. It has twenty 727s ready for flight in revenue service at an average cost per unit of $20,000,000. The total 727 valuation is, therefore, $400,000,000 for property factor denominator purposes.

3. It has nonflight tangible property (n.t.p.) valued at an original cost of $200,000,000.

4. It has the following annual payroll:

Flight personnel	$ 60,000,000
Nonflight personnel	40,000,000
Total	$100,000,000

5. From its operations, it has total receipts of $50,000,000, business net income of $1,000,000 and no nonbusiness income.

6. It has the following within State X:

a. 10% of its 747 flight departures (.10 × $432,000,000) $432,000,000

b. 20% of its 727 flight departures (.20 × $400,000,000) $80,000,000

c. 5% of its nonflight tangible property (n.t.p.) (.05 × $200,000,000) $10,000,000

d. 15% of its nonflight personnel (n.p.) payroll (.15 × $40,000,000) $6,000,000

7. State X has a corporate tax rate of 10%.

The airline's tax liability to State X would be determined as follows:

Property Factor:

$$\frac{43{,}200{,}000\ (747s) + 80{,}000{,}000\ (727s) + 10{,}000{,}000\ (n.t.p.)}{432{,}000{,}000\ (747s) + 400{,}000{,}000\ (727s) + 200{,}000{,}000\ (n.t.p.)} = \frac{133{,}200{,}000}{1{,}032{,}000{,}000} = .1291$$

Sales Factor:

$$\frac{43{,}200{,}000\ (747s) + 80{,}000{,}000\ (727s)}{432{,}000{,}000\ (747s) + 400{,}000{,}000\ (727s)} = \frac{123{,}200{,}000}{832{,}000{,}000} = .1481$$

Payroll Factor:

$$\frac{6{,}000{,}000\ (nonflight) + 8{,}880{,}000\ (.148 \times 60{,}000{,}000)\ (flight)}{100{,}000{,}000} = \frac{14{,}880{,}000}{100{,}000{,}000} = .1488$$

Average ratio: =

$$\frac{.1291 + .1481 + .1488}{3} = \frac{.4260}{3} = .1420$$

Taxable Income in State X: .1420 × $1,000,000 = $142,000

Tax Liability to State X: .10 × $142,000 = $14,200

Example 2: Same facts except that paragraphs 6 and 7 are changed to read:

6. It has the following within State Y:

a. 6% of its 747 flight departures (.6 × $432,000,000) $25,920,000

b. 31% of its 727 flight departures (.31 × $400,000,000) $124,000,000

c. 3% of its nonflight tangible property (.03 × $200,000,000) $6,000,000

d. 7% of its nonflight personnel payroll (.07 × $40,000,000) $2,800,000

7. State Y has a corporate tax rate of 6.5%.

The airline's tax liability to State Y would be determined as follows:

Property Factor:

$$\frac{25{,}920{,}000\ (747s) + 124{,}000{,}000\ (727s) + 6{,}000{,}000\ (n.t.p.)}{432{,}000{,}000\ (747s) + 400{,}000{,}000\ (727s) + 200{,}000{,}000\ (n.t.p.)} = \frac{155{,}920{,}000}{1{,}032{,}000{,}000} = .1511$$

Sales Factor:

$$\frac{25{,}920{,}000\ (747s) + 124{,}000{,}000\ (727s)}{432{,}000{,}000\ (747s) + 400{,}000{,}000\ (727s)} = \frac{149{,}920{,}000}{832{,}000{,}000} = .1802$$

Payroll Factor:

$$\frac{2{,}800{,}000\ (n.p.) + 10{,}812{,}000\ (.1802 \times 60{,}000{,}000)\ (flight)}{40{,}000{,}000 + 60{,}000{,}000} = \frac{13{,}612{,}000}{100{,}000{,}000} = .1361$$

Average Ratio

$$\frac{.1511 + .1802 + .1361}{3} = \frac{.4674}{3} = .1558$$

Taxable Income in State Y: .1558 × $1,000,000 = $155,800

Tax Liability to State Y: .065 × $155,800 = $10,127

Reg. IV.18.(f). Special Rules: Railroads.

[*Adopted July 16, 1981.*]

The following special rules are established in respect to railroads:

(1) In General. Where a railroad has income from sources both within and without this state, the amount of business income from sources within this state shall be determined pursuant to this regulation. In such cases, the first step is to determine what portion of the railroad's income constitutes "business" income and which portion constitutes "nonbusiness" income under Article IV.1 and Regulation

IV.1 thereunder. Nonbusiness income is directly allocable to specific states pursuant to the provisions of Article IV.5 to .8, inclusive. Business income is apportioned among the states in which the business is conducted pursuant to the property, payroll and sales apportionment factors set forth in this regulation. The sum of (1) the items of nonbusiness income directly allocated to this State, plus (2) the amount of business income attributable to this state constitutes the amount of the taxpayer's entire net income which is subject to tax by this state.

(2) Business and Nonbusiness Income. For definitions, rules and examples for determining business and nonbusiness income, see Reg. IV.1.

(3) Apportionment of Business Income.

(i) In General. The property factor shall be determined in accordance with Reg. IV.10.-.12., inclusive, the payroll factor in accordance with Reg. IV.13., and the sales factor in accordance with Reg. IV.14.-.17, inclusive, except as modified in this regulation.

(ii) The Property Factor.

A. Property Valuation. Owned property shall be valued at its original cost and property rented from others shall be valued at eight (8) times the net annual rental rate in accordance with Article IV.11. and Reg. IV.11. Railroad cars owned and operated by other railroads and temporarily used by the taxpayer in its business and for which a per diem or mileage charge is made are not included in the property factor as rented property. Railroad cars owned and operated by the taxpayer and temporarily used by other railroads in their business and for which a per diem charge is made by the taxpayer are included in the property factor of the taxpayer.

B. General Definitions. The following definitions are applicable to the numerator and denominator of the property factor:

1. "Original cost" is deemed to be the basis of the property for federal income tax purposes (prior to any federal income tax adjustments except for subsequent capital additions, improvements thereto or partial dispositions); or, if the property has no such basis, the valuation of such property for Interstate Commerce Commission purposes. If the original cost of property is unascertainable under the foregoing valuation of standards, the property is included in the property factor at its fair market value as of the date of acquisition by the taxpayer (Reg. IV.11.(a)).

2. "Rent" does not include the per diem and mileage charges paid by the taxpayer for the temporary use of railroad cars owned or operated by another railroad.

3. The "value" of owned real and tangible personal property shall mean its original cost. (See Article IV.11 and Reg. IV.11(a)).

4. "Average value" of property means the amount determined by averaging the values at the beginning and ending of the income tax year, but the (insert here the appropriate title of the administrative agency) may require the averaging of monthly values during the income year or such averaging as necessary to effect properly the average value of the railroad's property. (See Article IV.12. and Reg. IV.12.).

5. The "value" of rented real and tangible personal property means the product of eight (8) times the net annual rental rate. (See Art. IV.11. and Reg. IV.11.(b)).

6. "Net annual rental rate" means the annual rental rate paid by the taxpayer less any annual rental rate received by the taxpayer from subrentals.

7. "Property used during the income year" includes property which is available for use in the taxpayer's trade or business during the income year.

8. A "locomotive mile" is the movement of a locomotive (a self-propelled unit of equipment designed solely for moving other equipment) a distance of one mile under its own power.

9. A "car-mile" is a movement of a unit of car equipment a distance of one mile.

C. The Denominator and Numerator of the Property Factor. The denominator of the property factor shall be the average value of all of the taxpayer's real and tangible personal property owned or rented and used during the income year. The numerator of the property factor shall be the average value of the taxpayer's real and tangible personal property owned or rented and used in this state during the income year.

In determining the numerator of the property factor, all property except mobile or movable property such as passenger cars, freight cars, locomotives and freight containers which are located within and without this state during the income year shall be included in the numerator of the property factor in accordance with Article IV.10.-.12., inclusive, and Regulation IV.10.-.12, inclusive.

Mobile or movable property such as passenger cars, freight cars, locomotives and freight containers which are located within and without this state during the income year shall be included in the numerator of the property factor in the ratio which "locomotive-miles" and "car-miles" in the state bear to the total everywhere.

(iii) The Payroll Factor. The denominator of the payroll factor is the total compensation paid everywhere by the taxpayer during the income year for the production of business income. (See Article IV.13.-14. and Reg. IV.13.-.14). The numerator of the payroll factor is the total amount paid in this state during the income year by the taxpayer for compensation. With respect to all personnel except enginemen and trainmen performing services on interstate trains, compensation paid to such employees shall be included in the numerator as provided in Article IV.13.-.14 and Reg. IV.13.-.14.

With respect to enginemen and trainmen performing services on interstate trains, compensation paid to such employees shall be included in the numerator of the payroll factor in the ratio which their services performed in this state bear to their services performed everywhere. Compensation for services performed in this state shall be deemed to be the compensation reported or required to be reported by such employees for determination of their income tax liability to this state.

(iv) The Sales (Revenue) Factor.

A. In General. All revenue derived from transactions and activities in the regular course of the trade or business of the taxpayer which produces business income, except per diem and mileage charges which are collected by the taxpayer, is included in the denominator of the revenue factor. (See Art. IV.1. and Reg. IV.1.)

The numerator of the revenue factor is the total revenue of the taxpayer in this state during the income year. The total revenue of the taxpayer in this state during the income year, other than revenue from hauling freight, passengers, mail and express, shall be attributable to this state in accordance with Article IV.15.-.17. and Regulation IV.15.-.17.

B. Numerator of Sales (Revenue) Factor From Freight, Mail and Express. The total revenue of the taxpayer in this state during the income year for the numerator of the revenue factor from hauling freight, mail and express shall be attributable to this state as follows:

1. All receipts from shipments which both originate and terminate within this state; and

2. That portion of the receipts from each movement or shipment passing through, into, or out of this state is determined by the ratio which the miles traveled by such movement or shipment in this state bears to the total miles traveled by such movement or shipment from point of origin to destination.

C. Numerator of Sales (Revenue) Factor from Passengers. The numerator of the sales (revenue) factor shall include:

1. All receipts from the transportation of passengers (including mail and express handled in passenger service) which both originate and terminate within this state; and

2. That portion of the receipts from the transportation of interstate passengers (including mail and express handled in passenger service) determined by the ratio which revenue passenger miles in this state bear to the total everywhere.

Reg. IV.18.(g). Special Rules: Trucking Companies.

[*Adopted July 11, 1986; amended July 27, 1989.*]

The following special rules are established with respect to trucking companies:

(1) In General. As used in this regulation, the term "trucking company" means a motor common carrier, a motor contract carrier, or an express carrier which primarily transports tangible personal property of others by motor vehicle for compensation. Where a trucking company has income from sources both within and without this state, the amount of business income from sources within this state shall be determined pursuant to this regulation. In such cases, the first step is to determine what portion of the trucking company's income constitutes "business" income and what portion constitutes "nonbusiness" income under Article IV.1 of the Multistate Tax Compact and Regulation IV.1 thereunder. Nonbusiness income is directly allocable to specific states pursuant to the provisions of Article IV.5 to .8, inclusive. Business income is apportioned among the states in which the business is conducted and pursuant to the property, payroll, and sales apportionment factors set forth in this regulation. The sum of (i) the items of nonbusiness income directly allocated to this state and (ii) the amount of business income attributable to this state constitutes the amount of the taxpayer's entire net income which is subject to tax in this state.

(2) Business and Nonbusiness Income. For definitions, rules, and examples for determining business and nonbusiness income, see Regulation IV.1.

(3) Apportionment of Business Income.

(i) In General. The property factor shall be determined in accordance with Regulation IV.10 to .12, inclusive, the payroll factor in accordance with Regulation IV.13 to .14, and the sales factor in accordance with Regulation IV.15 to .17, inclusive, except as modified by this regulation.

(ii) The Property Factor.

A. Property Valuation. Owned property shall be valued at its original cost and property rented from others shall be valued at eight (8) times the net annual rental rate in accordance with Article IV.11 and Regulation IV.11.

B. General Definitions. The following definitions are applicable to the numerator and denominator of the property factor, as well as other apportionment factor descriptions:

1. "Average value" of property means the amount determined by averaging the values at the beginning and end of the income tax year, but the (insert here the title of the appropriate administrative agency) may require the averaging of monthly values during the income year or such averaging as is necessary to reflect properly the average value of the trucking company's property. (See Article IV.12 and Regulation IV.12.)

2. "Mobile property" means all motor vehicles, including trailers, engaged directly in the movement of tangible personal property.

3. A "mobile property mile" is the movement of a unit of mobile property a distance of one mile whether loaded or unloaded.

4. "Original cost" is deemed to be the basis of the property for federal income tax purposes (prior to any federal income tax adjustments, except for subsequent capital additions, improvements thereto, or partial dispositions); or, if the property has no such basis, the valuation of such property for Interstate Commerce Commission purposes. If the original cost of property is unascertainable under the foregoing valuation standards, the property is included in the property factor at its fair market value as of the date of acquisition by the taxpayer. (Regulation IV.11.(a).)

5. "Property used during the course of the income year" includes property which is available for use in the taxpayer's trade or business during the income year.

6. The "value" of owned real and tangible personal property means its original cost. (See Article IV.11 and Regulation IV.11.(a).)

7. The "value" of rented real and tangible personal property means the product of eight (8) times the net annual rental rate. (See Article IV.11 and Regulation IV.11.(b).)

C. The Denominator and Numerator of the Property Factor. The denominator of the property factor shall be the average value of all of the taxpayer's real and tangible personal property owned or rented and used during the income year. The numerator of the property factor shall be the average value of the taxpayer's real and tangible personal property owned or rented and used in this state during the income year. In the determination of the numerator of the property factor, all property, except mobile property as defined in this regulation, shall be included in the numerator of the property factor in accordance with Article IV.10 to .12, inclusive, and Regulation IV.10 to .12, inclusive.

Mobile property as defined in this regulation, which is located solely within this state during the income year shall be included in the numerator of the property factor.

Mobile property, as defined in this regulation, which is located within and without this state during the income year shall be included in the numerator of the property factor in the ratio which mobile property miles in the state bear to the total mobile property miles.

(iii) The Payroll Factor. The denominator of the payroll factor is the compensation paid everywhere by the taxpayer during the income year for the production of business income. (See Article IV.13 and .14 and Regulation IV.13 and .14.) The numerator of the payroll factor is the total compensation paid in this state during the income year by the taxpayer. With respect to all personnel, except those performing services within and without this state, compensation paid to such employees shall be included in the numerator as provided in Article IV.13 and .14 and Regulation IV.13 and .14.

With respect to personnel performing services within and without this state, compensation paid to such employees shall be included in the numerator of the payroll factor in the ratio which their services performed in this state bear to their services performed everywhere based on mobile property miles.

(iv) The Sales (Revenue) Factor.

A. In General. All revenue derived from transactions and activities in the regular course of the taxpayer's trade or business which produce business income shall be included in the denominator of the revenue factor. (See Article IV.1 and Regulation IV.1.)

The numerator of the revenue factor is the total revenue of the taxpayer in this state during the income year. The total state revenue of the taxpayer, other than revenue from hauling freight, mail, and express, shall be attributable to this state in accordance with Article IV.15 through .17 and Regulation IV.15 through .17.

B. Numerator of the Sales (Revenue) Factor From Freight, Mail, and Express. The total revenue of the taxpayer attributable to this state during the income year from hauling freight, mail, and express shall be:

1. Intrastate: All receipts from any shipment which both originates and terminates within this state; and,

2. Interstate: That portion of the receipts from movements or shipments passing through, into, or out of this state as determined by the ratio which the mobile property miles traveled by such movements or shipments in this state bear to the total mobile property miles traveled by movements or shipments from points of origin to destination.

(4) Records. The taxpayer shall maintain the records necessary to identify mobile property and to enumerate by state the mobile property miles traveled by such mobile property as those terms are used in this regulation. Such records are subject to review by [insert here the title of the appropriate administrative agency] or its agents.

(5) De Minimis Nexus Standard. Notwithstanding any provision contained herein, this Regulation IV.18.(g) shall not apply to require the apportionment of income to this state if the trucking company during the course of the income tax year neither:

a. owns nor rents any real or personal property in this state, except mobile property; nor

b. makes any pick-ups or deliveries within this state; nor

c. travels more than twenty-five thousand mobile property miles within this state; provided that the total mobile property miles traveled within this state during the income tax year do not exceed three percent of the total mobile property miles traveled in all states by the trucking company during that period; nor

d. makes more than twelve trips into this state.

Reg. IV.18.(h). Special Rules: Television and Radio Broadcasting.

[*Adopted August 31, 1990; amended April 25, 1996.*]

The following special rules are established in respect to the apportionment of income from television and radio broadcasting by a broadcaster that is taxable both in this state and in one or more other states.

(1) In General. When a person in the business of broadcasting film or radio programming, whether through the public airwaves, by cable, direct or indirect satellite transmission or any other means of communication, either through a network (including owned and affiliated stations) or through an affiliated, unaffiliated or independent television or radio broadcasting station, has income from sources both within and without this state, the amount of business income from sources within this state shall be determined pursuant to Article IV. of the Multistate Tax Compact and the regulations issued thereunder by this state, except as modified by this regulation.

(2) Business and Nonbusiness Income. For definitions, regulations and examples for determining whether income shall be classified as "business" or "nonbusiness" income, see Reg. IV.1.

(3) Definitions. The following definitions are applicable to the terms contained in this regulation, unless the context clearly requires otherwise.

(i) "Film" or "film programming" means any and all performances, events or productions telecast on television, including but not limited to news, sporting events, plays, stories or other literary, commercial, educational or artistic works, through the use of video tape, disc or any other type of format or medium.

Each episode of a series of films produced for television shall constitute a separate "film" notwithstanding that the series relates to the same principal subject and is produced during one or more tax periods.

(ii) "Outer-jurisdictional" property means certain types of tangible personal property, such as orbiting satellites, undersea transmission cables and the like, that are owned or rented by the taxpayer and used in the business of telecasting or broadcasting, but which are not physically located in any particular state.

(iii) "Radio" or "radio programming" means any and all performances, events or productions broadcast on radio, including but not limited to news, sporting events, plays, stories or other literary, commercial, educational or artistic works, through the use of an audio tape, disc or any other format or medium.

Each episode of a series of radio programming produced for radio broadcast shall constitute a separate "radio programming" notwithstanding that the series relates to the same principal subject and is produced during one or more tax periods.

(iv) "Release" or "in release" means the placing of film or radio programming into service. A film or radio program is placed into service when it is first broadcast to the primary audience for which the program was created. Thus, for example, a film is placed in service when it is first publicly telecast for entertainment, educational, commercial, artistic or other purpose. Each episode of a television or radio series is placed in service when it is first broadcast. A program is not placed in service merely because it is completed and therefore in a condition or state of readiness and availability for broadcast or, merely because it is previewed to prospective sponsors or purchasers.

(v) "Rent" shall include license fees or other payments or consideration provided in exchange for the broadcast or other use of television or radio programming.

(vi) A "subscriber" to a cable television system is the individual residence or other outlet which is the ultimate recipient of the transmission.

(vii) "Telecast" or "broadcast" (sometimes used interchangeably with respect to television) means the transmission of television or radio programming, respectively, by an electronic or other signal conducted by radiowaves or microwaves or by wires, lines, coaxial cables, wave guides, fiber optics, satellite transmissions directly or indirectly to viewers and listeners or by any other means of communications.

(4) Apportionment of Business Income.

(i) In General. The property factor shall be determined in accordance with Regulation IV.10. through 12., the payroll factor in accordance with Regulation IV.13. and 14., and the sales factor in accordance with Regulation IV.15. and 16., except as modified by this regulation.

(ii) The Property Factor.

A. In General.

1. In the case of rented studios, the net annual rental rate shall include only the amount of the basic or flat rental charge by the studio for the use of a stage or other permanent equipment such as sound recording equipment and the like; except that additional equipment rented from other sources or from the studio not covered in the basic or flat rental charge and used for one week or longer (even though rented on a day-to-day basis) shall be included. Lump-sum net rental payments for a period which encompasses more than a single income year shall be assigned ratably over the rental period.

2. No value or cost attributable to any outer-jurisdictional, film or radio programming property shall be included in the property factor at any time.

B. Property Factor Denominator.

1. All real property and tangible personal property (other than outer-jurisdictional and film or radio programming property), whether owned or rented, which is used in the business shall be included in the denominator of the property factor.

2. Audio or video cassettes, discs or similar medium containing film or radio programming and intended for sale or rental by the taxpayer for home viewing or listening shall be included in the property factor at

their original cost. To the extent that the taxpayer licenses or otherwise permits others to manufacture or distribute such cassettes, discs or other medium containing film or radio programming for home viewing or listening, the value of said cassettes, discs or other medium shall include the license, royalty or other fees received by the taxpayer capitalized at a rate of eight times the gross receipts derived therefrom during the income year.

3. Outer-jurisdictional, film and radio programming property shall be excluded from the denominator of the property factor.

C. Property Factor Numerator.

1. With the exception of outer-jurisdictional, film and radio programming property, all real and tangible personal property owned or rented by the taxpayer and used in this state during the tax period shall be included in the numerator of the property factor as provided in Regulation IV.10.(d).

2. Outer-jurisdictional, film and radio programming property shall be excluded from the numerator of the property factor.

Example: XYZ Television Co. has a total value of all of its property everywhere of $500,000,000, including a satellite valued at $50,000,000 that was used to telecast programming into this state and $150,000,000 in film property of which $1,000,000's worth was located in this state the entire tax year. The total value of real and tangible personal property, other than film programming property, located in this state for the entire income year was valued at $2,000,000; and the moveable and mobile property described in subparagraph C.1. was determined to be of a value of $4,000,000 and such moveable and mobile property was used in this state for 100 days. The total value of property to be attributed to this state would be determined as follows:

Value of property permanently in state:	$ 2,000,000
Value of mobile and moveable property (100/365 or .2739 × $4,000,000):	$ 1,095,600
Total value of property to be included in the state's property factor numerator (outer-jurisdictional and film property excluded):	$ 3,095,600
Total value of property to be used in the denominator ($500,000,000 – $200,000,000):	$300,000,000
Total property factor: ($3,095,600/$300,000,000):	.0103

(iii) The Payroll Factor.

A. Payroll Factor Denominator.

The denominator of the payroll factor shall include all compensation, including residual and profit participation payments, paid to employees during the income year, including that paid to directors, actors, newscasters and other talent in their status as employees.

B. Payroll Factor Numerator.

Compensation for all employees shall be attributed to the state or states as may be determined by the application of the provisions of Reg. IV.13. and 14.

(iv) The Sales Factor.

A. Sales Factor Denominator.

The denominator of the sales factor shall include the total gross receipts derived by the taxpayer from transactions and activity in the regular course of its trade or business, except receipts excluded under Reg. IV.18.(c).

B. Sales Factor Numerator.

The numerator of the sales factor shall include all gross receipts of the taxpayer from sources within this state, including, but not limited to the following:

1. Gross receipts, including advertising revenue, from television film or radio programming in release to or by television and radio stations located in this state.

2. Gross receipts, including advertising revenue, from television film or radio programming in release to or by a television or radio station (independent or unaffiliated) or network of stations for broadcast shall be attributed to this state in the ratio (hereafter "audience factor") that the audience for such station (or owned and affiliated stations in the case of networks) located in this state bears to the total audience for such station (or owned and affiliated stations in the case of networks).

The audience factor for television or radio programming shall be determined by the ratio that the taxpayer's in-state viewing (listening) audience bears to its total viewing (listening) audience. Such audience factor shall be determined either by reference to the books and records of the taxpayer or by reference to published rating statistics, provided the method used by the taxpayer is consistently used from year to year for such purpose and fairly represents the taxpayer's activity in the state.

3. Gross receipts from film programming in release to or by a cable television system shall be attributed to this state in the ratio (hereafter "audience factor") that the subscribers for such cable television system located in this state bears to the total subscribers of such cable television system. If the number of subscribers cannot be accurately determined from the books and records maintained by the taxpayer, such audience factor ratio shall be determined on the basis of the applicable year's subscription statistics located in published surveys, provided that the source selected is consistently used from year to year for that purpose.

4. Receipts from the sale, rental, licensing or other disposition of audio or video cassettes, discs, or similar medium intended for home viewing or listening shall be included in the sales factor as provided in Reg. IV.16.

Reg. IV.18.(i). Special Rules: [Reserved].

Reg. IV.18.(j). Special Rules: Publishing.

[*Adopted July 30, 1993.*]

The following special rules are established with respect to the apportionment of income derived from the publishing, sale, licensing or other distribution of books, newspapers, magazines, periodicals, trade journals or other printed material.

(1) In General. Except as specifically modified by this regulation, when a person in the business of publishing, selling, licensing or distributing newspapers, magazines, periodicals, trade journals or other printed material has income from sources both within and without this state, the amount of business income from sources within this state from such business activity shall be determined pursuant to [Article IV. of the Multistate Tax Compact and the regulations adopted thereunder].

(2) Definitions. The following definitions are applicable to the terms contained in this regulation, unless the context clearly requires otherwise.

(i) "Outer-jurisdictional property" means certain types of tangible personal property, such as orbiting satellites, undersea transmission cables and the like, that are owned or rented by the taxpayer and used in the business of publishing, licensing, selling or otherwise distributing printed material, but which are not physically located in any particular state.

(ii) "Print or printed material" includes, without limitation, the physical embodiment or printed version of any thought or expression including, without limitation, a play, story, article, column or other literary, commercial, educational, artistic or other written or printed work. The determination of whether an item is or consists of print or printed material shall be made without regard to its content. Printed material may take the form of a book, newspaper, magazine, periodical, trade journal or any other form of printed matter and may be contained on any medium or property.

(iii) "Purchaser" and "Subscriber" mean the individual, residence, business or other outlet which is the ultimate or final recipient of the print or printed material. Neither of such terms shall mean or include a wholesaler or other distributor of print or printed material.

(iv) "Terrestrial facility" shall include any telephone line, cable, fiber optic, microwave, earth station, satellite dish, antennae or other relay system or device that is used to receive, transmit, relay or carry any data, voice, image or other information that is transmitted from or by any outer-jurisdictional property to the ultimate recipient thereof.

(3) Apportionment of Business Income.

(i) The Property Factor.

A. Property Factor Denominator.

1. All real and tangible personal property, including outer-jurisdictional property, whether owned or rented, which is used in the business shall be included in the denominator of the property factor.

B. Property Factor Numerator.

1. All real and tangible personal property owned or rented by the taxpayer and used in this state during the tax period shall be included in the numerator of the property factor.

2. Outer-jurisdictional property owned or rented by the taxpayer and used in this state during the tax period shall be included in the numerator of the property factor in the ratio which the value of such property that is attributable to its use by the taxpayer in business activities in this state bears to the total value of such property that is attributable to its use in the taxpayer's business activities everywhere.

The value of outer-jurisdictional property to be attributed to the numerator of the property factor of this state shall be determined by the ratio that the number of uplinks and downlinks (sometimes referred to as "half-circuits") that were used during the tax period to transmit from this state and to receive in this state any data, voice, image or other information bears to the total number of uplinks and downlinks or half-circuits that the taxpayer used for transmissions everywhere.

Should information regarding such uplink and downlink or half-circuit usage not be available or should such measurement of activity not be applicable to the type of outer-jurisdictional property used by the taxpayer, the value of such property to be attributed to the numerator of the property factor of this state shall be determined by the ratio that the amount of time (in terms of hours and minutes of use) or such other measurement of use of outer-jurisdictional property that was used during the tax period to transmit from this state and to receive in this state any data, voice, image or other information bears to the total amount of time or other measurement of use that was used for transmissions everywhere.

3. Outer-jurisdictional property shall be considered to have been used by the taxpayer in its business activities within this state when such property, wherever located, has been employed by the taxpayer in any manner in the publishing, sale, licensing or other distribution of books, newspapers, magazines or other printed material and any data, voice, image or other information is transmitted to or from this state either through an earth station or terrestrial facility located in this state.

Example: One example of the use of outer-jurisdictional property is where the taxpayer either owns its own communications satellite or leases the use of uplinks, downlinks or circuits or time on a communications satellite for the purpose of sending messages to its newspaper printing facilities or employees in a state. The state or states in which any printing facility that receives the satellite communications is located and the state from which the communications were sent would, under this regulation, apportion the cost of the owned or rented satellite to their respective property factors based upon the ratio of the in-state use of said satellite to its total usage everywhere.

Assume that ABC Newspaper Co. owns a total of $400,000,000 of property everywhere and that, in addition, it owns and operates a communication satellite for the purpose of sending news articles to its printing plant in this state, as well as for communicating with its printing plants and facilities or news bureaus, employees and agents located in other states and throughout the world. Also assume that the total value of its real and tangible personal property that was permanently located in this state for the entire income year was valued at $3,000,000. Assume also that the total original cost of the satellite is $100,000,000 for the tax period and that of the 10,000 uplinks and downlinks of satellite transmissions used by the taxpayer during the tax period, 200 or 2% are attributable to its satellite communications received in and sent from this state. Assume further that the company's mobile property that was used partially within this state, consisting of 40 delivery trucks, were determined to have an original cost of $4,000,000 and such mobile property was used in this state for 95 days.

The total value of property to be attributed to this state would be determined as follows:

Value of property permanently in state:	$3,000,000
Value of mobile property: 95/365 or (.260274) × $4,000,000:	$1,041,096
Value of leased satellite property used in-state: (.02) × $100,000,000:	$2,000,000
Total value of property attributable to state:	$6,041,096
Total property factor %: $6,041,096/($500,000,000): . . .	1.2082%

(ii) The Payroll Factor.

The payroll factor shall be determined in accordance with Article IV.14. of the Multistate Tax Compact and the regulations promulgated thereunder.

(iii) The Sales Factor.

A. Sales Factor Denominator.

The denominator of the sales factor shall include the total gross receipts derived by the taxpayer from transactions and activity in the regular course of its trade or business, except receipts that may be excluded under Reg. IV.15 through 18.

B. Sales Factor Numerator.

The numerator of the sales factor shall include all gross receipts of the taxpayer from sources within this state, including, but not limited to, the following:

1. Gross receipts derived from the sale of tangible personal property, including printed materials, delivered or shipped to a purchaser or a subscriber in this state.

2. Except as provided in subparagraph (3)(iii)B.3., gross receipts derived from advertising and the sale, rental or other use of the taxpayer's customer lists or any portion thereof shall be attributed to this state as determined by the taxpayer's "circulation factor" during the tax period. The circulation factor shall be determined for each individual publication by the taxpayer of printed material containing advertising and shall be equal to the ratio that the taxpayer's in-state circulation to purchasers and subscribers of its printed material bears to its total circulation to purchasers and subscribers everywhere.

The circulation factor for an individual publication shall be determined by reference to the rating statistics as reflected in such sources as Audit Bureau of Circulations or other comparable sources, provided that the source selected is consistently used from year to year for such purpose. If none of the foregoing sources are available, or, if available, none is in form or content sufficient for such purposes, then the circulation factor shall be determined from the taxpayer's books and records.

3. When specific items of advertisements can be shown, upon clear and convincing evidence, to have been distributed solely to a limited regional or local geographic area in which this state is located, the taxpayer may petition, or the [Tax Administrator] may require, that a portion of such receipts be attributed to the sales factor numerator of this state on the basis of a regional or local geographic area circulation factor and not upon the basis of the circulation factor provided by subparagraph (3)(iii)B.2. Such attribution shall be based upon the ratio that the taxpayer's circulation to purchasers and subscribers located in this state of the printed material containing such specific items of advertising bears to its total circulation of such printed material to purchasers and subscribers located within such regional or local geographic area. This alternative attribution method shall be permitted only upon the condition that such receipts are not double counted or otherwise included in the numerator of any other state.

4. In the event that the purchaser or subscriber is the United States Government or that the taxpayer is not taxable in a State, the gross receipts from all sources, including the receipts from the sale of printed material, from advertising, and from the sale, rental or other use of the taxpayer's customer's lists, or any portion thereof that would have been attributed by the circulation factor to the numerator of the sales factor for such State, shall be included in the numerator of the sales factor of this State if the printed material or other property is shipped from an office, store, warehouse, factory, or other place of storage or business in this State.

Recommended Formula for the Apportionment and Allocation of Net Income of Financial Institutions

[Adopted November 17, 1994.]

Section 1. Apportionment and Allocation.

(a) Except as otherwise specifically provided, a financial institution whose business activity is taxable both within and without this state shall allocate and apportion its net income as provided in this [Act]. All items of nonbusiness income (income which is not includable in the apportionable income tax base) shall be allocated pursuant to the provisions of [ ]. A financial institution organized under the laws of a foreign country, the Commonwealth of Puerto Rico, or a territory or possession of the United States whose effectively connected income (as defined under the Federal Internal Revenue Code) is taxable both within this state and within another state, other than the state in which it is organized, shall allocate and apportion its net income as provided in this [Act].

(b) All business income (income which is includable in the apportionable income tax base) shall be apportioned to this state by multiplying such income by the apportionment percentage. The apportionment percentage is determined by adding the taxpayer's receipts factor (as described in Section 3 of this article), property factor (as described in Section 4 of this article), and payroll factor (as described in Section 5 of this article) together and dividing the sum by three. If one of the factors is missing, the two remaining factors are added and the sum is divided by two. If two of the factors are missing, the remaining factor is the apportionment percentage. A factor is missing if both its numerator and denominator are zero, but it is not missing merely because its numerator is zero.

(c) Each factor shall be computed according to the method of accounting (cash or accrual basis) used by the taxpayer for the taxable year.

(d) If the allocation and apportionment provisions of this [Act] do not fairly represent the extent of the taxpayer's business activity in this state, the taxpayer may petition for or the [State Tax Administrator] may require, in respect to all or any part of the taxpayer's business activity, if reasonable:

(1) separate accounting;

(2) the exclusion of any one or more of the factors,

(3) the inclusion of one or more additional factors which will fairly represent the taxpayer's business activity in this State; or

(4) the employment of any other method to effectuate an equitable allocation and apportionment of the taxpayer's income.

Section 2. Definitions.

As used in this [Act], unless the context otherwise requires:

(a) "**Billing address**" means the location indicated in the books and records of the taxpayer on the first day of the taxable year (or on such later date in the taxable year when the customer relationship began) as the address where any notice, statement and/or bill relating to a customer's account is mailed.

(b) "**Borrower or credit card holder located in this state**" means:

(1) a borrower, other than a credit card holder, that is engaged in a trade or business which maintains its commercial domicile in this state; or

(2) a borrower that is not engaged in a trade or business or a credit card holder whose billing address is in this state.

(c) "**Commercial domicile**" means:

(1) the headquarters of the trade or business, that is, the place from which the trade or business is principally managed and directed; or

(2) if a taxpayer is organized under the laws of a foreign country, or of the Commonwealth of Puerto Rico, or any territory or possession of the United States, such taxpayer's commercial domicile shall be deemed for the purposes of this [Act] to be the state of the United States or the District of Columbia from which such taxpayer's trade or business in the United States is principally managed and directed. It shall be presumed, subject to rebuttal, that the location from which the taxpayer's trade or business is principally managed and directed is the state of the United States or the District of Columbia to which the greatest number of employees are regularly connected or out of which they are working, irrespective of where the services of such employees are performed, as of the last day of the taxable year.

(d) "**Compensation**" means wages, salaries, commissions and any other form of remuneration paid to employees for personal services that are included in such employee's gross income under the Federal Internal Revenue Code. In the case of employees not subject to the Federal Internal Revenue Code, e.g., those employed in foreign countries, the determination of whether such payments would constitute gross income to such employees under the Federal Internal Revenue Code shall be made as though such employees were subject to the Federal Internal Revenue Code.

(e) **"Credit card"** means credit, travel or entertainment card.

(f) **"Credit card issuer's reimbursement fee"** means the fee a taxpayer receives from a merchant's bank because one of the persons to whom the taxpayer has issued a credit card has charged merchandise or services to the credit card.

(g) **"Employee"** means, with respect to a particular taxpayer, any individual who, under the usual common-law rules applicable in determining the employer-employee relationship, has the status of an employee of that taxpayer.

(h) **"Financial institution"** means: [insert state's definition here] [*for a starting point for the development of a definition, see Appendix A*].

(i) **"Gross rents"** means the actual sum of money or other consideration payable for the use or possession of property. "Gross rents" shall include, but not be limited to:

(1) any amount payable for the use or possession of real property or tangible property whether designated as a fixed sum of money or as a percentage of receipts, profits or otherwise,

(2) any amount payable as additional rent or in lieu of rent, such as interest, taxes, insurance, repairs or any other amount required to be paid by the terms of a lease or other arrangement, and

(3) a proportionate part of the cost of any improvement to real property made by or on behalf of the taxpayer which reverts to the owner or lessor upon termination of a lease or other arrangement. The amount to be included in gross rents is the amount of amortization or depreciation allowed in computing the taxable income base for the taxable year. However, where a building is erected on leased land by or on behalf of the taxpayer, the value of the land is determined by multiplying the gross rent by eight and the value of the building is determined in the same manner as if owned by the taxpayer.

(4) The following are not included in the term "gross rents":

(A) reasonable amounts payable as separate charges for water and electric service furnished by the lessor;

(B) reasonable amounts payable as service charges for janitorial services furnished by the lessor;

(C) reasonable amounts payable for storage, provided such amounts are payable for space not designated and not under the control of the taxpayer; and

(D) that portion of any rental payment which is applicable to the space subleased from the taxpayer and not used by it.

(j) **"Loan"** means any extension of credit resulting from direct negotiations between the taxpayer and its customer, and/or the purchase, in whole or in part, of such extension of credit from another. Loans include participations, syndications, and leases treated as loans for federal income tax purposes. Loans shall not include: properties treated as loans under Section 595 of the Federal Internal Revenue Code; futures or forward contracts; options; notional principal contracts such as swaps; credit card receivables, including purchased credit card relationships; non-interest bearing balances due from depository institutions; cash items in the process of collection; federal funds sold; securities purchased under agreements to resell; assets held in a trading account; securities; interests in a REMIC, or other mortgage-backed or asset-backed security; and other similar items.

(k) **"Loan secured by real property"** means that fifty percent or more of the aggregate value of the collateral used to secure a loan or other obligation, when valued at fair market value as of the time the original loan or obligation was incurred, was real property.

(l) **"Merchant discount"** means the fee (or negotiated discount) charged to a merchant by the taxpayer for the privilege of participating in a program whereby a credit card is accepted in payment for merchandise or services sold to the card holder.

(m) **"Participation"** means an extension of credit in which an undivided ownership interest is held on a *pro rata* basis in a single loan or pool of loans and related collateral. In a loan participation, the credit originator initially makes the loan and then subsequently resells all or a portion of it to other lenders. The participation may or may not be known to the borrower.

(n) **"Person"** means an individual, estate, trust, partnership, corporation and any other business entity.

(o) **"Principal base of operations"** with respect to transportation property means the place of more or less permanent nature from which said property is regularly directed or controlled. With respect to an employee, the "principal base of operations" means the place of more or less permanent nature from which the employee regularly (1) starts his or her work and to which he or she customarily returns in order to receive instructions from his or her employer or (2) communicates with his or her customers or other persons, or (3) performs any other functions necessary to the exercise of his or her trade or profession at some other point or points.

(p) **"Real property owned"** and **"tangible personal property owned"** mean real and tangible personal property, respectively, (1) on which the taxpayer may claim depreciation for federal income tax purposes, or (2) property to which the taxpayer holds legal title and on which no other person may claim depreciation for federal income tax purposes (or could claim depreciation if subject to federal income tax). Real and tangible personal property do not include coin, currency, or property acquired in lieu of or pursuant to a foreclosure.

(q) **"Regular place of business"** means an office at which the taxpayer carries on its business in a regular and systematic manner and which is continuously maintained, occupied and used by employees of the taxpayer.

(r) **"State"** means a state of the United States, the District of Columbia, the Commonwealth of Puerto Rico, any territory or possession of the United States or any foreign country.

(s) **"Syndication"** means an extension of credit in which two or more persons fund and each person is at risk only up to a specified percentage of the total extension of credit or up to a specified dollar amount.

(t) **"Taxable"** means either:

(1) that a taxpayer is subject in another state to a net income tax, a franchise tax measured by net income, a franchise tax for the privilege of doing business, a corporate stock tax (including a bank shares tax), a single business tax, or an earned surplus tax, or any tax which is imposed upon or measured by net income; or

(2) that another state has jurisdiction to subject the taxpayer to any of such taxes regardless of whether, in fact, the state does or does not.

(u) **"Transportation property"** means vehicles and vessels capable of moving under their own power, such as aircraft, trains, water vessels and motor vehicles, as well as any equipment or containers attached to such property, such as rolling stock, barges, trailers or the like.

Section 3. Receipts Factor.

(a) **General.** The receipts factor is a fraction, the numerator of which is the receipts of the taxpayer in this state during the taxable year and the denominator of which is the receipts of the taxpayer within and without this state during the taxable year. The method of calculating receipts for purposes of the denominator is the same as the method used in determining receipts for purposes of the numerator. The receipts factor shall include only those receipts described herein which constitute business income and are included in the computation of the apportionable income base for the taxable year.

(b) **Receipts from the lease of real property.** The numerator of the receipts factor includes receipts from the lease or rental of real property owned by the taxpayer if the property is located within this state or receipts from the sublease of real property if the property is located within this state.

(c) **Receipts from the lease of tangible personal property.**

(1) Except as described in paragraph (2) of this subsection, the numerator of the receipts factor includes receipts from the lease or rental of tangible personal property owned by the taxpayer if the property is located within this state when it is first placed in service by the lessee.

(2) Receipts from the lease or rental of transportation property owned by the taxpayer are included in the numerator of the receipts factor to the extent that the property is used in this state. The extent an aircraft will be deemed to be used in this state and the amount of receipts that is to be included in the numerator of this state's receipts factor is determined by multiplying all the receipts from the lease or rental of the aircraft by a fraction, the numerator of which is the number of landings of the aircraft in this state and the denominator of which is the total number of landings of the aircraft. If the extent of the use of any transportation property within this state cannot be determined, then the property will be deemed to be used wholly in the state in which the property has its principal base of operations. A motor vehicle will be deemed to be used wholly in the state in which it is registered.

(d) **Interest from loans secured by real property.**

(1) The numerator of the receipts factor includes interest and fees or penalties in the nature of interest from loans secured by real property if the property is located within this state. If the property is located both within this state and one or more other states, the receipts described in this subsection are included in the numerator of the receipts factor if more than fifty percent of the fair market value of the real property is located within this state. If more than fifty percent of the fair market value of the real property is not located within any one state, then the receipts described in this subsection shall be included in the numerator of the receipts factor if the borrower is located in this state.

(2) The determination of whether the real property securing a loan is located within this state shall be made as of the time the original agreement was made and any and all subsequent substitutions of collateral shall be disregarded.

(e) **Interest from loans not secured by real property.** The numerator of the receipts factor includes interest and fees or penalties in the nature of interest from loans not secured by real property if the borrower is located in this state.

(f) **Net gains from the sale of loans.** The numerator of the receipts factor includes net gains from the sale of loans. Net gains from the sale of loans includes income recorded under the coupon stripping rules of Section 1286 of the Internal Revenue Code.

(1) The amount of net gains (but not less than zero) from the sale of loans secured by real property included in the numerator is determined by multiplying such net gains by a fraction the numerator of which is the amount included in the numerator of the receipts factor pursuant to subsection (d) of this section and the denominator of which is the total amount of interest and fees or penalties in the nature of interest from loans secured by real property.

(2) The amount of net gains (but not less than zero) from the sale of loans not secured by real property included in the numerator is determined by multiplying such net gains by a fraction the numerator of which is the amount included in the numerator of the receipts factor pursuant to subsection (e) of this section and the denominator of which is the total amount of interest and fees or penalties in the nature of interest from loans not secured by real property.

(g) **Receipts from credit card receivables.** The numerator of the receipts factor includes interest and fees or penalties in the nature of interest from credit card receivables and receipts from fees charged to card holders, such as annual fees, if the billing address of the card holder is in this state.

(h) **Net gains from the sale of credit card receivables.** The numerator of the receipts factor includes net gains (but not less than zero) from the sale of credit card receivables multiplied by a fraction, the numerator of which is the amount included in the numerator of the receipts factor pursuant to subsection (g) of this section and the denominator of which is the taxpayer's total amount of interest and fees or penalties in the nature of interest from credit card receivables and fees charged to card holders.

(i) **Credit card issuer's reimbursement fees.** The numerator of the receipts factor includes all credit card issuer's reimbursement fees multiplied by a fraction, the numerator of which is the amount included in the numerator of the receipts factor pursuant to subsection (g) of this section and the denominator of which is the taxpayer's total amount of interest and fees or penalties in the nature of interest from credit card receivables and fees charged to card holders.

(j) **Receipts from merchant discount.** The numerator of the receipts factor includes receipts from merchant discount if the commercial domicile of the merchant is in this state. Such receipts shall be computed net of any cardholder charge backs, but shall not be reduced by any interchange transaction fees or by any issuer's reimbursement fees paid to another for charges made by its card holders.

(k) **Loan servicing fees.**

(1)(A) The numerator of the receipts factor includes loan servicing fees derived from loans secured by real property multiplied by a fraction the numerator of which is the amount included in the numerator of the receipts factor pursuant to subsection (d) of this section and the denominator of which is the total amount of interest and fees or penalties in the nature of interest from loans secured by real property.

(B) The numerator of the receipts factor includes loan servicing fees derived from loans not secured by real property multiplied by a fraction the numerator of which is the amount included in the numerator of the receipts factor pursuant to subsection (e) of this section and the denominator of which is the total amount of interest and fees or penalties in the nature of interest from loans not secured by real property.

(2) In circumstances in which the taxpayer receives loan servicing fees for servicing either the secured or the unsecured loans of another, the numerator of the receipts factor shall include such fees if the borrower is located in this state.

(l) **Receipts from services.** The numerator of the receipts factor includes receipts from services not otherwise apportioned under this section if the service is performed in this state. If the service is performed both within and without this state, the numerator of the receipts factor includes receipts from services not otherwise apportioned under this section, if a greater proportion of the income-producing activity is performed in this state based on cost of performance.

(m) **Receipts from investment assets and activities and trading assets and activities.**

(1) Interest, dividends, net gains (but not less than zero) and other income from investment assets and activities and from trading assets and activities shall be included in the receipts factor. Investment assets and activities and trading assets and activities include but are not

limited to: investment securities; trading account assets; federal funds; securities purchased and sold under agreements to resell or repurchase; options; futures contracts; forward contracts; notional principal contracts such as swaps; equities; and foreign currency transactions. With respect to the investment and trading assets and activities described in subparagraphs (A) and (B) of this paragraph, the receipts factor shall include the amounts described in such subparagraphs.

(A) The receipts factor shall include the amount by which interest from federal funds sold and securities purchased under resale agreements exceeds interest expense on federal funds purchased and securities sold under repurchase agreements.

(B) The receipts factor shall include the amount by which interest, dividends, gains and other income from trading assets and activities, including but not limited to assets and activities in the matched book, in the arbitrage book, and foreign currency transactions, exceed amounts paid in lieu of interest, amounts paid in lieu of dividends, and losses from such assets and activities.

(2) The numerator of the receipts factor includes interest, dividends, net gains (but not less than zero) and other income from investment assets and activities and from trading assets and activities described in paragraph (1) of this subsection that are attributable to this state.

(A) The amount of interest, dividends, net gains (but not less than zero) and other income from investment assets and activities in the investment account to be attributed to this state and included in the numerator is determined by multiplying all such income from such assets and activities by a fraction, the numerator of which is the average value of such assets which are properly assigned to a regular place of business of the taxpayer within this state and the denominator of which is the average value of all such assets.

(B) The amount of interest from federal funds sold and purchased and from securities purchased under resale agreements and securities sold under repurchase agreements attributable to this state and included in the numerator is determined by multiplying the amount described in subparagraph (A) of paragraph (1) of this subsection from such funds and such securities by a fraction, the numerator of which is the average value of federal funds sold and securities purchased under agreements to resell which are properly assigned to a regular place of business of the taxpayer within this state and the denominator of which is the average value of all such funds and such securities.

(C) The amount of interest, dividends, gains and other income from trading assets and activities, including but not limited to assets and activities in the matched book, in the arbitrage book and foreign currency transactions, (but excluding amounts described in subparagraphs (A) or (B) of this paragraph), attributable to this state and included in the numerator is determined by multiplying the amount described in subparagraph (B) of paragraph (1) of this subsection by a fraction, the numerator of which is the average value of such trading assets which are properly assigned to a regular place of business of the taxpayer within this state and the denominator of which is the average value of all such assets.

(D) For purposes of this paragraph, average value shall be determined using the rules for determining the average value of tangible personal property set forth in subsections (c) and (d) of Section 4.

(3) In lieu of using the method set forth in paragraph (2) of this subsection, the taxpayer may elect, or the [State Tax Administrator] may require in order to fairly represent the business activity of the taxpayer in this state, the use of the method set forth in this paragraph.

(A) The amount of interest, dividends, net gains (but not less than zero) and other income from investment assets and activities in the investment account to be attributed to this state and included in the numerator is determined by multiplying all such income from such assets and activities by a fraction, the numerator of which is the gross income from such assets and activities which are properly assigned to a regular place of business of the taxpayer within this state and the denominator of which is the gross income from all such assets and activities.

(B) The amount of interest from federal funds sold and purchased and from securities purchased under resale agreements and securities sold under repurchase agreements attributable to this state and included in the numerator is determined by multiplying the amount described in subparagraph (A) of paragraph (1) of this subsection from such funds and such securities by a fraction, the numerator of which is the gross income from such funds and such securities which are properly assigned to a regular place of business of the taxpayer within this state and the denominator of which is the gross income from all such funds and such securities.

(C) The amount of interest, dividends, gains and other income from trading assets and activities, including but not limited to assets and activities in the matched book, in the arbitrage book and foreign currency transactions (but excluding amounts described in subparagraphs (A) or (B) of this paragraph), attributable to this state and included in the numerator is determined by multiplying the amount described in subparagraph (B) of paragraph (1) of this subsection by a fraction, the numerator of which is the gross income from such trading assets and activities which are properly assigned to a regular place of business of the taxpayer within this state and the denominator of which is the gross income from all such assets and activities.

(4) If the taxpayer elects or is required by [the State Tax Administrator] to use the method set forth in paragraph (3) of this subsection, it shall use this method on all subsequent returns unless the taxpayer receives prior permission from the [State Tax Administrator] to use, or the [State Tax Administrator] requires a different method.

(5) The taxpayer shall have the burden of proving that an investment asset or activity or trading asset or activity was properly assigned to a regular place of business outside of this state by demonstrating that the day-to-day decisions regarding the asset or activity occurred at a regular place of business outside this state. Where the day-to-day decisions regarding an investment asset or activity or trading asset or activity occur at more than one regular place of business and one such regular place of business is in this state and one such regular place of business is outside this state, such asset or activity shall be considered to be located at the regular place of business of the taxpayer where the investment or trading policies or guidelines with respect to the asset or activity are established. Unless the taxpayer demonstrates to the contrary, such policies and guidelines shall be presumed to be established at the commercial domicile of the taxpayer.

(n) **All other receipts.** The numerator of the receipts factor includes all other receipts pursuant to the rules set forth in . . . [insert your state's regular situsing rules for the receipts not covered by this section.]

(o) **Attribution of certain receipts to commercial domicile.** All receipts which would be assigned under this section to a state in which the taxpayer is not taxable shall be included in the numerator of the receipts factor, if the taxpayer's commercial domicile is in this state.

Section 4. Property Factor.

(a) **General.** The property factor is a fraction, the numerator of which is the average value of real property and tangible personal property rented to the taxpayer that is located or used within this state during the taxable year, the average value of the taxpayer's real and tangible personal property owned that is located or used within this state during the taxable year, and the average value of the taxpayer's loans and credit card receivables that are located within this state during the taxable year, and the denominator of which is the average value of all such property located or used within and without this state during the taxable year.

(b) **Property included.** The property factor shall include only property the income or expenses of which are included (or would have been included if not fully depreciated or expensed, or depreciated or expensed to a nominal amount) in the computation of the apportionable income base for the taxable year.

(c) **Value of property owned by the taxpayer.**

(1) The value of real property and tangible personal property owned by the taxpayer is the original cost or other basis of such property for Federal income tax purposes without regard to depletion, depreciation or amortization.

(2) Loans are valued at their outstanding principal balance, without regard to any reserve for bad debts. If a loan is charged-off in whole or in part for Federal income tax purposes, the portion of the loan charged off is not outstanding. A specifically allocated reserve established pursuant to regulatory or financial accounting guidelines which is treated as charged-off for Federal income tax purposes shall be treated as charged-off for purposes of this section.

(3) Credit card receivables are valued at their outstanding principal balance, without regard to any reserve for bad debts. If a credit card receivable is charged-off in whole or in part for Federal income tax purposes, the portion of the receivable charged-off is not outstanding.

(d) **Average value of property owned by the taxpayer.** The average value of property owned by the taxpayer is computed on an annual basis by adding the value of the property on the first day of the taxable year and the value on the last day of the taxable year and dividing the sum by two. If averaging on this basis does not properly reflect average value, the [State Tax Administrator] may require averaging on a more frequent basis. The taxpayer may elect to average on a more frequent basis. When averaging on a more frequent basis is required by the [State Tax Administrator] or is elected by the taxpayer, the same method of valuation must be used consistently by the taxpayer with respect to property within and without this state and on all subsequent returns unless the taxpayer receives prior permission from the [State Tax Administrator] or the [State Tax Administrator] requires a different method of determining average value.

(e) **Average value of real property and tangible personal property rented to the taxpayer.**

(1) The average value of real property and tangible personal property that the taxpayer has rented from another and which is not

treated as property owned by the taxpayer for Federal income tax purposes, shall be determined annually by multiplying the gross rents payable during the taxable year by eight.

(2) Where the use of the general method described in this subsection results in inaccurate valuations of rented property, any other method which properly reflects the value may be adopted by the [State Tax Administrator] or by the taxpayer when approved in writing by the [State Tax Administrator]. Once approved, such other method of valuation must be used on all subsequent returns unless the taxpayer receives prior approval from the [State Tax Administrator] or the [State Tax Administrator] requires a different method of valuation.

(f) **Location of real property and tangible personal property owned by or rented to the taxpayer.**

(1) Except as described in paragraph (2) of this subsection, real property and tangible personal property owned by or rented to the taxpayer is considered to be located within this state if it is physically located, situated or used within this state.

(2) Transportation property is included in the numerator of the property factor to the extent that the property is used in this state. The extent an aircraft will be deemed to be used in this state and the amount of value that is to be included in the numerator of this state's property factor is determined by multiplying the average value of the aircraft by a fraction, the numerator of which is the number of landings of the aircraft in this state and the denominator of which is the total number of landings of the aircraft everywhere. If the extent of the use of any transportation property within this state cannot be determined, then the property will be deemed to be used wholly in the state in which the property has its principal base of operations. A motor vehicle will be deemed to be used wholly in the state in which it is registered.

(g) **Location of loans**

(1)(A) A loan is considered to be located within this state if it is properly assigned to a regular place of business of the taxpayer within this state.

(B) A loan is properly assigned to the regular place of business with which it has a preponderance of substantive contacts. A loan assigned by the taxpayer to a regular place of business without the state shall be presumed to have been properly assigned if—

(i) the taxpayer has assigned, in the regular course of its business, such loan on its records to a regular place of business consistent with Federal or state regulatory requirements;

(ii) such assignment on its records is based upon substantive contacts of the loan to such regular place of business; and

(iii) the taxpayer uses said records reflecting assignment of loans for the filing of all state and local tax returns for which an assignment of loans to a regular place of business is required.

(C) The presumption of proper assignment of a loan provided in subparagraph (B) of paragraph (1) of this subsection may be rebutted upon a showing by the [State Tax Administrator], supported by a preponderance of the evidence, that the preponderance of substantive contacts regarding such loan did not occur at the regular place of business to which it was assigned on the taxpayer's records. When such presumption has been rebutted, the loan shall then be located within this state if (i) the taxpayer had a regular place of business within this state at the time the loan was made; and (ii) the taxpayer fails to show, by a preponderance of the evidence, that the preponderance of substantive contacts regarding such loan did not occur within this state.

(2) In the case of a loan which is assigned by the taxpayer to a place without this state which is not a regular place of business, it shall be presumed, subject to rebuttal by the taxpayer on a showing supported by the preponderance of evidence, that the preponderance of substantive contacts regarding the loan occurred within this state if, at the time the loan was made the taxpayer's commercial domicile, as defined by subsection (c) of Section 2, was within this state.

(3) To determine the state in which the preponderance of substantive contacts relating to a loan have occurred, the facts and circumstances regarding the loan at issue shall be reviewed on a case-by-case basis and consideration shall be given to such activities as the solicitation, investigation, negotiation, approval and administration of the loan. The terms "solicitation", "investigation", "negotiation", "approval" and "administration" are defined as follows:

(A) *Solicitation.* Solicitation is either active or passive. Active solicitation occurs when an employee of the taxpayer initiates the contact with the customer. Such activity is located at the regular place of business which the taxpayer's employee is regularly connected with or working out of, regardless of where the services of such employee were actually performed. Passive solicitation occurs when the customer initiates the contact with the taxpayer. If the customer's initial contact was not at a regular place of business of the taxpayer, the regular place of business, if any, where the passive solicitation occurred is determined by the facts in each case.

(B) *Investigation.* Investigation is the procedure whereby employees of the taxpayer determine the credit-worthiness of the customer as well as the degree of risk involved in making a particular agreement. Such activity is located at the regular place of business which the taxpayer's employees are regularly connected with or working out of, regardless of where the services of such employees were actually performed.

(C) *Negotiation.* Negotiation is the procedure whereby employees of the taxpayer and its customer determine the terms of the agreement (e.g., the amount, duration, interest rate, frequency of repayment, currency denomination and security required). Such activity is located at the regular place of business which the taxpayer's employees are regularly connected with or working out of, regardless of where the services of such employees were actually performed.

(D) *Approval.* Approval is the procedure whereby employees or the board of directors of the taxpayer make the final determination whether to enter into the agreement. Such activity is located at the regular place of business which the taxpayer's employees are regularly connected with or working out of, regardless of where the services of such employees were actually performed. If the board of directors makes the final determination, such activity is located at the commercial domicile of the taxpayer.

(E) *Administration.* Administration is the process of managing the account. This process includes bookkeeping, collecting the payments, corresponding with the customer, reporting to management regarding the status of the agreement and proceeding against the borrower or the security interest if the borrower is in default. Such activity is located at the regular place of business which oversees this activity.

(h) **Location of credit card receivables.** For purposes of determining the location of credit card receivables, credit card receivables shall be treated as loans and shall be subject to the provisions of subsection (g) of this section.

(i) **Period for which properly assigned loan remains assigned.** A loan that has been properly assigned to a state shall, absent any change of material fact, remain assigned to said state for the length of the original term of the loan. Thereafter, said loan may be properly assigned to another state if said loan has a preponderance of substantive contact to a regular place of business there.

Section 5. Payroll Factor.

(a) **General.** The payroll factor is a fraction, the numerator of which is the total amount paid in this state during the taxable year by the taxpayer for compensation and the denominator of which is the total compensation paid both within and without this state during the taxable year. The payroll factor shall include only that compensation which is included in the computation of the apportionable income tax base for the taxable year.

(b) **Compensation relating to nonbusiness income and independent contractors.** The compensation of any employee for services or activities which are connected with the production of nonbusiness income (income which is not includable in the apportionable income base) and payments made to any independent contractor or any other person not properly classifiable as an employee shall be excluded from both the numerator and denominator of the factor.

(c) **When compensation paid in this state.** Compensation is paid in this state if any one of the following tests, applied consecutively, is met:

(1) The employee's services are performed entirely within this state.

(2) The employee's services are performed both within and without the state, but the service performed without the state is incidental to the employee's service within the state. The term "incidental" means any service which is temporary or transitory in nature, or which is rendered in connection with an isolated transaction.

(3) If the employee's services are performed both within and without this state, the employee's compensation will be attributed to this state:

(A) if the employee's principal base of operations is within this state; or

(B) if there is no principal base of operations in any state in which some part of the services are performed, but the place from which the services are directed or controlled is in this state; or

(C) if the principal base of operations and the place from which the services are directed or controlled are not in any state in which some part of the service is performed but the employee's residence is in this state.

Appendix A: Definition of Financial Institution.

The following definition of financial institution or a variation thereof could be made part of a statutory proposal or could be adopted by regulation if the state legislature has already delegated the authority to do so to the State Tax Administrator or other administrative officer. Again, the following provides a *starting point* for discussion purposes and the lack of a uniformly adopted definition by all of the states, while affecting competitive balance, is not critical to the main thrust of the apportionment proposal.

"Financial institution" means:

(1) Any corporation or other business entity registered under state law as a bank holding company or registered under the Federal Bank Holding Company Act of 1956, as amended, or registered as a savings and loan holding company under the Federal National Housing Act, as amended;

(2) A national bank organized and existing as a national bank association pursuant to the provisions of the National Bank Act, 12 U.S.C. §§21 et seq.;

(3) A savings association or federal savings bank as defined in the Federal Deposit Insurance Act, 12 U.S.C. §1813(b)(1);

(4) Any bank or thrift institution incorporated or organized under the laws of any state;

(5) Any corporation organized under the provisions of 12 U.S.C. §§611 to 631.

(6) Any agency or branch of a foreign depository as defined in 12 U.S.C. §3101;

(7) A state credit union the loan assets of which exceed $50,000,000 as of the first day of its taxable year.

(8) A production credit association organized under the Federal Farm Credit Act of 1933, all of whose stock held by the Federal Production Credit Corporation has been retired;

(9) Any corporation whose voting stock is more than fifty percent (50%) owned, directly or indirectly, by any person or business entity described in subsections (1) through (8) above other than an insurance company taxable under [insert applicable state statute] or a company taxable under [insert applicable state statute];

(10) A corporation or other business entity that derives more than fifty percent (50%) of its total gross income for financial accounting purposes from finance leases. For purposes of this subsection, a "finance lease" shall mean any lease transaction which is the functional equivalent of an extension of credit and that transfers substantially all of the benefits and risks incident to the ownership of property. The phrase shall include any "direct financing lease" or "leverage lease" that meets the criteria of Financial Accounting Standards Board Statement No. 13, "Accounting for Leases" or any other lease that is accounted for as a financing by a lessor under generally accepted accounting principles.

For this classification to apply,

(a) the average of the gross income in the current tax year and immediately preceding two tax years must satisfy the more than fifty percent (50%) requirement; and

(b) gross income from incidental or occasional transactions shall be disregarded;

or

(11) Any other person or business entity, other than [an insurance company taxable under ___], [a real estate broker taxable under ___], [a securities dealer taxable under ___] or [a ___ company taxable under ___], which derives more than fifty percent (50%) of its gross income from activities that a person described in subsections (2) through (8) and (10) above is authorized to transact. For the purpose of this subsection, the computation of gross income shall not include income from non-recurring, extraordinary items.

(12) The [State Tax Administrator] is authorized to exclude any person from the application of subsection (11) upon such person proving, by clear and convincing evidence, that the income-producing activity of such person is not in substantial competition with those persons described subsections (2) through (8) and (10) above.

Appendix C

Interstate Income Act (P.L. 86-272)

P.L. 86-272 became effective September 14, 1959, and was codified at 15 U.S.C. § § 381–384.

P.L. 86-272 is discussed at ¶ 705.01.

Title I
Imposition of Minimum Standard

Sec. 101. Imposition of Net Income Tax.

(a) No State, or political subdivision thereof, shall have power to impose, for any taxable year ending after the date of the enactment of this Act, a net income tax on the income derived within such State by any person from interstate commerce if the only business activities within such State by or on behalf of such person during such taxable year are either, or both, of the following:

(1) the solicitation of orders by such person, or his representative, in such State for sales of tangible personal property, which orders are sent outside the State for approval or rejection, and, if approved, are filled by shipment or delivery from a point outside the State; and

(2) the solicitation of orders by such person, or his representative, in such State in the name of or for the benefit of a prospective customer of such person, if orders by such customer to such person to enable such customer to fill orders resulting from such solicitation are orders described in paragraph (1).

(b) The provisions of subsection (a) shall not apply to the imposition of a net income tax by any State, or political subdivision thereof, with respect to—

(1) any corporation which is incorporated under the laws of such State; or

(2) any individual who, under the laws of such State, is domiciled in, or a resident of, such State.

(c) For purposes of subsection (a), a person shall not be considered to have engaged in business activities within a State during any taxable year merely by reason of sales in such State, or the solicitation of orders for sales in such State, of tangible personal property on behalf of such person by one or more independent contractors, or by reason of the maintenance of an office in such State by one or more independent contractors whose activities on behalf of such person in such State consist solely of making sales, or soliciting orders for sales, of tangible personal property.

(d) For purposes of this section—

(1) the term "independent contractor" means a commission agent, broker, or other independent contractor who is engaged in selling, or soliciting orders for the sale of, tangible personal property for more than one principal and who holds himself out as such in the regular course of his business activities; and

(2) the term "representative" does not include an independent contractor.

Sec. 102. Income Tax Prohibition on Interstate Commerce.

(a) No State, or political subdivision thereof, shall have power to assess, after the date of the enactment of this Act, any net income tax which was imposed by such State or political subdivision, as the case may be, for any taxable year ending on or before such date, on the income derived within such State by any person from interstate commerce, if the imposition of such tax for a taxable year ending after such date is prohibited by section 101.

(b) The provisions of subsection (a) shall not be construed—

(1) to invalidate the collection, on or before the date of the enactment of this Act, of any net income tax imposed for a taxable year ending on or before such date, or

(2) to prohibit the collection, after the date of the enactment of this Act, of any net income tax which was assessed on or before such date for a taxable year ending on or before such date.

Sec. 103. Definition of "Net Income Tax."

For purposes of this title, the term "net income tax" means any tax imposed on, or measured by, net income.

Sec. 104. Invalidity of Provision.

If any provision of this title or the application of such provision to any person or circumstance is held invalid, the remainder of this title or the application of such provision to persons or circumstances other than those to which it is held invalid, shall not be affected thereby.

Title II

Study and Report by Congressional Committees

Sec. 201. Authorization for Study on Interstate Commerce.

The Committee on the Judiciary of the House of Representatives and the Committee on Finance of the United States Senate, acting separately or jointly, or both, or any duly authorized subcommittees thereof, shall make full and complete studies of all matters pertaining to the taxation of interstate commerce by the States, territories, and possessions of the United States, the District of Columbia, and the Commonwealth of Puerto Rico, or any political or taxing subdivision of the foregoing.

Sec. 202. Study Results Reported.

The Committees shall report to their respective Houses the results of such studies together with their proposals for legislation on or before July 1, 1965.

Appendix D

New York Advisory Opinion, TSB-A-91(11)C

New York Advisory Opinion, TSB-A-91(11)C, was issued April 29, 1991, by the State of New York Commissioner of Taxation and Finance. This advisory opinion, concerning corporation taxes, came out of the Department of Taxation and Finance Taxpayer Services Division, Technical Services Bureau.

New York Advisory Opinion, TSB-A-91(11)C, is discussed at ¶ 715.01.

On August 6, 1990, a Petition [Petition No. C900806A] for Advisory Opinion was received from Mark S. Klein, Partner, Hodgson, Russ, Andrews, Woods & Goodyear, 1800 One M&T Plaza, Buffalo, New York 14203.

The issue raised by Petitioner, Mark S. Klein, is whether, under various situations described herein, a foreign corporation is subject to the franchise tax on utilities under section 186 of the Tax Law, the gross receipts tax under section 186-a of the Tax Law, and/or the franchise tax on business corporations under Article 9-A of the Tax Law, and if so, what receipts are subject to tax.

The underlying facts in each of the six situations described below are the same. A foreign (non-New York) corporation is engaged in the purchase and sale in bulk of natural gas. The foreign corporation negotiates for the purchase of natural gas from natural gas producers or wholesalers ("suppliers") under "requirements" contracts. Under a typical requirements contract the supplier makes available to the foreign corporation a maximum volume of gas. The foreign corporation takes title to as much of the natural gas as it can re-sell. The delivery point (the "point of sale") specified in the requirements contract with the supplier is the point at which the supplier's pipeline intersects the pipeline of an interstate distribution company.

The foreign corporation sells the natural gas to end-users. Generally an end-user is a business requiring large amounts of natural gas for heating and production. The agreement between the end-user and the foreign corporation is also a "requirements" contract. Under the terms of a typical requirements contract, the foreign corporation agrees to make available to the end-user a quantity of natural gas. The end-user takes title to all the gas it needs from the foreign corporation at the point of sale. The point of sale under the requirements contract with the end-user is also the point at which the supplier's pipeline intersects the interstate distribution company's pipeline.

The foreign corporation does not provide any transportation for the natural gas it purchases and sells. The supplier is required to "deliver" the natural gas to the point of sale (where the supplier's pipeline intersects the distribution company's pipeline). The end-user is required to separately contract with the interstate distribution company for transportation of the natural gas from the point of sale, through the interstate distribution company's pipeline and on to the end-user's facilities.

The foreign corporation is not related to the interstate distribution company. Nor is it related to any of the suppliers from which it purchases natural gas. The foreign corporation neither owns, leases nor has any contractual right to use the mains or pipes through which the natural gas flows.

The foreign corporation has title to the natural gas only for a moment, and only for the purpose of facilitating the transfer of title from the supplier to the user.

The foreign corporation is not subject to the supervision of the New York State Department of Public Service.

Unless otherwise stated below, the foreign corporation has no contact with New York State. Specifically, the foreign corporation does not maintain any office, any mail drop or any telephone listing within New York State.

SITUATION 1

Corporation A is a foreign corporation that purchases natural gas from suppliers and sells it to end-users.

Corporation A purchases all the natural gas from suppliers located outside of New York State. All negotiations for the purchase of natural gas occur outside of New York State.

Corporation A sells natural gas only to end-users located outside of New York State. All negotiations for the sale of the gas occur outside of New York State.

The points of sale with respect to the purchase and sale of natural gas by Corporation A are outside of New York State.

"Negotiations outside of New York State" include all negotiations and solicitations engaged in by employees or agents of the foreign corporations (corporations A–F, herein), where the employees or agents do not physically enter New York State for the purpose of soliciting or negotiating orders. Specifically included in "negotiations outside of New York" are negotiations and solicitations with suppliers or end-users located in New York State where the foreign corporations' employees and agents do not physically enter New York State, and where negotiations and solicitations with New York suppliers and/or end-users are engaged in via telecommunication or mail.

SITUATION 2

Corporation B purchases natural gas from suppliers located both inside and outside of New York State. All negotiations for the purchase of natural gas occur outside of New York State.

Corporation B sells the gas only to end-users located outside of New York State. All negotiations with end-users occur outside of New York State.

The points of sale with respect to both the purchase and sale of the natural gas by Corporation B are outside of New York State with respect to more than 50 percent of the natural gas Corporation B sells. However, the points of sale with respect to a significant (although not major) portion of the natural gas Corporation B purchases and sells are within New York State.

SITUATION 3

Corporation C purchases natural gas from suppliers located both inside and outside of New York State. All negotiations concerning the purchase of natural gas by Corporation C occur outside of New York State.

Corporation C sells to end-users located both inside and outside of New York. However, all negotiations concerning the sale of natural gas by Corporation C occur outside of New York State.

The points of sale with respect to the natural gas Corporation C purchases and sells are outside of New York more than 50 percent of the time.

SITUATION 4

Corporation D purchases natural gas from suppliers both inside and outside of New York. Negotiations between Corporation D and its suppliers occur both inside and outside of New York State, although

Corporation D does not have an office or any employees permanently situated in New York State. When negotiations in New York State are necessary, Corporation D sends one of its employees to New York State. Corporation D's employees do not enter New York State for any purpose other than to negotiate the purchase of natural gas from suppliers.

Corporation D sells the natural gas to end-users located both inside and outside of New York. All negotiations concerning the sale of natural gas to the end-users occur outside New York State.

The points of sale with respect to the purchase and sale of the natural gas by Corporation D are outside of New York State more than 50 percent of the time.

SITUATION 5

Corporation E purchases natural gas from suppliers located both inside and outside of New York State. All negotiations with suppliers concerning the purchase of natural gas occur outside of New York State.

The natural gas is sold by Corporation E to end-users located both inside and outside of New York State. More than 50 percent of the end-users purchasing natural gas from Corporation E are located in New York State. Corporation E retains an unrelated New York corporation (the "broker") to solicit the sale of natural gas to end-users located in New York State. The broker does not perform services for any other business. The broker is located in New York State, and performs all negotiations and solicitations with end-users located in New York.

However, all orders solicited by the broker must be sent to Corporation E's office (located outside of New York) for acceptance. Corporation E's employees do not enter New York State.

The points of sale with respect to the natural gas purchased and sold by Corporation E are outside of New York State over 50 percent of the time.

SITUATION 6

Corporation F purchases natural gas from suppliers located both inside and outside of New York State. However, all negotiations concerning Corporation F's purchase of natural gas occur outside of New York State.

Corporation F sells natural gas to end-users located both inside and outside of New York State. All negotiations and solicitations with respect to the sale of natural gas to New York end-users is accomplished through an unrelated New York corporation (the "broker") that performs similar services for other businesses. More than 50 percent of the end-users that purchase natural gas from Corporation F are located within New York State.

The points of sale with respect to the natural gas purchased and sold by Corporation F are outside of New York State more than 50 percent of the time.

Section 209.1 of Article 9-A of the Tax Law imposes an annual franchise tax on domestic or foreign corporations for the privilege of exercising a corporate franchise, doing business, employing capital, owning or leasing property in a corporate or organized capacity, or maintaining an office, in New York State. Section 209.4 of the Tax Law, provides that a corporation liable to tax under section 186 of Article 9 of the Tax Law is not subject to tax under Article 9-A.

Section 186 of the Tax Law imposes a franchise tax, on a corporation, joint stock company or association formed for or principally engaged in the business of supplying water, steam or gas, when delivered through mains or pipes, or electricity, or principally engaged in two or more such businesses, for the privilege of exercising its corporate franchise or carrying on its business in such corporate or organized capacity in New York State. The tax is computed as the sum of a percentage of gross earnings from all sources within New York State and a percentage of certain dividends paid.

To determine the classification and proper taxability of a corporation under either Article 9 or Article 9-A, an examination of the nature of the corporation's activities is necessary, regardless of the purposes for which the corporation was organized. See *McAllister Bros., Inc., v Bates,* 272 App Div 511, 517.

The determination of whether Petitioner is subject to tax under Article 9-A or Article 9, depends on what activity the taxpayer is *principally* engaged in. Ordinarily, a corporation is deemed to be principally engaged in the activity from which more than 50% of its receipts are derived. See, e.g. *Re Joseph Bucciero Contracting Inc.,* Adv Op St Comm, July 23, 1981, TSB-A-81(5)C.

In *Boundary Gas, Inc.,* Adv Op St Tax Comm, April 9, 1981, TSB-H-81(24), the Tax Commission determined that Boundary was not engaged in the business of supplying gas (and, thus, was not subject to tax under section 186 of the Tax Law) because (1) Boundary had no connection with the gas being sold other than holding bare legal title thereto for an instant of time; (2) Boundary did not take physical, possession or have any . . . . control or supervision of the gas; (3) Boundary did not own or operate any facilities of any nature whatsoever and was prohibited by its certificate of incorporation from either owning or constructing any facility; (4) Boundary was prohibited by its certificate of incorporation from selling gas to any entity which was not a shareholder of Boundary; and (5) all expenses of Boundary were reimbursed dollar for dollar by shareholders.

Whereas Boundary was nothing more than a paper corporation without substantive existence, herein, the foreign corporation in all situations is actively engaged in the business of purchasing and selling natural gas. The foreign corporation in all situations negotiates its own requirements contracts with suppliers and actually purchases the contracted natural gas. For the period of time that the foreign corporation owns the natural gas, it has title to such gas. The foreign corporation separately negotiates its own requirements contracts with end-users and sells the contracted natural gas to such end-users.

Herein, in each situation the foreign corporation is principally engaged in the business of supplying natural gas to end-users. Accordingly, if the foreign corporation is subject to franchise tax in New York State it will be subject to tax under section 186 of Article 9.

Under Public Law 86-272, a state may not impose a net income tax on income derived within a state from interstate commerce if the corporation's only activity within the state during the year is the corporation's solicitation of orders for sales of tangible personal property within the state. However, Public Law 86-272 is not applicable to section 186 of the Tax Law because such section imposes a tax on gross earnings not a tax on net income.

A state tax on interstate commerce is not unconstitutional if the tax is applied to an activity with a substantial nexus with the taxing state, is fairly apportioned, does not discriminate against interstate commerce, and is fairly related to the services provided by the state. *Complete Auto Transit, Inc. v Brady,* 430 US 274. While *Complete Auto* dealt with Commerce Clause issues, a tax that meets the *Complete Auto* test will also satisfy the Due Process requirements "that there be a 'minimal connection' between the interstate activities and the taxing state and a rational relationship between the income attributed to the State and the intrastate values of the enterprise". *Trinova Corporation v. Michigan Department of Treasury,* 498 US - ; 112 L Ed 2d 884.

The laws of New York State are presumed to be constitutional by the Commissioner of Taxation and Finance. There is no jurisdiction at the administrative level todeclare such laws unconstitutional; therefore, it must be presumed that the relevant sections of the law are constitutional to the extent that they relate to the imposition of the tax liability on petitioner.

Accordingly, the foreign corporation is subject to franchise tax under section 186 of the Tax Law if it is carrying on its business in New York State. To determine if the foreign corporation is carrying on its business in New York State, its activities in New York State must be analyzed.

Herein, the foreign corporation, s requirements contracts with its suppliers provide that the delivery point of the natural gas is the point of sale. At the point of sale, both legal possession and title pass to the foreign corporation. The foreign corporation sells its natural gas to end-users and that same point of sale (where the foreign corporation took possession and title) is the point the end-user takes possession and title. Accordingly, when the point of sale is in New York State, the foreign corporation is doing business in New York State.

Section 186 of the Tax Law provides that a corporation that carries on its business in New York State shall pay a tax of three-quarters of one percent on its gross earnings from all sources in New York State. Gross earnings, under section 186, means all receipts from the employment of capital without any deduction.

Herein, in Situations "2" through "6" the foreign corporation is subject to tax under section 186 of the Tax Law on its gross earnings from the sale of natural gas where the point of sale is located within New York State. However, if the foreign corporation sells natural gas to an end-user where the point of sale is in Louisiana, the gross earnings from such sale are not from a source in New York State. The end-user's subsequent contract with a pipeline company to transport the purchased natural gas to its destination, even if such destination is in New York State, is not relevant in determining the taxability of the foreign corporation selling the natural gas.

Section 186-a of the Tax Law imposes a tax on the furnishing of utility services. In the case of utilities not subject to the supervision of the New York State Department of Public Service, the tax is equal to three percent of the gross operating income of such a utility doing business in New York State which has annual gross operating income in excess of $500.

A utility includes every person (whether or not subject to the supervision of the Department of Public Service) who sells gas, electricity, steam, water, refrigeration, telephony or telegraphy, delivered through mains, pipes or wires, or furnishes gas, electric, steam, water, refrigeration, telephone or telegraph service, by means of mains, pipes, or wires, regardless of whether such activities are the main business of such person or are only incidental thereto.

The term "gross operating income" includes receipts from sales of gas, electricity, steam, water, refrigeration, telephony or telegraphy, and from the furnishing of gas, electric, steam, water, refrigerator, telephone or telegraph service, for ultimate consumption or use within New York State.

The section 186-a tax is not levied as a sale or use tax on the purchaser, but is a tax on the seller with respect to its activities as a utility in New York State. Herein, the foreign corporation is doing business in New York when its point of sale of natural gas is in New York State. Therefore, in Situations "2" through "6", the foreign corporation is subject to tax under section 186-a of the Tax Law on its gross operating income. Further, the foreign corporation's gross operating income includes receipts from the sale of natural gas where the point of sale is located in New York State. Where the point of sale is outside New York, for example, in Louisiana, the receipts from such sale are not included in gross operating income for purposes of section 186-a of the Tax Law.

In conclusion, the foreign corporation in all situations is in the business of supplying natural gas. Therefore, it is not subject to franchise tax under Article 9-A of the Tax Law, but is subject to franchise tax under section 186 of the Tax Law in Situations "2" through "6" since it is doing business in New York State. Likewise it is subject to tax under section 186-a of the Tax Law. In Situation "1" the foreign corporation is not doing business in New York State and is not subject to tax in New York State.

DATED: April 29, 1991

s/PAUL B. COBURN
Deputy Director
Taxpayer Services Division

NOTE: The opinions expressed in Advisory Opinions are limited to the facts set forth therein.

Appendix E

Court Decisions

The following seven court decisions have important implications to the state taxation of electric, natural gas, and other public utilties. The cases are reproduced in full and arranged alphabetically. A cross-reference to the text paragraph(s) where each case is discussed is shown at the start of each case.

- *Consolidated Fuel Corp. v. Director of Revenue*
- *General Motors Corp. v. Tracy*
- *Koch Fuels, Inc. v. Clark*
- *Mississippi River Fuel Corp. v. Hoffman*
- *Quill Corp. v. North Dakota*
- *Tennessee Gas Pipeline Co. v. Urbach*
- *The Williams Companies, Inc. v. Montana*

Consolidated Fuel Corp. v. Director of Revenue

[*Consolidated Fuel Corp.* is discussed at ¶ 510.01 and ¶ 715.04.]

Missouri Administrative Hearing Commission, No. 92-000230RV, April 29, 1993.

For petitioner: Johnny K. Richardson, Brydon, Swearengen & England, Jefferson City. For respondent: John M. Tomlin, Associate Counsel.

OttoOtto: Commissioner: Consolidated Fuel Corporation ("CFC") filed its complaint on February 21, 1992, challenging the Director of Revenue's assessments of use tax, interest, and additions issued after audit.

We convened a hearing on October 19, 1992, in Jefferson City. Johnny K. Richardson, of Brydon, Swearengen & England, Jefferson City, represented CFC. Associate counsel John M. Tomlin represented the Director. The parties elected to file written arguments; we received the last brief on March 2, 1993. Associate counsel Alana M. Barragan-Scott filed the brief for the Director.

Findings of Fact

1. CFC is a Texas corporation, headquartered at 17070 Dallas Parkway, Dallas, Texas. CFC is not authorized to do business in Missouri.

2. CFC is a wholesale supplier of natural gas. CFC sells natural gas directly to Missouri natural gas consumers. Such direct sales of natural gas are a recent development, pursuant to federal deregulation of the natural gas industry. CFC has been involved in direct gas sales for six years, in fifteen states.

3. The national natural gas distribution system is similar to a bank. Natural gas producers place natural gas into the nationwide natural gas pipeline system. The pipeline operators then "credit" the producers for an equivalent volume of gas, which the operators may withdraw from the system at some other time and place. The gas withdrawn is not physically the same gas as was deposited, although it is indistinguishable from it.

4. Traditionally, natural gas producers sold gas to local utility companies, such as Union Electric, who then sold the gas to consumers. Following deregulation, suppliers such as CFC purchase gas from the producers and sell it to the consumers directly, paying a transit fee to the local utility company equivalent to its profit under the traditional system. Direct purchasing can result in significant savings for the gas consumer.

5. CFC purchases natural gas from producers. By contract, CFC obtains title to the gas upon its entry into the interstate pipeline system. None of the gas is produced in Missouri.

6. CFC enters into contracts with natural gas consumers. Pursuant to the contracts, CFC's customers must notify CFC each month of the volume of gas desired for the following month. According to the contracts, title to the gas passes from CFC to its customers upon delivery.[1] CFC credits the customer for any unused gas each month, the accumulated credits—called a "gas bank"—being available to the customer at any time upon demand. If the customer uses more gas than ordered, it must buy the extra gas from CFC, up to the Maximum Monthly Volume. If a customer needs gas in excess of the Maximum Monthly Volume, it has to purchase it from the local utility company.

7. CFC had no pipelines or meters of its own. CFC contracted with pipeline operators to transport and meter its gas. According to these

[1] Respondent's Exhibit C, at page 3.

contracts, CFC retained title to the gas at all times. However, the risk of loss was on whoever actually possessed the gas at the time the loss occurred.[2] The gas delivered by CFC to its Missouri direct purchase customers was transported first by interstate pipeline and finally by the local utility company's existing distribution system. CFC's contracts with pipeline operators required the operators to receive gas on behalf of CFC at certain designated points and to deliver an equivalent volume of gas on CFC's behalf at certain other designated points, some of which were in Missouri. Each of CFC's Missouri customers authorized CFC in writing to arrange for transportation of directly purchased gas.

8. CFC directly billed all of its customers from its office in Dallas, Texas. Customers remitted payment directly to CFC in Dallas. CFC's invoices sometimes did and sometimes did not separately state transportation charges.

9. CFC contracted with Comet Industries, Inc., formerly known as Comet Electronics, Inc., of Kansas City, Missouri. Under the contract, Comet solicited Missouri and Kansas gas consumers on CFC's behalf. Comet did most soliciting by telephone, using prepared lists of potential consumers, but its employees did make some visits to CFC's Missouri customers. Neither Comet nor CFC ever used any media advertising. CFC did not authorize Comet to make any contracts on its behalf and Comet was not a party to any of CFC's contracts.

10. Comet screened potential customers for CFC, determining that their fuel needs and payment ability were suitable. Comet also serviced CFC's Missouri accounts, collecting current credit information, maintaining monthly contact with each customer, troubleshooting problems, and generally assisting CFC's customers on its behalf.

11. CFC provided training to certain Comet employees.

12. CFC had no office or other facility, employees, real property, or personal property in Missouri. CFC's only contacts with Missouri were by its agent Comet, and by telephone, the United States Mail, and common carrier—the interstate pipelines.

13. The Director audited CFC in November and December, 1991, and issued assessments of unpaid use tax, interest and additions, amounting to $79,180.61, for the period June 1989 through October 1991 ("the audit period"). The auditor concluded that CFC's Missouri sales for the audit period amounted to $17,539,657, of which $16,205,782 was not subject to tax. On the advice of the auditor, CFC solicited exemption certificates from its customers; the auditor ac-

[2] Respondent's Exhibit B, at page 3, paragraph 6.1.

cepted all of the certificates tendered prior to the conclusion of the audit.

14. Three of CFC's customers, Milnot, Guy's Foods, and Siegel-Robert, did not provide exemption certificates until after the conclusion of the audit. The Director did not accept these certificates. Three other customers, Kawasaki Motors, Chemtech Industries, and Lindberg Heat Treating Co., informed the Director that they themselves had paid the use tax due on the gas they purchased. The Director did not credit CFC for the tax paid by these three customers.

I Conclusions of Law

The Administrative Hearing Commission has jurisdiction over protests of use tax assessments issued by the Director of Revenue. Sections 144.261 [3] and 621.050.1, RSMo Supp. 1992. CFC bears the burden of proof. Section 621.050.2, RSMo Supp. 1992.

Our duty in a tax case is not to review the Director's decision, but to find the facts and to determine, by the application of existing law to those facts, the taxpayer's lawful tax liability for the period or transaction at issue. *J.C. Nichols Co. v. Director of Revenue,* 796 S.W.2d 16, 20-21 (Mo. banc 1990); *Bridge Data Co. v. Director of Revenue,* 794 S.W.2d 204, 207 (Mo. banc 1990); *Air Evac EMS, Inc. v. Director of Revenue,* 779 S.W.2d 573, 575-76 (Mo. banc 1989). In making our determination, we must strictly construe the taxing statutes against the taxing authority, *May Dep't Stores Co. v. Director of Revenue,* 791 S.W.2d 388, 389 (Mo. banc 1990) (*May Dep't Stores II*), but exemption provisions are subject to strict, though reasonable, construction against the claimant. *Director of Revenue v. Armco, Inc.,* 787 S.W.2d 722, 724 (Mo. banc 1990).

II Use Tax

The Director, after audit, issued use tax assessments to CFC for the period November 1986 through October 1991, amounting to $79,180.61 (approximately tax: $57,257.97; interest: $8,415.68; and additions: $14,314.53) on gross receipts of $1,333,874.94.[4]

Section 144.610.1 establishes a use tax on the storage, use, or consumption of tangible personal property in this state. Although it is the user—that is, the purchaser—who is liable for the tax, the out-of-state seller is obliged to collect and remit the tax. Sections 144.635, RSMo Supp. 1992, and 144.655.

---

[3] All statutory references, unless otherwise noted, are to the Revised Statutes of Missouri (RSMo), revision of 1986.

[4] CFC had no Missouri sales prior to June 1989.

Section 144.605(14), RSMo Supp. 1992, defines a "vendor" as "every person engaged in making sales of tangible personal property by mail order, by advertising . . . [or by] soliciting . . . sales[.]" CFC's activities are within the scope of this definition and we conclude that CFC is a vendor for the purposes of the Missouri use tax.

Although we agree that CFC is a vendor within the meaning of the use tax law, that is not the end of the analysis. CFC contends that the Commerce Clause of the United States Constitution bars Missouri from imposing the "vendor's use tax"—more properly, the use tax collection duty—upon it. We disagree.

The Commerce Clause imposes limitations on the power of the states to levy taxes on interstate commerce. Such taxes are permissible so long as the tax (1) is applied to an activity having a substantial nexus with the taxing state; (2) is fairly apportioned; (3) does not discriminate against interstate commerce; and (4) is fairly related to the services provided by the state. *Complete Auto Transit, Inc. v. Brady,* 430 U.S. 247, 279 (1977).

Where the tax liability concerned is the use tax collection duty, that is, the vendor's use tax, a special "bright line" rule replaces the first prong of the Complete Auto Transit test: a state may not impose the use tax collection duty upon an out-of-state seller whose only contact with the forum state is by common carrier or the United States Mail. *Quill Corp. v. North Dakota,* —U.S. —, 112 S.Ct. 1904, 1914-16 (1992); *National Bellas Hess, Inc. v. Department of Revenue of Illinois,* 386 U.S. 753 (1967). However, those are not the extent of CFC's contacts with Missouri. A seller who systematically solicits sales in a state through independent contractor agents has sufficient nexus with that state to support the use tax collection duty. *Tyler Pipe Indus., Inc. v. Washington State Dep't of Revenue,* 483 U.S. 232, 250 (1987); *Scripto, Inc. v. Carson,* 362 U.S. 207, 211 (1960). CFC systematically solicited sales in this state through its agent Comet. Thus, Missouri has sufficient nexus with CFC to impose the use tax collection duty on it.

The second prong of the *Complete Auto Transit* test demonstrates the Court's continuing concern that interstate activities might be subjected to a multiple tax burden. As the Court has stated, "A vice in a tax on . . . interstate business is the risk of multiple taxation; but . . . the burden is on the taxpayer to demonstrate it." *Standard Pressed Steel Co. v. Washington Dep't of Revenue,* 419 U.S. 560, 563 (1975); *General Motors Corp. v. Washington Dep't of Revenue,* 377 U.S. 436, 449 (1964). The Missouri Supreme Court has found Missouri's use tax to be fairly apportioned because it relieves taxpayers from the possibility of a multiple tax burden by a system of credits for taxes paid to other states. *Director of Revenue v. Superior Aircraft,* 734

S.W.2d 504, 507 (Mo. banc 1987). Likewise, the *Superior Aircraft* court concluded that Missouri's use tax did not discriminate against interstate commerce because "interstate and intrastate commerce are equally burdened" under the tax. *Id.*

The United States Supreme Court has held that "[t]he exploitation by foreign corporations of interstate opportunities under the protection and encouragement of local government offers a basis for taxation as unrestricted as that for domestic corporations." *Commonwealth Edison Co. v. Montana,* 453 U.S. 609, 623 (1981). CFC, by affirmatively acting to exploit economic opportunities in Missouri, has taken advantage of the orderly marketplace our state provides. A taxpayer that has affirmatively acted to take advantage of the benefits provided by the forum state must "pay its way." *General Motors Corp. v. Washington Dep't of Revenue,* 377 U.S. 436, 439 (1964); *Western Live Stock v. Bureau of Revenue,* 303 U.S. 250, 258 (1938). We conclude that Missouri's use tax collection duty is fairly related to the benefits and services provided by Missouri to CFC.

The Missouri Supreme Court has found that the legislature intended the Missouri use tax law to extend only as far as constitutionally permissible.[5] See *Superior Aircraft,* supra (in which the Court adopted the *Complete Auto Transit* test, by which it is determined whether a state tax is constitutionally permissible, as the test for whether the Missouri use tax attaches). Under the *Complete Auto Transit* test, Missouri may constitutionally impose the use tax collection duty upon CFC. Because it is constitutionally permissible, we conclude that the Missouri use tax collection duty attached to CFC's Missouri activities.

CFC relies upon *Burke & Sons Oil Co. v. Director of Revenue,* 757 S.W.2d 278 (Mo. App., WD. 1988), in which the court reversed this Commission's imposition of the use tax collection duty upon a Kansas fuel oil dealer. CFC's reliance is misplaced; *Burke* is significantly different from the present case. In *Burke,* the fuel dealer had no continuous physical presence in Missouri and his contacts with Missouri customers were mostly by mail, telephone, and common carrier. However, Burke did occasionally deliver fuel to Missouri customers in his truck. The court held that these excursions did not amount to nexus under the *Complete Auto Transit* test. CFC, on the other hand, solicits Missouri customers by an agent physically present in Missouri, conduct which the United States Supreme Court has expressly found to constitute sufficient nexus. *Scripto, Inc. v. Carson, supra.*

[5] Thus, the law is saved from constitutional invalidity.

CFC next contends that the tax impermissibly discriminates against interstate commerce. CFC offers the following example:

> If title to the gas had not been transferred by Petitioner to its customers until the gas arrived in Missouri, then there would be an interstate sale which concluded in Missouri. Since the sale took place in Missouri, there would be no use tax. Furthermore, the sale would not be subject to sales tax pursuant to the Missouri commerce clause, because it involved a sale between the states. Section 144.030.1.

Petitioner's Initial Brief at 4.

However, Missouri's use tax is not discriminatory. Contrary to CFC's assertion, the use tax does apply to Missouri retail sales. It applies, by its terms, to all persons who use, store or consume in this state tangible personal property purchased from a vendor. Section 144.610.1 and .2. It is only by virtue of the exemption at § 144.615(2) that Missourians do not pay both the use tax and the sales tax on their purchases. CFC is equally wrong in its assertion that imported goods, exempt from the sales tax under the "Missouri commerce clause" at § 144.030.1, RSMo Supp. 1992, are not subject to the use tax. Such transactions are within the scope of the use tax. Section 144.615(3); *American Bridge Co. v. Smith,* 179 S.W.2d 12 (Mo. 1944).

CFC also relies on *Quill Cob. v. North Dakota,* —U.S. —, 112 S.Ct. 1904, 1914-16 (1992), for the proposition that the rule of *Scripto, Inc. v. Carson, supra,* is no longer good law. CFC misunderstands—or misrepresents—Quill. *Quill* does not represent a new departure in Commerce Clause jurisprudence; Quill is a clarification of the present state of that law. More importantly, *Quill* expressly ratified the *Scripto* rule. *Supra,* at 1914-15.

CFC sold gas to Missouri consumers. The constitution permits Missouri to impose the use tax collection duty upon CFC and we conclude that the tax attaches.

III Exemption Certificates

CFC contends that the Director ought to have accepted certain exemption certificates tendered after the end of the audit. We disagree.

Section 144.210.1, RSMo Supp. 1992, requires a seller to "obtain and maintain exemption certificates signed by the purchaser or his agent as evidence for any exempt sales claimed[.]" [6] The value of such certificates is that, if taken in "good faith," they absolutely relieve the seller from any sales tax liability on the transaction. Sections 32.200 [Multistate Tax Compact], art. V, § 2, and 144.210.1, RSMo Supp. 1992.

---

[6] This section contained this requirement throughout the audit period. *See* 1978 Mo. Laws 447.

Neither statute nor case law defines "good faith" in § 32.200. We conclude that it means that the seller must have "[h]onesty of intention, and freedom from knowledge of circumstances which ought to put the holder [of the certificate] upon inquiry." *Blacks Law Dictionary* (6th ed. 1990) at 693; see *Gammaitoni v. Director of Revenue,* 786 S.W.2d 126, 131 (Mo. banc 1990). We conclude that the statute requires that the purchaser tender the certificate, and the seller accept it, in the regular course of business. "The taking of exemption certificates other than contemporaneously with the sale is not in the regular course of business and is a circumstance which, while not conclusive on the good faith issue, weighs against a finding of good faith." *Conagra Poultry Co. v. Director of Revenue,* no. 91-001914RV, [2 Mo.] St. Tax Rep. (CCH) [¶ 201-612] (Mo. Admin. Hearing Comm'n, Nov. 6, 1992), at 10.

The Missouri Supreme Court has held that the statutes concerning exemption certificates must be strictly construed against the claimant of the exemption. Armco, supra, at 724. This rule, as well as public policy, requires that the seller receive the certificate in the regular course of business, contemporaneously with the transaction to which the certificate relates: [7]

> Section 144.210.1 serves purposes of administrative convenience and resource efficiency[.] The taxpayer bears the burden of producing, and the Director is entitled to have, all of the evidence required to determine that an otherwise taxable transaction is not taxable before him when he makes his initial determination of tax liability[.] We believe that Section 144.210.1 imposes on the seller the duty to obtain and maintain exemption certificates from the purchaser and to have such certificates available for, and at the time of, the Director's audit[.]

Id.

The law does not require the Director to accept exemption certificates tendered after the end of the audit. The record suggests that the Director occasionally does so and that she has agreed to accept certain of the certificates at issue here. Such private agreements of the parties are of no concern to this Commission. Our duty is to apply the law to the facts; on this record, CFC is not entitled to the benefit of art. V, § 2 of the Compact for the exemption certificates tendered after the end of the audit by Milnot, Guy's Foods, and Siegel-Robert.

---

[7] In *Director of Revenue v. Armco, Inc.,* 787 S.W.2d 722 (Mo. banc 1990), the taxpayer's failure to have exemption certificates at the time of the audit resulted in its loss of the benefit of the exemptions. The legislature reacted to this stem result by amending § 144.210.1. The first amendment, 1990 Mo. Laws 582-83, permitted the taxpayer to obtain the exemption certificates anytime prior to the hearing before this Commission. The second amendment, resulting in the current form of the statute, abandoned the 1990 scheme and provides that, in the absence of exemption certificates, the taxpayer may simply prove that the transaction was exempt. 1991 Mo. Laws 848-49. The quoted language of *Armco* is just as applicable to the present version of § 144.210.1 as it was to the pre-1990 version.

We note, too, that CFC has made no attempt to show that the purchases made by Milnot, Guy's Foods, and Siegel-Robert were actually exempt under the law. Therefore, we do not consider the merits of the exemptions asserted in these exemption certificates.

IV Transportation Charges

CFC next argues that the measure of the use tax does not include transportation charges because these are fees for services which are not part of the sale.

Section 144.610.1 imposes the use tax "in an amount equivalent to the percentage imposed on the sales price in the sales tax law in section 144.020." The "sales price" is "the consideration including the charges for services . . . paid or given, or contracted to be paid or given, by the purchaser to the vendor for the tangible personal property, including any services that are a part of the sale[.]"

The issue, therefore, is whether the transportation charges were part of the sale. This matter is controlled by the intention of the parties to the transaction. *Brinson Appliance, Inc. v. Director of Revenue,* No. 74645 (Mo. banc, Dec. 18, 1992) slip op. at 3-4; *May Department Stores Co. v. Director of Revenue,* 748 S.W.2d 174, 175 (Mo. banc 1988) (*May Department Stores*). The parties' intent is determined by such objective indicia as the moment of passage of title, *Kurtz Concrete, Inc. v. Spradling,* 560 S.W.2d 858 (Mo. banc 1978), and whether the charges for the services under consideration are separately stated from the price of the goods. *May Department Stores I, supra.*

In the present case, the transportation charges were sometimes separately stated and sometimes not. CFC contends that the variation is without significance and that the parties never intended the transportation charges to be part of the sale of gas. Further, CFC contends that title passed to the customer upon the introduction of the gas into the interstate pipeline system. Thus, transportation occurred after title passed and, under the rule of *Kurtz Concrete,* the transportation charges are not part of the sale of the gas and, therefore, not taxable.

We must again disagree with CFC's analysis. Under the peculiar facts of this case, we do not think that the passage of title is significant. The record shows that tile gas received by the customer in Missouri is not the same gas that CFC placed into the pipeline; that is, it is not the same physical aggregation of molecules. Finding of Fact 3. The transaction is more similar to a banking transaction: the customer deposits money at one branch and may therefore withdraw the same amount of money at a different branch. The money withdrawn, equal in value and indistinguishable from the money deposited, is not the same money.

In *Brinson Appliance,* the court upheld our conclusion that the delivery charges at issue in that case were not subject to tax where:

> [T]he cost and means of delivery of the appliances were entirely up to the customer. The customer had the option to take the appliance from the store, hire a carrier, or use a carrier selected by Slyman Bros. At the same time, the seller derived no financial benefit from the delivery and undertook no risk for damage or loss during delivery.

Supra, slip op. at 4.

In the present case, by contrast, CFC's customers had no choice at all. There was only one carrier, the gas pipeline serving their location. By contract, CFC made all of the transportation arrangements for the customer. Finding of Fact 7. On these facts, we conclude that the transportation charges were always part of the sale, whether separately stated or not. "The mere fact that a charge is stated separately is not conclusive as to whether or not it is a part of the sale and taxable." *Oakland Park Inn vs. Director of Revenue of the State of Missouri,* 822 S.W.2d 425, 426 (Mo. banc 1992).

V Credit for Payments by Purchasers

CFC contends that three of its customers, Kawasaki Motors, Chemtech Industries, and Lindberg Heat Treating Co., self-assessed and paid use tax on the gas they purchased from CFC. The record contains no proof of this assertion and we must find against CFC on this point. At the hearing, the parties indicated that they had arrived at a method of resolving this issue outside our proceedings. As we stated earlier, such private agreements of the parties are of no concern to this Commission. Our duty is to apply the law to the facts; on this record, CFC has not carried its burden of proof.

VI Interest and Additions

The Director assessed interest and additions to tax against CFC in addition to unpaid use taxes. By challenging the assessments, CFC has necessarily challenged the imposition and calculation of these items. *Travelhost v. Director of Revenue,* 785 S.W.2d 541, 546 (Mo. banc 1990).

A Interest

Because we have found that the taxpayer is liable for unpaid use tax, it is automatically liable for interest under the law. Section 144.720.

B Additions to Tax

Section 144.665.1 provides for additions to tax whenever a taxpayer fails to timely file a return required by 144.600 et seq. Section 144.665.2 imposes additions for failure to timely pay the tax. In both cases, the additions may be excused when "it is shown that such failure is due to reasonable cause and not the result of willful neglect, evasion or fraudulent intent." Identical provisions at § 144.250.1 and .2 apply additions to the sales tax. The burden of proof is on the taxpayer. Section 621.050.2, RSMo Supp. 1992.

The Missouri Supreme Court has recently instructed us that, to avoid additions, the taxpayer need only show that its conduct was not characterized by "willful neglect," without any separate showing of "reasonable cause." *Hewitt Well Drilling & Pump Service, Inc., v. Director of Revenue,* No. 74891 (Mo. banc, Feb. 23, 1993) slip op. at 8. "Willful neglect" is (1) a failure to act as required by the taxing statutes (2) coupled with a lack of good faith. *Hewitt Well Drilling, supra,* at 9. We recall that "good faith" is "[h]onesty of intention, and freedom from knowledge of circumstances which ought to put the [taxpayer] upon inquiry." *Black's Law Dictionary* (6th ed. 1990) at 693.

Turning to the record, we note CFC did not file a use tax return or remit use tax at all, although the record shows that CFC sold goods for delivery and consumption in Missouri during the audit period. The taxpayer's claim that it acted out of its sincere belief that its conduct is not subject to the tax has not generally been acceptable to show a lack of willful neglect in the absence of a showing that the taxpayer sought and followed authoritative advice. In the past, we would have upheld the additions. See *Conagra Poultry Co. v. Director of Revenue,* No. 91-001914RV, [2 Mo.] St. Tax Rep. (CCH) [¶ 201-612] (Mo. Admin. Hearing Comm'n, Nov. 6, 1992); *Cityvision, Inc. et al v. Director of Revenue,* No's RS-85-0587 through 0591, [2 Mo.] St. Tax Rep. (CCH) Para. 201-155 (Mo. Admin. Hearing Comm'n, Nov. 12, 1987).

However, *Hewitt* seems to require that additions be supported by facts establishing actual purposeful tax evasion. This record establishes only that CFC was unknowledgeable and unconcerned about its possible Missouri use tax liability. We conclude that additions do not lie.

Summary

This Commission concludes that CFC has failed to show that the Director's assessment of unpaid use tax is erroneous. Interest is due on the unpaid tax by operation of law. We conclude that additions are not due because the record does not show that CFC acted intentionally, in bad faith, to avoid its known duty.

General Motors Corp. v. Tracy

[*General Motors Corp.* is discussed at ¶ 520 and ¶ 1005.]

U.S. Supreme Court, Dkt. 95-1232, 117 S.Ct. 811 (1997), February 18, 1997.

On writ of certiorari to the Supreme Court of Ohio. Affirmed.

JUSTICE SOUTER delivered the opinion of the Court.

The State of Ohio imposes its general sales and use taxes on natural gas purchases from all sellers, whether in-state or out-of-state, except regulated public utilities that meet Ohio's statutory definition of a "natural gas company." The question here is whether this difference in tax treatment between sales of gas by domestic utilities subject to regulation and sales of gas by other entities violates the Commerce Clause or Equal Protection Clause of the Constitution. We hold that it does not.

I

During the tax period at issue,[1] Ohio levied a 5% tax on the in-state sales of goods, including natural gas, see Ohio Rev. Code Ann. § § 5739.02, 5739.025 (Supp. 1990), and it imposed a parallel 5% use tax on goods purchased out-of-state for use in Ohio. See § 5741.02 (1986). Local jurisdictions were authorized to levy certain additional taxes that increased these sales and use tax rates to as much as 7% in some municipalities. See § 5739.025 (Supp. 1990); Reply Brief for Petitioner 13, n. 11.

Since 1935, when Ohio's first sales and use taxes were imposed, the State has exempted natural gas sales by "natural gas compan[ies]" from all state and local sales taxes. § 5739.02(B)(7) (Supp. 1990).[2] Under Ohio law, "[a]ny person . . . [i]s a natural gas company when engaged in the business of supplying natural gas for lighting, power, or heating purposes to consumers within this state." § 5727.01(D)(4) (1996); see also § 5727.01(E)(4) (Supp. 1990); § 5727.01(E)(8) (1986). It is undisputed that natural gas utilities (generally termed "local distribution companies" or LDCs) located in Ohio satisfy this definition of "natural gas company." The Supreme Court of Ohio has, however, interpreted the statutory term to exclude non-LDC gas sellers, such as producers and independent marketers, see *Chrysler Corp. v. Tracy,* 73 Ohio St. 3d

---

[1] The natural gas purchases that gave rise to petitioner's challenge were made during the period from October 1, 1986 to June 30, 1990.

[2] The exemption was originally codified at Ohio Gen. Code Ann. § 5546-2(6) (Baldwin 1952). As part of a general recodification in 1953, it was moved to Ohio Rev. Code Ann. § 5739.02(B)(7), where it remains today.

26, 652 N. E. 2d 185 (1995), and the State has accordingly treated their sales as outside the exemption and so subject to the tax.

The very question of such an exclusion, and consequent taxation of gas sales or use, reflects a recent stage of evolution in the structure of the natural gas industry. Traditionally, the industry was divisible into three relatively distinct segments: producers, interstate pipelines, and LDCs. This market structure was possible largely because the Natural Gas Act of 1938, 52 Stat. 821, 15 U. S. C. § 717 et seq. (NGA), failed to require interstate pipelines to offer transportation services to third parties wishing to ship gas. As a result, "interstate pipelines [were able] to use their monopoly power over gas transportation to create and maintain monopsony power in the market for the purchase of gas at the wellhead and monopoly power in the market for the sale of gas to LDCs." Pierce, The Evolution of Natural Gas Regulatory Policy, 10 Nat. Resources & Env't 53, 53-54 (Summer 1995) (hereinafter Pierce). For the most part, then, producers sold their gas to the pipelines, which resold it to utilities, which in turn provided local distribution to consumers. See, *e.g., Associated Gas Distributors v. FERC,* 824 F. 2d 981, 993 (CADC 1987), cert. denied, 485 U. S. 1006 (1988); Mogel & Gregg, Appropriateness of Imposing Common Carrier Status on Interstate Natural Gas Pipelines, 4 Energy L. J. 155, 157 (1983).

Congress took a first step toward increasing competition in the natural gas market by enacting the Natural Gas Policy Act of 1978, 92 Stat. 3350, 15 U. S. C. § 3301 *et seq.,* which was designed to phase out regulation of wellhead prices charged by producers of natural gas, and to "promote gas transportation by interstate and intrastate pipelines" for third parties. 57 Fed. Reg. 13271 (1992). Pipelines were reluctant to provide common carriage, however, when doing so would displace their own sales, see *Associated Gas Distributors v. FERC, supra,* at 993, and in 1985, the Federal Energy Regulatory Commission (FERC) took the further step of promulgating Order No. 436, which contained an "open access" rule providing incentives for pipelines to offer gas transportation services, see 50 Fed. Reg. 42408. In 1992, this evolution culminated in FERC's Order No. 636, which required all interstate pipelines to "unbundle" their transportation services from their own natural gas sales and to provide common carriage services to buyers from other sources that wished to ship gas. See 57 Fed. Reg. 13267.

Although FERC did not take the further step of requiring intrastate pipelines to provide local transportation services to insure that gas sold by producers and independent marketers could get all the way to the point of consumption,[3] under the system of open access to

[3] Section 1(b) of the NGA, 52 Stat. 821, 15 U. S. C. § 717(b), explicitly exempts "local distribution of natural gas" from federal regulation. In addition, the Hinshaw Amendment to the NGA, 15 U. S. C.

interstate pipelines that had emerged in the mid-1980s "larger industrial end-users" began increasingly to bypass utilities' local distribution networks by "construct[ing] their own pipeline spurs to [interstate] pipeline[s] . . . ." Fagan, From Regulation to Deregulation: The Diminishing Role of the Small Consumer Within the Natural Gas Industry, 29 Tulsa L. J. 707, 723 (1994). Bypass posed a problem for LDCs, since the departure of large end-users from the system left the same fixed costs to be spread over a smaller customer base. The State of Ohio consequently took steps in 1986 to keep some income from large industrial customers within the utility system by adopting regulations that allowed industrial end-users in Ohio to buy natural gas from producers or independent marketers, pay interstate pipelines for interstate transportation, and pay LDCs for local transportation. See *In re Commission Ordered Investigation of the Availability of Gas Transportation Service Provided by Ohio Gas Distribution Utilities to End-Use Customers,* No. 85-800-GA-COI (Ohio Pub. Util. Comm'n, April 15, 1986); see generally Natural Gas Marketing and Transportation Committee, 1990 Annual Report, in Natural Resources Energy and Environmental Law, 1990 Year in Review 57, 91-92, and n. 207 (1991).

This new market structure led to the question whether purchases from non-LDC sellers of natural gas qualified for the State sales tax exemption under Ohio Rev. Code Ann. 5739.02(B)(7) (Supp. 1990). In *Chrysler Corp. v. Tracy,* the Ohio Supreme Court held that they do not. The Court reasoned that independent marketers do not "suppl[y]" natural gas as required by § 5727.01(D)(4), because they do "not own or control any physical assets to . . . distribute natural gas." 73 Ohio St. 3d, at 28, 652 N. E. 2d, at 187. This determination of state law led in turn to the case before us now.

During the tax period in question here, petitioner General Motors Corporation (GMC) bought virtually all the natural gas for its Ohio plants from out-of-state marketers, not LDCs.[4] Respondent Tax Commissioner of Ohio applied the State's general use tax to GMC's purchases, and the State Board of Tax Appeals sustained that action. GMC appealed to the Supreme Court of Ohio on two grounds. GMC first contended that its purchases should be exempt from the sales tax because independent marketers fell within the statutory definition of "natural gas company." The State Supreme Court, citing its decision the same day in *Chrysler,* rejected this argument. See *General Motors*

(Footnote Continued)

§ 717(c), exempts from FERC regulation intrastate pipelines that operate exclusively in one State and with rates and service regulated by the State. See *ANR Pipeline Co. v. FERC,* 71 F. 3d 897, 898, n. 2 (CADC 1995). See also *infra,* at—.

[4] App. 156. Pursuant to Ohio's regulations authorizing LDCs to provide local transportation services, GMC took delivery of much of this gas from local utilities. *Id.,* 156-157.

Corp. v. Tracy, 73 Ohio St.3d 29, 30, 652 N. E. 2d 188, 189 (1995). GMC also argued that denying the tax exemption to sales by marketers violated the Commerce and Equal Protection Clauses. The Ohio court initially concluded that the State's regime did not violate the Commerce Clause because Ohio taxes sales by "compan[ies] that d[o] not own any production, transportation, or distribution equipment" at the same rate regardless of "whether [the companies sell] natural gas in-state or out-of-state." *Id.,* at 31, 652 N. E. 2d, at 190. The Court then stepped back to rule, however, that GMC lacked standing to bring its Commerce Clause challenge:

> On close inspection, GM actually argues that the commissioner's application burdens out-of-state vendors of natural gas. However, GM is not a member of that class and lacks standing to challenge the constitutionality of this application on that basis; our further comment on this question is inappropriate." *Ibid.*

Finally, the court dismissed GMC's Equal Protection claim as "submerged in its Commerce Clause argument." *Id.,* at 31-32, 652 N. E. 2d, at 190. We granted GMC's petition for certiorari to address the question of standing as well as the Commerce and Equal Protection Clause issues. 517 U. S.—(1996).

II

The Supreme Court of Ohio held GMC to be without standing to raise this Commerce Clause challenge because the company is not one of the sellers said to suffer discrimination under the challenged tax laws. But cognizable injury from unconstitutional discrimination against interstate commerce does not stop at members of the class against whom a state ultimately discriminates, and customers of that class may also be injured, as in this case where the customer is liable for payment of the tax and as a result presumably pays more for the gas it gets from out-of-state producers and marketers. Consumers who suffer this sort of injury from regulation forbidden under the Commerce Clause satisfy the standing requirements of Article III. See generally *Lujan v. Defenders of Wildlife,* 504 U. S. 555, 560-561 (1992).

On similar facts, we held in *Bacchus Imports, Ltd. v. Dias,* 468 U. S. 263 (1984), that in-state liquor wholesalers had standing to raise a Commerce Clause challenge to a Hawaii tax regime exempting certain alcohols produced in-state from liquor taxes. Although the wholesalers were not among the class of out-of-state liquor producers allegedly burdened by Hawaii's law, we reasoned that the wholesalers suffered economic injury both because they were directly liable for the tax and because the tax raised the price of their imported goods relative to the exempted in-state beverages. *Id.,* at 267; see also *Fulton Corp. v. Faulkner,* 516 U. S.—(1996) (in-state stockholder challenged tax regime imposing higher taxes on stock from issuers with out-of-state operations than on stock from purely in-state issuers); *West Lynn Creamery, Inc. v. Healy,* 512 U. S. 186 (1994) (in-state milk dealers challenged tax and subsidy scheme discriminating against out-of-state milk producers). *Bacchus* applies with equal force here, and GMC "plainly ha[s] standing to challenge the tax in this Court," *Bacchus Imports v. Dias, supra,* at 267. We therefore turn to the merits.

III

A

The negative or dormant implication of the Commerce Clause prohibits state taxation, see, *e.g., Quill Corp. v. North Dakota,* 504 U. S. 298, 312-313 (1992), or regulation, see, *e.g., Brown-Forman Distillers Corp. v. New York State Liquor Authority,* 476 U. S. 573, 578-579 (1986), that discriminates against or unduly burdens interstate commerce and thereby "imped[es] free private trade in the national marketplace," *Reeves, Inc. v. Stake,* 447 U. S. 429, 437 (1980). GMC claims that Ohio's differential tax treatment of natural gas sales by marketers and regulated local utilities constitutes "facial" or "patent" discrimination in violation of the Commerce Clause, and it argues that differences in the nature of the businesses of LDCs and interstate marketers cannot justify Ohio's differential treatment of these in-state and out-of-state entities. Although the claim is not that the Ohio tax scheme distinguishes in express terms between in-state and out-of-state entities, GMC argues that by granting the tax exemption solely to LDCs, which are in fact all located in Ohio, the State has "favor[ed] some in-state commerce while disfavoring all out-of-state commerce," Brief for Petitioner 16. That is, because the favored entities are all located within the State, "the tax exemption did not need to be drafted explicitly along state lines in order to demonstrate its discriminatory design," *Amerada Hess Corp. v. Director, Div. of Taxation, N. J. Dept. of Treasury,* 490 U. S. 66, 76 (1989). Assessing these arguments requires an understanding of the historical development of the contemporary retail market for natural gas, to which we referred before and now turn in greater detail.

B

Since before the Civil War, gas manufactured from coal and other commodities had been used for lighting purposes, and of course it was understood that natural gas could be used the same way. See Dorner, Initial Phases of Regulation of the Gas Industry, in 1 Regulation of the Gas Industry §§2.03–2.06 (American Gas Assn. 1996) (hereinafter Dorner). By the early years of this century, areas in "proximity to the gas field[s]," *West v. Kansas Natural Gas Co.,* 221 U. S. 229, 246

(1911), did use natural gas for fuel, but it was not until the 1920's that the development of high-tensile steel and electric welding permitted construction of high-pressure pipelines to transport natural gas from gas fields for distant consumption at relatively low cost. Pierce 53. By that time, the States' then-recent experiments with free market competition in the manufactured gas and electricity industries had dramatically underscored the need for comprehensive regulation of the local gas market. Companies supplying manufactured gas proliferated in the latter half of the 19th century and, after initial efforts at regulation by statute at the state level proved unwieldy, the States generally left any regulation of the industry to local governments. See Dorner §§2.03, 2.04. Many of those municipalities honored the tenets of laissez-faire to the point of permitting multiple gas franchisees to serve a single area and relying on competition to protect the public interest. *Ibid.* The results were both predictable and disastrous, including an initial period of "wasteful competition,"[5] followed by massive consolidation and the threat of monopolistic pricing.[6] The public suffered through essentially the same evolution in the electric industry.[7] Thus, by the time natural gas became a widely marketable commodity, the States had learned from chastening experience that public streets could not be continually torn up to lay competitors' pipes, that investments in parallel delivery systems for different fractions of a local market would limit the value to consumers of any price competition, and that competition would simply give over to monopoly in due course. It seemed virtually an economic necessity for States to provide a single, local franchise with a business opportunity free of competition from any source, within or without the State, so long as the creation of exclusive franchises under state law could be balanced by regulation and the imposition of obligations to the consuming public upon the franchised retailers.

---

[5] During this period, "[t]he public grew weary of the interminable rate wars which were invariably followed by a period of recoupment during which the victorious would attempt to make the price of the battle of the consumers by way of increased rates. Investors suffered heavy losses through the manipulation of fly-by-night paper concerns operating with 'nuisance' franchises. . . . Everybody suffered the inconvenience of city streets being constantly torn up and replaced by installation and relocation of duplicate facilities. The situation in New York City alone, prior to the major gas company consolidations, threatened municipal chaos.'" Dorner § 2.03, (quoting Welch, The Odyssey of Gas—A Record of Industrial Courage, 24 Pub. Utils. Fortnightly, 500, 501-502 (1939)).

[6] Reticence was not the order of the day. When, for example, the last two surviving gas companies supplying the citizens of Brooklyn announced their merger in October 1883, they also announced that gas prices would immediately double. Dorner § 2.03.

[7] The electric industry burgeoned following Thomas Edison's patent on the first incandescent electric lamp in 1878. Dorner, Beginnings of the Gas Industry, in 1 Regulation of the Gas Industry § 1.06 (American Gas Assn. 1996). Again, after an initial period of unsuccessful regulation by state statute, States mostly left regulation of the electric industry to municipal or local government. Swartwout, Current Utility Regulatory Practice from a Historical Perspective, 32 Nat. Res. J. 289, 298 (1992). "[M]ultiple franchises were handed out, and duplicative utility systems came into being." *Id.*, at 299. The results were "ruinous and short lived." *Ibid.* For example, 45 mostly overlapping franchises were granted for electric utility operation in Chicago between 1882 and 1905. By 1905, however a single monopoly entity had emerged from the chaos, and customers ended up paying monopoly prices. *Id.*, at 300.

Almost as soon as the States began regulating natural gas retail monopolies, their power to do so was challenged by interstate vendors as inconsistent with the dormant Commerce Clause. While recognizing the interstate character of commerce in natural gas, the Court nonetheless affirmed the States' power to regulate, as a matter of local concern, all direct sales of gas to consumers within their borders, absent congressional prohibition of such state regulation. See, *e.g., Pennsylvania Gas Co. v. Public Serv. Comm'n of N. Y.,* 252 U. S. 23, 28-31 (1920); *Public Util. Comm'n of Kan. v. Landon,* 249 U. S. 236, 245-246 (1919). At the same time, the Court concluded that the dormant Commerce Clause prevents the States from regulating interstate transportation or sales for resale of natural gas. See, *e.g., Missouri ex rel. Barrett v. Kansas National Gas Co.,* 265 U. S. 298, 307-310 (1924); *Pennsylvania v. West Virginia,* 262 U. S. 553, 596-600, reaffirmed on rehearing, 263 U. S. 350 (1923). See generally *Illinois Natural Gas Co. v. Central Ill. Public Service Co.,* 314 U. S. 498, 504-505 (1942) (summarizing prior cases distinguishing between permissible and impermissible state regulation of commerce in natural gas). Thus, the Court never questioned the power of the States to regulate retail sales of gas within their respective jurisdictions. Dorner § 2.06.[8]

When federal regulation of the natural gas industry finally began in 1938, Congress, too, clearly recognized the value of such state-regulated monopoly arrangements for the sale and distribution of natural gas directly to local consumers. Thus, § 1(b) of the NGA, 15 U. S. C. § 717(b), explicitly exempted "local distribution of natural gas" from federal regulation, even as the NGA authorized the Federal Power Commission (FPC) to begin regulating interstate pipelines. Congress's purpose in enacting the NGA was to fill the regulatory void created by

[8] In *Arkansas Elec. Cooperative Corp. v. Arkansas Pub. Serv. Comm'n,* 461 U. S. 375 (1983), "we rejected the bright-line distinction between wholesale and retail sales drawn by these older cases and concluded that state regulation of wholesale sales of electricity transmitted in interstate commerce is not precluded by the Commerce Clause. Reasoning that utilities should not be insulated from our contemporary dormant Commerce Clause jurisprudence by formalistic judge-made rules, *id.,* at 391, we looked instead to 'the nature of the state regulation involved, the objective of the state, and the effect of the regulation upon the national interest in the commerce,'" *id.,* at 390 (quoting *Illinois Natural Gas Co. v. Central Ill. Public Service Co.,* 314 U. S. 498, 505 (1942)), to determine whether States have a sufficient interest in regulating wholesale rates within their borders, and had no problem concluding that States do indeed have such an interest, with the result that state regulation of wholesale rates is not precluded by the Commerce Clause (in the absence of preemptive congressional action), *id.,* at 394-395. While the holding of *Arkansas Electric* thereby expanded both the permissible scope of state utility regulation and judicial recognition of the important state interests in such regulation, the reasoning of the case equally implies that state regulation of retail sales is not, as a constitutional matter, immune from our ordinary Commerce Clause jurisprudence, and to the extent that our earlier cases may have implied such immunity they are no longer good law. Nothing in *Arkansas Electric* undermines the earlier cases' recognition of the powerful state interest in regulating sales to domestic consumers buying at retail, however, which we reaffirm here. In addition, *Arkansas Electric* does not disturb the relevance of the wholesale/retail distinction for construing the jurisdictional provisions of statutes such as the NGA, which we discuss immediately below. See *id.,* at 380, and n. 3; see also *Schneidewind v. ANR Pipeline Co.,* 485 U. S. 293, 300-301 (1988) ("The NGA confers upon FERC exclusive jurisdiction over the transportation and sale of natural gas in interstate commerce for resale").

the Court's earlier decisions prohibiting States from regulating interstate transportation and sales for resale of natural gas, while at the same time leaving undisturbed the recognized power of the States to regulate all in-state gas sales directly to consumers. *Panhandle Eastern Pipe Line Co. v. Public Serv. Comm'n of Ind.*, 332 U. S. 507, 516-522 (1947). Thus, the NGA "was drawn with meticulous regard for the continued exercise of state power, not to handicap or dilute it in any way," *id.*, at 517-518; "the scheme was one of cooperative action between federal and state agencies" to "protect consumers against exploitation at the hands of natural gas companies," *id.*, at 520 (internal quotation marks omitted); and "Congress' action . . . was an unequivocal recognition of the vital interests of the states and their people, consumers and industry alike, in the regulation of rates and service," *id.*, at 521; see also *Panhandle Eastern Pipe Line Co. v. Michigan Pub. Serv. Comm'n,* 341 U. S. 329, 334 (1951) ("Direct sales [of natural gas] for consumptive use were designedly left to state regulation" by the NGA). Indeed, the Court has construed § 1(b) of the NGA as altogether exempting state regulation of in-state retail sales of natural gas from attack under the dormant Commerce Clause:

> The declaration [in the NGA], though not identical in terms with the one made by the McCarran Act, 59 Stat. 33, 15 U. S. C. § 1011, concerning continued state regulation of the insurance business, is in effect equally clear, in view of the [NGA's] historical setting, legislative history and objects, to show intention for the states to continue with regulation where Congress has not expressly taken over. Cf. *Prudential Ins. Co. v. Benjamin,* 328 U. S. 408 [(1946) (upholding discriminatory state taxation of out-of-state insurance companies as authorized by the McCarran Act)]." *Panhandle-Indiana, supra,* at 521.

And Congress once again acknowledged the important role of the States in regulating intrastate transportation and distribution of natural gas in 1953 when, in the wake of a decision of this Court permitting the FPC to regulate intrastate gas transportation by LDCs, see *Federal Power Comm'n v. East Ohio Gas Co.*, 338 U. S. 464 (1950), Congress amended the NGA to "leav[e] jurisdiction" over "companies engaged in the distribution" of natural gas "exclusively in the States, as always has been intended." S. Rep. No. 817, 83d Cong., 1st Sess., 1-2 (1953); see 15 U. S. C. § 717(c).

For 40 years, the complementary federal regulation of the interstate market and congressionally approved state regulation of the intrastate gas trade thus endured unchanged in any way relevant to this case. The resulting market structure virtually precluded competition between LDCs and other potential suppliers of natural gas for direct sales to consumers, including large industrial consumers. The simplicity of this dual system of federal and state regulation began to erode in 1978, however, when Congress first encouraged interstate pipelines to provide transportation services to end users wishing to ship gas,[9] and thereby moved toward providing a real choice to those consumers who were able to buy gas on the open market and were willing to take it free of state-created obligations to the buyer. The upshot of congressional and regulatory developments over the next 15 years was increasing opportunity for a consumer in that class to choose between gas sold by marketers and gas bundled with rights and benefits mandated by state regulators as sold by LDCs. But amidst such changes, two things remained the same throughout the period involved in this case. Congress did nothing to limit the States' traditional autonomy to authorize and regulate local gas franchises, and the local franchised utilities (though no longer guaranteed monopolies as to all natural gas demand) continued to provide bundled gas to the vast majority of consumers who had neither the capacity to buy on the interstate market nor the resilience to forgo the reliability and protection that state regulation provided.

To this day, all 50 States recognize the need to regulate utilities engaged in local distribution of natural gas.[10] Ohio's treatment of its

---

[9] For a more complete description of these changes in federal regulatory policy, and the relevant modifications of Ohio regulation of local utilities that they prompted, see *supra* at—. P

[10] Alabama: Ala. Code §§37-4-1(7)(b) (Supp. 1996); see generally §§37-1-80 through 37-1-105 (1992 and Supp. 1996); Alaska: Alaska Stat. Ann. §§42.05.141, 42.05.291, 42.05.990(4)(D) (1989 and Supp. 1995); see generally §§42.05.010-42.05.995; Arizona: Ariz. Rev. Stat. Ann. §§40-201.4, 40-203 (1996); see generally §§40-201 through 40-495; Arkansas: Ark. Code Ann. §§23-1-101(4)(A)(i), 23-4-101 (1987 and Supp. 1995); see generally §§23-1-101 through 23-4-637; California: Cal. Pub. Util. Code Ann. §§216, 701 (West 1975 and Supp. 1996); see generally §§201-2101; Colorado: Colo. Rev. Stat. §§40-1-103(1)(a), 40-3-101 (1993); see generally §§40-1-101 through 40-8.5-107 (1993 and Supp. 1996); Connecticut: Conn. Gen. Stat. Ann. §§16-1(a)(4), (9), 16-6b (West 1988 and Supp. 1996); see generally §§16-1 through 16-50f; Delaware: Del Code Ann., Tit. 26, §§102(2) (Supp. 1996); see generally, Tit. 26, §§101 through 511 (1989 and Supp. 1996); District of Columbia: D.C. Code Ann. §§43-203, 43-212 (1990); see generally §§43-101 through 43-1107 (1990 and Supp. 1996); Florida: Fla. Stat. Ann. §§366.02(1), 366.03 (West Supp. 1997); see generally §§366.01 through 366.14 (West 1968 and Supp. 1997); Georgia: Ga. Code Ann. §46-2-20(a) (1992); see generally §§46-2-20 through 46-2-94 (1992 and Supp. 1996); Hawaii: Haw. Rev. Stat. Ann. §§269-1, 269-6, 269-16 (Michie 1992 and Supp. 1996); see generally §§269-1 through 269-32; Idaho: Idaho Code §§61-129, 61-501, 61-502 (1994); see generally §§61-101 through 61-714; Illinois: Ill. Comp. Stat. ch. 220, §§5/3-105, 5/4-101, 5/9-101 (1994); see generally ch. 220, §§5/1-101 through 5/10-204; Indiana: Ind. Code. §§8-1-2-1, 8-1-2-4, 8-1-2-87 (West Supp. 1996); see generally §§8-1-2-1 through 8-1-2-127; Iowa: Iowa Code Ann. 476.1 (West Supp. 1996); see generally §§476.1 through 476.66 (West 1991 and Supp. 1996); Kansas: Kan. Stat. Ann. §§66-104, 66-1,200 through 66-1,208 (1985 and Supp. 1995); Kentucky: Ky. Rev. Stat. Ann. §278.010(3)(c) (Baldwin 1992); see generally §§278.010 through 278.450; Louisiana: La. Rev. Stat. Ann. §33:4161 (West 1988); see generally §§33:4161 through 33:4174, 33:4301 through 33:4308, 33:4491 through 33:4496 (West 1988 and Supp. 1996); Maine: Me. Rev. Stat. Ann. Tit. 35-A, §§102, 103, 301 (1988 and Supp. 1996-1997); see generally Tit. 35-A, §§101-1210; Maryland: Md. Ann. Code, Art. 78, §§1, 2(o) (1991); see generally Art. 78, §§1 through 2, 23 through 27A, 51 through 54K, 68 through 88 (1991 and Supp. 1994); Massachusetts: Mass. Gen. Laws §§164:1, 164:93, 164:94 (1994); see generally ch. 164, §§1 through 128; Michigan: Mich. Comp. Laws Ann. §§460.6-460.6b (West 1991 and Supp. 1996-1997); see generally §§460.1 through 460.8; Minnesota: Minn. Stat. Ann. §§216B.02(4), 216B.03 (West 1992); see generally §§216B.01 through 216B.67 (1994 and Supp. 1995); Mississippi: Miss. Code Ann. §§77-3-3(d)(ii), 77-3-5 (1991 and Supp. 1996); see generally §§77-3-1 through 77-3-307; Missouri: Mo. Rev. Stat. §§386.020, 393.130 (1994); see generally §§386.010 through 386.710, 393.010 through 393.770; Montana: Mont. Code Ann. §§69-3-101, 69-3-102, 69-3-201

gas utilities has been a typical blend of limitation and affirmative obligation. Its natural gas utilities, during the period in question, bore with a variety of requirements: they had to submit annual forecasts of future supply and demand for gas, Ohio Rev. Code Ann. § 4905.14 (Supp. 1990), comply with a range of accounting, reporting, and disclosure rules, § § 4905.14, 4905.15 (1977 and Supp. 1990), and get permission from the State Public Utilities Commission to issue securities and even enter certain contracts, § § 4905.40, 4905.41, 4905.48. The "just and reasonable" rates to which they were restricted, see § § 4905.22, 4905.32, 4909.15, 4909.17, included a single average cost of gas, see Ohio Admin. Code 4901:1-14 Ohio Monthly Record (Nov. 1991), together with a limited return on investment.[11] The LDCs could not exact "a greater or lesser compensation for any services rendered . . . than [exacted] . . . from any other [customer] for doing a like and contemporaneous service under substantially the same circumstances and conditions." Ohio Rev. Code Ann. § 4905.33 (Supp. 1990).

(Footnote Continued)

(1995); see generally § § 69-3-101 through 69-3-713; Nebraska: Neb. Rev. Stat. § § 14-1103 through 14-1103.1, 19-4601 through 19-4623 (1991); Nevada: Nev. Rev. Stat. Ann. § 704.020(2)(a) (1995); see generally § § 704.001 through 704.320, 704.755; New Hampshire: N. H. Rev. Stat. Ann. § § 362:2, 374:1, 374:2 (1995); see generally § § 378:1 through 378:42; New Jersey: N.J. Stat. Ann. 48:2-13 (West Supp. 1996); see generally § § 48:2-13 through 48:2-91, 48:9-5 through 48:9-32 (West 1969 and Supp. 1996-1997); New Mexico: N.M. Stat. Ann. § § 62-3-3, 62-6-4, 62-8-1 (1993 and Supp. 1996); see generally § § 62-1-1 through 62-13-14; New York: N.Y. Pub. Serv. Law § 65 (McKinney 1989); see generally § § 30 through 52, 64 through 77 (McKinney 1989 and Supp. 1996); North Carolina: N.C. Gen. Stat. § § 62-3(23), 62-30 (1989 and Supp. 1996); see generally § § 62-1 through 62-171; North Dakota: N.D. Cent. Code § § 49-02-01, 49-02-02, 49-04-02 (1978 and Supp. 1995); see generally § § 49-02-01 through 49-07-06; Ohio: Ohio Rev. Code Ann. § § 4905.03(A)(6), 4905.04, 4905.22 (1991); see generally § § 4901.01-4909.99 (Baldwin 1991 and Supp. 1995); Oklahoma: Okla. Stat., Tit. 17, § § 15, 152, 160.1 (West 1986 and Supp. 1997); Oregon: Ore. Rev. Stat. § § 757.005, 757.020, 756.040 (1991); see generally § § 756.010 through 757.991; Pennsylvania: Pa. Cons. Stat. Tit. 66, § § 102, 501, 1301 (Purdon 1979 and Supp. 1996-1997); see generally Tit. 66, § § 101 through 2107; Rhode Island: R.I. Gen. Laws 39-1-2(7), 39-1-3(a) (Supp. 1996); see generally § § 39-1-1 through 39-2-19 (1990 and Supp. 1996); South Carolina: S.C. Code Ann. § § 58-5-10(3), 58-5-210 (1976 and Supp. 1995); see generally § § 58-5-10 through 58-5-1070; South Dakota: S.D. Codified Laws § § 49-34A-1, 49-34A-4, 49-34A-6 (1993 and Supp. 1996); see generally § § 49-34A-1 through 49-34A-78; Tennessee: Tenn. Code Ann. § § 65-4-101, 65-5-201 (Supp. 1996); see generally § § 65-4-101 through 65-5-205 (1993 and Supp. 1996); Texas: Tex. Rev. Civ. Stat. Ann. Art 6050, § 1(a)(4), Art. 6053 (Vernon Supp. 1996-1997); see generally Arts. 6050 through 6066g (Vernon 1962 and Supp. 1996-1997); Utah: Utah Code Ann. § § 54-2-1(8), 54-3-1, 54-4-1 (1994 and Supp. 1996); see generally § § 54-2-1 through 54-4-30; Vermont: Vt. Stat. Ann., Tit. 30, § 215 (1986); Virginia: Va. Code Ann. § § 56-232, 56-234 (1995); see generally § § 56-232 through 56-260.1 (1995 and Supp. 1996); Washington: Wash. Rev. Code § § 80.04.010, 80.28.020 (West 1991 and Supp. 1996-1997); see generally § § 80.04.010 through 80.04.520, 80.28.010 through 80.28.260; West Virginia: W. Va. Code § 24-2-1 (1992); see generally § § 24-1-1 through 24-5-1 (1992 and Supp. 1996); Wisconsin: Wis. Stat. Ann. § § 196.01(5), 196.02, 196.03 (West 1992 and Supp. 1996-1997); see generally § § 196.01 through 196.98; Wyoming: Wyo. Stat. § § 37- 1-101(a)(vi)(D), 37-2-112 (1996); see generally § § 37-1-101 through 37-6-107.

[11] Ohio's Amended Substitute House Bill 476, signed into law in 1996, requires the state Public Utilities Commission to exempt certain sales of natural gas and/or related services by an LDC from this rate regulation if the Commission finds that the LDC is subject to effective competition with respect to such service and that the customers for such service have reasonably available alternatives, Ohio Rev. Code Ann. § 4929.04, as amended by H. R. 476, § 1, effective Sept. 17, 1996. Although this law had not been enacted at the time of the purchases involved in this case, petitioner contended at oral argument that during the tax period in question here, Ohio permitted some natural gas sales by public utilities at unregulated, negotiated rates, and that those sales were not subject to sales tax. The record provides no support for this contention, and the constitutionality of Ohio exempting from state sales tax utility sales that are not price-regulated is therefore not before the Court in this case.

The State also required LDCs to serve all members of the public, without discrimination, throughout their fields of operations. See, *e.g., Industrial Gas Co. v. Public Utilities Comm'n of Ohio,* 135 Ohio St. 408, 21 N. E. 2d 166 (1939). They could not "pick out good portions of a particular territory, serve only select customers under private contract, and refuse service . . . to . . . other users," *id.,* at 413, 21 N. E. 2d, at 168, or terminate service except for reasons defined by statute and by following statutory procedures, Ohio Rev. Code Ann. § § 4933.12, 4933.121 (Supp. 1990). When serving "human needs" consumers including "residential [and] other customers . . . where the element of human welfare [was] the predominant factor," *In re Commission Ordered Investigation of the Availability of Gas Transportation Service Provided by Ohio Gas Distribution Utilities to End-Use Customers,* No. 85-800-GA-COI (Ohio Pub. Util. Comm'n, Aug. 1, 1989), Ohio LDCs were required to provide a firm backup supply of gas, see *ibid.,* and administer specific protective schemes, as by helping to assure a degree of continued service to low-income customers despite unpaid bills. See, *e.g.,* Ohio Admin. Code 4901:1-18 (Ohio Monthly Record Nov. 1991).

IV

The fact that the local utilities continue to provide a product consisting of gas bundled with the services and protections summarized above, a product thus different from the marketer's unbundled gas, raises a hurdle for GMC's claim that "Ohio's differential tax treatment of natural gas utilities and independent marketers violates our 'virtually *per se* rule of invalidity,'" *Associated Industries of Mo. v. Lohman,* 511 U. S. 641, 647 (1994) (quoting *Armco Inc. v. Hardesty,* 467 U. S. 638, 642 (1984)), prohibiting facial discrimination against interstate commerce.

A

Conceptually, of course, any notion of discrimination [12] assumes a comparison of substantially similar entities. Although this central as-

[12] Although GMC raises only a "facial discrimination" challenge to Ohio's tax scheme, our cases have indicated that even nondiscriminatory state legislation may be invalid under the dormant Commerce Clause, when, in the words of the so-called *Pike* undue burden test, "the burden imposed on [interstate] commerce is clearly excessive in relation to the putative local benefits," *Pike v. Bruce Church, Inc.,* 397 U. S. 137, 142 (1970). There is, however, no clear line between these two strands of analysis, *Brown-Forman Distillers Corp. v. New York State Liquor Authority,* 476 U. S. 573, 579 (1986), and several cases that have purported to apply the undue burden test (including *Pike* itself) arguably turned in whole or in part on the discriminatory character of the challenged state regulations, see, *e.g., Pike, supra,* at 145 (declaring packing order "virtually *per se* illegal" because it required business operation to be performed in-state); *Kassel v. Consolidated Freightways Corp. of Del.,* 450 U. S. 662, 677 (1981) (plurality opinion of Powell, J.) (noting that in adopting invalidated truck-length regulation the State "seems to have hoped to limit the use of its highways by deflecting some through traffic"); *id.,* at 679-687 (Brennan, J., concurring in judgment) (emphasizing that truck-length regulation should be invalidated solely in view of its protectionist purpose); see generally, Regan, The Supreme Court and State Protectionism: Making Sense of the Dormant Commerce Clause, 84 Mich. L. Rev. 1091 (1986). Nonetheless, a small number of our cases have invalidated state laws under the dormant Commerce Clause that appear to have been genuinely nondiscriminatory, in

sumption has more often than not itself remained dormant in this Court's opinions on state discrimination subject to review under the dormant Commerce Clause, when the allegedly competing entities provide different products, as here, there is a threshold question whether the companies are indeed similarly situated for constitutional purposes. This is so for the simple reason that the difference in products may mean that the different entities serve different markets, and would continue to do so even if the supposedly discriminatory burden were removed. If in fact that should be the case, eliminating the tax or other regulatory differential would not serve the dormant Commerce Clause's fundamental objective of preserving a national market for competition undisturbed by preferential advantages conferred by a State upon its residents or resident competitors. In Justice Jackson's now-famous words:

> Our system, fostered by the Commerce Clause, is that every farmer and every craftsman shall be encouraged to produce by the certainty that he will have free access to every market in the Nation, that no home embargoes will withhold his exports, and no foreign state will by customs duties or regulations exclude them. Likewise, every consumer may look to the free competition from every producing area in the Nation to protect him from exploitation by any. Such was the vision of the Founders; such has been the doctrine of this Court which has given it reality. *H.P. Hood & Sons, Inc. v. Du Mond,* 336 U. S. 525, 539 (1949).

See also, *e.g., Wyoming v. Oklahoma,* 502 U. S. 437, 469 (1992) (SCALIA, J. dissenting) ("Our negative Commerce Clause jurisprudence grew out of the notion that the Constitution implicitly established a national free market . . ."); *Reeves, Inc. v. Stake,* 447 U. S., at 437 (The dormant Commerce Clause prevents "state taxes and regulatory measures impeding free private trade in the national marketplace"); *Hunt v. Washington State Apple Advertising Comm'n,* 432 U. S. 333, 350 (1977) (referring to "the Commerce Clause's overriding requirement of a national 'common market'"). Thus, in the absence of

(Footnote Continued)

the sense that they did not impose disparate treatment on similarly situated in-state and out-of-state interests, where such laws undermined a compelling need for national uniformity in regulation. See *Bibb v. Navajo Freight Lines, Inc.*, 359 U. S. 520 (1959) (conflict in state laws governing truck mud flaps); *Southern Pacific Co. v. Arizona ex rel. Sullivan,* 325 U. S. 761 (1945) (train lengths); see also *CTS Corp. v. Dynamics Corp. of America,* 481 U. S. 69, 88 (1987) ("This Court's recent Commerce Clause cases also have invalidated statutes that may adversely affect interstate commerce by subjecting activities to inconsistent regulations"); L. Brilmayer, Conflict of Laws § 3.2.3, pp. 144-148 (2d ed. 1995) (discussing Court's review of conflicting state laws under the dormant Commerce Clause). In the realm of taxation, the requirement of apportionment plays a similar role by assuring that interstate activities are not unjustly burdened by multistate taxation. See generally *Oklahoma Tax Comm'n v. Jefferson Lines, Inc.*, 514 U. S.—,—(1995) (slip op., at 9-10) (discussing "internal" and "external" consistency tests for apportionment of state taxes). Of course, the fact that Ohio exempts local utilities from its sales and use taxes could not support any claim of undue burden in this nondiscriminatory sense, since the exemption itself does not give rise to conflicting regulation of any transaction or result in mal-apportionment of any tax.

actual or prospective competition between the supposedly favored and disfavored entities in a single market there can be no local preference, whether by express discrimination against interstate commerce or undue burden upon it, to which the dormant Commerce Clause may apply. The dormant Commerce Clause protects markets and participants in markets, not taxpayers as such.

Our cases have, however, rarely discussed the comparability of taxed or regulated entities as operators in arguably distinct markets; the closest approach to the facts here occurred in *Alaska v. Arctic Maid,* 366 U. S. 199 (1961). In *Arctic Maid,* a 4% tax on the value of salmon taken from territorial waters by so-called freezer ships and frozen for transport and later canning outside the State was challenged as discriminatory in the face of a 1% tax on the value of fish taken from territorial waters and frozen by on-shore cold storage facilities for later sale on the domestic fresh-frozen fish market. The State prevailed on the Court's holding that the claimants and cold storage facilities served separate markets, did not compete with one another, and thus could not properly be compared for Commerce Clause purposes. The proper comparison, the Court held, was between the freezer ships and domestic salmon canners, who shipped interstate into the same markets served by the freezer ships. Since the canners were taxed even more heavily than the freezer ships, there was no unfavorable burden upon the latter. *Id.,* at 204. Although the Court's opinion did not discuss the possibility that competition in the domestic fresh-frozen market might have occurred in the absence of the tax disparity between the two types of salmon freezers, the freezer ships had made no attempt to compete in that market and neither claimed nor demonstrated an interest in entering it. See Brief for Respondents in *Alaska v. Arctic Maid,* O. T. 1960, No. 106, pp. 27-33.

Arctic Maid provides a partial analogy to this case. Here, natural gas marketers did not serve the Ohio LDCs' core market of small, captive users, typified by residential consumers who want and need the bundled product. See, *e.g.,* Darr, A State Regulatory Strategy for the Transitional Phase of Gas Regulation, 12 Yale J. on Reg. 69, 99 (1995) ("[T]he large core residential customer base is bound to the LDC in what currently appears to be a natural-monopoly relationship"); App. 199 (a marketer from which GMC purchased gas does not hold itself out to the general public as a gas supplier, but rather selectively contacts industrial end users that it has identified as potentially profitable customers). While this captive market is not geographically distinguished from the area served by the independent marketers, it is defined economically as comprising consumers who are captive to the need for bundled benefits. These are buyers who live on sufficiently tight budgets to make the stability of rate important, and who cannot readily bear the risk of losing a fuel supply in harsh natural or economic weather. See, *e.g., Consolidated Edison Co. of N. Y. v. FERC,* 676 F. 2d 763, 766, n. 5 (CADC 1982) ("[R]esidential users [of natural gas cannot] switch temporarily to other fuels and so they must endure cold homes" if their gas supply is interrupted); A. Samuels, Reliability of Natural Gas Service for Captive End-Users Under the Federal Energy Regulatory Commission's Order No. 636, 62 Geo. Wash. L. Rev. 718, 749 (1994) ("Gas service disruptions lasting just a few days can cause severe health risks to captive end-users"). They are also buyers without the high volume requirements needed to make investment in the transaction costs of individual purchases on the open market economically feasible. Pierce, Intrastate Natural Gas Regulation: An Alternative Perspective, 9 Yale J. on Reg. 407, 409-410 (1992) ("Purchasing gas service [from marketers] requires considerable time and expertise. Its benefits are likely to exceed its costs only for consumers who purchase very large quantities of gas"). The demands of this market historically arose free of any influence of differential taxation (since there was none during the pre-1978 period when only LDCs generally served end-users), and because the market's economic characteristics appear to be independent of any effect attributable to the State's sales taxation as imposed today, there is good reason to assume that any pricing changes that could result from eliminating the sales tax differential challenged here would be inadequate to create competition between LDCs and marketers for the business of the utilities' core home market.

On the other hand, one circumstance of this case is unlike what *Arctic Maid* assumed, for there is a possibility of competition between LDCs and marketers for the noncaptive market. Although the record before this Court reveals virtually nothing about the details of that competitive market, in the period under examination it presumably included bulk buyers like GMC, which have no need for bundled protection, see, *e.g.*, State Issue: Atlanta Gas Light Takes Step to Abandon Gas Sales by Unbundling Services for Non-Core Customers, Foster Natural Gas Report, June 20, 1996, p. 22 (indicating that prior to "unbundling" marketers accounted for 80% of sales to large commercial and industrial users in Georgia), and consumers of middling volumes of natural gas who found some value in Ohio's state-imposed protections but not enough to offset lower price at some point, see, *e.g.*, Pierobon, Small Customers: The Yellow Brick Road to Deregulation?, 134 Pub. Utils. Fortnightly, No. 6, pp. 14, 15 (1996) (marketers' efforts in California are increasingly directed to attracting consumers in the "small commercial sector," including "schools, hospitals, hotels, restaurants, laundromats, and master-metered apartments," which currently purchase bundled gas from utilities); Salpukas, New Choices for Natural Gas: Retailers Find Users Puzzled as Industry Deregulates, N.Y. Times, Oct. 23, 1996, pp. D1, D4 (indicating that some natural gas marketers in New York City are attempting to lure "mom-and-pop businesses like restaurants and dry-cleaners" away from LDCs, with mixed success). Eliminating the sales tax differential at issue here might well intensify competition between LDCs and marketers for customers in this noncaptive market.

B

In sum, the LDCs' bundled product reflects the demand of a market neither susceptible to competition by the interstate sellers nor likely to be served except by the regulated natural monopolies that have historically supplied its needs. So far as this market is concerned, competition would not be served by eliminating any tax differential as between sellers, and the dormant Commerce Clause has no job to do. There is, however, a further market where the respective sellers of the bundled and unbundled products apparently do compete and may compete further. Thus, the question raised by this case is whether the opportunities for competition between marketers and LDCs in the noncaptive market requires treating marketers and utilities as alike for dormant Commerce Clause purposes. Should we accord controlling significance to the noncaptive market in which they compete, or to the noncompetitive, captive market in which the local utilities alone operate? Although there is no *a priori* answer, a number of reasons support a decision to give the greater weight to the captive market and the local utilities' singular role in serving it, and hence to treat marketers and LDCs as dissimilar for present purposes. First and most important, we must recognize an obligation to proceed cautiously lest we imperil the delivery by regulated LDCs of bundled gas to the noncompetitive captive market. Second, as a court we lack the expertness and the institutional resources necessary to predict the effects of judicial intervention invalidating Ohio's tax scheme on the utilities' capacity to serve this captive market. Finally, should intervention by the National Government be necessary, Congress has both the resources and the power to strike the balance between the needs of the competitive and captive markets.

ONE

Where a choice is possible, as it is here, the importance of traditional regulated service to the captive market makes a powerful case against any judicial treatment that might jeopardize LDCs' continuing capacity to serve the captive market. Largely as a response to the monopolistic shakeout that brought an end to the era of unbridled competition among gas utilities, regulation of natural gas for the principal benefit of householders and other consumers of relatively small quantities is the rule in every State in the Union. Congress has also long recognized the desirability of these state regulatory regimes. *Supra,* at—. Indeed, half a century ago we concluded that the NGA altogether exempts state regulation of retail sales of natural gas (including in-state sales to large industrial customers) from the strictures of the dormant Commerce Clause, see *Panhandle Eastern Pipe Line Co. v. Public Serv. Comm'n of Ind.,* 332 U. S. 507 (1947), and to this day, notwithstanding the national regulatory revolution, Congress has done nothing to limit its unbroken recognition of the state regulatory authority that has created and preserved the local monopolies.[13] The clear implication is that Congress finds the benefits of the bundled product for captive local buyers well within the realm of what the States may reasonably promote and preserve.

This Court has also recognized the importance of avoiding any jeopardy to service of the state-regulated captive market, and in circumstances remarkably similar to those of the present case. In *Panhandle Eastern Pipe Line Co. v. Michigan Pub. Serv. Comm'n,* 341 U. S. 329 (1951), Ford Motor Company had entered a contract with an interstate pipeline for supply of gas at Ford's plant in Dearborn, Michigan, thus bypassing the local distribution company. The Michigan Public Service Commission ordered the pipeline to cease and desist from making direct sales of natural gas to the State's industrial customers without a certificate of public convenience and necessity, and the pipeline brought a Commerce Clause challenge to the Commission's action. The Court observed that

> [a]ppellant asserts a right to compete for the cream of the volume business without regard to the local public convenience or necessity. Were appellant successful in this venture, it would no doubt be reflected adversely in [the LDC's] over-all costs of service and its rates to customers whose only source of supply is [the LDC]. This clearly presents a situation of . . . vital interest to the State of Michigan. *Id.,* at 334.

In view of the economic threat that competition for large industrial consumers posed to gas service to small captive users, the Court again reaffirmed its long-standing doctrine upholding the States' power to regulate all direct in-state sales to consumers, even if such regulation resulted in an outright prohibition of competition for even the largest end users. *Id.,* at 336-337; see also *Panhandle-Indiana, supra* (uphold-

[13] In the present case, the parties have not briefed the question whether the present amended version of the NGA and related federal legislation continues the express Commerce Clause exemption for state regulation and taxation of retail natural gas sales recognized in *Panhandle-Indiana,* and we do not decide this issue. We note, however, that the language of § 1(b) of the NGA, which the *Panhandle-Indiana Court* construed as creating the exemption, itself remains unchanged. (Compare 52 Stat. 821 with 15 U. S. C. § 717(b) (1994).)

ing state regulation of direct sales to large industrial users as not preempted by the NGA or precluded by the dormant Commerce Clause).[14]

The continuing importance of the States' interest in protecting the captive market from the effects of competition for the largest consumers is underscored by the common sense of our traditional recognition of the need to accommodate state health and safety regulation in applying dormant Commerce Clause principles. State regulation of natural gas sales to consumers serves important interests in health and safety in fairly obvious ways, in that requirements of dependable supply and extended credit assure that individual buyers of gas for domestic purposes are not frozen out of their houses in the cold months. We have consistently recognized the "legitimate state pursuit of such interests as compatible with the Commerce Clause, which was 'never intended to cut the States off from legislating on all subjects relating to the health, life, and safety of their citizens, though the legislation might indirectly affect the commerce of the country.'" *Huron Portland Cement Co. v. Detroit,* 362 U. S. 440, 443-444 (1960) (quoting *Sherlock v. Alling,* 93 U. S. 99, 103 (1876)). Just so may health and safety considerations be weighed in the process of deciding the threshold question whether the conditions entailing application of the dormant Commerce Clause are present.[15]

TWO

The size of the captive market, its noncompetitive character, the values served by its traditional regulation: all counsel caution before making a choice that could strain the capacity of the States to continue to demand the regulatory benefits that have served the home market of low-volume users since natural gas became readily available. Here we have to assume that any decision to treat the LDCs as similar to the interstate marketers would change the LDCs' position in the noncaptive market in which (we are assuming) they compete, at least at the margins, by affecting the overall size of the LDCs' customer base. As we recognized in *Panhandle,* a change in the customer base could affect

---

[14] Under today's altered market structure, see *supra,* at—, several courts of appeals have held that the NGA confers jurisdiction on FERC, rather than the States, to regulate such bypass arrangements for supplying gas to large industrial consumers when the sale of gas itself occurs outside the State and an interstate pipeline merely transports the gas to the industrial consumer for delivery in-state. See *Cascade Natural Gas Corp. v. FERC,* 955 F. 2d 1412, 1414-1422 (CA10 1992); *Michigan Consolidated Gas Co. v. Panhandle Eastern Pipe Line Co.,* 887 F. 2d 1295, 1299-1301 (CA6 1989), cert. denied, 494 U. S. 1079 (1990); *Michigan Consolidated Gas Co. v. FERC,* 883 F. 2d 117, 121-122 (CADC 1989), cert. denied, 494 U. S. 1079 (1990). We express no view on the correctness of these decisions.

[15] Of course, if a State discriminates against out-of-state interests by drawing geographical distinctions between entities that are otherwise similarly situated, such facial discrimination will be subject to a high level of judicial scrutiny even if it is directed toward a legitimate health and safety goal. See, *e.g., Philadelphia v. New Jersey,* 437 U. S. 617, 626-628 (1978); *Dean Milk Co. v. Madison,* 340 U. S. 349, 353-354 (1951).

the LDCs' ability to continue to serve the captive market where there is no such competition.

To be sure, what in fact would happen as a result of treating the marketers and LDCs alike we do not know. We might assume that eliminating the tax on marketers' sales would leave those sellers stronger competitors in the noncaptive market, especially at the market's boundaries, and that any resulting contraction of the LDCs' total customer base would increase the unit cost of the bundled product. We might also suppose that the State would not respond to our decision by subjecting the LDCs and marketers both to the same sales tax now imposed on marketers alone, since the utilities are already subject to a complicated scheme of property taxation quite different from the tax treatment of the marketers.[16] It seems, in fact, far more likely that eliminating the tax challenged here would portend, among other things, some reduction of the total taxes levied against LDCs, in order to strengthen their position in trying to compete with marketers in the non-captive market.

The degree to which these very general suggestions might prove right or wrong, however, is not really significant; the point is simply that all of them are nothing more than suggestions, pointedly couched in terms of assumption or supposition. This is necessarily so, simply because the Court is institutionally unsuited to gather the facts upon which economic predictions can be made, and professionally untrained to make them. See, *e.g., Fulton Corp. v. Faulkner,* 516 U. S.—,—(1996) (slip op., at 16-17), and authorities cited therein; Hunter, Federalism and State Taxation of Multistate Enterprises, 32 Emory L. J. 89, 108 (1983) ("It is virtually impossible for a court, with its limited resources, to determine with any degree of accuracy the costs to a town, county, or state of a particular industry"); see also Smith, State Discriminations Against Interstate Commerce, 74 Cal. L. Rev. 1203, 1211 (1986) (noting that "[e]ven expert economists" may have difficulty determining "whether the overall economic benefits and burdens of a regulation favor local inhabitants against outsiders"). We are consequently ill-qualified to develop Commerce Clause doctrine dependent on any such predictive judgments, and it behooves us to be as reticent about projecting the effect of applying the Commerce Clause here, as we customarily are in declining to engage in elaborate analysis

[16] For example, public utilities pay personal property tax on 88% of true value, Ohio Rev. Code Ann. § 5727.111 (1996), while marketers pay personal property tax on 25% of their true value, § 5711.22(D). Public utilities also pay a special tax assessment for the expenses of the Public Utility Commission, § 4905.10 (1991), and for the expenses of the Ohio Consumer Counsel, § 4911.18. Moreover, natural gas utilities must pay a gross receipts tax of 4.75% on gas sales, § 5727.38 (1996), while marketers pay none. Independent marketers, for their part, are subject to a franchise tax, § 5733.01, that does not apply to utilities, § 5733.09(a). Thus, this sales and use tax challenge would not be the last available to marketers and their customers; the franchise tax, which also does not apply to utilities, is presumably next in line.

of real-world economic effects, *Fulton Corp., supra,* at—(slip op., at 16-17), or to consider subtle compensatory tax defenses, *Oregon Waste Systems, Inc. v. Department of Environmental Quality of Ore.,* 511 U. S. 93, 105 (1994). The most we can say is that modification of Ohio's tax scheme could subject LDCs to economic pressure that in turn could threaten the preservation of an adequate customer base to support continued provision of bundled services to the captive market. The conclusion counsels against taking the step of treating the bundled gas seller like any other, with the consequent necessity of uniform taxation of all gas sales.

THREE

Prudence thus counsels against running the risk of weakening or destroying a regulatory scheme of public service and protection recognized by Congress despite its noncompetitive, monopolistic character. Still less is that risk justifiable in light of Congress's own power and institutional competence to decide upon and effectuate any desirable changes in the scheme that has evolved. Congress has the capacity to investigate and analyze facts beyond anything the judiciary could match, joined with the authority of the commerce power to run economic risks that the judiciary should confront only when the constitutional or statutory mandate for judicial choice is clear. See, *e.g., Bush v. Lucas,* 462 U. S. 367, 389 (1983) (Congress "may inform itself through factfinding procedures such as hearings that are not available to the courts"). One need not adopt Justice Black's extreme reticence in Commerce Clause jurisprudence to recognize in this instance the soundness of his statement that a challenge like the one before us "call[s] for Congressional investigation, consideration, and action. The Constitution gives that branch of government the power to regulate commerce among the states, and until it acts I think we should enter the field with extreme caution." *Northwest Airlines v. Minnesota,* 322 U. S. 292, 302 (1943) (concurrence). This conclusion applies a fortiori here, because for a half-century Congress has been aware of our conclusion in *Panhandle Eastern Pipe Line Co. v. Public Serv. Comm'n of Ind.,* 332 U. S. 507 (1947), that the NGA exempts state regulation of in-state retail natural gas sales from the dormant Commerce Clause and in the years following that decision has only reaffirmed the power of the States in this regard.

* * *

Accordingly, we conclude that Ohio's regulatory response to the needs of the local natural gas market have resulted in a noncompetitive bundled gas product that distinguishes its regulated sellers from independent marketers to the point that the enterprises should not be considered "similarly situated" for purposes of a claim of facial discrimination under the Commerce Clause. GMC's argument that the State discriminates between regulated local gas utilities and unregulated marketers must therefore fail.

C

GMC also suggests that Ohio's tax regime "facially discriminates" because the State's sales and use tax exemption would not apply to sales by out-of-state LDCs. See, *e.g.*, Reply Brief for Petitioner at 2, n. 1. As respondent points out, however, the Ohio courts might well extend the challenged exemption to out-of-state utilities if confronted with the question. Indeed, in *Carnegie Natural Gas Co. v. Tracy,* No. 94-K-526 (Ohio Bd. Tax App. Nov. 17, 1995), reported in Ohio Tax Rep. (CCH) at ¶ 402-254, the Ohio Board of Tax Appeals accepted the argument of a Pennsylvania public utility that insofar as the out-of-state utility sold natural gas to Ohio consumers it qualified as a utility under Ohio Rev. Code Ann. § 5727.01 and was therefore exempt from the State's corporate franchise tax. Out-of-state public utilities may therefore also qualify for Ohio's sales and use tax exemption. Because "we have never deemed a hypothetical possibility of favoritism to constitute discrimination that transgresses constitutional commands," *Associated Industries of Mo. v. Lohman,* 511 U. S., at 654, this argument, too, must be rejected.

V

Finally, GMC claims that Ohio's tax regime violates the Equal Protection Clause by treating LDCs' natural gas sales differently from those of producers and marketers. Once again, the hurdle facing GMC is a high one, since state tax classifications require only a rational basis to satisfy the Equal Protection Clause. See, *e.g., Amerada Hess Corp. v. Director, Div. of Taxation, N. J. Dept. of Treasury,* 490 U. S., at 80. Indeed, "in taxation, even more than in other fields, legislatures possess the greatest freedom in classification." *Madden v. Kentucky,* 309 U. S. 83, 88 (1940).

It is true, of course, that in some peculiar circumstances state tax classifications facially discriminating against interstate commerce may violate the Equal Protection Clause even when they pass muster under the Commerce Clause. See *Metropolitan Life Ins. Co. v. Ward,* 470 U. S. 869, 874-883 (1985).[17] But as we explain in Part IV, *supra,* Ohio's differential tax treatment of LDC and independent marketer sales does

[17] *Ward* involved an Alabama statute that facially discriminated against interstate commerce by imposing a lower gross premiums tax on in-state than out-of-state insurance companies. The case did not present a Commerce Clause violation only because Congress, in enacting the McCarran-Ferguson Act, 15 U. S. C. §§ 1011-1015, intended to authorize States to impose taxes that burden interstate commerce in the insurance field. *Ward,* 470 U. S., at 880. We nonetheless invalidated Alabama's classification because "neither of the two purposes furthered by the [statute] . . . is legitimate under the Equal Protection Clause . . . ." *Id.,* at 883.

not facially discriminate against interstate commerce. And in any event, there is unquestionably a rational basis for Ohio's distinction between these two kinds of entities.

* * *

We conclude that Ohio's differential tax treatment of public utilities and independent marketers violates neither the Commerce Clause nor the Equal Protection Clause and that petitioners' claims are without merit otherwise. The judgment of the Supreme Court of Ohio is affirmed.

It is so ordered.

JUSTICE SCALIA, concurring.

I join the Court's opinion, which thoroughly explains why the Ohio tax scheme at issue in this case does not facially discriminate against interstate commerce. I write separately to note my continuing adherence to the view that the so-called "negative" Commerce Clause is an unjustified judicial invention, not to be expanded beyond its existing domain. "The historical record provides no grounds for reading the Commerce Clause to be other than what it says—an authorization for Congress to regulate Commerce." *Tyler Pipe Industries, Inc. v. Washington State Dept. of Revenue,* 483 U. S. 232, 263 (1987) (SCALIA, J., concurring in part and dissenting in part).

I have previously stated that I will enforce on stare decisis grounds a "negative" self-executing Commerce Clause in two situations: (1) against a state law that facially discriminates against interstate commerce, and (2) against a state law that is indistinguishable from a type of law previously held unconstitutional by this Court. *West Lynn Creamery, Inc. v. Healy,* 512 U. S. 186, 210 (1994) (SCALIA, J., concurring in judgment); *Itel Containers Int'l Corp. v. Huddleston,* 507 U. S. 60, 78 (1993) (SCALIA, J., concurring in part and concurring in judgment) (collecting cases). Although petitioner contends that Ohio facially discriminates against interstate commerce with respect to natural gas sales, its argument is based on a novel premise: that private marketers engaged in the sale of natural gas are similarly situated to public utility companies. Nothing in this Court's negative Commerce Clause jurisprudence compels that conclusion. To hold that States must tax gas sales by these two types of entities equally would broaden the negative Commerce Clause beyond its existing scope, and intrude on a regulatory sphere traditionally occupied by Congress and the States.

JUSTICE STEVENS, dissenting.

In Ohio, as in other States, regulated utilities selling natural gas—referred to by the Court as "LDCs"—operate in two markets, one that is monopolistic and one that is competitive.

In the first, they sell a "noncompetitive bundled gas product," *ante,* at 32, to small consumers who have no practical alternative source of supply. The LDCs' dominant position in that market justifies detailed regulation of their activities in order to protect consumers from the risk of exploitation by a seller with monopoly power. See *ante,* at 14-20. The basic purpose of that regulation is to protect consumers, not to subsidize the LDCs.

The second market in which LDCs sell natural gas is a competitive market in which large customers like the General Motors Corporation have alternative sources of supply. Although Ohio possesses undoubted power to regulate the activities of all sellers in that market, *Panhandle Eastern Pipe Line Co. v. Michigan Pub. Serv. Comm'n,* 341 U. S. 329 (1951), it has not done so in any manner relevant here. The purchasers in this competitive market do not need the protections afforded by the state regulation of the monopolistic market, see *ante,* at 23, and the benefits provided by these regulations will thus not affect a competitive consumer's choice of seller. Customers like GMC are not "captive to the need for bundled benefits," *ante,* at 22. Nor do the burdens imposed by the regulations have a significant impact on LDCs' activities within this market. Thus, while the gas sold by LDCs on the competitive market may be subject to the same regulations as the gas sold in the non-competitive market, the different impact of the regulations on the economic decisions of both consumers and sellers makes it appropriate to characterize all gas sold in that market as "unbundled gas," see *ante,* at 20. Although the physical composition of the gas sold in the two markets is identical, I agree with what I understand the Court to be assuming, namely that as a matter of economics "bundled gas" and "unbundled gas" should be viewed as different products. See *ante,* at 20, 22-24.

It is not uncommon for a firm with a monopolistic position in one market also to sell a second product in a competitive market. See, *e.g., International Business Machines Corp. v. United States,* 298 U. S. 131 (1936). Even regulated monopolies such as electric utilities may distribute goods, such as light bulbs, in a competitive market. See, *e.g., Cantor v. Detroit Edison Co.,* 428 U. S. 579 (1976). There is no reason why an LDC might not develop a product line, such as thermostats or gas furnaces, to sell in the competitive market for such products. I do not believe that the fact that the LDC is heavily regulated in the "bundled gas" market would justify granting it a special preference in the market for thermostats or gas furnaces. Nor do I discern a significant relevant difference between competition in "unbundled gas" and competition in thermostats or gas furnaces.

It may well be true that without a discriminatory tax advantage in the competitive market, the LDCs would lose business to interstate competitors and therefore be forced to increase the rates charged to small local consumers. This circumstance may require the States to find new, and nondiscriminatory, methods for accommodating the needs of small consumers for regular and reasonably priced natural gas service. As the Court recognizes, speculation about the "real-world economic effects" of a decision like this one is beyond our institutional competence. See *ante,* at 31. Such speculation is not, therefore, a sufficient justification for a tax exemption that discriminates against interstate commerce. *Bacchus Imports, Ltd. v. Dias,* 468 U. S. 263 (1984).

Accordingly, while I agree with Parts II and IV of the Court's opinion, I respectfully dissent from the judgment.

Koch Fuels, Inc. v. R. Gary Clark

[*Koch Fuels* is discussed at ¶ 710 and ¶ 715.02.]

Koch Fuels, Inc. v. R. Gary Clark, in His Capacity as Tax Administrator for the State of Rhode Island.

Rhode Island Supreme Court, No. 93-714-M.P., May 23, 1996, 676 A.2d 330.

Present: Weisberger C.J., Murray, Lederburg, and Bourcier, JJ.

Weisberger, C.J.

OPINION

This case came before us on a petition for certiorari filed by Koch Fuels, Inc. (Koch), seeking a review of a judgment entered by the District Court. The District Court judgment sustained a final decision rendered by R. Gary Clark, the Tax Administrator of the State of Rhode Island (tax administrator), imposing a gross-earnings tax on sales of fuel oil by Koch to New England Power; New England Power is the parent company of Narragansett Electric Company (Narragansett). After reviewing the record before us, we affirm the District Court's judgment.

The facts of this case are not in dispute. Koch is a Delaware corporation with headquarters in Wichita, Kansas; it is engaged in the sale and distribution of fuel oil. On several occasions between the years 1982 and 1984, Koch sold fuel oil to New England Power to be used for the generation of electricity at Narragansett's electric generating plant in Providence, Rhode Island. These occasions were the only instances in which Koch had any business contact with any entity in Rhode Island. The fuel oil sold to Narragansett originated in Texas, Pennsylvania, or Massachusetts. All shipments were delivered via common carriers using barges or vessels to bring the oil through Narragansett Bay to the Port of Providence.

The terms of each of the sales contracts were negotiated and agreed upon via telecommunications between Koch's representatives in Texas or in New Jersey and New England Power's representatives in Westborough, Massachusetts. Narragansett received invoices for and paid the purchase price of the fuel oil outside Rhode Island. The terms of each of the sales contracts were f.o.b. Providence, indicating that title, possession, and risk of loss surrounding the fuel-oil shipments passed from Koch to Narragansett at the flange, namely, the point where the vessel's oil outflow pipe interlocks the oil terminal's inflow pipe in Rhode Island.

At all times relevant to the sales made to New England Power, Koch did not have employees in Rhode Island and did not rent, lease, or own real property within Rhode Island. Koch did, however, register to do business in Rhode Island and paid Rhode Island corporate taxes in the years it sold fuel oil to New England Power.

On March 11, 1988, the Rhode Island Division of Taxation (tax division) issued Koch a notice-of-deficiency determination regarding five of the six fuel-oil deliveries made by Koch to Narragansett under the Gross-Earnings Tax Act, G.L. 1956 § 44-44-1, as amended by P.L. 1983, ch. 2, art. 4, § 1.[1] This deficiency amounted to $311,358.57 including penalties and interest.

On March 14, 1988, Koch made a timely request for an administrative hearing. The matter was heard at a formal administrative hearing on August 26, 1988. The tax administrator on the recommendation of the hearing officer issued a final order on April 7, 1989, affirming the tax assessment against Koch.

On May 8, 1989, Koch paid the tax division the full assessment of $366,604.88, which represents the amount of the contested assessment plus statutory interest accrued thereon. Subsequently, on May 9, 1989, Koch filed a complaint seeking de novo review of the tax division's decision in the District Court pursuant to G.L.1956 § 8-8-24.

The District Court rendered its decision on December 7, 1993, affirming the tax administrator's assessment. In its decision the District Court found that the tax assessment at issue did not violate either the due-process clause of the Fourteenth Amendment or the Commerce Clause of Article I, section 8, clause 3, of the United States Constitution. It also found that Koch was an "importer" within the meaning of the Gross-Earnings Tax Act and was therefore correctly assessed pursuant to that act.

On December 23, 1993, Koch filed a petition for writ of certiorari in this court, seeking review of the District Court's judgment. We granted Koch's petition on September 8, 1994. On certiorari, Koch challenges the District Court's analysis based on the commerce clause and its determination that Koch was an "importer" within the meaning of the Gross-Earnings Tax Act. We shall therefore confine our consideration in similar fashion to the propriety of the District Court's analysis based on the commerce clause and its interpretation of the Rhode Island Gross-Earnings Tax Act.

As an initial matter we shall address whether the gross-earnings tax imposed upon Koch may be considered a "sales or use" tax. We

[1] That statute has since been repealed.

note that the District Court, in its decision rendered on December 7, 1993, characterized the tax at issue as a sales or use tax. Upon review of the relevant statute, we are of the opinion that the District Court did not err in reaching such a result.

Section 44-41-1(a), entitled "Gross Earnings Tax of Petroleum Companies," imposes on petroleum companies "an annual tax rate of one percent (1%) of gross earnings *** derived *** from the *sale* of petroleum products in this state." (Emphasis added.) The term "gross earnings" is defined as "those earnings from *sales* of its tangible personal property (inventory sold in the ordinary course of business) where shipments are made to points within the state *** [but] does not include those earnings from *sales* to out-of-state customers for marketing, distribution or consumption outside this state." (Emphasis added.) Section 44-41-1(b). It is clear that although the tax at issue is defined by the Legislature as a "gross earnings" tax, its application pursuant to the statute imposes a tax upon specific sales transactions in Rhode Island. The tax mandated by the statute therefore has the practical effect of a sales or use tax. See *Complete Auto Transit,. Inc. v. Brady,* 430 U.S. 274, 279, 97 S. Ct. 1076, 1079, 51 L. Ed. 2d 326, 331 (1977) (the United States Supreme Court noted that when confronted with commerce-clause challenges of state taxes, it considered "not the formal language of the tax statute but rather its practical effect"). We are therefore of the opinion that the District Court correctly characterized the tax at issue as a sales or use tax.

We shall now turn to Koch's contention that the gross-earnings tax imposed by the relevant statute violates the commerce clause. The United States Supreme Court articulated a four-part test for determining the validity of a state tax under the commerce clause in *Complete Auto.* In that case, the Court provided that a state tax will pass commerce-clause scrutiny when the "tax [1] is applied to an activity with a substantial nexus with the taxing State, [2] is fairly apportioned, [3] does not discriminate against interstate commerce, and [4] is fairly related to the services provided by the State." 430 U.S. at 279, 97 S. Ct. at 1079, 51 L. Ed. 2d at 331. In applying this four-pronged test to the instant case, we are not persuaded by Koch's contentions that the gross-earnings tax at issue was violative of the commerce clause.

In regard to the first prong of the test Koch argues that its fuel-oil sales in Rhode Island lacked the substantial nexus required in a commerce-clause analysis. Relying on *Quill Corp. v. North Dakota,* 504 U.S. 298, 112 S. Ct. 1904, 119 L. Ed. 2d 91 (1992), Koch contends that because the gross-earnings tax at issue is a sales or use tax, the first prong of the test is satisfied only if the taxpayer maintained a physical presence in the taxing state. Koch argues that since it does not have a physical presence in Rhode Island, its activities lack a substantial nexus with Rhode Island. Although we do not dispute the applicability of *Quill Corp.* to the instant case, we are not persuaded by Koch's contentions that it did not maintain a physical presence in this state.

In *Quill Corp.* the Court considered the imposition of state use tax upon a mail-order vendor of office supplies under both the due process analysis and the commerce-clause analysis. In regard to the commerce-clause analysis, the Court upheld its holding in *National Bellas Hess, Inc. v. Department of Revenue of Illinois,* 386 U.S. 753, 87 S. Ct. 1389, 18 L. Ed. 2d 505 (1967), and determined that a state cannot constitutionally impose a sales and use tax upon a seller unless the seller maintained a physical presence in the taxing state. *Quill Corp.,* 504 U.S. at 314, 112 S. Ct. at 1914, 119 L. Ed. 2d at 108. In instances wherein a taxpayer did "no more than communicate with customers in the State by mail or common carrier as part of a general interstate business," the Court stressed that that taxpayer did not have a substantial nexus with the taxing state.

In the instant case we are of the opinion that Koch's activities amounted to more than mere "communication with its customers in the State by mail or common carrier." We first note that Koch shipped approximately 25.6 million gallons of oil into Rhode Island over the course of three years with a total value of approximately $18 million. It retained total control over the shipments of oil throughout delivery. Koch retained title, possession, and risk of loss over the oil up until the point it reached the flange in Providence. Koch was in continuous contact and control with both the common carrier and Narragansett and was in a position to cancel the delivery if contract performance was not met by Narragansett. Although Koch did not own the vessels that carried its fuel oil into Rhode Island, Koch's fuel oil represented the entire and exclusive cargo of the vessel. On the basis of Koch's complete control over the oil shipments, the exclusive nature of the common carrier's contract, the unique nature of the cargo, and the fact that the sales were consummated upon delivery in Rhode Island, we are of the opinion that Koch's activities created in practical effect a physical presence within this state. Given Koch's physical presence in Rhode Island, we agree with the District Court's conclusion that Koch had sufficient contact with the state to satisfy the substantial-nexus requirement of the *Complete Auto* test.

Koch next asserts that the gross-earnings tax is unfairly apportioned, thereby violating the second prong of the *Complete Auto* test. The apportionment prong of the analysis serves to "prohibit taxes that pass an unfair share of the tax burden onto interstate commerce." *Quill Corp.,* 504 U.S. at 313, 112 S.Ct. at 1913, 119 L.Ed.2d at 107. In

Goldberg v. Sweet, 488 U.S. 252, 261, 109 S.Ct. 582, 589, 102 L.Ed.2d 607, 616 (1989), the Court stated that "we determine whether a tax is fairly apportioned by examining whether it is internally and externally consistent." *See also Armco, Inc. v. Hardesty,* 467 U.S. 638, 644, 104 S.Ct. 2620, 2623, 81 L.Ed.2d 540, 555-56 (1984); *Container Corp. of America v. Franchise Tax Board,* 463 U.S. 159, 169-70, 103 S.Ct. 2933, 2942-43, 77 L.Ed.2d 545, 556 (1983).

"To be internally consistent, a tax must be structured so that if every State were to impose an identical tax, no multiple taxation would result." *Goldberg,* 488 U.S. at 261, 109 S.Ct. at 589, 102 L.Ed.2d at 617. "[T]he internal consistency test [therefore] focuses on the text of the challenged statute and hypothesizes a situation where other States have passed an identical statute." *Id.* In the instant case the gross-earnings tax applies only to those fuel-oil sales consummated in Rhode Island. We are of the opinion that such a tax is internally consistent, for if every state taxed only those fuel-oil sales consummated in the state, only one state would be able to tax each sale. *See id.* (the tax at issue is internally consistent where only one state would be able to tax those interstate phone calls which are charged to an in-state service address).

We next turn to the external-consistency requirement. That requirement asks "whether the State has taxed only that portion of the revenues from the interstate activity which reasonably reflects the in-state component of the activity being taxed." *Goldberg,* 488 U.S. at 262, 109 S.Ct. at 589, 102 L.Ed.2d at 617 (citing *Container Corp.,* 463 U.S. at 169-70, 103 S.Ct. at 2942-43, 77 L.Ed.2d at 555-56). Here Koch argues that the gross-earnings tax is unfairly apportioned because it taxes the entire transaction without taking into account other activities associated with the transaction that occurred outside Rhode Island. We are not persuaded by Koch's contentions and are of the opinion that the gross-earnings tax at issue is externally consistent.

In the instant case the gross-earnings tax applies only to those sales that are consummated within Rhode Island. Although Koch maintains that its sales of petroleum oil within this state were a result of numerous negotiations outside Rhode Island, the District Court found that "[such] communications between the parties outside Rhode Island do not amount to an apportionment problem that violates the Commerce Clause." We agree with the District Court. Although it appears that Koch would have this court apportion the sale on the basis of its contract negotiations outside Rhode Island, such an apportionment would be administratively unwieldy. We note that fair apportionment does not require a state to adopt a tax which would "pose genuine administrative burdens." *American Trucking Associations, Inc. v.*

Scheiner, 483 U.S. 266, 296, 107 S.Ct. 2829, 2847, 97 L.Ed.2d 226, 251 (1987). Accordingly, we are not persuaded by Koch's contentions. Because the gross-earnings tax is both externally and internally consistent, we are of the opinion that the gross-earnings tax is fairly apportioned.

We turn next to the third prong of the test, which prohibits a state from imposing a discriminatory tax on interstate commerce. Koch asserts that the gross-earnings tax discriminates against interstate commerce because it imposes a tax on income from interstate transactions only. Koch argues that the gross-earnings tax has a discriminatory effect on out-of-state petroleum companies because even though it taxes their sales coming into Rhode Island, Rhode Island petroleum companies are free to make sales out of state that are not subject to the gross-earnings tax.

We have held that the failure of a party challenging the constitutionality of a taxing statute to present evidence of its discriminatory effect is fatal to the claim of unconstitutionality. *Seibert v. Clark,* 619 A.2d 1108, 1116 (R.I. 1993). Here, the District Court found that Koch had failed to demonstrate the discriminatory effect of the gross-earnings tax. The District Court specifically noted that Koch produced no evidence whatsoever to support its discrimination argument. On review of the record we also note the absence of any evidence to show that the gross-earnings tax discriminates against out-of-state petroleum companies in favor of Rhode Island petroleum companies. On this basis we must reject Koch's discriminatory-effect assertions.

We now reach the fourth prong of the test, namely, whether the tax at issue is fairly related to the presence and activities of the taxpayer within the state. Koch argues that the assessment from the gross-earnings tax is not fairly related to the services provided to Koch by Rhode Island. Koch asserts that because it has neither employees nor property within Rhode Island, it does not directly receive benefits related to the tax at issue. Koch further argues that because the fuel oil was shipped into Rhode Island on common carriers which it did not own, any state-financed benefits, such as the creation and the management of navigable waterways, benefited the common carrier only.

Like the substantial-nexus prong of the *Complete Auto* test, the reasonable-relation prong serves to "limit the reach of State taxing authority so as to ensure that State taxation does not unduly burden interstate commerce." *Quill Corp.,* 504 U.S. at 313, 112 S.Ct. at 1913, 119 L.Ed.2d at 107. This prong imposes the "additional limitation that the measure of the tax must be reasonably related to the extent of the contact, since it is the activities or presence of the taxpayer in the State that may properly be made to bear a 'just share of state tax burden.'"

Commonwealth Edison Co. v. Montana, 453 U.S. 609, 626, 101 S. Ct. 2946, 2958, 69 L. Ed. 2d 884, 900 (1981). Moreover, "[t]he tax which may be imposed on a particular interstate transaction need not be limited to the cost of the services incurred by the State on account of that particular activity. *** On the contrary, 'interstate commerce may be required to contribute to the cost of providing all governmental services, including those services from which it arguably receives no direct "benefit." ' " *Goldberg,* 488 U.S. at 267, 109 S.Ct. at 592, 102 L.Ed.2d at 620-21.

In the instant case Koch's assertions that it is not the beneficiary of services provided by Rhode Island is untenable. We are persuaded by the District Court's findings that the tax imposed on Koch is reasonably related to the services provided by Rhode Island. As the District Court correctly indicated, Rhode Island provided shipping facilities to Koch and maintained emergency equipment in case of an environmental disaster. The risk of an environmental disaster, and its attendant costs, are based upon the amount of oil imported into and sold in Rhode Island. We note that Koch had shipped approximately 25.6 million gallons of fuel oil into Rhode Island over the course of three years. Given the frequency of Koch's sales in Rhode Island and the amount of fuel oil shipped into Rhode Island, Koch's claim that it did not benefit from the services provided by Rhode Island is without merit. Accordingly we believe that the District Court correctly concluded that the gross-earnings tax is fairly related to the services received by Koch.

In light of the foregoing, we are of the opinion that the tax imposed by the Gross-Earnings Tax Act is consistent with the commerce clause. The tax at issue is applied to an activity with a substantial nexus with Rhode Island, is fairly apportioned, does not discriminate against interstate commerce, and is fairly related to services which Rhode Island provides to Koch. We therefore reject Koch's contentions that the District Court erred in its analysis under the commerce clause.

Koch also asserts that the District Court erred in determining that it was an "importer" under the language of the Gross-Earnings Tax Act. Koch argues that an importer is the person to whom the goods are sent. Since the goods in the instant case were sent to Narragansett, Koch argues, Narragansett was the importer of fuel oil into Rhode Island. We are not persuaded by Koch's contentions.

It is well-settled doctrine that when a statute is clear and free from ambiguity, it is the obligation of this court to give effect to its clearly expressed intent. *Gilbane Co. v. Poulas,* 576 A.2d 1195, 1196 (R.I. 1990). In such circumstances we must accord the words of the statute their literal and plain meaning. *Marran v. Baird,* 635 A.2d 1174, 1180 (R.I. 1994); *City of Warwick v. Aptt,* 497 A.2d 721, 724 (R.I. 1985).

The language of § 44-41-1 is clear and unequivocal. It unambiguously states that a "petroleum company" means "every corporation formed for or engaged in the business of importing or causing to be imported by a person other than a [petroleum] corporation subject to tax under this section into this state for sale in this state, extracting, producing, refining, manufacturing or compounding petroleum." Pursuant to the tax administrator's regulations under the Gross-Earning Tax Act, "an entity is engaged in the business of importing petroleum in Rhode Island if it owns petroleum located outside Rhode Island and ships it or causes it to be shipped to a point within Rhode Island for sale in Rhode Island." *Emergency Rules, Re: Gross Earnings Tax of Petroleum Companies,* Rule II (Oct. 18, 1992). The plain meaning of the term "importer" is a "[p]erson who brings (i.e., imports) goods into [a] country from [a] foreign country." *Black's Law Dictionary,* 755 (6th ed. 1990). Clearly under this definition Koch is the party bringing the product from another state into Rhode Island.

As the District Court correctly indicated, Koch caused the oil to be imported into Rhode Island. Through its own actions Koch conducted the negotiations which resulted in the fuel-oil sales' consummation in Rhode Island. Additionally, because Koch held title, risk of loss, and possession of the fuel oil up until the time the fuel oil passed the flange in Providence, it clearly possessed the fuel oil at the time it was "brought" into the state. Accordingly, we believe that the District Court correctly determined that Koch was an importer within the meaning of the Gross-Earnings Tax Act. We therefore reject Koch's contentions that Narragansett was the importer in the instant case.

For the reasons stated herein, the petition for certiorari is denied and the writ heretofore issued is quashed. The judgment of the District Court is affirmed, and the papers of the case may be remanded to the District Court with our decision endorsed thereon.

Justice Flanders did not participate.

Mississippi River Fuel Corp. v. Hoffman

[*Mississippi River Fuel* is discussed at ¶ 420.01.]

MISSISSIPPI RIVER FUEL CORPORATION, Appellee, v. Elmer J. HOFFMAN, State Treasurer, et al., Appellants

Supreme Court of Illinois., No. 33148, Sept. 23, 1954. As Modified on Denial of Rehearing Jan. 18, 1955, 123 N.E.2d 503

Latham Castle, Atty. Gen. (John L. Davidson, Jr., Springfield, William C. Wines, Raymond S. Sarnow, A. Zola Groves, Chicago, M. Brooks Byus, Jacksonville, Robert E. McGlynn, East St. Louis, and Richard L. Cooper, Springfield, of counsel), for appellants.

Kramer, Campbell, Costello & Wiechert, and Norman J. Gundlach, East St. Louis, Dougherty & White, New York City, and Hendren & Andrae, Jefferson City, Mo., for appellee.

BRISTOW, Chief Justice.This is an appeal from a decree of the eircuit court of St. Clair County enjoining Elmer J. Hoffman, State Treasurer, and Richard J. Lyons, Director of the Department of Revenue, from paying into the State Treasury moneys collected from the appellee, Mississippi River Fuel Corporation, under the supposed authority of section 2 of the Gas Revenue Tax Act. Ill.Rev.Stat.1953, chap. 120, par. 467.17.

That act imposes upon persons engaged in the business of distributing, supplying, furnishing or selling gas to persons for use or consumption and not for resale, a tax at the rate of 3 per cent of the gross receipts from such business, after June 30, 1945. It provides further: 'However, such taxes are not imposed with respect to any business in interstate commerce, or otherwise to the extent to which such business may not, under the constitution and statutes of the United States, be made the subject of taxation by this State.'

The amount here involved, $1,100,700.44, covering a period of something over a year, was paid by the appellee under written protest, after which appellee filed its complaint, asking for a temporary and a permanent injunction, restraining the predecessors in office of the defendants above named from paying the money over into the State Treasury. On December 8, 1952, the trial court issued a restraining order as prayed, without notice.

Appellants' motion to vacate this order was denied December 24, 1952. Thereafter, after hearing, the trial court, on October 30, 1953, entered the decree here appealed from, by which decree it restrained appellants from paying into the State Treasury the funds so collected and from making any further attempt to assess or collect from the appellee any tax claimed to be due under the statute above referred to.

Appellee, Mississippi River Fuel Corporation, is a Delaware corporation organized in 1928 for the purpose, among other things, of transporting natural gas from gas fields near Monroe, Louisiana, to the St. Louis, Missouri, area. In 1929 it constructed a pipeline west of and approximately parallel to the Mississippi River, from a point near Monroe, Louisiana, to point in Missouri somewhat south of the city of St. Louis, from which latter point the line was extended easterly across the Mississippi River into Illinois and thence northerly to a point opposite the northern part of the city of St. Louis, from which latter point two lines were extended westerly across the Mississippi River into St. Louis for delivery of natural gas to Laclede Gas Company, which serves gas in that city. Appellee's pipeline, for the most part, is 22 inches in diameter, dropping down to 18 inches and 16 inches as it extends northerly in Illinois.

On 1947 a second line was built across the Mississippi River into Randolph County, Illinois. This line turns in a northerly direction, somewhat east of the city of East St. Louis, and connects with the original line, at a point south of the city of Alton, Illinois.

From these two lines gas is sold to 23 industrial customers, whose plants are located along the lines and who buy the gas for their own use. In addition, appellee sells, and delivers from these lines, natural gas to two Illinois public utility companies, Illinois Power Company and Union Electric Power Company, which resell most of the gas to the general public in Madison and St. Clair Counties in Illinois, retaining some of it for their own use as boiler fuel. The sales by appellee to these public utility companies are involved in the present dispute only to the extent that they purchase some of the gas for use under their own boilers. Appellee asserts that these sales are made in interstate commerce and are not taxable by this State. Appellants, on the other hand, contend that the sales to the industrial customers are not sales in interstate commerce, but are intrastate in character, and as such, are subject to taxation under the statute referred to. In the alternative, they contend, somewhat less aggressively, that, even if the sales are in interstate commerce, the tax is not discriminatory and is not an undue burden upon that commerce, and hence is valid.

All of the gas is sold by the appellee to these customers under written contracts, which are in evidence. As to some of it, appellee is firmly obligated to make delivery; as to a very considerable part of the gas, appellee reserves the right to interrupt delivery under conditions provided in the contracts.

There is some conflict of statement between the parties as to the exact nature of the things done in Illinois by appellee. We find appellants asserting, apparently by way of emphasizing the local character of appellee's activities, that, in addition to selling and delivering the gas to the industrial customers in question, appellee in some way 'prepares' and 'transforms' the gas in Illinois for delivery to its Illinois customers. This appellee denies. There is no basis for appellants' assertion. We have examined the evidence in the record on this point, and we find the testimony to be uncontradicted to the effect that the gas is delivered in the same form in which it is transported through appellee's pipelines from the fields, and that at the point of delivery, the gas is not reduced by appellee to such a pressure as to make it usable by the customer. The industrial customers receive the gas at 25 to 150 pounds pressure per square inch, which, as the record shows, is much in excess of the pressure at which it can be utilized. Such pressure reduction as is necessary to make the gas usable is done in every case by the customer.

Appellants devote a considerable part of their argument to a discussion of an attempt which is being made by appellee to create a gas storage field in Illinois in an exhausted gas field in Monroe County. It is enough to say that even if appellee had fully succeeded in this endeavor and if some of the gas sold to its industrial customers had for a time been held in storage in the places mentioned, it would not, in our opinion, detract in any way from the interstate character of the whole transaction. A freight train carrying an interstate shipment may pause for a long time at a railroad siding in the course of the shipment without changing the interstate character of the whole act. It is well known, at least to those acquainted with the natural gas pipeline industry, that in several parts of the county such gas storage fields exist, and it has never been supposed that the existence and use of this method of underground storage has in any way detracted from or minimized the interstate character of the business of such pipeline companies.

There are other irrelevancies in appellants' argument. It is unimportant, as we view it, that appellee furnishes to some of its customers apparatus for burning fuel other than natural gas. The interruptible gas service which appellee renders presupposes that other fuels will be used during periods of such interruption, and for the protection of its interstate gas business, appellee is entirely justified in facilitating the use of such other fuels by the means mentioned.

The same considerations apply to appellants' argument that appellee's business is in some way reduced to a local intrastate one by reason of the fact that appellee sometimes finds it advisable to 'pack' gas in its pipelines at higher than normal pressure. Such 'packing' is treated by appellants as identical with 'storage.' What we have said above with respect to underground storage of gas as a proper and useful part of interstate commerce disposes of this question of 'packing.' We may point out, however, that the record shows that even when the lines are packed with gas at an unusually high pressure for some temporary reason, the gas continues to flow in the pipes.

We do not propose to discuss in detail all of the authorities cited by the parties, as we find one or two of them to be controlling. In the case of *Panhandle Eastern Pipeline Co. v. Public Service Commission of Indiana,* 332 U.S. 507, 68 S.Ct. 190, 193, 92 L.Ed. 128, the court was considering the character of sales of gas by an interstate pipeline company (Panhandle) directly to industrial customers of the State of Indiana. Commenting upon the character of these sales, it said: 'Nor do we question that these sales are interstate transactions. The contrary suggestion left open in the state supreme court's treatment rests upon the view that gas transported interstate takes on the character of a commodity which has come to rest or broken bulk when it leaves the main transmission line and, under reduced pressure, enters branch lines or laterals irrevocably on its way to final distribution or consumption. Those merely mechanical considerations are no longer effective, if ever they were exclusively, to determine for regulatory purposes the interstate or intrastate character of the continuous movement and resulting sales we have here. Thus gas furnished to local utilities for resale is supplied unquestionably, both as to transportation and as to sale, in interstate commerce. Yet it is subjected to practically identical changes in pressure with the gas sold by appellant directly for industrial use. Neither practical common sense nor constitutional sense would tolerate holding that reduction in pressure makes the industrial sales to Anchor-Hocking wholly intrastate for purposes of local regulation while deliveries at similar pressures to utility companies remain exclusively interstate. Variations in main pressure are not the criterion of the states' regulatory powers under the commerce clause. Cf. *Interstate Natural Gas Co. v. Federal Power Comm.,* 331 U.S. 682, 689, 67 S.Ct. 1482, 1486, 91 L.Ed. 1742. The sales here were clearly in interstate commerce.'

The present case presents an exactly parallel situation, as we view it. The sales by appellee to its industrial customers for their own use are shown by the record to be made in exactly the same way and under exactly the same conditions as the sales made by appellee to the two public utility companies who purchase the gas for resale. The physical acts done in Illinois are identical in both cases, as we read the testimony, yet appellants in their argument frankly concede that the sales to the two public utilities are sales in interstate commerce while they deny that result as to the sales to the industries.

Mississippi River Fuel

Appellants have allowed themselves to become confused between interstate commerce in its constitutional aspect and that part of interstate commerce which Congress chose to take under Federal regulation by the Federal Natural Gas Act of 1938, 15 U.S.C.A. s 717 et seq. In that act Congress gave to the Federal Power Commission power to regulate rates and all other aspects of sales of gas by interstate pipelines to purchasers for resale, the purchasers being, in general, local public utility companies. But in that act, Congress refrained from giving to the Federal Power Commission power to regulate the rates for gas sold by interstate pipelines to customers who took gas for their own use. (See Panhandle case.) But this statutory distinction which Congress elected to make certainly did not mean, as appellants seem to deduce, that the sales for resale were sales in interstate commerce while the sales to industries for their own use were not. Jurisdiction over both types of sales could without question have been given by Congress to the Federal Power Commission had it chosen. It was because of this statutory choice, by Congress that the Panhandle case quoted from above was decided as it was. The quoted language from the opinion in that case shows as plainly as possible that the United States Supreme Court fully recognizes the interstate character of industrial gas sales such as are here involved. The very recent case of *Phillips Petroleum Co. v. State of Wisconsin,* 347 U.S. 672, 74 S.Ct. 794, decided June 7, 1954, accords in principle with the Panhandle decision. There it was held that the Phillips Petroleum Company in selling gas to an interstate pipeline, was dong an act which amounted to participation in interstate transportation of gas and hence was subject to the Federal Power Commission. The late case of *Michigan-Wisconsin Pipeline Co. v. Calvert,* 347 U.S. 157, 74 S.Ct. 396, is in principle the same. It also was a case where a local producer of gas introduced it into an interstate pipeline. The court held a Texas State tax on the gathering of the gas to be invalid as a burden on the interstate transaction of selling and delivering the gas to the pipeline. The court said, 74 S.Ct. at page 401, 'The recurring problem is to resolve a conflict between the Constitution's mandate that trade between the states be permitted to flow freely without unnecessary obstruction from any source, and the state's rightful desire to require that interstate business bear its proper share of the costs of local government in return for benefits received. Some have thought that the wisest course would be for this Court to uphold all state taxes not patently discriminatory, and wait for Congress to adjust conflicts when and as it wished. But this view has not prevailed, and the Court has therefore been forced to decide in many varied factual situations whether the application of a given state tax to a given aspect of interstate activity violates the Commerce Clause. It is now well settled that a tax imposed on a local activity related to interstate commerce is valid if, and only if, the local activity is not such an integral part of the interstate process, the flow of commerce, that it cannot realistically be separated from it. *Memphis Natural Gas Co. v. Stone,* 1948, 335 U.S. 80, 87, 68 S.Ct. 1475, 1478, 92 L.Ed. 1832; *Western Live Stock v. Bureau of Revenue, supra,* 303 U.S. (250), at page 258, 58 S.Ct. (546), at page 550 (82 L.Ed. 823). And if a genuine separation of the taxed local activity from the interstate process is impossible, it is more likely that other states through which the commerce passes or into which it flows can with equal right impose a similar levy on the goods, with the net effect of prejudicing or unduly burdening commerce.' *Puget Sound Stevedoring Co. v. Tax Commission,* 1937, 302 U.S. 90, 58 S.Ct. 72, 82 L.Ed. 68. These holdings render pertinent the decision in *Puget Sound Stevedoring Co. v. Tax Commission,* 302 U.S. 90, 58 S.Ct. 72, 82 L.Ed. 68, in which the court held that the act of loading or unloading of goods at the beginning or end of an admittedly interstate or foreign act of transportation of a cargo is a part of the transportation itself and cannot be taxed by the State in which the act is done. The court said: 'The business of appellant, insofar as it consists of the loading and discharge of cargoes by longshoremen subject to its own direction and control, is interstate or foreign commerce. Transportation of a cargo by water * * * is impossible or futile unless the thing to be transported is put aboard the ship and taken off at destination. * * * The business of loading and unloading being interstate or foreign commerce, the state of Washington is not at liberty to tax the privilege of doing it by exacting in return therefor a percentage of the gross receipts. 302 U.S. at pages 92, 94, 58 S.Ct. at pages 73, 74.

That the Puget Sound Co. case represents the settled law on this subject may be inferred from the language in *Michigan-Wisconsin Pipeline Co. v. Calvert,* where the court referred to the act of taking gas into an interstate gas pipeline as an operation of 'loading.' 347 U.S. 157, 74 S.Ct. 396.

We will deal only briefly with that part of appellants' argument in which they contend that, even if these industrial sales are sales in interstate commerce, the tax is valid because it does not constitute an undue burden upon that commerce or discriminate against it. We are aware that the United States Supreme Court has at times used language which indicates that where interstate commerce is only collaterally involved a State tax may be levied if it does not constitute an 'unreasonable interference by the state' or does not 'unduly burden' the interstate commerce. We do not find that it has ever given a definitive meaning to this general language. We have no means of knowing when a tax burden is 'undue' or 'unreasonable.' It seems to us that the language referred to cannot possibly have any application to a case like the present one where the tax is directly imposed upon the very act of sale which constitutes an integral and essential part of the interstate commerce in question. If the State of Illinois can take 3 per cent of the proceeds of such sale by way of tax, it could presumably take more, up to some unknown and unascertainable point where the burden would clearly become 'undue' or 'unreasonable.' The present case involves the sum of $1,000,000 which, in our view, represents a substantial burden upon the payer regardless of its size or resources.

Appellee, in its argument, analyzes the case of *Sprout v. South Bend,* 227 U.S. 163, 48 S.Ct. 502, 72 L.Ed. 833, and refers to it as authority for the propositions that 'the state must not impose a tax solely on account of the interstate business done,' and that 'an occupation tax cannot be levied by a state upon a business devoted exclusively to interstate commerce.' We believe that, by indirection at least, the case supports both of these propositions, and they completely answer appellants' argument that the tax here can be sustained as nondiscriminatory. All of the business done by appellee in Illinois is shown to be interstate in character, and the disputed tax is levied directly upon and on account of a part of that interstate business.

Appellants place much reliance on the case of *Norton Co. v. Department of Revenue,* 340 U.S. 534, 71 S.Ct. 377, 95 L.Ed. 517, Id., 405 Ill. 314, 90 N.E.2d 737. We view the holding in this case differently. The Norton Company, a Massachusetts corporation, manufactured and sold abrasive machines and supplies. Under consent from the State of Illinois to do business therein, it operated a branch office and warehouse in Chicago, Illinois, from which it made local sales at retail. All sales to Illinois customers were not over the counter sales, but the State collected a tax on the entire gross income. In the Chicago warehouse the company carried 3000 most frequently purchased items. From them it served its cash customers. The Chicago office performed other functions, helpful to other classes of customers, namely, for those without credit; those who ordered items not carried in the local stock; those who desired special equipment. It received their order and forwarded it to the home office. For many Illinois customers it acted as an intermediary to reduce freight charges. Upon receipt of the order in Worcester, the goods were packaged and marked and allowed to accumulate until a carload lot could be consigned to the Chicago office, where the separate orders were reconsigned. The Chicago agency thus intervened between the seller and all vendees, and performed a valuable service in their selling operation. Upon such procedure, both this court and the United States Supreme Court held that the questioned tax was within constitutional bounds. However, there were sales wherein orders were sent directly to Worcester by the customer and the goods were shipped directly to the customer from Worcester. On these items of interstate commerce this court was reversed and the United States Supreme Court held that they were not taxable. Appellee's operation in the instant case does not have the local and retail characteristics present in the merchandising scheme of the Norton Company. Other cases relied upon by appellants are likewise distinguishable.

A State, of course, may levy ad valorem taxes upon the property of an interstate gas pipeline or other interstate carrier, *Braniff Airways, Inc. v. Nebraska State Board of Equalization,* 347 U.S. 590, 74 S.Ct. 757, the cases cited, and appellee's property is shown to be so taxed like other property in Illinois.

The sales by appellee to its 23 industrial customers as well as the sales of gas to the two public utility companies for their own use, even though not subject to rate control by the Federal Power Commission, are very clearly sales in interstate commerce and hence cannot be taxes by the State of Illinois. The money heretofore collected should be returned to appellee and no further comparable collection should be attempted. The decree of the circuit court of St. Clair County was right and is affirmed.

Decree affirmed.

SCHAEFER, Justice (dissenting).Section 2 of the act, which is quoted in the court's opinion, makes it clear that the issue here is whether this tax is forbidden by the commerce clause of the Federal constitution or by Federal statute. That issue is not determined by deciding simply that Mississippi's activities constitute a 'business in interstate commerce.' The court's treatment of the case leaves out of account the fact that the validity of similar taxes has often been decided in terms of their economic effect and their tendency to impose undue burdens upon interstate transactions. See Powell, More Ado About Gross Receipts Taxes, 60 Harv.L.Rev. 501, 710; Barrett, State Taxation of Interstate Commerce, 4 Vand.L.Rev. 496.

There are, I think, significant characteristics of this tax and of the transactions before us which have been overlooked. This tax cannot discriminate against interstate commerce, for it applies to all sales of gas for use or consumption. Nor does this tax give rise to any possibility of multiple taxation, for the taxable event is the sale 'for use or consumption and not for resale.' The transaction which gives rise to tax liability is thus the transaction which terminates all commerce, interstate and intrastate.

Under its contracts with its industrial customers Mississippi has undertaken to maintain equipment in Illinois. It owns and services equipment inside the plants of its industrial customers for the purpose of carrying out these contracts. The purchaser pays only for what is delivered at its local plant in Illinois; all of the risks of loss in transit are borne by Mississippi. Mississippi holds a franchise from the State of Illinois to engage in business in Illinois. The tax here involved is not measured by gross receipts upon all of Mississippi's sales of gas in Illinois, but only by receipts from those sales which are for use or consumption and which thus eliminate the gas as a future subject of commerce.

In its sales to industrial consumers which are here involved, Mississippi competes directly with public utilities which are unquestionably subject to the tax when they sell gas to their customers. Instead of discriminating against interstate commerce, the present tax does no more than to impose upon Mississippi's transactions the identical burden which is borne by competing sellers of the same commodity within the State. If Mississippi's sales to industrial customers cannot be reached by the tax, I see nothing which would prevent other utilities in Illinois from purchasing gas outside the State, bringing it within the State, and selling it for use or consumption here, free of the tax.

The cases on which the court relies are not, in my opinion, controlling. The tax invalidated in *Michigan-Wisconsin Pipe Line Co. v. Calvert,* 347 U.S. 157, 74 S.Ct. 396, was one imposed by the State of origin upon the 'taking' of gas into a pipeline for immediate interstate transmission. Apart from other differences, taxes by the State of origin have not been treated as equivalent to those imposed by the State of destination since their effect is different. See, *e.g., McGoldrick v. Berwind-White Coal Mining Co.,* 309 U.S. 33, 60 S.Ct. 388, 84 L.Ed. 565; *Gwin, White & Prince v. Henneford,* 305 U.S. 434, 59 S.Ct. 325, 83 L.Ed. 272; *Freeman v. Hewit,* 329 U.S. 249, 67 S.Ct. 274, 91 L.Ed. 265; *Panhandle Eastern Pipe Line Co. v. Public Service Comm.,* 332 U.S. 507, 68 S.Ct. 190, 92 L.Ed. 128, dealt with regulation, not taxation, and the actual holding in that case sustained the power of the State to regulate the direct sales in interstate commerce which were there involved. Under the commerce clause the limits upon State power to regulate are not necessarily identical with those upon State power to tax; but so far as the regulation cases are at all relevant, they argue in favor of State power rather than against it.

The tax here imposed is in material respects identical with that which was sustained in *East Ohio Gas Co. v. Tax Commission,* 283 U.S. 465, 51 S.Ct. 499, 75 L.Ed. 1171. See also *Southern Natural Gas Corp. v. Alabama,* 301 U.S. 148, 57 S.Ct. 696, 81 L.Ed. 970; *Memphis Natural Gas Co. v. Beeler,* 315 U.S. 649, 62 S.Ct. 857, 86 L.Ed. 1090. Prior to the East Ohio decision, the Supreme Court had already taken the position with regard to State regulatory powers that unlike sales of gas to utilities for resale, direct sales for consumption were within the area of State control. *Public Utilities Comm. v. Landon,* 249 U.S. 236, 39 S.Ct. 268, 63 L.Ed. 577; *Pennsylvania Gas Co. v. Public Service Comm.,* 252 U.S. 23, 40 S.Ct. 279, 64 L.Ed. 43; cf. *Missouri ex rel. Barrett v. Kansas Natural Gas Co.,* 265 U.S. 298, 44 S.Ct. 544, 68 L.Ed. 1027. So far as the East Ohio decision may be thought to rest on such 'mechanical' considerations as reduction in pressure, it is now of doubtful authority. See *Illinois Natural Gas Co. v. Central Illinois Public Service Co.,* 314 U.S. 498, 504-506, 62 S.Ct. 384, 86 L.Ed. 371; *Panhandle Eastern Pipe Line Co. v. Public Service Comm.,* 332 U.S. 507, 512-513, 68 S.Ct. 190, 92 L.Ed. 128; but cf. *Federal Power Comm. v. East Ohio Gas Co.,* 338 U.S. 464, 469-473, 70 S.Ct. 266, 94 L.Ed. 268. But subsequent cases have not rejected the 'wholesale-retail' criterion for determining the permissible reach of State power.

The theory employed in the East Ohio opinion to sustain the tax was that interstate commerce ended when distribution to the consumer began, the same theory which had been employed to sustain State regulation in the Landon case. As the majority opinion here notes, subsequent pronouncements of the Supreme Court have reverted to the different standard employed in *Pennsylvania Gas Co. v. Public Service Comm.,* 252 U.S. 23, 30-31, 40 S.Ct. 279, 64 L.Ed. 434, and the present view seems to be that these direct sales are interstate commerce, and that the State's power to control them rests on the fact that these sales are 'essentially local' in character. *Panhandle Eastern Pipe Line Co. v. Public Service Comm.,* 332 U.S. 507, 523-524, 68 S.Ct. 190, 92 L.Ed. 128; *Panhandle Eastern Pipe Line Co. v. Michigan Public Service Comm.,* 341 U.S. 329, 71 S.Ct. 777, 95 L.Ed. 993; *Illinois Natural Gas Co. v. Central Illinois Public Service Co.,* 314 U.S. 498, 504-506, 62 S.Ct. 384, 86 L.Ed. 371. More significant than this change in theory, perhaps, is the fact that whether sales of this kind have been regarded as interstate or intrastate, State power to regulate them has been sustained. I do not think, therefore, that subsequent decisions justify disregarding the East Ohio holding.

Last year this court held that Mississippi's direct sales were not subject to regulation by the State. *Mississippi River Fuel Corp. v. Illinois Commerce Comm.,* 1 Ill.2d 509, 116 N.E.2d 394. The result of that decision was to give the appellee a favored economic position as against competing local utilities. Today the court creates a similar result by holding these same sales immune to taxation. I do not believe that the commerce clause requires that interstate commerce be given more than equal treatment. The decree below should be reversed.

HERSHEY, J., concurs in the foregoing dissenting opinion.

Mississippi River Fuel

Quill Corporation v. North Dakota

[*Quill* is discussed at ¶ 505.02 and ¶ 705.]

Quill Corporation v. North Dakota, by and through its Tax Commissioner, Keitkamp.

United States Supreme Court, Docket No. 91-194, May 26, 1992, 504 U.S. 298, 112 S.Ct. 1904, reversing North Dakota Supreme Court, May 7, 1991, 470 NW2d 203

STEVENS, Justice:

This case, like *National Bellas Hess, Inc. v. Department of Revenue of Ill.*, 386 U.S. 753 (1967), involves a State's attempt to require an out-of-state mail-order house that has neither outlets nor sales representatives in the State to collect and pay a use tax on goods purchased for use within the State. In *Bellas Hess* we held that a similar Illinois statute violated the Due Process Clause of the Fourteenth Amendment and created an unconstitutional burden on interstate commerce. In particular, we ruled that a "seller whose only connection with customers in the State is by common carrier or the United States mail" lacked the requisite minimum contacts with the State. *Id.*, at 758.

In this case the Supreme Court of North Dakota declined to follow *Bellas Hess* because "the tremendous social, economic, commercial, and legal innovations" of the past quarter-century have rendered its holding "obsole[te]." 470 N.W.2d 203, 208 (1991). Having granted certiorari, 502 U.S. __, we must either reverse the State Supreme Court or overrule *Bellas Hess*. While we agree with much of the State Court's reasoning, we take the former course.

I

Quill is a Delaware corporation with offices and warehouses in Illinois, California, and Georgia. None of its employees work or reside in North Dakota and its ownership of tangible property in that State is either insignificant or nonexistent.[1] Quill sells office equipment and supplies; it solicits business through catalogs and flyers, advertisements in national periodicals, and telephone calls. Its annual national sales exceed $200,000,000, of which almost $1,000,000 are made to about 3,000 customers in North Dakota. It is the sixth largest vendor of office

[1] In the trial court, the State argued that because Quill gave its customers an unconditional 90-day guarantee, it retained title to the merchandise during the 90-day period after delivery. The trial court held, however, that title passed to the purchaser when the merchandise was received. See App. to Pet. for Cert. A40-A41. The State Supreme Court assumed for the purposes of its decision that that ruling was correct. 470 N.W.2d 203, 217, n. 13. The State Supreme Court also noted that Quill licensed a computer software program to some of its North Dakota customers that enabled them to check Quill's current inventories and prices and to place orders directly. *Id.*, at 216-217. As we shall explain, Quill's interests in the licensed software does not affect our analysis of the due process issue and does not comprise the "substantial nexus" required by the Commerce Clause. See *infra* n. 8.

supplies in the State. It delivers all of its merchandise to its North Dakota customers by mail or common carrier from out-of-state locations.

As a corollary to its sales tax, North Dakota imposes a use tax upon property purchased for storage, use or consumption within the State. North Dakota requires every "retailer maintaining a place of business in" the State to collect the tax from the consumer and remit it to the State. N.D. Cent. Code § 57-40.2-07 (Supp. 1991). In 1987 North Dakota amended the statutory definition of the term "retailer" to include "every person who engages in regular or systematic solicitation of a consumer market in th[e] state." § 57-40.2-01(6). State regulations in turn define "regular or systematic solicitation" to mean three or more advertisements within a 12-month period. N.D. Admin. Code § 81-04.1-01-03.1 (1988). Thus, since 1987, mail-order companies that engage in such solicitation have been subject to the tax even if they maintain no property or personnel in North Dakota.

Quill has taken the position that North Dakota does not have the power to compel it to collect a use tax from its North Dakota customers. Consequently, the State, through its Tax Commissioner, filed this action to require Quill to pay taxes (as well as interest and penalties) on all such sales made after July 1, 1987. The trial court ruled in Quill's favor, finding the case indistinguishable from *Bellas Hess*; specifically, it found that because the State had not shown that it had spent tax revenues for the benefit of the mail-order business, there was no "nexus to allow the state to define retailer in the manner it chose." App. to Pet. for Cert. A41.

The North Dakota Supreme Court reversed, concluding that "wholesale changes" in both the economy and the law made it inappropriate to follow *Bellas Hess* today. 470 N.W.2d, at 213. The principal economic change noted by the court was the remarkable growth of the mail-order business "from a relatively inconsequential market niche" in 1967 to a "goliath" with annual sales that reached "the staggering figure of $183.3 billion in 1989." *Id.*, at 208, 209. Moreover, the court observed, advances in computer technology greatly eased the burden of compliance with a "welter of complicated obligations" imposed by state and local taxing authorities. *Id.*, at 215 (quoting *Bellas Hess*, 386 U.S., at 759-760).

Equally important, in the court's view, were the changes in the "legal landscape." With respect to the Commerce Clause, the court emphasized that *Complete Auto Transit, Inc. v. Brady*, 430 U.S. 274 (1977), rejected the line of cases holding that the direct taxation of interstate commerce was impermissible and adopted instead a "consistent and rational method of inquiry [that focused on] the practical effect of [the] challenged tax." *Mobil Oil Corp. v. Commissioner of Taxes of Vt.,* 445 U.S. 425, 443 (1980). This and subsequent rulings, the court maintained, indicated that the Commerce Clause no longer mandated the sort of physical-presence nexus suggested in *Bellas Hess.*

Similarly, with respect to the Due Process Clause, the North Dakota court observed that cases following *Bellas Hess* had not construed "minimum contacts" to require physical presence within a State as a prerequisite to the legitimate exercise of state power. The State Court then concluded that "the Due Process requirement of a 'minimal connection' to establish nexus is encompassed within the *Complete Auto* test" and that the relevant inquiry under the latter test was whether "the state has provided some protection, opportunities, or benefit for which it can expect a return." 470 N.W.2d, at 216.

Turning to the case at hand, the State Court emphasized that North Dakota had created "an economic climate that fosters demand for" Quill's products, maintained a legal infrastructure that protected that market, and disposed of 24 tons of catalogs and flyers mailed by Quill into the State every year. *Id.,* at 218-219. Based on these facts, the court concluded that Quill's "economic presence" in North Dakota depended on services and benefits provided by the State and therefore generated "a constitutionally sufficient nexus to justify imposition of the purely administrative duty of collecting and remitting the use tax." *Id.,* at 219.[2]

II

As in a number of other cases involving the application of state taxing statutes to out-of-state sellers, our holding in *Bellas Hess* relied on both the Due Process Clause and the Commerce Clause. Although the "two claims are closely related," *Bellas Hess,* 386 U.S., at 756, the clauses pose distinct limits on the taxing powers of the States. Accordingly, while a State may, consistent with the Due Process Clause, have the authority to tax a particular taxpayer, imposition of the tax may nonetheless violate the Commerce Clause. See, *e.g., Tyler Pipe Industries, Inc. v. Washington State Dept. of Revenue,* 483 U.S. 232 (1987).

The two constitutional requirements differ fundamentally, in several ways. As discussed at greater length below, see *infra,* at Part IV, the Due Process Clause and the Commerce Clause reflect different constitutional concerns. Moreover, while Congress has plenary power to regulate commerce among the States and thus may authorize state actions that burden interstate commerce, see *International Shoe Co. v.*

[2] The court also suggested that, in view of the fact that the "touchstone of Due Process is fundamental fairness" and that the "very object" of the Commerce Clause is protection of interstate business against discriminatory local practices, it would be ironic to exempt Quill from this burden and thereby allow it to enjoy a significant competitive advantage over local retailers. 470 N.W.2d, at 214-215.

Washington, 326 U.S. 310, 315 (1945), it does not similarly have the power to authorize violations of the Due Process Clause.

Thus, although we have not always been precise in distinguishing between the two, the Due Process Clause and the Commerce Clause are analytically distinct.

> 'Due process' and 'commerce clause' conceptions are not always sharply separable in dealing with these problems. . . . To some extent they overlap. If there is a want of due process to sustain the tax, by that fact alone any burden the tax imposes on the commerce among the states becomes 'undue.' But, though overlapping, the two conceptions are not identical. There may be more than sufficient factual connections, with economic and legal effects, between the transaction and the taxing state to sustain the tax as against due process objections. Yet it may fall because of its burdening effect upon the commerce. And, although the two notions cannot always be separated, clarity of consideration and of decision would be promoted if the two issues are approached, where they are presented, at least tentatively as if they were separate and distinct, not intermingled ones. *International Harvester Co. v. Department of Treasury,* 322 U.S. 340, 353 (1944) (Rutledge, J., concurring in part and dissenting in part).

Heeding Justice Rutledge's counsel, we consider each constitutional limit in turn.

III

The Due Process Clause "requires some definite link, some minimum connection, between a state and the person, property or transaction it seeks to tax," *Miller Bros. Co. v. Maryland,* 347 U.S. 340, 344-345 (1954), and that the "income attributed to the State for tax purposes must be rationally related to 'values connected with the taxing State.' " *Moorman Mfg. Co. v. Bair,* 437 U.S. 267, 273 (1978) (citation omitted). Here, we are concerned primarily with the first of these requirements. Prior to *Bellas Hess,* we had held that that requirement was satisfied in a variety of circumstances involving use taxes. For example, the presence of sales personnel in the State,[3] or the maintenance of local retail stores in the State,[4] justified the exercise of that power because the seller's local activities were "plainly accorded the protection and services of the taxing State." *Bellas Hess,* 386 U.S., at 757. The furthest extension of that power was recognized in *Scripto, Inc. v. Carson,* 362 U.S. 207 (1960), in which the Court upheld a use tax despite the fact that all of the seller's in-state solicitation was performed by independent contractors. These cases all involved some sort of physical presence within the State, and in *Bellas Hess* the Court suggested that such presence was not only sufficient for jurisdiction under the Due Process Clause, but also necessary. We expressly de-

[3] *Felt & Tarrant Mfg. Co. v. Gallagher,* 306 U.S. 62 (1939).

[4] *Nelson v. Sears, Roebuck & Co.,* 312 U.S. 359 (1941).

clined to obliterate the "sharp distinction . . . between mail order sellers with retail outlets, solicitors, or property within a State, and those who do no more than communicate with customers in the State by mail or common carrier as a part of a general interstate business." 386 U.S., at 758.

Our due process jurisprudence has evolved substantially in the 25 years since *Bellas Hess,* particularly in the area of judicial jurisdiction. Building on the seminal case of *International Shoe Co. v. Washington,* 326 U.S. 310 (1945), we have framed the relevant inquiry as whether a defendant had minimum contacts with the jurisdiction "such that the maintenance of the suit does not offend 'traditional notions of fair play and substantial justice.' " *Id.,* at 316 (quoting *Milliken v. Meyer,* 311 U.S. 457, 463 (1940)). In that spirit, we have abandoned more formalistic tests that focused on a defendant's "presence" within a State in favor of a more flexible inquiry into whether a defendant's contacts with the forum made it reasonable, in the context of our federal system of government, to require it to defend the suit in that State. In *Shaffer v. Heitner,* 433 U.S. 186, 212 (1977), the Court extended the flexible approach that *International Shoe* had prescribed for purposes of *in personam* jurisdiction to *in rem* jurisdiction, concluding that "all assertions of state-court jurisdiction must be evaluated according to the standards set forth in *International Shoe* and its progeny."

Applying these principles, we have held that if a foreign corporation purposefully avails itself of the benefits of an economic market in the forum State, it may subject itself to the State's in personam jurisdiction even if it has no physical presence in the State. As we explained in *Burger King Corp. v. Rudzewicz,* 471 U.S. 462 (1985):

> Jurisdiction in these circumstances may not be avoided merely because the defendant did not *physically* enter the forum State. Although territorial presence frequently will enhance a potential defendant's affiliation with a State and reinforce the reasonable foreseeability of suit there, it is an inescapable fact of modern commercial life that a substantial amount of business is transacted solely by mail and wire communications across state lines, thus obviating the need for physical presence within a State in which business is conducted. So long as a commercial actor's efforts are 'purposefully directed' toward residents of another State, we have consistently rejected the notion that an absence of physical contacts can defeat personal jurisdiction there. *Id.,* at 476 (emphasis in original).

Comparable reasoning justifies the imposition of the collection duty on a mail-order house that is engaged in continuous and widespread solicitation of business within a State. Such a corporation clearly has "fair warning that [its] activity may subject [it] to the jurisdiction of a foreign sovereign." *Shaffer v. Heitner,* 433 U.S., at 218 (STEVENS, J., concurring in judgment). In "modern commercial life" it matters little that such solicitation is accomplished by a deluge of catalogs rather than a phalanx of drummers: the requirements of due process are met irrespective of a corporation's lack of physical presence in the taxing State. Thus, to the extent that our decisions have indicated that the Due Process Clause requires physical presence in a State for the imposition of duty to collect a use tax, we overrule those holdings as superseded by developments in the law of due process.

In this case, there is no question that Quill has purposefully directed its activities at North Dakota residents, that the magnitude of those contacts are more than sufficient for due process purposes, and that the use tax is related to the benefits Quill receives from access to the State. We therefore agree with the North Dakota Supreme Court's conclusion that the Due Process Clause does not bar enforcement of that State's use tax against Quill.

IV

Article I, §8, cl. 3 of the Constitution expressly authorizes Congress to "regulate Commerce with foreign Nations, and among the several States." It says nothing about the protection of interstate commerce in the absence of any action by Congress. Nevertheless, as Justice Johnson suggested in his concurring opinion in *Gibbons v. Ogden,* 9 Wheat. 1, 231-232, 239 (1824), the Commerce Clause is more than an affirmative grant of power; it has a negative sweep as well. The clause, in Justice Stone's phrasing, "by its own force" prohibits certain state actions that interfere with interstate commerce. *South Carolina State Highway Dept. v. Barnwell Bros., Inc.,* 303 U.S. 177, 185 (1938).

Our interpretation of the "negative" or "dormant" Commerce Clause has evolved substantially over the years, particularly as that clause concerns limitations on state taxation powers. See generally, P. Hartman, Federal Limitations on State and Local Taxation §§2:9-2:17 (1981). Our early cases, beginning with *Brown v. Maryland,* 12 Wheat. 419 (1827), swept broadly, and in *Leloup v. Port of Mobile,* 127 U.S. 640, 648 (1888), we declared that "no State has the right to lay a tax on interstate commerce in any form." We later narrowed that rule and distinguished between direct burdens on interstate commerce, which were prohibited, and indirect burdens, which generally were not. See, *e.g., Sanford v. Poe,* 69 F. 546 (CA6 1895), aff'd *sub nom. Adams Express Co. v. Ohio State Auditor,* 165 U.S. 194, 220 (1897). *Western Live Stock v. Bureau of Revenue,* 303 U.S. 250, 256-258 (1938), and subsequent decisions rejected this formal, categorical analysis and adopted a "multiple-taxation doctrine" that focused not on whether a tax was "direct" or "indirect" but rather on whether a tax subjected interstate commerce to a risk of multiple taxation. However, in *Freeman v. Hewit,* 329 U.S. 249, 256 (1946), we embraced again the formal distinction between direct and indirect taxation, invalidating Indiana's imposition of a gross receipts tax on a particular transaction because that application would "impos[e] a direct tax on interstate sales." Most recently, in *Complete Auto Transit, Inc. v. Brady,* 430 U.S. 274, 285 (1977), we renounced the *Freeman* approach as "attaching constitutional significance to a semantic difference." We expressly overruled one of *Freeman*'s progeny, *Spector Motor Service, Inc. v. O'Connor,* 340 U.S. 602 (1951), which held that a tax on "the privilege of doing interstate business" was unconstitutional, while recognizing that a differently denominated tax with the same economic effect would not be unconstitutional. *Spector,* as we observed in *Railway Express Agency, Inc. v. Virginia,* 358 U.S. 434, 441 (1959), created a situation in which "magic words or labels" could "disable an otherwise constitutional levy." *Complete Auto* emphasized the importance of looking past "the formal language of the tax statute [to] its practical effect," *Complete Auto,* 430 U.S., at 279, and set forth a four-part test that continues to govern the validity of state taxes under the Commerce Clause.[5]

Bellas Hess was decided in 1967, in the middle of this latest rally between formalism and pragmatism. Contrary to the suggestion of the North Dakota Supreme Court, this timing does not mean that *Complete Auto* rendered *Bellas Hess* "obsolete." Complete Auto rejected *Freeman* and *Spector*'s formal distinction between "direct" and "indirect" taxes on interstate commerce because that formalism allowed the validity of statutes to hinge on "legal terminology," "draftsmanship and phraseology." 430 U.S., at 281. *Bellas Hess* did not rely on any such labeling of taxes and therefore did not automatically fall with *Freeman* and its progeny.

While contemporary Commerce Clause jurisprudence might not dictate the same result were the issue to arise for the first time today, *Bellas Hess* is not inconsistent with *Complete Auto* and our recent cases. Under *Complete Auto*'s four-part test, we will sustain a tax against a Commerce Clause challenge so long as the "tax [1] is applied to an activity with a substantial nexus with the taxing State, [2] is fairly apportioned, [3] does not discriminate against interstate commerce, and [4] is fairly related to the services provided by the State."

---

[5] Under our current Commerce Clause jurisprudence, "with certain restrictions, interstate commerce may be required to pay its fair share of state taxes." *D.H. Holmes Co. v. McNamara,* 486 U.S. 24, 31 (1988); see *also Commonwealth Edison Co. v. Montana,* 453 U.S. 609, 623-624 (1981) ("[i]t was not the purpose of the commerce clause to relieve those engaged in interstate commerce from their just share of [the] state tax burden even though it increases the cost of doing business") (internal quotation and citation omitted).

430 U.S., at 279. *Bellas Hess* concerns the first of these tests and stands for the proposition that a vendor whose only contacts with the taxing State are by mail or common carrier lacks the "substantial nexus" required by the Commerce Clause.

Thus, three weeks after *Complete Auto* was handed down, we cited *Bellas Hess* for this proposition and discussed the case at some length. In *National Geographic Society v. California Bd. of Equalization,* 430 U.S. 551, 559 (1977), we affirmed the continuing vitality of *Bellas Hess'* "sharp distinction . . . between mail-order sellers with [a physical presence in the taxing] State and those . . . who do no more than communicate with customers in the State by mail or common carrier as part of a general interstate business." We have continued to cite *Bellas Hess* with approval ever since. For example, in *Goldberg v. Sweet,* 488 U.S. 252, 263 (1989), we expressed "doubt that termination of an interstate telephone call, by itself, provides a substantial enough nexus for a State to tax a call. See *National Bellas Hess* . . . (receipt of mail provides insufficient nexus)." See *also D. H. Holmes Co. v. McNamara,* 486 U.S. 24, 33 (1988); *Commonwealth Edison Co. v. Montana,* 453 U.S. 609, 626 (1981); *Mobil Oil Corp. v. Commissioner of Taxes,* 445 U.S., at 437; *National Geographic Society,* 430 U.S., at 559. For these reasons, we disagree with the State Supreme Court's conclusion that our decision in *Complete Auto* undercut the *Bellas Hess* rule.

The State of North Dakota relies less on *Complete Auto* and more on the evolution of our due process jurisprudence. The State contends that the nexus requirements imposed by the Due Process and Commerce Clauses are equivalent and that if, as we concluded above, a mail-order house that lacks a physical presence in the taxing State nonetheless satisfies the due process "minimum contacts" test, then that corporation also meets the Commerce Clause "substantial nexus" test. We disagree. Despite the similarity in phrasing, the nexus requirements of the Due Process and Commerce Clauses are not identical. The two standards are animated by different constitutional concerns and policies.

Due process centrally concerns the fundamental fairness of governmental activity. Thus, at the most general level, the due process nexus analysis requires that we ask whether an individual's connections with a State are substantial enough to legitimate the State's exercise of power over him. We have, therefore, often identified "notice" or "fair warning" as the analytic touchstone of due process nexus analysis. In contrast, the Commerce Clause, and its nexus requirement, are informed not so much by concerns about fairness for the individual defendant as by structural concerns about the effects of state regulation on the national economy. Under the Articles of Confederation,

State taxes and duties hindered and suppressed interstate commerce; the Framers intended the Commerce Clause as a cure for these structural ills. See generally The Federalist Nos. 7, 11 (A. Hamilton). It is in this light that we have interpreted the negative implication of the Commerce Clause. Accordingly, we have ruled that that Clause prohibits discrimination against interstate commerce, see, *e.g., Philadelphia v. New Jersey,* 437 U.S. 617 (1978), and bars state regulations that unduly burden interstate commerce, see, *e.g., Kassel v. Consolidated Freightways Corp. of Del.,* 450 U.S. 662 (1981).

The *Complete Auto* analysis reflects these concerns about the national economy. The second and third parts of that analysis, which require fair apportionment and non-discrimination, prohibit taxes that pass an unfair share of the tax burden onto interstate commerce. The first and fourth prongs, which require a substantial nexus and a relationship between the tax and State-provided services, limit the reach of State taxing authority so as to ensure that State taxation does not unduly burden interstate commerce.[6] Thus, the "substantial-nexus" requirement is not, like due process' "minimum-contacts" requirement, a proxy for notice, but rather a means for limiting state burdens on interstate commerce. Accordingly, contrary to the State's suggestion, a corporation may have the "minimum contacts" with a taxing State as required by the Due Process Clause, and yet lack the "substantial nexus" with that State as required by the Commerce Clause.[7]

The State Supreme Court reviewed our recent Commerce Clause decisions and concluded that those rulings signalled a "retreat from the formalistic constrictions of a stringent physical presence test in favor of a more flexible substantive approach" and thus supported its decision not to apply *Bellas Hess.* 470 N.W.2d, at 214 (citing *Standard Pressed Steel Co. v. Department of Revenue of Wash.,* 419 U.S. 560 (1975), and *Tyler Pipe Industries, Inc. v. Washington State Dept. of Revenue,* 483 U.S. 232 (1987)). Although we agree with the State Court's assessment

---

[6] North Dakota's use tax illustrates well how a state tax might unduly burden interstate commerce. On its face, North Dakota law imposes a collection duty on every vendor who advertises in the State three times in a single year. Thus, absent the *Bellas Hess* rule, a publisher who included a subscription card in three issues of its magazine, a vendor whose radio advertisements were heard in North Dakota on three occasions, and a corporation whose telephone sales force made three calls into the State, all would be subject to the collection duty. What is more significant, similar obligations might be imposed by the Nation's 6,000-plus taxing jurisdictions. See *National Bellas Hess, Inc. v. Department of Revenue of Ill.,* 386 U.S. 753, 759-760 (1967) (noting that the "many variations in rates of tax, in allowable exemptions, and in administrative and record-keeping requirements could entangle [a mail-order house] in a virtual welter of complicated obligations") (footnotes omitted); see *also* Shaviro, An Economic and Political Look at Federalism in Taxation, 90 Mich. L. Rev. 895, 925-926 (1992).

[7] We have sometimes stated that the "*Complete Auto* test, while responsive to Commerce Clause dictates, encompasses as well . . . Due Process requirement[s]." *Trinova Corp v. Michigan Dept. of Treasury,* 498 U.S. ___, ___ (1991) (slip op. 12). Although such comments might suggest that every tax that passes contemporary Commerce Clause analysis is also valid under the Due Process Clause, it does not follow that the converse is as well true: a tax may be consistent with Due Process and yet unduly burden interstate commerce. See, *e.g., Tyler Pipe Industries, Inc. v. Washington State Dept. of Revenue,* 483 U.S. 232 (1987).

of the evolution of our cases, we do not share its conclusion that this evolution indicates that the Commerce Clause ruling of *Bellas Hess* is no longer good law.

First, as the State Court itself noted, 470 N.W.2d, at 214, all of these cases involved taxpayers who had a physical presence in the taxing State and therefore do not directly conflict with the rule of *Bellas Hess* or compel that it be overruled. Second, and more importantly, although our Commerce Clause jurisprudence now favors more flexible balancing analyses, we have never intimated a desire to reject all established "bright-line" tests. Although we have not, in our review of other types of taxes, articulated the same physical-presence requirement that *Bellas Hess* established for sales and use taxes, that silence does not imply repudiation of the *Bellas Hess* rule.

Complete Auto, it is true, renounced *Freeman* and its progeny as "formalistic." But not all formalism is alike. *Spector*'s formal distinction between taxes on the "privilege of doing business" and all other taxes served no purpose within our Commerce Clause jurisprudence, but stood "only as a trap for the unwary draftsman." *Complete Auto,* 430 U.S., at 279. In contrast, the bright-line rule of *Bellas Hess* furthers the ends of the dormant Commerce Clause. Undue burdens on interstate commerce may be avoided not only by a case-by-case evaluation of the actual burdens imposed by particular regulations or taxes, but also, in some situations, by the demarcation of a discrete realm of commercial activity that is free from interstate taxation. *Bellas Hess* followed the latter approach and created a safe harbor for vendors "whose only connection with customers in the [taxing] State is by common carrier or the United States mail." Under *Bellas Hess,* such vendors are free from state-imposed duties to collect sales and use taxes.[8]

Like other bright-line tests, the *Bellas Hess* rule appears artificial at its edges: whether or not a State may compel a vendor to collect a sales or use tax may turn on the presence in the taxing State of a small sales force, plant, or office. Cf. *National Geographic Society v. California Bd. of Equalization,* 430 U.S. 551 (1977); *Scripto, Inc. v. Carson,* 362 U.S. 207 (1960). This artificiality, however, is more than offset by the benefits of a clear rule. Such a rule firmly establishes the boundaries of legitimate state authority to impose a duty to collect sales and

[8] In addition to its common-carrier contacts with the State, Quill also licensed software to some of its North Dakota clients. See *supra* n. 1. The State "concedes that the existence in North Dakota of a few floppy diskettes to which Quill holds title seems a slender thread upon which to base nexus." Brief for Respondent 46. We agree. Although title to "a few floppy diskettes" present in a State might constitute some minimal nexus, in *National Geographic Society v. California Bd. of Equalization,* 430 U.S. 551, 556 (1977), we expressly rejected a " 'slightest presence' standard of constitutional nexus." We therefore conclude that Quill's licensing of software in this case does not meet the "substantial nexus" requirement of the Commerce Clause.

use taxes and reduces litigation concerning those taxes. This benefit is important, for as we have so frequently noted, our law in this area is something of a "quagmire" and the "application of constitutional principles to specific state statutes leaves much room for controversy and confusion and little in the way of precise guides to the States in the exercise of their indispensable power of taxation." *Northwestern States Portland Cement Co. v. Minnesota,* 358 U.S. 450, 457-458 (1959).

Moreover, a bright-line rule in the area of sales and use taxes also encourages settled expectations and, in doing so, fosters investment by businesses and individuals.[9] Indeed, it is not unlikely that the mail-order industry's dramatic growth over the last quarter-century is due in part to the bright-line exemption from state taxation created in *Bellas Hess.*

Notwithstanding the benefits of bright-line tests, we have, in some situations, decided to replace such tests with more contextual balancing inquiries. For example, in *Arkansas Electric Cooperative Corp. v. Arkansas Pub. Serv. Comm'n,* 461 U.S. 375 (1983), we reconsidered a bright-line test set forth in *Public Utilities Comm'n of R.I. v. Attleboro Steam & Electric Co.,* 273 U.S. 83 (1927). *Attleboro* distinguished between state regulation of *wholesale* sales of electricity, which was constitutional as an "indirect" regulation of interstate commerce, and state regulation of *retail* sales of electricity, which was unconstitutional as a "direct regulation" of commerce. In *Arkansas Electric,* we considered whether to "follow the mechanical test set out in *Attleboro,* or the balance-of-interests test applied in our Commerce Clause cases." *Arkansas Electric Cooperative Corp.,* 461 U.S., at 390-391. We first observed that "the principle of *stare decisis* counsels us, here as elsewhere, not lightly to set aside specific guidance of the sort we find in *Attleboro.*" *Id.,* at 391. In deciding to reject the *Attleboro* analysis, we were influenced by the fact that the "mechanical test" was "anachronistic," that the Court had rarely relied on the test, and that we could "see no strong reliance interests" that would be upset by the rejection of that test. *Id.,* at 391-392. None of those factors obtains in this case. First, the *Attleboro* rule was "anachronistic" because it relied on formal distinctions between "direct" and "indirect" regulation (and on

[9] It is worth noting that Congress has, at least on one occasion, followed a similar approach in its regulation of state taxation. In response to this Court's indication in *Northwestern States Portland Cement Co. v. Minnesota,* 358 U.S. 450, 452 (1959), that, so long as the taxpayer has an adequate nexus with the taxing State, "net income from the interstate operations of a foreign corporation may be subjected to state taxation," Congress enacted Pub. L. 86-272, codified at 15 U.S.C. § 381. That statute provides that a State may not impose a net income tax on any person if that person's "only business activities within such State [involve] the solicitation of orders [approved] outside the State [and] filled . . . outside the State." 15 U.S.C. § 381. As we noted in *Heublein, Inc. v. South Carolina Tax Comm'n,* 409 U.S. 275, 280 (1972), in enacting § 381, "Congress attempted to allay the apprehension of businessmen that 'mere solicitation' would subject them to state taxation . . . Section 381 was designed to define clearly a lower limit for the exercise of [the State's power to tax]. *Clarity that would remove uncertainty was Congress' primary goal.*" (Emphasis supplied.)

the regulatory counterparts of our *Freeman* line of cases); as discussed above, *Bellas Hess* turned on a different logic and thus remained sound after the Court repudiated an analogous distinction in *Complete Auto.* Second, unlike the *Attleboro* rule, we have, in our decisions, frequently relied on the *Bellas Hess* rule in the last 25 years, see *supra,* at 11, and we have never intimated in our review of sales or use taxes that *Bellas Hess* was unsound. Finally, again unlike the *Attleboro* rule, the *Bellas Hess* rule has engendered substantial reliance and has become part of the basic framework of a sizeable industry. The "interest in stability and orderly development of the law" that undergirds the doctrine of *stare decisis,* see *Runyon v. McCrary,* 427 U.S. 160, 190-191 (1976) (STEVENS, J., concurring), therefore counsels adherence to settled precedent.

In sum, although in our cases subsequent to *Bellas Hess* and concerning other types of taxes we have not adopted a similar bright-line, physical-presence requirement, our reasoning in those cases does not compel that we now reject the rule that *Bellas Hess* established in the area of sales and use taxes. To the contrary, the continuing value of a bright-line rule in this area and the doctrine and principles of *stare decisis* indicate that the *Bellas Hess* rule remains good law. For these reasons, we disagree with the North Dakota Supreme Court's conclusion that the time has come to renounce the bright-line test of *Bellas Hess.*

This aspect of our decision is made easier by the fact that the underlying issue is not only one that Congress may be better qualified to resolve,[10] but also one that Congress has the ultimate power to resolve. No matter how we evaluate the burdens that use taxes impose on interstate commerce, Congress remains free to disagree with our conclusions. See *Prudential Insurance Co. v. Benjamin,* 328 U.S. 408 (1946). Indeed, in recent years Congress has considered legislation that would "overrule" the *Bellas Hess* rule.[11] Its decision not to take action in this direction may, of course, have been dictated by respect for our holding in *Bellas Hess* that the Due Process Clause prohibits States from imposing such taxes, but today we have put that problem to rest. Accordingly, Congress is now free to decide whether, when, and to what extent the States may burden interstate mail-order concerns with a duty to collect use taxes.

[10] Many States have enacted use taxes. See App. 3 to Brief for Direct Marketing Association as *Amicus Curiae.* An overruling of *Bellas Hess* might raise thorny questions concerning the retroactive application of those taxes and might trigger substantial unanticipated liability for mail-order houses. The precise allocation of such burdens is better resolved by Congress rather than this Court.

[11] See, *e.g.,* H.R. 2230, 101st Cong., 1st Sess. (1989); S. 480, 101st Cong., 1st Sess. (1989); S. 2368, 100th Cong., 2d Sess. (1988); H.R. 3521, 100th Cong., 1st Sess. (1987); S. 1099, 100th Cong., 1st Sess. (1987); H. R. 3549, 99th Cong., 1st Sess. (1985); S. 983, 96th Cong., 1st Sess. (1979); S. 282, 93d Cong., 1st Sess. (1973).

Indeed, even if we were convinced that *Bellas Hess* was inconsistent with our Commerce Clause jurisprudence, "this very fact [might] giv[e us] pause and counse[l] withholding our hand, at least for now. Congress has the power to protect interstate commerce from intolerable or even undesirable burdens." *Commonwealth Edison Co. v. Montana,* 453 U.S. 609, 637 (1981) (WHITE, J., concurring). In this situation, it may be that "the better part of both wisdom and valor is to respect the judgment of the other branches of the Government." *Id.,* at 638.

The judgment of the Supreme Court of North Dakota is reversed and the case is remanded for further proceedings not inconsistent with this opinion.

It is so ordered.

JUSTICE WHITE, concurring in part and dissenting in part.

Today the Court repudiates that aspect of our decision in *National Bellas Hess, Inc. v. Department of Revenue of Ill.,* 386 U.S. 753 (1967), which restricts, under the Due Process Clause of the Fourteenth Amendment, the power of the States to impose use tax collection responsibilities on out-of-state mail order businesses that do not have a "physical presence" in the State. The Court stops short, however, of giving *Bellas Hess* the complete burial it justly deserves. In my view, the Court should also overrule that part of *Bellas Hess* which justifies its holding under the Commerce Clause. I, therefore, respectfully dissent from Part IV.

I

In Part IV of its opinion, the majority goes to some lengths to justify the *Bellas Hess* physical presence requirement under our Commerce Clause jurisprudence. I am unpersuaded by its interpretation of our cases. In *Bellas Hess,* the majority placed great weight on the interstate quality of the mail order sales, stating that "it is difficult to conceive of commercial transactions more exclusively interstate in character than the mail order transactions here involved." *Bellas Hess, supra,* at 759. As the majority correctly observes, the idea of prohibiting States from taxing "exclusively interstate" transactions had been an important part of our jurisprudence for many decades, ranging intermittently from such cases as *Case of State Freight Tax,* 15 Wall. 232, 279 (1873), through *Freeman v. Hewit,* 329 U.S. 249, 256 (1946), and *Spector Motor Service, Inc. v. O'Connor,* 340 U.S. 602 (1951). But though it recognizes that *Bellas Hess* was decided amidst an upheaval in our Commerce Clause jurisprudence, in which we began to hold that "a State, with proper drafting, may tax exclusively interstate commerce so long as the tax does not create any effect forbidden by the Commerce Clause," *Complete Auto Transit, Inc. v. Brady,* 430 U.S.

274, 285 (1977), the majority draws entirely the wrong conclusion from this period of ferment.

The Court attempts to paint *Bellas Hess* in a different hue from *Freeman* and *Spector* because the former "did not rely" on labeling taxes that had "direct" and "indirect" effects on interstate commerce. See *ante,* at 10-11. Thus, the Court concludes, *Bellas Hess* "did not automatically fall with *Freeman* and its progeny" in our decision in *Complete Auto.* See *id.,* at 11. I am unpersuaded by this attempt to distinguish *Bellas Hess* from *Freeman* and *Spector,* both of which were repudiated by this Court. See *Complete Auto, supra,* at 288-289, and n.15. What we disavowed in *Complete Auto* was not just the "formal distinction between 'direct' and 'indirect' taxes on interstate commerce," *ante,* at 10, but also the whole notion underlying the *Bellas Hess* physical presence rule—that "interstate commerce is immune from state taxation." *Complete Auto, supra,* at 288.

The Court compounds its misreading by attempting to show that *Bellas Hess* "is not inconsistent with *Complete Auto* and our recent cases." *Ante,* at 11. This will be news to commentators, who have rightly criticized *Bellas Hess.*[1] Indeed, the majority displays no small amount of audacity in claiming that our decision in *National Geographic Society v. California Bd. of Equalization,* 430 U.S. 551, 559 (1977), which was rendered several weeks after *Complete Auto,* reaffirmed the continuing vitality of *Bellas Hess.* See *ante,* at 11.

Our decision in that case did just the opposite. *National Geographic* held that the National Geographic Society was liable for use tax collection responsibilities in California. The Society conducted an out-of-state mail order business similar to the one at issue here and in *Bellas Hess,* and in addition, maintained two small offices in California that solicited advertisements for National Geographic Magazine. The Society argued that its physical presence in California was unrelated to its mail order sales, and thus that the *Bellas Hess* rule compelled us to hold that the tax collection responsibilities could not be imposed. We expressly rejected that view, holding that the "requisite nexus for requiring an out-of-state seller [the Society] to collect and pay the use tax is not whether the duty to collect the use tax relates to the seller's activities carried on within the State, but simply whether the facts demonstrate 'some definite link, some minimum connection, between (the State and) the *person* . . . it seeks to tax.' " 430 U.S., at 561 (citation omitted).

[1] See, *e.g.,* P. Hartman, Federal Limitations on State and Local Taxation § 10.8 (1981); Hartman, Collection of Use Tax on Out-of-State Mail-Order Sales, 39 Vand. L. Rev. 993, 1006-1015 (1986); Hellerstein, Significant Sales and Use Tax Developments During the Past Half Century, 39 Vand. L. Rev. 961, 984-985 (1986); McCray, Overturning *Bellas Hess:* Due Process Considerations, 1985 B.Y.U.L. Rev. 265, 288-290; Rothfeld, Mail Order Sales and State Jurisdiction to Tax, 53 Tax Notes 1405, 1414-1418 (1991).

By decoupling any notion of a *transactional* nexus from the inquiry, the *National Geographic* Court in fact repudiated the free trade rationale of the *Bellas Hess* majority. Instead, the *National Geographic* Court relied on a due process-type minimum contacts analysis that examined whether a link existed between the seller and the State wholly apart from the seller's in-state transaction that was being taxed. Citations to *Bellas Hess* notwithstanding, see 430 U.S., at 559, it is clear that rather than adopting the rationale of *Bellas Hess,* the *National Geographic* Court was instead politely brushing it aside. Even were I to agree that the free trade rationale embodied in *Bellas Hess'* rule against taxes of purely interstate sales was required by our cases prior to 1967, therefore, I see no basis in the majority's opening premise that this substantive underpinning of *Bellas Hess* has not since been disavowed by our cases.[2]

II

The Court next launches into an uncharted and treacherous foray into differentiating between the "nexus" requirements under the Due Process and Commerce Clauses. As the Court explains, "[d]espite the similarity in phrasing, the nexus requirements of the Due Process and Commerce Clauses are not identical. The two standards are animated by different constitutional concerns and policies." *Ante,* at 12. The due process nexus, which the Court properly holds is met in this case, see *ante,* at Part III, "concerns the fundamental fairness of governmental activity." *Ante,* at 12. The Commerce Clause nexus requirement, on the other hand, is "informed not so much by concerns about fairness for the individual defendant as by structural concerns about the effects of state regulation on the national economy." *Ibid.*

Citing *Complete Auto,* the Court then explains that the Commerce Clause nexus requirement is not "like due process' 'minimum-contacts' requirement, a proxy for notice, but rather a means for limiting state burdens on interstate commerce." *Ante,* at 13. This is very curious, because parts two and three of the *Complete Auto* test, which require fair apportionment and nondiscrimination in order that interstate commerce not be unduly burdened, now appear to become the animating features of the nexus requirement, which is the first prong of the

[2] Similarly, I am unconvinced by the majority's reliance on subsequent decisions that have cited *Bellas Hess.* See *ante,* at 11. In *D.H. Holmes Co. v. McNamara,* 486 U.S. 24, 33 (1988), for example, we distinguished *Bellas Hess* on the basis of the company's "significant economic presence in Louisiana, its many connections with the State, and the direct benefits it receives from Louisiana in conducting its business." We then went on to note that the situation presented was much more analogous to that in *National Geographic Society v. California Bd. of Equalization,* 430 U.S. 551 (1977). See *id.,* at 33-34. In *Commonwealth Edison Co. v. Montana,* 453 U.S. 609, 626 (1981), the Court cited *Bellas Hess* not to revalidate the physical presence requirement, but rather to establish that a "nexus" must exist to justify imposition of a state tax. And finally, in *Mobil Oil Corp. v. Commissioner of Taxes,* 445 U.S. 425, 437 (1980), the Court cited *Bellas Hess* for the due process requirements necessary to sustain a tax. In my view, these citations hardly signal the continuing support of *Bellas Hess* that the majority seems to find persuasive.

Complete Auto inquiry. The Court freely acknowledges that there is no authority for this novel interpretation of our cases and that we have never before found, as we do in this case, sufficient contacts for due process purposes but an insufficient nexus under the Commerce Clause. See *ante,* at 13-14, and n.6.

The majority's attempt to disavow language in our opinions acknowledging the presence of due process requirements in the *Complete Auto* test is also unpersuasive. See *ante,* at 13-14, n. 6 (citing *Trinova Corp. v. Michigan Dept. of Treasury,* 498 U.S. __, __ (1991) (slip op., at __)). Instead of explaining the doctrinal origins of the Commerce Clause nexus requirement, the majority breezily announces the rule and moves on to other matters. See *ante,* at 13-14. In my view, before resting on the assertion that the Constitution mandates inquiry into two readily distinct "nexus" requirements, it would seem prudent to discern the origins of the "nexus" requirement in order better to understand whether the Court's concern traditionally has been with the fairness of a State's tax or some other value.

The cases from which the *Complete Auto* Court derived the nexus requirement in its four-part test convince me that the issue of "nexus" is really a due process fairness inquiry. In explaining the sources of the four-part inquiry in *Complete Auto,* the Court relied heavily on Justice Rutledge's separate concurring opinion in *Freeman v. Hewit,* 329 U.S. 249 (1946), the case whose majority opinion the *Complete Auto* Court was in the process of comprehensively disavowing. Instead of the formalistic inquiry into whether the State was taxing interstate commerce, the *Complete Auto* Court adopted the more functionalist approach of Justice Rutledge in *Freeman.* See *Complete Auto,* 430 U.S., at 280-281. In conducting his inquiry, Justice Rutledge used language that by now should be familiar, arguing that a tax was unconstitutional if the activity lacked a sufficient connection to the State to give "jurisdiction to tax," *Freeman, supra,* at 271; or if the tax discriminated against interstate commerce; or if the activity was subjected to multiple tax burdens. 329 U.S., at 276-277. Justice Rutledge later refined these principles in *Memphis Natural Gas Co. v. Stone,* 335 U.S. 80 (1948), in which he described the principles that the *Complete Auto* Court would later substantially adopt: "[I]t is enough for me to sustain the tax imposed in this case that it is one clearly within the state's power to lay insofar as any limitation of due process or 'jurisdiction to tax' in that sense is concerned; it is nondiscriminatory . . .; [it] is duly apportioned . . .; and cannot be repeated by any other state." 335 U.S., at 96-97 (concurring opinion) (footnotes omitted).

By the time the Court decided *Northwestern States Portland Cement Co. v. Minnesota,* 358 U.S. 450 (1959), Justice Rutledge was no longer on the Court, but his view of the nexus requirement as grounded in the Due Process Clause was decisively adopted. In rejecting challenges to a state tax based on the Due Process and Commerce Clauses, the Court stated that "[t]he taxes imposed are levied only on that portion of the taxpayer's net income which arises from its activities within the taxing State. These activities form a sufficient 'nexus between such a tax and transactions within a state for which the tax is an exaction.' " *Id.,* at 464 (citation omitted). The Court went on to observe that "[i]t strains reality to say, in terms of our decisions, that each of the corporations here was not sufficiently involved in local events to forge 'some definite link, some minimum connection' sufficient to satisfy due process requirements." *Id.,* at 464-465 (quoting *Miller Bros. v. Maryland,* 347 U.S. 340, 344-345 (1954)). When the Court announced its four-part synthesis in *Complete Auto,* the nexus requirement was definitely traceable to concerns grounded in the Due Process Clause, and not the Commerce Clause, as the Court's discussion of the doctrinal antecedents for its rule made clear. See *Complete Auto, supra,* at 281-282, 285. For the Court now to assert that our Commerce Clause jurisprudence supports a separate notion of nexus is without precedent or explanation.

Even were there to be such an independent requirement under the Commerce Clause, there is no relationship between the physical presence/nexus rule the Court retains and Commerce Clause considerations that allegedly justify it. Perhaps long ago a seller's "physical presence" was a sufficient part of a trade to condition imposition of a tax on such presence. But in today's economy, physical presence frequently has very little to do with a transaction a State might seek to tax. Wire transfers of money involving billions of dollars occur every day; purchasers place orders with sellers by fax, phone, and computer linkup; sellers ship goods by air, road, and sea through sundry delivery services without leaving their place of business. It is certainly true that the days of the door-to-door salesperson are not gone. Nevertheless, an out-of-state direct marketer derives numerous commercial benefits from the State in which it does business. These advantages include laws establishing sound local banking institutions to support credit transactions; courts to insure collection of the purchase price from the seller's customers; means of waste disposal from garbage generated by mail order solicitations; and creation and enforcement of consumer protection laws, which protect buyers and sellers alike, the former by ensuring that they will have a ready means of protecting against fraud, and the latter by creating a climate of consumer confidence that inures to the benefit of reputable dealers in mail order transactions. To create, for the first time, a nexus requirement under the Commerce Clause independent of that established for due process purposes is one thing; to attempt to justify an anachronistic notion of physical presence in economic terms is quite another.

III

The illogic of retaining the physical presence requirement in these circumstances is palpable. Under the majority's analysis, and our decision in *National Geographic,* an out-of-state seller with one salesperson in a State would be subject to use tax collection burdens on its entire mail order sales even if those sales were unrelated to the salesperson's solicitation efforts. By contrast, an out-of-state seller in a neighboring State could be the dominant business in the putative taxing State, creating the greatest infrastructure burdens and undercutting the State's home companies by its comparative price advantage in selling products free of use taxes, and yet not have to collect such taxes if it lacks a physical presence in the taxing State. The majority clings to the physical presence rule not because of any logical relation to fairness or any economic rationale related to principles underlying the Commerce Clause, but simply out of the supposed convenience of having a bright-line rule. I am less impressed by the convenience of such adherence than the unfairness it produces. Here, convenience should give way. Cf. *Complete Auto, supra,* at 289, n.15 ("We believe, however, that administrative convenience . . . is insufficient justification for abandoning the principle that 'interstate commerce may be made to pay its way' ").

Also very questionable is the rationality of perpetuating a rule that creates an interstate tax shelter for one form of business—mail order sellers—but no countervailing advantage for its competitors. If the Commerce Clause was intended to put businesses on an even playing field, the majority's rule is hardly a way to achieve that goal. Indeed, arguably even under the majority's explanation for its "Commerce Clause nexus" requirement, the unfairness of its rule on retailers other than direct marketers should be taken into account. See *ante,* at 12 (stating that the Commerce Clause nexus requirement addresses the "structural concerns about the effects of state regulation on the national economy"). I would think that protectionist rules favoring a $180 billion-a-year industry might come within the scope of such "structural concerns." See Brief for State of New Jersey as *Amicus Curiae* 4.

IV

The Court attempts to justify what it rightly acknowledges is an "artificial" rule in several ways. See *ante,* at 15. First, it asserts that the *Bellas Hess* principle "firmly establishes the boundaries of legitimate state taxing authority and reduces litigation concerning state taxation." *Ibid.* It is very doubtful, however, that the Court's opinion can achieve its aims. Certainly our cases now demonstrate two "bright-line" rules for mail order sellers to follow: under the physical presence requirement reaffirmed here they will not be subjected to use tax collection if they have no physical presence in the taxing State; under the *National Geographic* rule, mail order sellers will be subject to use tax collection if they have some presence in the taxing State even if that activity has no relation to the transaction being taxed. See *National Geographic,* 430 U.S., at 560-562. Between these narrow lines lies the issue of what constitutes the requisite "physical presence" to justify imposition of use tax collection responsibilities.

Instead of confronting this question head-on, the majority offers only a cursory analysis of whether Quill's physical presence in North Dakota was sufficient to justify its use tax collection burdens, despite briefing on this point by the State.[3] See Brief for Respondent 45-47. North Dakota contends that even should the Court reaffirm the *Bellas Hess* rule, Quill's physical presence in North Dakota was sufficient to justify application of its use tax collection law. Quill concedes it owns software sent to its North Dakota customers, but suggests that such property is insufficient to justify a finding of nexus. In my view, the question of Quill's actual physical presence is sufficiently close to cast doubt on the majority's confidence that it is propounding a truly "bright-line" rule. Reasonable minds surely can, and will, differ over what showing is required to make out a "physical presence" adequate to justify imposing responsibilities for use tax collection. And given the estimated loss in revenue to States of more than $3.2 billion this year alone, see Brief for Respondent 9, it is a sure bet that the vagaries of "physical presence" will be tested to their fullest in our courts.

The majority next explains that its "bright-line" rule encourages "settled expectations" and business investment. *Ante,* at 15-16. Though legal certainty promotes business confidence, the mail order business has grown exponentially despite the long line of our post-*Bellas Hess* precedents that signalled the demise of the physical presence requirement. Moreover, the Court's seeming but inadequate justification of encouraging settled expectations in fact connotes a substantive economic decision to favor out-of-state direct marketers to the detriment of other retailers. By justifying the *Bellas Hess* rule in terms of "the mail order industry's dramatic growth over the last quarter-century," *ante,* at 16, the Court is effectively imposing its own economic preferences in deciding this case. The Court's invitation to Congress to

[3] Instead of remanding for consideration of whether Quill's ownership of software constitutes sufficient physical presence under its new Commerce Clause nexus requirement, the majority concludes as a matter of law that it does not. See *ante,* n. 8. In so doing, the majority rebuffs North Dakota's challenge without setting out any clear standard for what meets the Commerce Clause physical presence nexus standard and without affording the State an opportunity on remand to attempt to develop facts or otherwise to argue that Quill's presence is constitutionally sufficient.

legislate in this area signals that its preferences are not immutable, but its approach is different from past instances in which we have deferred to state legislatures when they enacted tax obligations on the State's share of interstate commerce. See, *e.g., Goldberg v. Sweet,* 488 U.S. 252 (1989); *Commonwealth Edison Co. v. Montana,* 453 U.S. 609 (1981).

Finally, the Court accords far greater weight to *stare decisis* than was given to that principle in *Complete Auto* itself. As that case demonstrates, we have not been averse to overruling our precedents under the Commerce Clause when they have become anachronistic in light of later decisions. See *Complete Auto,* 430 U.S., at 288-289. One typically invoked rationale for *stare decisis*—an unwillingness to upset settled expectations—is particularly weak in this case. It is unreasonable for companies such as Quill to invoke a "settled expectation" in conducting affairs without being taxed. Neither Quill nor any of its *amici* point to any investment decisions or reliance interests that suggest any unfairness in overturning *Bellas Hess.* And the costs of compliance with the rule, in light of today's modern computer and software technology, appear to be nominal. See Brief for Respondents 40; Brief for State of New Jersey as *Amicus Curiae* 18. To the extent Quill developed any reliance on the old rule, I would submit that its reliance was unreasonable because of its failure to comply with the law as enacted by the North Dakota state legislature. Instead of rewarding companies for ignoring the studied judgments of duly-elected officials, we should insist that the appropriate way to challenge a tax as unconstitutional is to pay it (or in this case collect it and remit it or place it in escrow) and then sue for declaratory judgment and refund.[4] Quill's refusal to comply with a state tax statute prior to its being held unconstitutional hardly merits a determination that its reliance interests were reasonable.

The Court hints, but does not state directly, that a basis for its invocation of *stare decisis* is a fear that overturning *Bellas Hess* will lead to the imposition of retroactive liability. *Ante,* at 18, and n.10. See *James B. Beam Distilling Co. v. Georgia,* 501 U.S. ___ (1991). As I thought in that case, such fears are groundless because no one can "sensibly insist on automatic retroactivity for any and all judicial decisions in the federal system." *Id.,* at ___ (WHITE, J., concurring in judgment). Since we specifically limited the question on which certiorari was granted in order not to consider the potential retroactive effects of overruling *Bellas Hess,* I believe we should leave that issue for another day. If indeed fears about retroactivity are driving the Court's decision in this case, we would be better served, in my view, to address

[4] For the federal rule, see *Flora v. United States,* 357 U.S. 63 (1958); see generally J. Mertens, Law of Federal Income Taxation § 58A.05 (1992). North Dakota appears to follow the same principle. See *First Bank of Buffalo v. Conrad,* 350 N. W. 2d 580, 586 (N.D. 1984) (citing 72 Am. Jur. 2d § 1087).

those concerns directly rather than permit them to infect our formulation of the applicable substantive rule.

Although Congress can and should address itself to this area of law, we should not adhere to a decision, however right it was at the time, that by reason of later cases and economic reality can no longer be rationally justified. The Commerce Clause aspect of *Bellas Hess,* along with its due process holding, should be overruled.

JUSTICE SCALIA, with whom JUSTICE KENNEDY and JUSTICE THOMAS join, concurring in part and concurring in the judgment.

National Bellas Hess, Inc. v. Department of Revenue of Ill., 386 U.S. 753 (1967), held that the Due Process and Commerce Clauses of the Constitution prohibit a State from imposing the duty of use-tax collection and payment upon a seller whose only connection with the State is through common carrier or the United States mail. I agree with the Court that the Due Process Clause holding of *Bellas Hess* should be overruled. Even before *Bellas Hess,* we had held, correctly I think, that state regulatory jurisdiction could be asserted on the basis of contacts with the State through the United States mail. See *Travelers Health Assn. v. Virginia ex rel. State Corp. Comm'n,* 339 U.S. 643, 646-650 (1950) (Blue Sky laws). It is difficult to discern any principled basis for distinguishing between jurisdiction to regulate and jurisdiction to tax. As an original matter, it might have been possible to distinguish between jurisdiction to tax and jurisdiction to compel collection of taxes as agent for the State, but we have rejected that. *National Geographic Soc. v. California Bd. of Equalization,* 430 U.S. 551, 558 (1977); *Scripto, Inc. v. Carson,* 362 U.S. 207, 211 (1960). I agree with the Court, moreover, that abandonment of *Bellas Hess*'s due process holding is compelled by reasoning "[c]om-parable" to that contained in our post-1967 cases dealing with state jurisdiction to adjudicate. *Ante,* at 8. I do not understand this to mean that the due process standards for adjudicative jurisdiction and those for legislative (or prescriptive) jurisdiction are necessarily identical; and on that basis I join Parts I, II, and III of the Court's opinion. Compare *Asahi Metal Industry Co. v. Superior Court,* 480 U.S. 102 (1987) with *American Oil Co. v. Neill,* 380 U.S. 451 (1965).

I also agree that the Commerce Clause holding of *Bellas Hess* should not be overruled. Unlike the Court, however, I would not revisit the merits of that holding, but would adhere to it on the basis of *stare decisis. American Trucking Assns., Inc. v. Smith,* 496 U.S. 167, 204 (1990) (SCALIA, J., concurring in judgment). Congress has the final say over regulation of interstate commerce, and it can change the rule of *Bellas Hess* by simply saying so. We have long recognized that the doctrine of *stare decisis* has "special force" where "Congress remains free to alter what we have done." *Patterson v. McLean Credit Union,* 491 U.S. 164, 172-173 (1989). See *also Hilton v. South Carolina Pub. Railways Comm'n,* 502 U.S. __, __ (1991) (slip op., at 4); *Illinois Brick Co. v. Illinois,* 431 U.S. 720, 736 (1977). Moreover, the demands of the doctrine are "at their acme . . . where reliance interests are involved," *Payne v. Tennessee,* 501 U.S. __, __ (1991) (slip op., at 18). As the Court notes, "the *Bellas Hess* rule has engendered substantial reliance and has become part of the basic framework of a sizeable industry," *ante,* at 17.

I do not share JUSTICE WHITE's view that we may disregard these reliance interests because it has become unreasonable to rely upon *Bellas Hess, post,* at 11-12. Even assuming for the sake of argument (I do not consider the point) that later decisions in related areas are inconsistent with the principles upon which *Bellas Hess* rested, we have never acknowledged that, but have instead carefully distinguished the case on its facts. See, *e.g., D. H. Holmes Co. v. McNamara,* 486 U.S. 24, 33 (1988); *National Geographic Soc., supra,* at 559. It seems to me important that we retain our ability—and, what comes to the same thing, that we maintain public confidence in our ability—sometimes to adopt new principles for the resolution of new issues without abandoning clear holdings of the past that those principles contradict. We seemed to be doing that in this area. Having affirmatively suggested that the "physical presence" rule could be reconciled with our new jurisprudence, we ought not visit economic hardship upon those who took us at our word. We have recently told lower courts that "[i]f a precedent of this Court has direct application in a case, yet appears to rest on reasons rejected in some other line of decisions, [they] should follow the case which directly controls, leaving to this Court the prerogative of overruling its own decisions." *Rodriguez de Quijas v. Shearson/American Express, Inc.,* 490 U.S. 477, 484 (1989). It is strangely incompatible with this to demand that private parties anticipate our overrulings. It is my view, in short, that reliance upon a square, unabandoned holding of the Supreme Court is always justifiable reliance (though reliance alone may not always carry the day). Finally, the "physical presence" rule established in *Bellas Hess* is not "unworkable," *Patterson, supra,* at 173; to the contrary, whatever else may be the substantive pros and cons of the rule, the "bright-line" regime that it establishes, see *ante,* at 15-16, is unqualifiedly in its favor. JUSTICE WHITE's concern that reaffirmance of *Bellas Hess* will lead to a flurry of litigation over the meaning of "physical presence," see *post,* at 10, seems to me contradicted by 25 years of experience under the decision.

For these reasons, I concur in the judgment of the Court and join Parts I, II, and III of its opinion.

Tennessee Gas Pipeline Co. v. Urbach

[*Tennessee Gas Pipeline* is discussed at ¶ 1015 n. 10.]

Tennessee Gas Pipeline Company v. Michael H. Urbach, as Commissioner of the Department of Taxation and Finance of the State of New York, et al.

New York Court of Appeals, 3 No. 71, 2001 N.Y. LEXIS 1109, May 1, 2001.

Reversing Supreme Court, Appellate Division, Third Judicial Department, No. 86152, May 25, 2000 (¶ 403–¶ 670).

Christopher L. Doyle, for appellant.

Andrew D. Bing, for respondents.

WESLEY, J.:

When Congress passed the Natural Gas Policy Act of 1978 (*see,* 15 USC § 3301, *et seq.*), it set in motion the deregulation of the natural gas industry. At that time, interstate pipeline companies enjoyed market control of prices as they provided the only means for the sale and distribution of gas from the wellhead to local distribution companies (regulated utilities in New York).[1] In 1992, the Federal Energy Regulatory Commission (FERC) completed the transition when it ordered all interstate pipelines to "unbundle" their transportation services from their gas sales (FERC Order No. 636, 57 Fed Reg 13267). The pipelines became common carriers of natural gas (*see, e.g., Matter of Texas E. Transmission Corp. v Tax Appeals Tribunal,* 95 NY2d 323, 325-329). Large industrial buyers could now buy natural gas directly from suppliers, bypassing local utilities. The gas is delivered by pipeline, or more commonly, by a New York gas utility. Pursuant to FERC-approved tariffs, the cost of the transport paid by the user is separate from the purchase price of the gas.

Allowing industrial end users to bypass local utilities and purchase gas outside the State created a tax problem for New York. The State's system of natural gas taxation was developed prior to deregulation and focused on utilities and other entities that sold gas within New York. Section 186 of the Tax Law imposes a corporate franchise tax on any corporation, joint stock company or association "formed for or principally engaged in the business of supplying water, steam or gas, when delivered through mains or pipes" (Tax Law § 186[1]). The tax (.75%) is

[1] The effect of the deregulation on the structure and organization of the natural gas industry is detailed in *General Motors Corp. v Tracy,* 519 US 278, 283–297.

assessed against "gross earnings from all sources within this state" (*id.*). In addition, Tax Law § 186-a imposes a tax (3.5%) on the gross income or gross operating income of gas sellers for gas sales for "ultimate consumption or use" in New York (Tax Law § 186-a[1], [2][c], [2][d]). Although utilities are prohibited from identifying taxes assessed pursuant to section 186-a on a customer's bill (*see,* Tax Law § 186-a[6]), both taxes are passed through to gas customers by the utility's gross receipts tax assessment in its rate charged to customers pursuant to its Public Service Commission tariff (*see, Matter of Brooklyn Union Gas Co. v Commissioner of Taxation & Fin.*, 255 AD2d 80, 82; *see also,* L 1991, ch 166, § 149). Deregulation allowed end users to avoid the "pass-through" taxes by buying gas from out-of-State producers.

In an attempt to recapture those taxes and to "equalize" the tax burden on all gas consumers, the Legislature enacted the Natural Gas Import Tax (L 1991, ch 166, §§ 147-149). The tax (4.25% of the price paid) is imposed "on the privilege or act of importing gas services [gas provided through pipes or mains] or causing gas services to be imported into this state for [the importer's] own use or consumption in this state" (Tax Law § 189[2][a]).[2] At the time the Legislature enacted section 189, it took note that the taxes imposed by sections 186 and 186-a are passed on to consumers; that the legislation required the Public Service Commission to continue the pass-through; and that section 189 was "an attempt to impose on those consumers who purchase gas services outside this state a comparable fair tax burden" (L 1991, ch 166, § 149).[3]

Tennessee Gas is a natural gas pipeline company that acts primarily as a transporter of natural gas. Its pipeline originates in Texas and Louisiana and runs through New York into New England. Tennessee is regulated by FERC and operates under a FERC tariff. Tennessee has a number of pumping facilities along its pipeline that increase the pressure in the line. Ten of these facilities are located in New York. The compressors are powered by natural gas (compressor fuel) that is drawn off the line. Pursuant to Tennessee's tariff, ownership of the compressor gas passes at the point where the gas enters Tennessee's pipeline outside New York. Tennessee is therefore a "gas importer" under Tax Law § 189.

---

[2] If gas is delivered to the importer in New York by a utility, it is required to collect the tax on behalf of the State from the importer based on an "annual average gas price," and the importer is allowed a quarterly refund to the extent that the amount collected by the utility exceeds the importer's actual tax liability based on the price paid for the gas (Tax Law § 189 [3][a]).

[3] In 2000, the Legislature phased out Tax Law § 189, gradually decreasing the tax rate to zero percent by 2005 and repealing the tax effective January 1, 2005 (L 2000, ch 63, Part Y, §§ 6, 6-a, 49[b]). The rate reduction and repeal of Tax Law § 189 matched the rate reductions resulting from the repeal of Tax Law § 186 and the phase-out of Tax Law § 186-a (L 2000, ch 63, Part Y, §§ 3, 4).

Although Tennessee filed reports with FERC for the period November 30, 1991 through November 30, 1996, it did not pay any section 189 tax on compressor fuel consumed in New York. The State Tax Department audited Tennessee's FERC filings and determined that Tennessee owed $1.6 million in section 189 taxes, plus interest and penalties. Following an exchange of letters between Tennessee and the Department, and prior to any proceedings before the Tax Tribunal, Tennessee commenced this declaratory judgment action challenging its status as a gas importer under the statute and the facial constitutionality of section 189. Each side moved for summary judgment. Supreme Court dismissed Tennessee's complaint for failure to exhaust its administrative remedies and characterized Tennessee's challenge to the statute as based on its specific application to Tennessee's New York activities. Tennessee appealed.

The Appellate Division noted that the purpose of the statute is to equalize the tax burdens of natural gas consumers in New York. It agreed with Supreme Court that Tennessee's challenge was actually directed at the statute's application to Tennessee's activities in New York and that a facial challenge to the statute was not merited. Tennessee again appealed, and we now reverse and declare the statute unconstitutional on its face.

Tennessee argues, and the Attorney General concedes, that the import tax discriminates against interstate commerce.[4] The statute provides differential treatment of in-State and out-of-State economic interests that benefit the former and burden the latter (*see, Oregon Waste Sys. v Department of Envtl. Ouality,* 511 US 93, 99); it imposes a tax on the out-of-State purchase of gas consumed in New York while not taxing in-State purchases of gas used in New York. State laws that discriminate against interstate commerce on their facie are "virtually *per se* invalid" (*id.*).

Where a tax is facially discriminatory it may survive Commerce Clause scrutiny if the State can show that the tax "advances a legitimate local purpose that cannot adequately be served by reasonable nondiscriminatory alternatives" (*id.,* at 101, *see also, City of New York*

[4] The Commerce Clause provides that "[t]he Congress shall have Power *** [t]o regulate Commerce *** among the several States" (US Const, art I, § 8, cl 3). Though phrased as a positive grant of regulatory power to Congress, the United States Supreme Court has long interpreted the Commerce Clause to have a "negative" or "dormant" implication that prevents States from unduly interfering with interstate commerce (*see, Oklahoma Tax Commn. v Jefferson Lines, Inc.,* 514 US 175, 179; *Oregon Waste Sys. v Department of Envtl. Quality,* 511 US 93, 98). By our count, this is the fifth time in the last four years we have ruled on a taxing scheme under the Commerce Clause (*Matter of Texas E. Transmission Corp. v Tax Appeals Tribunal,* 95 NY2d 323; *City of New York v State of New York,* 94 NY2d 577; *Matter of Tamagni v Tax Appeals Tribunal,* 91 NY2d 530, *cert denied* 525 US 931; *Homier Distrib. Co. v City of Albany,* 90 NY2d 153).

v *State of New York,* 94 NY2d 577, 596-597). The State contends that the import tax survives Tennessee's Commerce Clause challenge because the tax complements the taxes imposed under sections 186 and 186-a.

Certain "complementary" or "compensatory" taxes may satisfy Commerce Clause scrutiny even though they discriminate against interstate commerce (*Oregon Waste, supra,* at 102). A valid complementary tax must satisfy three criteria. First, it must identify the intrastate tax burden for which it attempts to compensate. Second, the interstate tax must "roughly approximate," but not exceed, the amount of the tax on intrastate commerce. Third, the events on which both taxes are imposed must be " 'substantially equivalent;' that is they must be sufficiently similar in substance to serve as mutually exclusive 'prox[ies]' for each other" (*Oregon Waste, supra,* at 103 [quoting *Armco, Inc. v Hardesty,* 467 US 638, 643]; *see also, Homier Distr. Co. v City of Albany,* 90 NY2d 153, 163). As United States Supreme Court Justice Cardozo noted, under a truly compensatory tax scheme "the stranger from afar is subject to no greater burdens as a consequence of ownership than the dweller within the gates. The one pays upon one activity or incident, and the other upon another, but the sum is the same when the reckoning is closed" (*Henneford v Silas Mason Co.,* 300 US 577, 584).

Tennessee concedes that the Legislature's stated intent in enacting Tax Law § 189 was to level the tax field for gas consumers in New York regardless of the location of their gas source. However, Tennessee vigorously contests that section 189 is in fact a valid compensatory tax.

If the import tax roughly approximates, but does not exceed, the amount of the tax on intrastate commerce, it passes the second prong of the compensatory tax test (*see, Oregon Waste, supra,* at 103). Here, the tax rates imposed on consumers who purchase gas in-State are the same as those who purchase gas elsewhere—the sum of the in-State tax rates equals the import tax rate. Tennessee argues, however, that the taxes are not "imposed" on consumers of natural gas in both instances and, thus, the resulting taxes cannot roughly approximate each other. The import tax is directly assessed on the importer/consumer, and the in-State tax is imposed on the utility or seller, which then passes those taxes through to the consumer. The State argues that, therefore, economic incidence of the tax is the same. Tennessee cautions that this type of "economic incidence analysis" will draw the Court into the thicket of analyzing and comparing different markets to determine if the tax burden imposed on interstate activity roughly approximates, but does not exceed, the intrastate tax burden (*see, Fulton Corp. v Faulkner,* 516 US 325, 336-338).

There is no doubt that the taxes in question here are imposed, in fact, on the same activity—the use of natural gas in New York. Significantly, the Legislature noted (and mandated the Public Service Commission to continue) the "pass-through" practice of utilities with regard to sections 186 and 186-a taxes when it enacted the import tax (L 1991, ch 166, § 149).[5] The taxes paid by the utilities are based, in part, on revenues derived from gas sales. The tax therefore reflects the "cost" of gas purchased in New York by utility customers. Moreover, because the in-State taxes are imposed on a receipt tax basis (including transportation costs charged to utility customers for delivering the gas in-State along with income from any other source), the taxes imposed under sections 186 and 186-a will never be less than the import tax on comparable volumes of gas.

The practical effect of the statutes is the same—consumers carry the tax burden for the use of natural gas in New York. Thus, we need not engage in the difficult quantitative assessment of the extent to which a discriminatory tax supports in-State economic activity—which may be highly speculative—in order to reach our decision.

Tennessee also notes that not all gas consumers who buy their gas in New York pay the pass-through taxes because some gas suppliers are not regulated by the Public Service Commission and therefore are not required to pass the tax through to their customers. In support of its contention, Tennessee offered two affidavits from suppliers who are not regulated by the Public Service Commission and a list of unregulated marketers that were certified to sell gas in New York as of March 1999. The Attorney General counters that Tennessee has failed to identify that portion of the gas market served by non-regulated sellers. Indeed, the Attorney General points to Public Service Commission documents that show, for the tax period in question, unregulated sellers served only 4,000 small customers (*see,* New York State Public Service Commission, Department of Public Service, 1995-1996 Annual Report, at 13).[6] Tennessee's submissions do not convince us that sales of gas subject to sections 186 and 186-a pass-through taxes as compared to unregulated sales establish the " 'substantial distinctions and real injuries' " necessary in a Commerce Clause challenge (*Associated In-*

---

[5] Our courts have also recognized the use of the revenue tax surcharge as an element of Public Service Commission tariffs (*see, Matter of Brooklyn Union Gas Co., supra,* 255 AD2d, at 82).

[6] In 1996, there were approximately 4,578,511 gas customers in New York (*see,* Financial Statistics of the Major Investor-Owned Utilities in NYS (The "Five Year Book"), New York State Dept. of Pub. Svc., 1999, Tables 9C, 6G [also available on-line at http://www.dps.state.ny.us/welcome99.html]). Thus, unregulated sellers served less than .1% of all gas customers statewide.

dus. of Mo. v Lohman, 511 US 641, 654 [quoting *Gregg Dyeing Co. v Query.,* 286 US 472, 481]). The Supreme Court has never "deemed a hypothetical possibility of favoritism to constitute discrimination that transgresses constitutional commands" (*Associated Indus., supra,* at 654).

The third element of a valid compensatory tax is that the events on which the taxes are imposed must be " 'substantially equivalent;' they must be sufficiently similar in substance to serve as mutually exclusive 'prox[ies]' for each other" (*Oregon Waste, supra,* 511 US 93, at 103 [citation omitted]). Tennessee correctly points out that sections 186 and 186-a are franchise taxes. They are imposed on corporations for the privilege of doing business in New York while section 189 is an import tax. Tennessee asserts that the taxing events are so different that they cannot reasonably be seen as taxing similar economic activity. The Attorney General compares the statute to sales and use taxes.

A State can impose a sales tax for sales within the State and a use tax on goods purchased outside the State and consumed within the State provided the use tax does not exceed the sales tax. Although the taxing events are different (purchase or use), they completely cover one area of economic activity--the taxation of all tangible property used or consumed in-State regardless of where the property is acquired (*see, Associated Indus. of Mo. v Lohman,* 511 US 641, *supra; see also, Henneford v Silas Mason Co.,* 300 US 577, *supra*). However, the Supreme Court has been cautious to note that its "most recent cases have shown extreme reluctance to recognize new compensating categories" (*Fulton Corp., supra,* 516 US, at 338).

A new category is not required here. As noted earlier, the taxable events are, in fact, the sale of gas in New York and the use of imported gas in New York. Although the in State taxes are calculated, not by the price paid for the product, but by the gross income/receipts of the seller, they are in essence, taxes from the sales of gas because of the nature of the passthrough. The taxes are also mutually exclusive; the consumer either buys the gas in-State or imports it--the taxes cannot overlap. The State has thus met its burden of establishing that Tax Law § 189 is a valid compensatory tax.

Tennessee's last challenge to the import tax is premised on "fair apportionment." The central purpose of fair apportionment "is to ensure that each State taxes only its fair share of an interstate transaction" (*Goldberg v Sweet,* 488 US 252, 260-261) and to minimize the likelihood that an interstate transaction will be improperly burdened by multiple taxation (*see, Oklahoma Tax Commn. v Jefferson Lines,*

Inc., supra, 514 US, at 184-185; *Matter of Tamagni v Tax Appeals Tribunal, supra,* 91 NY2d, at 541). To determine the threat of malapportionment, the Supreme Court has employed "internal" and "external" consistency tests (*Oklahoma Tax Commn., supra,* at 185).

Tennessee limits its challenge; to whether the taxes in question are internally consistent.

> Internal consistency is preserved when the imposition of a tax identical to the one in question by every other State would add no burden to interstate commerce that intrastate commerce would not also bear. This test asks nothing about the degree of economic reality reflected by the tax, but simply looks to the structure of the tax at issue to see whether its identical application by every State in the Union would place interstate commerce at a disadvantage as compared with commerce intrastate. A failure of internal consistency shows as a matter of law that a State is attempting to take more than its fair share of taxes from the interstate transaction (*id.*).

Tennessee correctly argues that the taxes in question run afoul of the internal consistency test. If consumers buy gas in a State with a provision identical to Tax Law § 186, they would pay a pass-through tax even though they exported the gas to New York and consumed it here.[7] Because the import tax contains no credit for taxes assessed on the purchase of gas out-of-State, a double tax occurs; the statute crosses over from a permissible exercise of the State's taxing powers to an unconstitutional burden on interstate commerce.

The State attempts to save the tax by pointing to the enactment language of section 189 (*see,* L 1991, ch 166, § 149). In that provision, the Legislature appears to have anticipated the constitutional flaw we now identify. It notes that "if a court of final, competent jurisdiction should adjudge the privilege taxation imposed by this act too be infirm because of the lack of an appropriate credit for tax imposed by another jurisdiction on the sale of the gas service therein then, in such event, *such appropriate credit,* to the extent of the tax imposed by this act, shall be *deemed to be available* in the *manner provided by such court of final,* competent jurisdiction" (*id.* [emphasis added]).

The Attorney General would have us employ the savings language only if Tennessee can establish that it did indeed pay a pass-through tax like that imposed by section 186 in the State it purchased the compressor gas. But this is a facial challenge: the internal consistency test is measured by hypothetically employing the taxes in question as if

---

[7] Contrary to Tennessee's assertion, Tax Law § 186-a applies only to gross income from sales of gas to be used or consumed in New York. Therefore, that provision does not present any internal inconsistency.

they existed in all States; there is no "as applied" escape hatch from the test as the Attorney General seems to argue (*see, Goldberg v Sweet, supra,* 488 US, at 261). The savings provision would appear to remedy the flaw in section 189 by providing a credit for any double taxation. However, we find the savings provision invalid here because it requires the Court to define the parameters of the credit and the manner in which it will be implemented. This violates fundamental separation of powers principles. The savings provision would require us to rewrite the statute and create quasi-judicial tax regulations. We are not well suited as an institution for such a task.

Accordingly, the order of the Appellate Division should be reversed, with costs, and Tax Law §§ 189, 189-a and 189-b declared unconstitutional as violative of the Commerce Clause of the United States Constitution.

Order reversed, with costs, and Tax Law §§ 189, 189-a and 189-b declared unconstitutional as violative of the Commerce Clause of the United States Constitution. Opinion by Judge Wesley. Chief Judge Kaye and Judges Smith, Levine, Ciparick, Rosenblatt and Graffeo concur.

Williams Companies, Inc. v. Montana

[*Williams Companies* is discussed at ¶ 410.01 n. 9 and ¶ 715.03.]

The Williams Companies, Inc. and Subsidiaries v. The Department of Revenue of the State of Montana.

Montana State Tax Appeal Board, No. CT-1996-1, December 31, 1998.

Appeal from a decision of the Department of Revenue. Denied.

FINDINGS OF FACT, CONCLUSIONS OF LAW, ORDER and OPPORTUNITY FOR JUDICIAL REVIEW

The above-entitled appeal was heard July 27, 1998 in the City of Helena, Montana, in accordance with an order of the State Tax Appeal Board of the State of Montana (hereinafter referred to as the "Board"). The notice of the hearing was given as required by law. The Appellant was represented by attorneys Terry B. Cosgrove, Maryann B. Gall, and Rose Mary Ham. The Respondent was represented by attorneys Brendan Beatty and David Woodgerd.

At this time and place, testimony was presented and exhibits were received. The hearing was continued and reconvened on December 11, 1998 in the City of Helena, Montana for the purpose of hearing a Respondent's surrebuttal witness.

The Board having fully considered the testimony, exhibits, and all things and matters presented to it for its consideration by all parties, and being well and fully advised finds and concludes as follows:

STATEMENT OF THE ISSUE

The issue before this Board is whether Northwest Alaskan Pipeline Company, a wholly owned subsidiary of THE WILLIAMS COMPANIES, INC., has taxable nexus with the State of Montana, providing a basis for an assessment of additional taxes and interest as determined by the Montana Department of Revenue.

FINDINGS OF FACT

1. Due, proper, and sufficient notice was given of this matter, the hearing, and of the time and place of the hearing. All parties were afforded opportunity to present evidence, oral and documentary.

2. This Board has jurisdiction to hear and decide this matter.

3. The Department of Revenue (hereinafter referred to as "DOR") conducted an audit of The Williams Companies, Inc. and Subsidiaries (hereinafter referred to as "Williams") for the tax years ending Decem-

ber 31, 1987 through December 31, 1993. As a result of this audit the DOR issued a Notice of Proposed Assessment by letter of July 25, 1995.

4. Following an informal conference and review with the Appellant, the DOR through Mr. Lynn Chenowith, Bureau Chief of the Corporation Tax Bureau, upheld assessments as set forth in a letter of November 17, 1995 that stated, in pertinent part:

> It is the division's determination that Northwest Alaskan Pipeline Company has sufficient activities in the state of Montana to create nexus and that natural gas destination sales made into the state of Montana have been correctly included in the Montana Sales Numerator for all years of the audit.

5. Northwest Alaskan Pipeline Company (hereinafter referred to as "NWA"), is a wholly owned subsidiary of Williams, a Delaware corporation.

6. Northwest Border Pipeline Company (hereinafter referred to as "NWB") is also a wholly owned subsidiary of Williams. NWB owns 12.25% of the Northern Border Natural Gas Pipeline which enters Montana from Canada near Port of Morgan, Montana. (Jt Ex 44)

7. The Appellant filed an objection with the DOR Director; and the Appellant filed an appeal with this Board.

8. Pursuant to § 15-1-211(6)(b) Montana Code Annotated, the Director of the Department of Revenue elected not to review the department's decision in this matter.

9. In addition to the objection identified in Finding 2, the Appellant's Petition of January 11, 1996 contained an additional five objections to the DOR's final determination as set forth in the DOR's letter of November 17, 1995; the Appellant's Second (and final) Amended Petition of March 9, 1998 set out a single issue as identified in Finding 2 and set out in the Statement of the Issue of this decision.

10. NWA was formed to hold the partnership interests of the Alaskan Northwest Natural Gas Transportation Company (hereinafter referred to as "ANNGTC"), which was the partnership company formed to build the Alaska portion of the Alaskan Natural Gas Transportation System (hereinafter referred to as "ANGTS").

11. During the Audit Period, NWA's primary business was acting as managing partner of the ANNGTC. (Jt Ex 37) NWA also held an import permit, issued by the Federal Energy Regulatory Commission (hereinafter referred to as "FERC"), which permitted NWA to import 800 million cubic feet of Canadian natural gas into the United States each day. (Jt Ex 10)

12. The federal governments of Canada and the United States required parties selling gas from Canada to hold export permits issued by Canada's National Energy Board and import permits issued by the United States FERC. (Tr I pg 33)

13. NWA secured the import permit from FERC which permitted it to purchase 800 million cubic feet of Canadian gas each day from Pan-Alberta Gas at the International Boundary, import the gas into the United States, and resell the gas to several U.S. purchasers. (Tr II pg 42, Jt Ex 10)

14. NWA entered into Gas Purchase and Gas Sales agreements with Pan-Alberta and the U.S. purchasers. The contracts specifically provided that when NWA purchased the gas, it held title to, and was deemed to be in control and possession of, the gas. The contracts provided that NWA would deliver the gas to the U.S. purchasers in the United States. (Jt Ex 11, 12, Ex R-17, Tr III pg 9)

15. NWA reported its Eastern Leg natural gas sales as Montana sales on its Montana Corporation License Tax Returns for the years 1987 to 1991. (Jt Ex 15, 16, 17)

16. NWA has no employees. (Tr II pg 210) NWA does not own any gas pipeline, compressor stations, or other pipeline parts. (Tr II pg 199)

17. NWA owned tangible personal property in Montana on a continuous basis at all times during the audit period. (Tr I pg 154, II pg 218, III pg 187, 188, IV pg 196) NWA sold and delivered tangible personal property to its purchasers in Montana during the audit period. (Tr IV pg 196, 197)

18. Any proposed findings not adopted by this Board are hereby rejected by this Board.

APPELLANT'S CONTENTIONS

19. Appellant's counsel summarized the two primary bases upon which the DOR assessment was appealed: 1) NWA does not have nexus with the State of Montana; and 2) NWA ". . . . has always operated on a no-profit no-gain basis" operating as an accommodation as ". . . . part of a large national and international energy project". (Tr I pgs 7-8)

20. Cuba Wadlington, Jr., former vice president of NWA, testified that NWA was formed to hold the partnership interests of the 15 partners of ANNGTC, the partnership company formed to build the Alaska portion of the ANGTS. He stated that Pan-Alberta Gas Limited owned the export permit needed to sell Canadian gas to NWA at the international border. (Tr I pgs 14-15)

21. Mr. Wadlington testified the U.S. Congress passed the Alaska Natural Gas Transportation Act (hereinafter referred to as "ANGTA")

that provided the means of selection of the transportation system to move gas from Prudhoe Bay, Alaska to the lower 48 states; and there were essentially three proposals (Jt Ex 7). The proposal selected was the Alcan II project: the section from Prudhoe Bay to the Alaskan/ Canadian border was owned by a partnership of U.S. companies; and the sections from that border to the U.S. border of the lower 48 states were owned by Canadian interests. An international treaty reflected joint U.S. and Canadian approval of the system, but it was a private enterprise project. (Tr I pg 19-30)

22. Mr. Wadlington stated the section that is pertinent to this appeal, the Eastern Leg of the ANGTS, started at Caroline Junction and went through Monchy, Saskatchewan and was intended to run all the way to Illinois but actually stopped at Ventura, Iowa (Jt Ex 8) where it could connect with U.S. pipeline systems for further distribution. (The Western Leg started at the British Columbia international border and was to run to southern California.) While environmental approvals and funding were being sought for the Alaskan and northern Canadian sections, it was decided to pre-build a portion of the system in order to move Canadian natural gas on that pre-built portion into the United States to meet energy demands. The pre-built Canadian portion of the pipeline was built by Foothills Pipeline, a subsidiary of NOVA; and Mr. Wadlington testified there was no affiliation between Foothills or NOVA with Williams or NWA. The Canadian portion ends at the Canadian/U.S. international border. The U.S. portion of the pre-built system was Northern Border Pipeline Company and started at the international boundary and terminated in Ventura, Iowa. Mr. Wadlington stated it was anticipated the revenues from the pre-built portion would provide income that would help partners provide equity contributions to the Alaskan partnership when the Alaskan portion of the system was built. (Tr I pg 20-30)

23. Mr. Wadlington stated the Federal Power Commission, now known as the Federal Energy Regulatory Commission (FERC), had the regulatory authority over the proposed Alaskan natural gas transportation; and on April 5, 1978, NWA filed an application for authorization to import natural gas from Canada and, subsequently, received that import permit. (Jt Ex 9) Mr. Wadlington stated NWA was the entity to apply because buyers of the gas believed NWA was most likely to receive authorization due to its relationship with the Canadian partners in the Alaskan project and with the Canadian government.

Mr. Wadlington testified NWA did not have any use for the natural gas as it didn't have any end-use customers. The market for the gas on the Eastern Leg of the pipeline was through three customers: Northern Natural Gas, United Gas Pipeline, and Panhandle Eastern.

Joint Exhibit 10-A was identified by Mr. Wadlington as a series of all the authorizations to allow the gas to be imported at the international boundary between Canada and the United States and sold to U.S. buyers. The Eastern Leg of the pipeline went into service in September, 1982. (Tr I pg 20, 32-35, 37)

24. Mr. Wadlington explained that the portion of the pipeline from Prudhoe Bay to Caroline Junction has not been built because events subsequent to 1978 made the economics of building substantially difficult to justify; it is anticipated this will be reversed at a future time when economics support resumption of building plans. (Tr I pg 36-37)

25. Mr. Wadlington stated NWA did not build nor was it involved in the building of the Eastern Leg of the pipeline. He stated NWA does not have an ownership interest in the pre-built system. He explained the original ownership of Northern Border Pipeline Company, the U.S. pipeline that interconnects with the Canadian portion of the system at Monchy, Saskatchewan, was a partnership involving Enron (formerly Northern Natural), Williams, Duke Energy (formerly Panhandle Eastern) and United Gas Pipeline. Northern Plains, a subsidiary of Northern (now a subsidiary of Northern's parent Enron) operates the Northern Border Pipeline, that is, the day-to-day business activities and the natural gas transmission. Mr. Wadlington stated that, during the audit period, Williams had a 12 percent interest in Northern Border Pipeline. (Tr I pg 38-39, 54)

26. Mr. Wadlington testified that NWA does not take possession of the Canadian natural gas in the state of Montana. He explained, ". . . . the gas is delivered through the Foothills system to the international boundary. Northwest Alaskan buys the gas from Pan-Alberta at the international boundary and instantaneously sells the gas at the international boundary to the three U.S. buyers, that being Panhandle, Northern, and United . . . . if you could take a snapshot in time . . . . the gas stops in place for a matter-of-second period of time, and several transactions take place while it is stopped in place at the international boundary . . . . a sell by Pan-Alberta, a purchase by Northwest, by NWA, and a re-sell by NWA to United, Panhandle, and Northern." In another explanation, Mr. Wadlington stated, "We take title and get rid of title in what I call this dead zone. And the dead zone being the international boundary. Because if we had title inside the United States, that would mean that we had title of the gas while it was on the Northern Border Pipeline. Therefore, we would be responsible for transportation charges on the Northern Border Pipeline. . . . It is sort of in a nano second time frame." And then that gas moves on down

the Northern Border system and as it is moving . . . . it is crossing Montana.

Mr. Wadlington added, "NWA has never made a profit from the conduit role that it plays with respect to this overall transaction. It was never intended by the parties that NWA make a profit, and it has never made a profit." Mr. Wadlington added that NWA has never contributed any operating profit to Williams. "In fact, NWA has, as a practical matter, been a cost to Williams. Even though the administrative cost under the import arrangement was recouped by NWA, but NWA has had to allocate time or personnel to . . . . an entity and an exercise wherein it doesn't earn a profit . . . . Not only has it never made any money, I personally view it as having cost Williams over time, because we have used scarce resources in order to administer the deal." (Tr I pg 43-44, 55)

27. Mr. Kenneth A. Williams served in several capacities with the Federal Power Commission and, subsequently, FERC during the period 1979 through 1986. Mr. Williams stated, at the time the import application was made by NWA, the FERC was concerned that whatever project it authorized for the pre-built portion of the pipeline, ". . . . it would be consistent ultimately with the Alaskan project . . . . that whatever it authorized would not be incompatible, but would actually enhance the development of the Alaskan project." He testified the imports from Canada and the pre-build of the Alaskan natural gas transportation facilities were authorized by FERC. Mr. Williams stated NWA was involved due to the fact that FERC was concerned about the Alaskan project and ". . . . it wanted to make certain that it didn't do anything or that nothing was done that disjointed this. . . ." and "not being simply a pre-build to get some gas down from Canada. . . ." Mr. Williams added that if each company intending to market Canadian gas in the U.S. had to secure import authorization, the duplicative effort for those companies and for FERC would have been considerable. "And so it made sense to have one party to have the import authorization and make all the filings with the FERC." (Tr I pg 72, 90-93)

28. Mr. Williams testified the FERC ". . . . regulates companies that transport or sell gas in interstate commerce." NWA ". . . . was a company that didn't have facilities in the U.S., but made a sale within the international border and that gas was ultimately transported by the purchaser in interstate commerce. And so that was subject to FERC jurisdiction . . . ."

Mr. Williams stated that the regulated company, in this case NWA, was required to file with the FERC proposed charges for the gas it was importing. To the cost of the Canadian gas, NWA was permitted to add administrative costs. It was required to provide to FERC, twice yearly, the details of the development of those costs. Additionally, there was a true-up mechanism whereby the actual costs and estimated costs would be recovered in a future period. He stated ". . . . the only thing they were allowed to recover was their actual cost." As the Canadian pricing changed, the National Energy Board of Canada approved a "demand charge" that included Pan-Alberta's costs of negotiating contracts with producers, the costs of gathering the gas, and the costs of transporting the gas on the Foothills pipeline. NWA would then add its administrative costs into that demand charge.

Mr. Williams stated that, during the audit period, the Canadian government permitted individual U.S. shippers to negotiate directly with Pan-Alberta, resulting in different prices. He clarified that a "shipper" is a customer of Pan-Alberta and a shipper on the Northern Border Pipeline system. He stated there was no provision for earnings by NWA in its re-sell of the imported gas to the U.S. purchasers or shippers. NWA did not propose to add any type of profit. He stated that, insofar as FERC was concerned, ". . . . the only type of margin or mark-up for earnings has to be on investment. And since NWA had no investment, there was no basis for any type of earnings." Mr. Williams clarified "investment" as ". . . . investment in facilities. And those facilities can be the pipeline, meters, compressors, any number of things." (Tr I pg 96-102)

29. Mr. Kenneth K. Craig is the manager of planning and analysis in the financial group of Pan-Alberta. He stated Pan-Alberta had no role in the initial ANGTS and became involved only when the pre-build became a viable project. During the audit period, Pan-Alberta obtained gas from its pool of producers and NWA was Pan-Alberta's customer for this Canadian natural gas which allowed Pan-Alberta to deal with one customer and NWA ". . . . performed the import authorization role". Mr. Craig added, ". . . . it allowed the downstream customers to have a FERC-approved cost that they could recognize and pass . . . . through their rates in the United States."

Mr. Craig testified that, under the 1978 gas purchase agreement between Pan-Alberta Gas Limited and NWA (Jt Ex 11), NWA as the buyer of gas from Pan-Alberta was a "middle man" or the ". . . . term that I use from the commercial background I have is a flipper. What we do, Pan-Alberta exports under national Energy Board approved license, on the international border, to Northwest Alaskan, who in turn flips it simultaneously to the U.S. customers, after utilizing their import authorization."

Mr. Craig added that NWA ". . . . does not have possession of the gas, because there is nothing they can do with it at that point, where we called it a nano second . . . . where they transfer title from Pan-Alberta gas to the U.S. customers. In order to take possession of the gas, they would have to have something, some place to put it, something to do with it . . . . they do not have transportation . . . . storage, something like that . . . . they do not have possession . . . . they have title to the gas." (Tr I pg 121, 123-130)

30. Mr. Craig testified that, in the period 1989 through 1993, Pan-Alberta undertook a series of negotiations with all three of their major U. S. customers. The result was that all three ceased to buy natural gas from Pan-Alberta, as deregulation of the natural gas industry in the U.S. made it no longer necessary to sell gas to pipeline companies for distribution companies and marketers were buying the gas directly. The contracts were assumed by the wholly-owned subsidiary of Pan-Alberta in the United States: Pan-Alberta Gas U.S. Inc. (hereinafter referred to as "PAG-US"). Mr. Craig stated that PAG-US had, at any given time, ". . . . between 40 and 75 customers on the East Leg." (Tr I pg 131-134)

31. Mr. Craig stated that, during the 1987 through 1989 period, when the customers were United, Panhandle, and Northern Natural, the customers would make a nomination for the amount of gas supply requested. He explained, "My understanding of the word nomination means the request by somebody for an amount of natural gas." He stated, "The buyers would make their requests known to Northern Border Pipeline . . . . the pipeline that would have to transport their supplies. At the same time, they would either fax or phone the order to Pan-Alberta Gas . . . ." The pipeline would also contact Pan-Alberta to ensure the quantity of gas nominated was agreed upon. He added, "So, in other words, Northern Border would aggregate the amount of gas required by all Pan-Alberta customers and request that amount of gas from Foothills Pipelines . . . ." which would ". . . . then go to NOVA to request that amount of gas from NOVA . . . ." ensuring Pan-Alberta sufficient qualities of gas to meet the nominations.

Mr. Craig stated that the nomination process did not change when Pan-Alberta took over the contracts from the original three customers. He added that NWA ". . . . never was and still is not involved in the nomination process . . . ." He explained, that Pan-Alberta Gas prepares statements related to their customers' nominations which it sends to NWA, outlining their sales revenue and, at the same time, Pan-Alberta is invoicing NWA for the gas sold. On the statement are the costs that are required to move the gas from the Canadian border where NWA sells the gas to the downstream customers and details those costs so NWA knows what its net costs would be at the Canadian border. To that amount NWA adds its administrative costs. Mr. Craig stated there was never a billing function in Montana; the invoices and statements are sent to NWA's Tulsa office. NWA invoices PAG-US; PAG-US pays NWA which, in turn, deducts its costs and electronically transfers the remaining funds to Pan-Alberta Gas in Canada. (Tr I pg 134-138)

32. Mr. Craig testified that Pan-Alberta Gas. under its contract that is Joint Exhibit 11, delivers its gas on the international border between Canada and the United States. In response to a question of who owns the gas after the sale that occurs in Canada, he stated: ". . . . this is the conundrum you get into in the definition of the international boundary . . . ." and NWA ". . . . is just one piece of this quadruple change that occurs at the international border. So I believe that Northwest Alaskan takes possession of that gas after it is exported, under license from Canada . . . . it has been exported from Canada. It has not yet been imported into the United States. So we are in this dead zone that Mr. Wadlington brought up."

He further explained, "Pan-Alberta Gas does not, cannot own that gas in the United States. So we export it, then we sell it, then it is imported, and then it is sold by Northwest Alaskan." So there is no clear definition that says . . . . Pan-Alberta has sold that gas in Canada or the United States. The contractual language says the sale is made on the international boundary. When asked for further clarification as to where the sales transaction occurs, Mr. Craig responded, "The gas is sold on the international border, after export from Canada and before import to the United States." Mr. Craig agreed when asked if he believed that the "international border" was not in either Canada or the United States. (Tr I pg 144-145,148-149)

33. Mr. Craig testified that, during the audit years, the U.S. customers took title to the gas in the United States and the sales occurred in Montana; however, NWA did not deliver the natural gas into Montana. He stated, "The term "deliver," in my mind, connotates (sic) the movement of natural gas from a point to another point, however small that may be. In order to do that, Northwest Alaska would have to have a transportation agreement with a pipeline or another medium to move that natural gas in order to deliver it." Mr. Craig further explained that the goods are not moved, but rather only the title to the goods are transferred. The gas is delivered between two pipelines, one of which has a transportation contract with Pan-Alberta on the Canadian side; and the other one has transportation agreements with the three downstream customers. He stated that, without being moved, the gas is imported on that thin line of the international border on the United States side. (Tr I pg 151-153,155-156)

34. Harry N. Hobbs, vice-president of transportation and public affairs, and secretary of Foothills Pipeline, Ltd. testified about the transportation of Canadian natural gas on that portion of the pipeline system. He stated that Foothills delivers approximately one-third of all natural gas exports to the United States.

Foothills connects with Northern Border Pipeline Company at the international border. He described the location of the gas metering station 20 meters north of the international boundary and stated that NWA has no facilities on this portion of the pipeline. Foothills does not consider NWA to be a shipper on this pipeline, and NWA is not billed by Foothills for transportation of any natural gas on its system. He stated that customers are billed for transportation of natural gas from the point of receipt to the delivery point. The final point of delivery on the Foothills system is the international boundary between Canada and the United States. (Tr I pgs 166-184)

Mr. Hobbs testified that NWA was not an owner of natural gas on the Eastern Leg of the Foothills system and that NWA never had an inventory of natural gas stored on Foothills. Mr. Hobbs stated that he is aware NWA imports natural gas under its authorizations and re-sells that gas to its repurchasers.

35. Mr. Raymond D. Neppl, Northern Plains Natural Gas Company vice-president of regulatory affairs, testified for the appellant. Although formally employed by Northern Plains, his work is dedicated to the Northern Border Pipeline Company, the owner and operator of the pipeline system from the Montana-Saskatchewan border to its points in Iowa.

He testified concerning the international border and the significance of the change in jurisdiction between the National Energy Board in Canada and the FERC in the U.S. He stated that Northern Border has never considered NWA as a shipper on the Northern Border system nor has NWA had storage of any inventory on that system.

He responded to a question concerning the NWA sales of natural gas, "it would be my understanding, I believe that the sales authority would be a U.S. jurisdiction." (Tr I pg 239)

36. Mr. Scott K. Coburn is director of throughput management for Northern Border, although he is an employee of Northern Plains Natural Gas Company. Mr. Coburn testified as to "in-line title transfers" of natural gas. He explained that, when receipt and delivery occur at the same point one can have "zero mileage under that kind of a scenario." (Tr II pg 22) He stated that Northern Border has never charged NWA for transportation of natural gas because NWA is not a "shipper" on the pipeline, and NWA has no contract to do so on

Northern Border's system. He testified that NWA plays no role in the "nomination" process for natural gas quantities being transported on the pipeline system.

Mr. Coburn referred to the commonality of title transfers of natural gas. He stated that ". . . we've seen title transfers communicated to us that maybe are twelve or thirteen parties long . . . ." (Tr II pg 32)

Mr. Coburn described the relationship of the Port of Morgan to the international boundary as, "I would say that international boundary, Port of Morgan, just butts up right against each other. If you want to say that Port of Morgan is in Montana, yes, because I think you have to say that because that's a jurisdictional point on our system." (Tr II pg 47)

Mr. Coburn explained how the gas measurement, nomination process and billing of shippers eventually includes NWA. "Pan-Alberta Gas, for part of the period, Northern Border, Pan-Alberta--or Panhandle Eastern, and United for part of the period. Then in turn those customers have to pay--they're required to pay Northwest Alaskan. So our documentation that we produce for billing our customers turns--produces the information you're searching to find. How does Northwest Alaskan know how it's--It's communicated from our shippers to Northwest Alaskan, which in turn Northwest Alaskan communicates back to the Canadian party." (Tr II pg 75)

37. Mr. Glenn Shearer was employed by United Gas Pipeline Company during the audit period at issue in this appeal. United Gas was a purchaser of the imported natural gas. He testified to very little contact with NWA but to at least monthly meetings with Pan-Alberta Gas. United Gas paid NWA for the gas received due to import/export license requirements even though the prices were negotiated with Pan-Alberta.

Mr. Shearer considered that United took possession of the gas at the international border at Mile Post 0.00 and "That point is in the United States, yes." (Tr II pg 92)

RESPONDENT'S CONTENTIONS

38. Exhibit J-29 is a FERC form number two filed by NWA for the year ended December 31, 1987. DOR witness Mr. George Donkin referred to that exhibit as one reviewed by him in making the determination that NWA sells natural gas in Montana. He testified that a statement on page 522 of the report states, "Respondent, (respondent is Northwest Alaskan) receives natural gas from Pan-Alberta Gas, Ltd. at Kingsgate, British Columbia and Monchy, Saskatchewan, both on the US/Canadian border. The natural gas is delivered to US customers on

the US side of the border (Idaho and Montana)." Mr. Donkin stated that, for each of the years included in the audit period, the FERC form number two filings indicate the same point of delivery. (Tr III pg 17)

39. Mr. Donkin supported his testimony concerning the point of delivery by referring to the FERC form number sixteen, a required report that is an annual sales and requirements report. That form indicates that "delivery point" for NWA customers in the US is "Morgan Port, Phillips County, and these are all in Montana." (Tr III pg 20)

40. Mr. Donkin stated that specification of title delivery point in purchase contracts is necessary because "regulatory requirements can be affected by where the point of delivery takes place. Jurisdictional issues can arise as to whether it's interstate or intrastate." (Tr III pg 29)

41. The NWA natural gas resale contracts with its customers passes the responsibility to arrange for transportation of the purchased gas and paying for the transportation on to the purchaser. (Ex J-12)

42. NWA is regulated under the Natural Gas Act. If NWA sold natural gas only outside the United States FERC regulation would not be required. FERC does have jurisdiction over the importation of natural gas.

43. Revenue Agent Brian Staley testified as to the audit at issue in this appeal. He stated one of the reasons the audit was performed is that, prior to the audit, "the Williams Companies was filing separate company returns in the state of Montana. Each of their subsidiaries that had business was filing returns on a separate company basis under that separate company's name. And part of that audit was to go and determine if that was the correct filing method for these companies, or if they should be included in a unitary combined return and file just one return." (Tr IV pg 97)

There are other reasons for the audit that Mr. Staley explained: another subsidiary of Williams "had an interest in the Northern Border pipeline"; for the years "1987 through 1991 Northern Alaska Pipeline Company had filed and reported sales to Montana of a large amount, and in 1992 and 1993, the sales reported on those returns dropped to zero." (Tr IV pg 98)

44. The Williams Companies conceded to the fact of filing as unitary in a letter dated February 1, 1995 from David Wulf to Mr. Staley. (Post audit report)

BOARD'S DISCUSSION

The issue before this Board is whether Northwest Alaskan Pipeline Company, a wholly owned subsidiary of THE WILLIAMS COMPANIES, INC., has taxable nexus with the State of Montana, providing a basis for an assessment of additional taxes and interest as determined by the Montana Department of Revenue.

To determine the issue of nexus, NWA must have a connection or definite link with Montana, and the assessment levied must reflect NWA's activity in the state. One element central to that determination is where the transfer of the Canadian gas occurs.

At the hearing before this Board, the appellant argued that the purchase by NWA of the Canadian gas from Pan-Alberta, the import of that gas, and the transfer to Northern Border Pipeline occurred "simultaneously" or in a "nanosecond" or in a "dead zone" between the United States and Canada; and a witness for the appellant stated: The gas is sold on the international border, after export from Canada and before import to the United States."

The Board rejects the idea that the transactions occur simultaneously. The importer, NWA, imports gas prior to sale and, irrespective of the fact that the sale might occur immediately thereafter, NWA does indeed have possession for a period of time, whether that is for a nanosecond or some other period of time. There was no credible evidence presented to substantiate the proffered theory that the international border is a "dead zone" in which the transactions occurred.

The appellant, Williams Companies, Inc. and subsidiaries, argues that one of its subsidiaries, specifically NWA, is not engaged in business in Montana. It supports that argument by reliance on its claim that NWA is not organized to, nor has it ever, made a profit. It follows that argument with the conclusion that, if NWA is not profitable, it is not subject to Montana Corporation License Tax.

NWA is a wholly owned subsidiary of Williams. Williams is also the parent of its wholly owned subsidiary, Northwest Border Pipeline Company. Northwest Border Pipeline Company owns 12.5% of the Northern Border Natural Gas Pipeline which enters Montana near the Port of Morgan, Montana.

Williams went to great length to establish the fact that NWA is not considered a shipper on the pipeline system in either Canada or the United States; and, of course, NWA does not need to be a shipper, since it is buying and selling the product, the seller and the purchaser would be considered the shippers. The sales contracts make the purchaser responsible for the transportation of the gas, so the cost of transportation is not borne by NWA.

Without NWA and its import authority, there presumably would be no customers for Northwest Border Pipeline Co. or for the Williams natural gas business. Whether NWA itself makes a profit is a reflection of the structure under which it was established to operate. The appellant provided numerous witnesses to underscore the point that NWA was never established to make a profit. NWA's purpose is, however, to ensure there will be product available to meet its business related entities and its parent Williams' customers needs for natural gas.

The role of NWA in this large project cannot be defined by its profitability status. The authorization by FERC for NWA to "import and resell" up to 800,000 Mcf of natural gas per day places NWA in the primary position of the entity which, in fact, makes the remainder of the system and the business generated by it possible, necessary, and a reality. Without NWA in the present structure, there would not be the generation of further business activity down the line to U.S. customers.

The appellant argues that the actions of purchaseexport and import-sell occur at a point that is neither in Canada or the U.S. NWA is subject to FERC regulation. FERC authorizes NWA to import and resell natural gas. NWA is required to file reports monthly, semi-annually, and annually with the FERC. FERC would not have regulatory authority beyond the U.S. border. If the actions of NWA were, in fact, beyond the boundaries of the U.S., FERC would not have jurisdiction. NWA is the first owner of the natural gas subject to FERC regulation and, as such, the transactions are recognized as occurring in FERC jurisdiction within the U.S. Because of geography it follows then that, if the transactions occur within the U.S., they are occurring in Montana.

NWA, being a wholly owned subsidiary of Williams, is controlled by Williams. Both parties made it clear that NWA has no property or payroll in Montana. Williams testified that NWA is not a shipper on the pipeline system and it argues, if NWA is not a "shipper", it only follows that NWA has no gas in the pipeline. NWA does not need to be designated as a shipper because it sells the gas to pipeline customers who do pay for transportation of the gas.

If NWA has no gas in the pipeline at any point, at any time, then it presumably has nothing to sell. We know that is not the situation since the record is clear that NWA buys ans sells natural gas. That is its function, its reason for existence, and without ownership of gas to sell it would definitely not be able to perform its function. If that occurred, it would have substantial impact on its parent, The Williams Companies, Inc.

The relationship of Williams and NWA is clear in that an employee of Williams Gas Pipeline Central is also NWA's Manager of Operations. He confirmed that, while NWA has no employees, agents, or independent contractors in Montana, it does take title to Canadian gas. As has already been stated, we also know that NWA then sells that gas and gives up title to the purchaser.

The Corporation License Tax is not a sales or use tax. It is a license fee paid by those subject to the tax based on business activity within the state. Corporations "created, organized, or existing under and pursuant to the laws, agreements, or declarations of trust of any state, county, or the United States . . ." pay the tax only on that income attributable to Montana. The fact that NWA is directly controlled by the parent and is engaged in business in Montana makes it subject to the tax. Neither Williams nor NWA is operating as a mail order house for retail sales of various products. One product is bought by a major importer of that product and sold to its customers. Those business transactions occur in Montana. Where the product that was purchased in Montana is eventually destined does not negate that fact that these sales by NWA were made in Montana.

CONCLUSIONS OF LAW

1. The State Tax Appeal Board has jurisdiction over this appeal. § 15-2-302, Montana Code Annotated.

2. **15-31-101. Organizations subject to tax.**

(1) The term "corporation" includes associations, joint-stock companies, common-law trusts and business trusts which do business in an organized capacity, and all other corporations whether created, organized, or existing under and pursuant to the laws, agreements, or declarations of trust of any state, country, or the United States.

(2) The terms "engaged in business" and "doing business" both mean actively engaging in any transaction for the purpose of financial or pecuniary gain or profit.

(3) Except as provided in 15-31-103 or 33-2-705(4) or as may be otherwise specifically provided, every corporation engaged in business in the state of Montana shall annually pay to the state treasurer as a license fee for the privilege of carrying on business in this state the percentage or percentages of its total net income for the preceding taxable year at the rate set forth in this chapter. In the case of corporations having income from business activity which is taxable both within and outside of this state, the license fee must be measured by the net income derived from or attributable to Montana sources as determined under part 3. Except as

provided in 15-31-502, this tax is due and payable on the 15th day of the 5th month following the close of the taxable year of the corporation. However, the tax becomes a lien as provided in this chapter on the last day of the taxable year in which the income was earned and is for the privilege of carrying on business in this state for the taxable year in which the income was earned. (Montana Code Annotated)

3. **15-31-311. Sales factor for sales in this state.**

(1) Sales of tangible personal property are in this state if:

(a) the property is delivered or shipped to a purchaser, other than the United States government, within this state regardless of the f.o.b. point or other conditions of the sale; or

(b) the property is shipped from an office, store, warehouse, factory, or other place of storage in this state and:

(I) the purchaser is the United States government; or

(ii) the taxpayer is not taxable in the state of the purchaser.

(2) Sales, other than sales of tangible personal property, are in this state if:

(a) the income-producing activity is performed in this state; or

(b) the income-producing activity is performed both in and outside this state and a greater proportion of the income-producing activity is performed in this state than in any other state, based on costs of performance. (Montana Code Annotated)

4. *42.26.255 SALES OF TANGIBLE PERSONAL PROPERTY*

(1) Gross receipts from the sales of tangible personal property (except sales to the United States Government; see ARM 42.26.256) are in this state:

(a) if the property is delivered or shipped to a purchaser within this state regardless of the f.o.b. point or other conditions of sale; or

(b) if the property is shipped from an office, store, warehouse, factory, or other place of storage in this state and the taxpayer is not taxable in the state of the purchaser.

(2) Property shall be deemed to be delivered or shipped to a purchaser within this state if the recipient is located in this state, even though the property is ordered from outside this state.

(3) Property is delivered or shipped to a purchaser within this state if the shipment terminates in this state, even though the property is subsequently transferred by the purchaser to another state. (ADMINISTRATIVE RULES OF MONTANA)

5. Based upon the foregoing testimony and evidence, this appeal is hereby denied and the decision of the Department of Revenue is hereby affirmed.

ORDER

IT IS THEREFORE ORDERED by the State Tax Appeal Board of the State of Montana that the corporate assessment and interest as determined by the Department of Revenue is properly due and owing by THE WILLIAMS COMPANIES, INC. and SUBSIDIARIES.

Index

References are to paragraph (¶) numbers unless page is indicated.

References are to paragraph (¶) numbers unless page is indicated.

M

N

O

T